Introduction to Eastern Thought

Introduction to Eastern Thought

Marietta Stepaniants

EDITED BY JAMES BEHUNIAK
TRANSLATED BY ROMMELA KOHANOVSKAYA

ALTAMIRA
PRESS

A Division of
ROWMAN & LITTLEFIELD PUBLISHERS, INC.
Walnut Creek • Lanham • New York • Oxford

To Asya and Sasha

ALTAMIRA PRESS
A Division of Rowman & Littlefield Publishers, Inc.
1630 North Main Street, #367
Walnut Creek, CA 94596
www.altamirapress.com

Rowman & Littlefield Publishers, Inc.
4720 Boston Way,
Lanham, MD 20706

12 Hid's Copse Road
Cumnor Hill, Oxford OX2 9JJ, England

British Library Cataloguing in Publication Information Available

Library of Congress Cataloging-in-Publication Data

Stepaniants, M. T. (Marietta Tigranovna)
[Vostochnaia filosofia. English]
Introduction to eastern thought / Marietta Stepaniants ; translated from the Russian by Rommela Kohanovskaya ; edited by James Behuniak.
p. cm.
Includes bibliographical references and index.
ISBN 0-7425-0433-6 (cloth : alk. paper) — ISBN 0-7425-0434-4 (pbk. : alk. paper)
1. Philosophy, Asian. I. Behuniak, James. II. Title.

B121.S7413 2002
181—dc21 00-054825

Printed in the United States of America

∞™ The paper used in this publication meets the minimum requirements of American National Standard for Information Sciences—Permanence of Paper for Printed Library Materials, ANSI/NISO Z39.48-1992.

Contents

Foreword

Professor Marietta Stepaniants, director of the Center for Oriental Philosophies Studies at the Institute of Philosophy of the Russian Academy of Sciences, is in many ways uniquely qualified to present non-Western philosophical traditions to Western students of philosophy. Having authored ten books and edited more than twenty volumes in both Western and, mainly, Muslim philosophy, and having spent many months living in non-Western countries, Stepaniants is widely recognized internationally as one of the most outstanding interpreters of Asian thought. Both in her writing and in conversation, she is able to present extremely difficult ideas, often quite alien to Westerners, with clarity and deep understanding. Stepaniants's work, however, is not merely scholarly: she is passionately concerned with cross-cultural political and social issues, and this passion informs both her work and her life.

In 1989 she was the first scholar from Russia to participate in the East-West Philosophers' Conference program held at the University of Hawaii. She so impressed her colleagues here and the sponsors of the program that she was invited back in 1995 to direct the next conference held on the theme of justice and democracy. The conference was highly successful, and once again she was invited back to help organize the conference held in January 2000 on technology and cultural values. Stepaniants is very much a public intellectual devoted to cross-cultural understanding. She believes strongly, and I dare say rightly, that open, civil, and critical exchanges by philosophers from different cultural backgrounds on important, topical issues can enrich all parties to the conversation. I am confident this volume will exhibit her wisdom and her commitment to further cross-cultural understanding among Western students of philosophy.

Eliot Deutsch
University of Hawaii

Preface

A number of textbooks are available for instructors who teach and for students who take interest in Eastern philosophies. At least four deserve mention here: Stuart C. Hacket, *Oriental Philosophy: A Westerner's Guide to Eastern Thought* (Madison: University of Wisconsin Press, 1979); John M. Koller, *Oriental Philosophies* (2d ed., New York: Scribner, 1985); Daniel Bonevac and Stephen Phillips, eds., *Understanding Non-Western Philosophy: Introductory Readings* (Mountain View, Calif.: Mayfield, 1993); Eliot Deutsch, *Introduction to World Philosophies* (Englewood Cliffs, N.J.: Prentice Hall, 1997).

The subject is so vast and complicated, however, that I believe there is still room (even a need) for more attempts to provide exposure to the main Eastern philosophical traditions. This book is different from these other works in several respects.

First of all, this work is a translation of the *first* textbook on Oriental philosophies ever published in Russia. Hence, it offers a unique glance at the Russian approach. The notion of the "Orient" has always been broader in Russia than in the West. Accordingly, in the category of "Eastern" philosophies, the Islamic tradition is included alongside the Chinese and Indian.

Second, the reader may be surprised to find that the Islamic tradition is presented here in more detail than the other two traditions. This is justified by the fact that philosophical trends of thought in the world of Islam have commonly been excluded from textbooks of this kind. My intention is to do justice to this rich tradition as well as to provide readers with some knowledge helpful to an understanding of what is currently taking place in this active and challenging part of the world. I should also admit that Islamic thought has been the main focus of my personal academic interests and work since the 1960s.

Third, the interpretive part of the book is organized *topically.* In other words, I have chosen not to present detailed histories of the Indian, Chinese, and Islamic traditions in terms of names, schools, systems, and so on. Quite a few definitive and extensive works have been published on these subjects to date. The generic conventions of this text call for a different approach, one that surrenders the unrealizable aspiration to "capture all the sounds" inherent in certain Eastern traditions, and instead convey to the reader a "harmony of those sounds," that is, a general assessment of the matter under consideration.

While omitting a specific "sound" it would hardly be possible to cast off the larger "chords," the role of which, in this text, is to designate by section certain key notions—those concerning the general structure of the universe, the place and mission of the human being within it, and the means and ways to apprehend the Truth. Because this work involves a concurrent study of Indian, Chinese, and Islamic traditions, it will inevitably entail a "polyphony" that at first may look rather inaccessible to the uninitiated, but my hope is that it will eventually be appreciated by my readership.

Fourth, the theme of the concluding essay is one quite unique for the common textbooks. It considers the encounter of East and West, focusing on the cultural transformation of traditional societies and their philosophical responses to modernity. Observations concerning the prospects for reformation in Eastern religions and the nature of fundamentalist trends of thought should be of particular interest.

Fifth, the interpretive sections of this book are not written in accord with the Anglo-American analytic tradition. Because it is an *introductory* level text, I have tried to present non-Western ways of thinking in a manner that might capture the interest of younger readers and motivate them toward further and much deeper studies in this field. My own teaching experience has shown that students are inclined to continue with their studies of Eastern philosophies when at the introductory stage I succeed in presenting them this rather exotic and "alien" material in as sympathetic a way possible, trying to get as close as I can to an insider's view of Eastern thought.

It is well known that the conventional concept of "Eastern" philosophy was introduced into scholarly circulation by those thinkers predisposed to be only "at home with the Greeks."[1] This explains the inclination to cover all philosophical ideas propounded by representatives of apparently dissimilar cultural traditions with one word: "Eastern." This common category has come to embrace thinkers whose worldviews are bound to be distinct by virtue of their emergence under different natural, geographical, historical, and cultural conditions. Yet for the sake of convenience I too use this term from time to time in expounding these traditions, which in certain respects have turned out to be similar enough and thereby distinguishable from "Western" philosophy. In particular I would highlight that, throughout their centuries-old history, each of these traditions failed to distinguish itself fully from religious thought and practice, and to thereby "structure thought from within itself."

The second part of the book includes important primary sources organized chronologically. These sources have been selected to illustrate, and promote a deeper understanding of, the main points presented in the interpretive portion of the book. Each source is presented in its turn with a short introduction.

The reader might be disappointed to find that a glossary has not been included. I purposely did not include one in order to avoid almost inevitable simplifications of terms and notions. In my opinion an index is preferable, because terms and notions can then be traced throughout the volume in different contexts, such that readers may receive a many-sided and more adequate treatment of the term or notion they desire to understand.

ACKNOWLEDGMENTS

The publication of this book was made possible due to my fortunate association with two academic communities. First, the Center for Oriental Philosophies Studies at the Institute of Philosophy, Russian Academy of Sciences in Moscow, where I have been working since my graduation in 1959. My Russian colleagues have always shared their knowledge with me and have been ready to critically review my writings. I am especially indebted to Andrey Smirnov, Vladimir Shokhin, Victoria Lysenko, Evgenia Frolova, and Grigory Tkachenko for their attentive reading and critical review of the Russian version of the manuscript.

No less important for me in recent years has been my association with the Department of Philosophy at the University of Hawaii. It was my honor to be appointed director of the seventh (1995) and eighth (2000) East-West Philosophers' Conferences. The conference is a tradition in Honolulu that traces back to 1939, and it has given me the opportunity to visit Hawaii six times. The moral support and wide erudition in the field of comparative studies and Eastern philosophical traditions presented by faculty members (in particular, by Professors Eliot Deutsch, Roger T. Ames, and Arindam Chakrabarty) were of great importance to me as I coped with the many problems I was to face in the process of preparing the manuscript.

This book was prepared during the years when, along with my compatriots, I faced hard times. The unfailing support of the late Dr. Hung Wo Ching and his family, Helen and Edwin Lee, Connie Heart, and Patricia Eames encouraged me and helped me stay optimistic.

I am very thankful to AltaMira Press and to Erik J. Hanson personally for his encouragement and interest in this project.

I wish to express my gratitude to the publishers who graciously permitted me to reprint the texts included in part two of the book. And, finally, the penetrating comments and the insightful recommendations of the referees contributed significantly to the refinement of the book's content and its composition.

NOTE

1. *Hegel's Lectures on the History of Philosophy,* 3 vols. London: Routledge & Kegan Paul, 1974, vol. 1, p. 150.

I

INTERPRETIVE ESSAYS

1

The Birth of Philosophy

The middle of the first millennium B.C. proved to be a milestone in human history, when in two ancient civilizations, namely India and China, philosophy came into existence virtually simultaneously with its rise in Greece. Historians have yet to explain why this intellectual explosion should have occurred precisely in the sixth century B.C. Yet, today we are aware that there were many economic, social, political, and—last but not least—intellectual preconditions that paved the way for this landmark. The factors conducive to the increasingly intellectual atmosphere and the birth of philosophy itself included a leap in the development of production forces, the emergence of commodity and money relationships, the collapse of tribal structures, the emergence of the first states, the growing opposition to traditional religions and criticism of conventional moral standards, the advancement of a critical spirit, and the development of scientific knowledge.

These common features in the genesis of philosophy, however, did not exclude differences in the approach to systematizing philosophical knowledge in the various centers of civilization.

THE AGE OF *ŚRAMAṆAS*

In India the rise of philosophy involved an opposition to Brahmanism, which had assimilated tribal creeds and customs and was based on the Vedic rituals codified in the four *Saṃhitās*, or *Vedas* (*Veda* meaning "knowledge"), collections of scriptures and ritual charms. Later on, each Veda came to embrace *brāhmaṇas*, descriptions of rites and interpretations of ritual texts; then *āraṇyakas* ("forest" texts), intended as reading material for forest hermits; and finally Upaniṣads (derived from the word combination "To sit down at the feet of the guru"), texts of esoteric, primarily cosmogonic, *opposition to the brahmans, the highest caste*

śramaṇas =

knowledge. The entire complex of the Vedic scriptures was regarded as *śruti,* "divine revelation." The brahmans, members of the highest caste, were regarded as the true connoisseurs and interpreters of the Vedic wisdom. The rupture of tribal relationships, however, and a crisis in patrimonial morality, shook the unwavering authority of the brahman priests and the unfaltering belief in the rites they cultivated. The preachers who led an ascetic life became the first "heretics" who challenged the omnipotence of the brahmans and the ritualistic routines. These early opponents were called *śramaṇas,* "selfless zealots."

More than just thought and opposition

The sixth and fifth centuries B.C. saw the emergence of diverse trends of thought opposed to Brahmanism, among them *Ājīvika* (a naturalistic-fatalistic teaching), Jainism, and Buddhism. The *śramaṇa* schools gave rise to the main philosophical systems that subsequently gained ground in India. The first evidence of an independent systematic exposition of Indian philosophy can be found in the *sūtras* (pithy statements and aphorisms, dating from the second through the fourth centuries). Further developments in Indian philosophy took place within the framework of the *darśana,*[1] embracing the following six classical systems: Sāṃkhya, Yoga, Nyāya, Vaiśeṣika, Mīmāṃsā, and Vedānta all oriented toward the authority of the Vedas. There were also these unorthodox trends: the materialistic Cārvāka (also known as Lokāyata), Jainism, and Buddhism.

THE "WARRING STATES" PERIOD IN CHINA   *CHINA*

In many respects the formation of ancient Chinese philosophy proceeded in a fashion similar to that of ancient India. The shattering of traditional communal relationships resulting from economic development, the appearance of money and private property, and the advance of scientific knowledge and medicine also served to create fertile soil for cultural transformations in China. It is noteworthy that here as well ascetic vagrant sages, appearing as the first "opposition members" during the "Ch'ang ko" (Warring States) period, paved the way for the "golden age" of Chinese philosophy. Although philosophical ideas can occasionally be discovered in the earliest cultural masterpieces, such as the Upaniṣads and parts of the Ṛgveda in India, and the *Shih-ching* (*The Book of Poetry*) and *I-ching* (*The Book of Changes*) in China, philosophical schools in both regions took shape in approximately the sixth century B.C. Moreover, in both regions, after having developed anonymously for a long period of time, philosophy began around this time to become associated with specific names, such as Gautama Siddhartha, the historical Buddha; Mahāvīra Vardhamāna, the founder of Jainism; Confucius, the first Chinese philosopher; Lao-tzu, a Taoist sage, and others.

Whereas in India numerous philosophical schools in one way or another were associated mainly with Brahmanism and Buddhism, it was the Confucian orthodoxy that prevailed in China. In India, differences among individual schools failed to lead to the official recognition of any particular philosophical trend, while Confucianism in the second century B.C. received the official status of a state ideology in China, holding that status up until the early twentieth century. Along with Confucianism, the most influential rival trends of thought among the so-called hundred schools of the time included Taoism and Buddhism.

ARABIAN PEOPLE ISLAM

THE BEGINNING OF INTERNAL POLEMICS IN ISLAM

Islamic philosophy is a medieval phenomenon and, therefore, its emergence and development differ significantly from similar processes in the ancient civilizations of India and China. The intellectual history of the Arabian people began, in fact, with the rise of Islam in the early seventh century. The Muslim religion originated from the interaction of Arabian culture and the Christian and Judaic ideas that had gained wide currency in Arabia by the end of the sixth century. Islam's monotheistic teachings reflected radical changes that occurred as a result of the disintegration of tribal relationships and the establishment of a common state for all Arabs. The institution of *umma*, a commune composed of the followers of the prophet Muḥammad, represented the first association of Arab peoples on the basis of a factor other than kinship and blood relationship, signaling the emergence of a state structure.

Islamic teachings were founded on the Koran and the Sunna.[2] While these texts were "canonized" by the late ninth century, neither the Muslim holy book nor their tradition was capable of answering all the questions posed by life, especially in the rapidly developing and expanding Muslim society of the day. Hence, there appeared some auxiliary "root sources," namely *qiyās* (judgments by analogy) and *ijmāʿ* (the consensus of all believers), which allowed a broader interpretation of the Koran and the Sunna. Eventually, Muslim exegetics (or to be more precise, jurisprudence) formed the four schools of *madhābs*, two of which (the Ḥanafī and the Shāfiʿī) were liberal, whereas the remaining two (the Ḥanbalī and the Mālikī) were conservative. The conservative views of the Mālikīs, for example, are aptly expressed in the following statement attributed to the founder of that school, Mālik b. ʿAnas (d. 795): "Faith is a duty while questioning is heresy." Rivalry between these two polar trends in Muslim exegetics, one liberal and one conservative, gave rise to Kalām, Islamic scholastic theology.

It was not only internal polemics that gave rise to Kalām. The need to rebuff the criticism leveled at Islam both by idolaters and the neighboring

Christians and Jews made the Mutakallimūn, the proponents of scholastic theology, turn to logical argumentation.

The appearance of philosophical schools in the Arabian East is directly linked to the efforts of early translators. The Syrian Christians were the first to introduce the works of Greek thinkers to the Arabs. The greatest impact on the development of Muslim philosophy was exerted through the translation of the treatises of one Greek philosopher in particular, Aristotle; hence there has emerged the notion of an "Oriental Peripateticism."[3]

Debates surrounding the origin and character of Oriental Peripateticism still continue in scholarly circles. For a long time the idea of the exclusively epigonic nature of Arabic philosophy prevailed in European literature. Hegel claimed that it represented no self-sufficient "singular step in the development of philosophy." According to Ernest Renan, "everything the Semitic East and the Middle Ages had in the field of philosophy in the proper sense of the word they had borrowed from the Greeks."

The teachings developed by the Peripatetics of the Muslim East were founded on certain "neoplatonic" readings of Aristotle.[4] It is partly due to the fact that their familiarization with Aristotle's ideas were filtered through two neoplatonic influenced texts, the *Theology of Aristotle* and the *Liber de Causis*, both of which were translated into Arabic on the initiative of al-Kindī, the first "philosopher of the Arabs." The *Theology of Aristotle* contained excerpts from Plotinus's *Enneads* (4–6) as well as separate texts by Aristotle himself; as for the *Liber de Causis*, it reproduced Proclus's treatise, the *Elements of Theology.*

The development of Islamic philosophy along neoplatonic lines is not due to negligence, credulity, nor ignorance on the part of Arabic Peripatetics, much less is it accounted for by a lack of "critical abilities." The assimilation of neoplatonic ideas rather than a more "pure" Aristotelianism had been their conscious, willful choice.

THE GENESIS OF PHILOSOPHY EAST AND WEST: SOME POINTS OF CONTRAST

In contrast to Greece, the transition from mythology to philosophy in India and China was based on an explicit and extremely deep-rooted ritual structure.

In India, sacrifice is the core of ritual. The Vedas, āraṇyakas, and Upaniṣads, the texts that gave rise to later theoretical constructs, had been oriented not so much toward cognition as toward eschatological practice, first and foremost. The writers of these texts were primarily interested in the path of attaining immortality rather than in proving or disproving its actual existence. They were seeking immortality through a special kind of ritualistic knowledge, one characterized by prolonged and active remembrance of a certain image (mythologeme, etc.) used to accompany certain external, verbal, and bodily ritualistic acts. The physical rituals were gradually replaced by strictly verbal and mental ones.

The mental rituals have been maintained and cultivated by "gurus," a special class of teachers. Hence, this tutorial tradition came to be acclaimed as the principal means of communicating knowledge in India.

Likewise, the Chinese attached paramount importance to ritual in the most diverse spheres of life. Its role in the rise of philosophy proved decisive, more so as, according to widespread opinion, the Chinese had no "genuine" mythology at all; first, because the mythological tradition in this case was commonly associated with concrete historical personalities and heroes and, second, because their mythology was mainly represented in the form of separate narrative fragments, rather than a full-blown, integral mythology.

In contrast to the Indian approach, where, as mentioned above, rituals had practical eschatological implications, for the Chinese, rituals were oriented toward keeping order in the phenomenal world and adjusting it to the world of unmanifested things. Ritual was designed to achieve harmonious relations between heaven and nature, earth and society, and among human beings. Revealed here is its explicitly social orientation.

It is significant that a special role in achieving this harmony has been assigned to music. The notion of the "prime sound" is invariably present in all surviving fragments pertaining to cosmogony. This is how it was expressed in the *Lu-shih ch'un-ch'iu*, a kind of encyclopedia of spiritual culture prevailing during the rise of Chinese civilization: "The sources of musical sound are far and deep-rooted. It emerges with that pitch-intensity going back to the unmanifested great absolute [Tao]. The Great Tao gives rise to the twofold prototypes (*liang-i*), which in turn presents the twofold *yin-yang* correlation. While changing, this correlation, by virtue of the polarization of the two basic energies, the *yin* and the *yang*, gets intensified, producing the individual sound image. Intermingling like *hungtung*,[5] sound images split and then produce a new formation, and so on; all of this we define as an immutable law of the heaven-nature."[6]

The Chinese cosmogonic model describes the emanating world as a harmonious musical scale (*lu*) in which the tonic center is the "Tone of the Yellow Bell," acting as an analogy to the Tao.

According to the Chinese, music is a mysterious gift passed down from the archaic heroes who had inherited it from their divine forefathers. Music embodies "the knowledge of ancestors," which is stated in numerical correlations.[7]

Because of the resonance of the prime sound, ritual music is right and proper. It is harmonious as an ideal musical scale. Nevertheless, just as a musical instrument needs regular tuning, ritual music is subject to damage from outside effects and, therefore, requires routine correction (*ssu*). This tuning-correction is performed by the sage (*sheng jen*) acting as a kind of root tone within a social group.[8]

The root tone is set by a center emitting any sound. The farther from the center, the greater probability of distortion, a deviation from the true order. For this reason a return to the source, to the past, predetermines the Chinese cultural disposition in general and their rational discourse in particular. The path to knowledge is oriented not toward the discovery of something novel but toward a return to the past, a certain "data bank," which was at the disposal of the ancestors in antiquity.

The unshakable authority of ritual and its decisive role in the genesis of Indian and Chinese philosophical thought preconditioned the rigorous confines of philosophical discourse. In contrast to mythology that, with its characteristic flight of human fancy, provided for a multifarious perception of the world and raised the possibility of employing more diversified forms of discussion and theoretical method, a rigid system of rituals restricted such diversity, binding reflection firmly to tradition.

The mechanism blocking innovation in the Islamic world was of a different kind, though in this case, too, the genesis of philosophy was not directly linked to mythology. The Arabic textual sources contain extremely scarce data pertaining to mythmaking among Arab populations. The Arabs' theoretical reflections virtually begin with their conversion to Islam, and the basic tenets of Islamic teaching (the explicit fatalistic credo, the belief in the finality of Muḥammad's prophecy, the establishment of the shari'ah as Allāh's law not subject to any revision, etc.) predisposed them toward a canonical style of thinking. One should keep in mind that the right to independent judgment (*ijtihād*) was banned two centuries after the emergence of Islam. Even "the learned among the philosophers do not permit discussion or disputation about the principles of religion," it is said, asserting that there are "things which surpass human understanding, but must be acknowledged although their causes are unknown."[9]

The above, of course, does not necessarily imply that deviation from tradition, divergence of opinion, and varied reflexive trends were out of the question in the East. Yet, as the history of spiritual culture in the regions under consideration testifies, the normative style of thinking prevailed up to the late eighteenth century.

Finally, summing up what has been said in this chapter, we cannot but fully agree with the authors of another recent effort to overcome Western centricity and look at the history of philosophy in a more profound, diversified way: "Thus, philosophy, broadly conceived, came into the world, not once but a number of times, in various places. Only our own ignorance and prejudice prevent us from entertaining the possibility that rich schools of philosophy and sophisticated argumentation once flourished through the world."[10]

FURTHER READING

Indian Tradition

Dasgupta, S. N. *A History of Indian Philosophy.* 5 vols. Delhi: Motilal Banarsidas, 1988.

Koller, J. *The Indian Way.* Albany: SUNY Press, 1982.

Mohanty, J. N. "A History of Indian Philosophy." In *A Companion to World Philosophies,* ed. Eliot Deutsch and Ron Bontekoe. Oxford: Blackwell, 1999.

Potter, K. *Guide to Indian Philosophy.* Boston: Hall, 1988.

Chinese Tradition

Fung Yu-Lan. *A History of Chinese Philosophy.* 2 vols. Trans. D. Bodde. Princeton, N.J.: Princeton University Press, 1952.

Hall, D. L., and R. T. Ames. *Anticipating China: Thinking through the Narratives of Chinese and Western Culture.* Albany: SUNY Press, 1995.

Needam, J. *Science and Civilization in China.* 2 vols. Cambridge: Cambridge University Press, 1956.

Schwartz, B. I. *The World of Thought in Ancient China.* Cambridge: Harvard University Press, 1956.

Tu Weiming. "Chinese Philosophy: A Synoptic View." In *A Companion to World Philosophies,* ed. Eliot Deutsch and Ron Bontekoe. Oxford: Blackwell, 1999.

Islamic Tradition

de Boer, T. J. *The History of Philosophy in Islam.* Trans. E. R. Jones. London: Luzac, 1970.

Corbin, H. *History of Islamic Philosophy.* Trans. Liadain Sherrad. London: Kegan Paul International, 1993.

Fakhry, M. *A History of Islamic Philosophy,* 2nd ed. New York: Columbia University Press, 1983.

Leaman, O. *An Introduction to Medieval Islamic Philosophy.* Cambridge: Cambridge University Press, 1985.

Sharif, M. M., ed. *A History of Muslim Philosophy.* 2 vols. Wiesbaden: Harrassowitz, 1963–66.

NOTES

1. *Darśana*, a word translatable literally as "vision," denotes what, for the early Indian thinkers, constituted the philosophical pursuit: the achievement and articulation of a certain "view" of ultimate reality.

2. The word "Sunna" denotes the "tradition" that surrounds the prophet Muḥammad himself, consisting of certain utterances, actions, and judgments attributed to him.

3. "Peripatetic" is a word referring broadly to Aristotelian schools. It is derived from the word "Peripatos," which is the name for the shady covered walkways that were located on the grounds of Aristotle's own school, the Lyceum.

4. The most important component of "neoplatonic" thought in this regard is the "Doctrine of Emanation," according to which an all-pervasive "One" completely generates or "emanates" the whole of reality. Two of the greatest neoplatonists were Plotinus and Proclus.

5. *Hungtung* denotes the incipient, chaotic state from which order emerges. Literally, it refers to the boiling contents of a popular soup, what we know as wonton.

6. For details see Tkachenko, G. A. *Cosmos, Music, Ritual: Myths and Aesthetics in Lu-shih ch'un-ch'iu.* Moscow: Vostochnaya literatura, 1990, p. 41.

7. Ibid., p. 45.

8. Ibid., pp. 60–61.

9. Averroes. *Tahāfut al-Tahāfut* (*The Incoherence of the Incoherence*). Trans. Simon Van Den Bergh. In 2 vols. Vol. 1. London: Luzac & Co., 1954, p. 322.

10. Solomon, R. C., and Higgins, K. M. *A Short History of Philosophy.* New York: Oxford University Press, 1996, pp. 5–6.

2

The Universe: Its Origin and Structure

What preoccupied the minds of early philosophers and what issues aroused not only discussions and polemics but fierce debates among them? As long as a thinking person lives on this earth, he or she will be unfailingly haunted by the same questions, and these appear to be the eternal problems of philosophy, namely: what is this world and what is the mission of one's own existence in it?

THE UNIVERSE IN INDIAN MYTHOLOGY

Myths do not draw a distinction between the real and the illusory by detaching the human person from the surrounding world—quite the reverse. They animate the latter, imparting human qualities to it. The earliest myths invariably associate the origins of the cosmos with biological birth. The Indians depicted it as a marriage ceremony between Heaven and Earth. The ancient Chinese viewed it as the emergence of two forces out of the shapeless abyss, bringing order into the world: the male (*yang*) spirit became the ruler of Heaven while the female (*yin*) governed Earth.

As long as a human being faced evil, ordinarily seen as a manifestation of natural elements, it was explained exclusively by supernatural forces. As evil was increasingly done by humans themselves, however, either by alien peoples or fellow tribesmen, conventional notions came to be questioned. Human suffering in its various forms gave an impetus to reflection and a search for the deep-rooted causes of evil. In this respect, the legend of Buddha is most symbolic. The son of a prince of the Shakyas whose family name was Gautama, he lived a happy and prosperous life until once, going outside the palace, he saw a crippled person, an old man, a funeral procession and, finally, an ascetic. These four encounters overwhelmed Gautama, who had never before been aware of any misery existing in the world, and compelled him to leave the palace and take up the life of a wandering ascetic. He achieved enlightenment after six years of doubts and quests. Gautama turned into Buddha, the awakened one, having understood that a human life meant suffering, which had its causes, and there was a chance to be saved from it by undertaking the road leading to its cessation (these are the "Four Noble Truths" of Buddhism).

What Was in the Beginning?

Dissatisfied with a mythological description of the world's origins, ancient thinkers such as Uddālaka Āruṇi, one of the sages from the Upaniṣads, began asking themselves cosmogonic questions: "But how, indeed, . . . could it be thus? . . . how could Being be produced from Nonbeing?" And their answer was: "On the contrary, . . . in the beginning this was Being alone, one only, without a second. And what else could its root be than food? And in the same manner, . . . with food as an offshoot, seek for water as the root; with water, . . . as an offshoot, seek for heat as the root; with heat, . . . as an offshoot, seek for Being as its root. All these creatures, . . . have their root in Being. They have Being as their abode, Being as their support" (Chāndogya Upaniṣad VI. 2, 2; 8, 4).[1] Renouncing mythological explanations of "creation," the philosophers asserted "causality" as the underlying principle in the origin of the world.

In the final analysis, notions about the cosmos, the world, and the order of things arising from it depend on one's understanding of the "Beginning." Traditionally, most Indian philosophers treated the "Beginning" as the Absolute or the Supreme Principle defying definition or description. Thus, in the earliest Upaniṣads, it is called *ansara*, that is, "indestructible," characterized in the following way: "It is neither gross nor fine, neither short nor long, neither glowing red (like fire) nor adhesive (like water). (It is) neither shadow nor darkness, neither air nor space, unattached, without taste, without smell, without eyes, without ears, without voice, without mind, without radiance, without breath, without a mouth, without measure, having no within and no without" (Brihad-Āranyaka Upaniṣad III. 8, 8).[2]

The *Mahābhārata*, an epic poem that develops the protophilosophy of the Vedas and Upaniṣads, contains some philosophical texts. Thus, in the Bhagavad Gītā (the most famous book of the *Mahābhārata*), there is a scene shortly before a battle between the two warring clans in which Krishna explains to Arjuna (the epic hero, who is facing the dramatic question of life and death and the purpose and essence of human life) the difference between true being and earthly existence. The first is the Supreme Brahman, "the Being submerged in eternity," the unborn and the imperishable pervading this world and at the same time going beyond its confines ("transcending and not manifested in its secret essence"):

> "Know that to be imperishable, by which all this is pervaded; for none can bring about the destruction of this indestructible substance. All these bodies pertaining to the imperishable, indefinable and eternal soul are spoken of as perishable, therefore, Arjuna, fight" (II: 17–18).

The tendency to treat the Absolute in negative terms explains a puzzling phenomenon known as "the silence of the Upaniṣads." As to what the genuine nature of Brahman is, Buddha (who by principle refused to discuss metaphysical problems) also failed to provide an answer. It should be noted that the seemingly inevitable and logically justifiable question about the beginning of the world is virtually nonexistent in Buddhism. According to legend, Siddhartha used to say that he was interested neither in who had directed the arrow nor whence it had been darted, for the chief goal for him was how to deliver a man from the suffering inflicted by this arrow. Further on, the Buddhists came to acknowledge the notion of an ultimate reality, even though their approach to these matters is far from self-evident.

Some Buddhist schools treat Being as a multiplicity of dharmas, certain immutable realities; and others assert that ultimate reality is emptiness devoid of any attributes and, therefore, not to be regarded as either Being or Nonbeing, nor as both Being and Nonbeing, nor as Nonbeing and not Nonbeing. Still others believe in an infinite "storehouse consciousness" out of which emerge dharma-like ripples on the surface of the ocean.

On the whole, one could say that the most typical approach to the Absolute prevailing in most Indian philosophical schools was to treat it not as a personified deity but rather as an impersonal, metaphysical principle. Some scholars believe that herein lies the difference between it and Greek philosophy, which views the Absolute and Creation in a more concrete way.

What is the Beginning? The answer to this question could not be exhaustive without associating it to the actual realities derived from it. What is the phenomenal world? What are its origins? What could be changed and improved in it, and what is the human mission in it? These questions have preoccupied the minds of all philosophers irrespective of the time and place.

The Indian philosophical tradition is distinguished by a great variety of answers to ontological questions. Here we can identify the following three principal approaches: philosophical pluralism, monism, and dualism.

The Pluralistic Ontology of Vaiśeṣika

Let us begin with the latter as represented in the Vaiśeṣika teaching: one of the oldest systems, perhaps even the very first, that tried to define the logical structure of Being in terms of philosophical categories, which was unprecedented for India.

The Vaiśeṣika doctrine acknowledged the presence of God in the cosmogonic process. However, according to it, God (*Īśvara*), rather than creating the universe from nothing, "supervises" its prime elements, which are as eternal as Himself. Eventually, it is *adṛṣṭas* (literally, the "invisible" factors) incarnating not merely the divine intention but the inexorable "law of karma," giving rise to atomic motion.

Let us unpack the above statement. First of all, what are *mahābhūtas*, these cosmic "prime elements" mentioned as early as the Upaniṣads? The classical Vaiśeṣika lists the following five great elements: earth, water, fire, air, and *ākāśa* (which correlates to the ear, the sense organ of hearing). The latter addition is explained by the fact that many Vaiśeṣikas assumed that the criteria for the great elements lay in their correlation with *indriyas*, sensory organs dissociated from the body. The five substances, beginning with earth, are generated by the material elements of these *indriyas* and endowed with particular properties, each perceived by the respective outer *indriya*. The addition of sound to the category of cosmic elements was in line with a tenet common for all Brahmanic philosophical systems. According to the Vedas, sound had the status of a self-contained ontological phenomenon.

The *mahābhūtas* or "prime elements" appear in the following two basic forms: *cause*, understood as the division of atoms during the period of a cosmic night and at the beginning of Creation; and *effect*, the bodies, sense organs, and objects, all composed of those atoms. The idea of atoms as the smallest material units is nonexistent in the Vedic tradition. Atomistic concepts in India first emerged in the principal schools following the non-Vedic tradition, that is, Buddhism, Jainism, and Ājīvika. The Vaiśeṣika teaching classifies atoms by natural elements (the exception being *ākāśa*, "ether," a shapeless element). Atoms differ in quality according to the specific properties of each element. The atoms of earth are endowed with the sense of smell, taste, color, and touch; the atoms of water, with those of taste, color, and touch; the atoms of fire, with color and touch; and the atoms of air, with the sense of touch alone. Atoms cannot move without an impetus from without. During the act of Creation that impetus was given by the supreme god *Īśvara* through *adṛṣṭas*, or "invisible factors."

It is believed that initially the Vaiśeṣika doctrine was purely a philosophy of nature and, therefore, interested primarily in the structure of Being and its material causality. This approach, however, did not blend well with the general Indian preoccupation with issues of soteriological relevance. For this reason, a later classical Vaiśeṣika placed emphasis on *adṛṣṭas* filling the gap between material and moral causes. The latter came to prevail over material causes that sometimes acted within the context of moral ones.

According to the Vaiśeṣika, the doctrine of *adṛṣṭas* carried threefold significance: a cosmological significance, by giving a prime impetus to the beginning of Creation, setting atoms into motion; a physical significance, as unobservable causes of natural drifts; and finally its ethical significance. One of the fundamental differences between the Vaiśeṣika atomism and that of the early Greek Democritus consists precisely in the latter's approach to the genesis of the universe as a natural mechanical process (the rise and fall of the worlds depending on the perpetual merging and division of atoms). This contrasts with the Vaiśeṣika doctrine that it is the realization of dharma and governed by moral laws. Conventionally speaking, according to the Vaiśeṣika doctrine, atoms depending on *adṛṣṭas* draw on a moral rather than a physical conception of the world. For the adherents to the Vaiśeṣika system, the world processes are determined not by mechanical causes, such as the collision of atoms, but by moral ones, that is, the retribution for human actions, including the law of karma, acting through *adṛṣṭas.*

The Monistic System of Śaṅkara

The founder of the monistic doctrine of Advaita-Vedānta (*advaita* meaning "nonduality" and *Vedānta* meaning "completion of the Vedas"), is considered the antithesis to Vaiśeṣika doctrine. Śaṅkara subjected all the non-Vedantic philosophical systems to severe criticism, particularly Vaiśeṣika. In his polemics with the latter, his prime aim was to refute its atomistic teaching.

Major divergences between Advaita-Vedānta and Vaiśeṣika can be summed up as follows. First, Śaṅkara stressed the infinite nature of substance in contrast to its atomic discreteness as proclaimed by the Vaiśeṣika school. Second, he asserted the identity of cause and effect contrary to the Vaiśeṣika position, according to which effect was the beginning of something new, something not present in the cause. Third, Śaṅkara recognized Brahman and not *adṛṣṭas* as the prime cause of all things.

According to Śaṅkara, the universe is an enchanting interplay of *māyā*, a magical illusion of sorts that sheds a veil over Brahman, which is immutable. Like a piece of rope in the hands of a fakir is mistaken for a snake, and a shell seems to be a piece of silver from afar, the manifest world is illusory, too. The supreme Brahman is devoid of any properties—it is ever self-identical. As for the illusion of the world, it arises as a result of *māyā*, which is in its essence nothing but ignorance (*avidyā*).

The world came into being not as a result of some cause, since cause and effect are identical. "Effects" are merely names for the existent and the immutable.

In one of his commentaries, Śaṅkara speaks of metal objects, stressing that they "originate from speech," implying that they are real not as some definite objects, but only to the extent of their presence in the nature of metal. To quote Śaïkara further on, "the modification originates from speech, it is merely a kind of name."[3]

According to Śaṅkara, "the state of the manifested names and forms differs from that of the unmanifested ones. Therefore, though the effect remains identical with the cause even before the creation, from the standpoint of the difference of the states the effect is regarded as non-existent before the act of creation . . . because it is accepted in the world that something exists when it is manifested through names and forms, so, conceding to ordinary views, we say that the world did not exist before its manifestation through names and forms."[4]

Śaṅkara believes that it is the soul differing from the rest of the manifest world that shares a similar ontological status with God (*Īśvara*): "The eternity of the soul is known from *śruti* through the absence of modification to it and the absence of origin of immutable Brahman which may exist as Brahman and as individual soul."[5]

The soul, *jīva*, being identical with Brahman, is eternal, beginningless and indestructible. Yet, a multiplicity of souls exists at the level of the empirical world, which is obligated to its preceding evolution unfolding wholly in the sphere of *avidyā* and imparting to the soul its individuality, that is, a condensed history of its past births. As long as the soul remains within the body-mind-sense system, it merely looks like Brahman and, therefore, it is multiple, never fully merging with Brahman.

Śaṅkara offers one more explanation for the individuation and multiplicity of souls. The united *ākāśa* (i.e., ether) seems to be split because of earthen pots set apart. After the pots are removed, the initial unity of *akasa* is reinstated. In the same way, "all the cause of the disjunction of the souls . . . lies in the adjunctive limitations, originating from buddhi[6] and the like, just as the cause of the dividing of clear ether lies in its connection with earthen pots."[7]

The soul is identical with one's consciousness viewed in the Advaita as an eternal, self-evident reality. The matter involves "pure" consciousness differing from what occurs in a waking or dreaming state because of limitations arising from ignorance. Only when the latter are fading away, in a deep sleep, does the soul regain its own integral entity, as if merging with Brahman.

The soul is intrinsically alien to any fuss, being set into action by its transient, "bodily tools." According to Śaṅkara's reasoning, "In this world a carpenter is unhappy when he has in his hands the instruments of his work—

a small axe and the like—and only having returned home, having put down the instruments, being self-contained, inactive, and non-engaged, is this carpenter happy. So it is with the *ātman* connected with duality, which is brought about by *avidyā*, staying in dreaming or waking state; this ātman is an agent and therefore unhappy. But the same ātman, having returned to its own being, that is, to the higher Brahman, for the sake of the destruction of tiredness, free from the chain of cause and effect, inactive, is happy and stays self-luminous, clear."[8]

Advaita-Vedānta was the last of the six Brahmanic teachings to imbibe the preceding intellectual legacy, including the concepts devised by unorthodox systems such as Jainism and Buddhism.

The Western model that comes nearest to Śaṅkara's teaching is the mysticism of Meister Eckhart. The views of these two thinkers are strikingly similar. Compare, for example, the following statement made by Śaṅkara, "All the modifications—those of the cause, the effect, and so on—exist only insofar that before them exists their foundation—their own nature in the form of *ātman*, or pure consciousness,"[9] with that of Eckhart: "Essence is his foothill, the ability to cognize is the temple of God."[10]

The Dualistic Position of Sāṃkhya

Dualism received its fullest treatment in Sāṃkhya, the oldest Indian philosophical system. The earlier Sāṃkhya denied the very existence of the Creator, claiming that there was no proof of God's existence, for any perception of Him could not be regarded as empirical testimony, neither could it be deduced from pure reasoning.

The classical Sāṃkhya school acknowledges the presence of two autonomous prime realities: *puruṣa* (consciousness) and *prakṛti* (nature). *Puruṣa* is the perceptive principle in which "consciousness" (*ckaitanya*) is not an attribute but its very essence. It is a kind of eternal consciousness, pure spirit lying outside the world of objects. As for *prakṛti*, it is the First Cause of the objective world. In contrast to the immutable *puruṣa*, *prakṛti* is in the process of perpetual transformation.

Although *prakṛti* is the integral entity, it is composed of three *guṇas*, or "fundamental forces." These constitute neither its qualities nor attributes, being its substantial elements comparable to three ropes (the very word *guṇa* meaning literally both "thread" or "string" and a "fundamental quality" or "property") interwoven into one cable.

What are these three *guṇas*? The first one, *rajas*, symbolizes activity and effort; the second, *tamas*, is identical with anything stable, immobile, and inert; and the third, *sattva*, denotes equilibrium, peace, and consciousness. In *prakṛti*, all three *guṇas* act simultaneously, albeit in varying proportion to one another. Their interaction is commonly compared to a lamp: they are as the wick, the oil, and the flame, three components of the single process of burning.

The merging of *puruṣa* and *prakṛti* upsets the latter's balance and gives rise to movement and change. In the first instance, *mahat*, the great seed of the manifest universe emerges from *prakṛti*. It represents the awakening of nature from the cosmic slumber and the first manifestation of thought, therefore it is also called *buddhi* (intellect). In its turn, intellect generates *ahaṅkāra*, a sort of principle of individuality from which matter generates living creatures. *ahaṅkāra*, under the prevalence of the *sattva* elements in it, gives rise to five organs of cognition, five organs of action, and an organ of both cognition and action (*manas*). In cases where the *tamas guṇa* predominates in *ahaṅkāra*, it produces the five finest elements, potencies of sound, touch, color, taste, and smell (*tanmātras*). These five finest elements give rise to the following five material elements: ether (*ākāśa*), air, fire, water, and earth. All in all, the Sāṃkhya system comes to encompass twenty-five fundamental principles.

THE SELF-DEVELOPING UNIVERSE OF THE CHINESE

The philosophical understanding of the Beginning in Chinese thought differs fundamentally from the Western cosmogonic approach. According to the latter, the Beginning is defined by an order imposed from without and produced out of a certain chaos by a transcendental force represented by either the Creator or the First Cause. According to the Chinese tradition, "a myriad things," or "the ten thousand things," as they are conventionally called, have no common origin and do not make up a uniformly governed world.

Here are just two citations from *Chuang Tzu* (third century B.C.), the most extensive and authoritative philosophical treatise of ancient China, which has laid down the foundations of the Taoist tradition: "All things are living but the roots are invisible. . . . They merely appear with the gateway unseen," and "Everything emerges by itself and there is no 'self' giving birth to another. The self cannot bring forth things and the latter are incapable of delivering the self. The self exists on its own in the same way as the others do." As a matter of fact, the above denotes the typical Chinese worldview, which is opposed to ontology (in the customary sense of the word).

The Chinese appear to be generally disinclined to reflect over the concepts of Being and Nonbeing. Existence, to their mind, is an infinite cyclical process: "It was through the Tao that the heavens first revolved and the earth was made fast: the successive revolutions failed not. The waters eternally flowed without ceasing and were conterminous with creation. The winds blew; the clouds steamed. There was nothing which should not be."[11] Many texts, including the one cited above, state that "Without apparent doing, things came into existence under the inspiration of the Tao,"[12] at the same time asserting that "The Supreme Tao begets all creation but keeps itself as though it did not exist, i.e., makes no boast of it. It produces all phenomena, yet without appearing as the controller."[13] Such statements are not incompatible because the Tao is conventionally understood not as the transcendental Absolute, but as a supreme principle, a law underlying the self-developing universe. According to the *Tao Te Ching,* "The Great Tao flows everywhere. It may go left or right. All things depend on it for life, and it does not turn away from them. . . . All things come to it. . . ."[14] Hence, it would be more accurate to treat Chinese "ontology" as an ontology of events rather than substances. For precisely this reason, the need for tools of categorization and definitions of "quality," "attribute," and the like are virtually eliminated.

I-ching: The "Book of Changes"

Traditional Chinese notions about the world process were codified in an earlier mentioned text, the *I-ching* (*Book of Changes*), which had a paradigmatic impact on the whole of Chinese culture. According to Yulian K. Shchutsky, an eminent scholar and the translator of the *Book of Changes* into Russian, it is quite probable that initially this book was used as a manual for prophecy in the ancient practices of fortune-telling and later served as a source for philosophical reasoning because its hardly comprehensible and mysterious archaic language gave wide scope for creative philosophical thought. The fortune-telling practices, using yarrow stalks, turtle shell, or the shoulder bones of cattle, which dated back to the late second and early first millennia B.C., gradually turned into a numerological system of mathematic-like operations with numbers and geometric figures intended to sort out the "ten thousand things" according to their properties. This system makes up the root text of the *I-ching,* which is divided into three layers. The first layer includes the names of hexagrams and divinational formulas. The hexagrams (which number sixty-four) are graphic symbols composed of six superimposed broken and unbroken horizontal lines in varying combinations. The *yao* lines are the signs of the universal energies bringing order into the world: the masculine *yang* (in the form of an unbroken line) was regarded as an active force symbolizing light, and the feminine *yin* (the broken line) embodied the essentially passive, dark force. Most likely, these hexagrams were used to represent customary notions before the appearance of a more extensive written language in China.

The basic structure of the *I-ching* system is formed by the eight trigrams (*pa-kua*), combinations of three lines. According to Chen I-Chuan (1033–1107), one of the renowned commentators of the *Book of Changes,* "In ancient times, the sages instituted the system of the Changes in order to follow the principle of nature and destiny. . . . (Each hexagram) embraced the three powers (Heaven, Earth, and Man) and doubled them."[15] The eight trigrams, denoting *yang*, *yin*, water, fire, metal, wood, land, and cereals, are genetically linked with what the Chinese call the "Ten Heavenly Stems."

The second layer of the text is composed of aphorisms to accompany the hexagrams, and the third layer contains aphorisms that correspond to the separation of the *yao* lines. The commentarial section of the *Book of Changes*, known as the "Ten Wings" (although often attributed to Confucius), in all probability dates from a later period and was compiled by his successors (in approximately the sixth century B.C. through the first century A.D.), who eventually managed to ingrain the perception of the world that had been evolved in *I-ching* as a theoretical foundation for the traditional Chinese world outlook.

Despite a vast amount of commentaries on the *I-ching* existing both in China and elsewhere, the *Book of Changes*, according to Vasily Alexeyev, a foremost Russian sinologist, remains a sealed book of revelation. In one of the sections of the Ten Wings, the essence of the symbols used in *I-ching* is explained in the following way: "Anciently, when the sages made the Changes, it was with the principles underlying the natures (of human beings and things), and the ordinances for them appointed (by heaven). With this view they exhibited in them the way of heaven calling (the lines) *yin* and *yang*; the way of earth, calling them the weak (or soft) and the strong (or hard); and the way of human beings, under the names of benevolence and righteousness. Each trigram embraced these three Powers; and being repeated, its full form consisted of six lines. A distinction was made between the places assigned to the *yin* and *yang* lines, which were variously occupied, now by the strong and now by the weak forms. . . . The numbering of the past is a natural process; the knowledge of the coming is anticipation. Therefore in the Changes we have both anticipation and the natural process."[16]

Naturally, the later commentators and interpreters sought to decipher the text of *I-ching* by drawing on the concepts that corresponded to the current level of their own thinking. Some of them gleaned the seeds of mathematical knowledge in the hexagrams (Liu Wei-hua); others linked them with astronomical and astrological observations close to the Babylonian concepts of the celestial spheres, or perhaps even borrowed therefrom; still others, for example Carl Jung, believed that the *kua* had codified the universal set of archetypes, or innate mental structures. According to the Russian philosopher Artem Kobzev, the trigrams, hexagrams, and their components in all possible combinations make up the universal hierarchy of classification schemes, embracing in visual symbols each and any aspect of reality: parts of space, spans of time, natural elements, numbers, colors, the body organs, and social and family relations.[17]

Generally speaking, despite the encoded nature of the archaic text in the *Book of Changes,* it clearly reveals a "sober" and scrutinizing view of the world surrounding the human person, whose life experiences prove at least the following undisputable factor: the process of world development has neither end nor beginning and its basic characteristic is the persistence of change: the indestructible, concurrent conflict and unity of opposites.

The Naturalistic Origin of the Myriad Things

Later classical texts identified the Beginning with the origin of the "ten thousand things." Tung Chung-shu (circa 180–120 B.C.), rated in the Middle Ages as the "Confucius of the Han Period," defines in his *Ch'un-ch'iu fan-lu* the "beginning" as the "One," the "origin of the myriad things" existing "before Heaven and Earth."[18]

Chinese thinkers offered different interpretations of life development from the "beginningless" Beginning. Take for example the reasoning of Wang Wu (A.D. 76–157), whose views, notable for their eclectic nature, incorporate ideas borrowed from various trends in Chinese thought: "In the remote past during the period of the great emptiness there existed the primordial, formless, and indefinable *chi*[19] composed of substances merged into the One. It could not be restrained, nor governed. That went on for a long time, but then all of a sudden it began to change, dividing into the pure and the obscure, which turned into *yin* and *yang.* These two already had a shape; *yin* and *yang* coming into right proportion in the world brought Heaven and Earth into being. When the heavenly *chi* joined with the earthly *chi,* it gave birth to all beings. A harmonious blend of *yin* and *yang* brought forth a human being for the latter to govern all other beings."[20]

The Will of Heaven

Along with the more popular naturalistic philosophical views, theistic-like ideas that asserted the presence of a transcendental force creating the world and ruling it also enjoyed wide currency among the Chinese. Sometimes this ruling force was attributed to the Tao, but more frequently it was associated with *T'ien* (heaven). Thus, according to the adepts of the Mohist school founded by Mo Tzu (479–400 B.C.), heaven "loves the world universally and seeks to bring mutual benefit to all creatures. . . . There is not so much as the tip of a hair that is not the work of heaven."[21] Moreover, in the Mohist interpretation, heaven assumes the punitive functions against those adverse to its "will." The violation of this will entails severe punishment in the form of heavenly omens, natural anomalies, or cataclysms, all indicative of heaven's "displeasure." It concerns not only natural but also social phenomena: "He who obeys the will of heaven . . . will surely win reward. But he who disobeys the will of heaven . . . will surely incur punishment."[22]

The materialistic approach to heaven was not absent, either. The most revealing in this respect are the views of Wang Ch'ung (circa A.D. 27–97). In his polemic with the Confucians, Wang Ch'ung maintained that heaven was not at all a nebulous and incorporeal entity. Drawing on the findings of astronomy and mathematical calculations, he insisted that "heaven (*T'ien* or 'Nature') gives force and distributes material force universally into all things. . . . Heaven is material force."[23]

The Confucian Synthesis

Despite the diversity of views in the Chinese intellectual tradition, one should acknowledge the prevalence of the official Confucian doctrine that emerged during the reign of the Han dynasty and remained in force for two millennia in the history of the Chinese Empire. This doctrine was established by the thinker Tung Chung-shu, mentioned above.

The "Confucius of the Han Period" recognized the existence of the Tao as the Supreme One or the First Principle preceding heaven. According to Confucianism, the Tao is identical with *te,* the manifestation of the potentials of the world. The latter is imbued with the primary units, *chi,* in its two energetic aspects, *yang* and *yin,* whose interaction gives rise to diversity in the world. Heaven consists of the following five agents: wood, fire, earth, metal, and water. Earth occupies the center among these elements, whose order is predetermined by heaven. The latter also gives birth to the human being, who by nature might be either good or evil. It is easy to see that the official doctrine of Confucianism made a synthesis of the tenets borrowed from the various ancient Chinese schools and was designed to reconcile them and secure a certain ideological unity indispensable for maintaining the stability of the Empire.

THE UNIVERSE IN ISLAMIC TRADITION

Muslim philosophers, in their reasoning about the "Beginning," invariably referred to *tawḥīd,* the principal Islamic dogmata that proclaimed their strict monotheism. The *tawḥīd* is codified in the Koranic formula "There is no god but Allāh" (and it would be, in fact, more precise to translate this as "There is no god but God").

The Mu'tazilites' Negative Theology

Religious philosophers such as the Mu'tazilites (from the Arabic *mu'tazilah* meaning "seceders") categorically rejected any attempts at an anthropomorphic conception of God. Anthropomorphism is formally prohibited in Islam (censoring the visual depiction of God or the Prophets), although certain text in the Koran provides quite ample inspiration for it, by maintaining, for example, that "God . . . is firmly established on the Throne" (Sura VII, ayat 54; Sura 20, ayat 5) or that "Some faces, that Day will beam; Looking towards their Lord" (75:22). The Mu'tazilites were unanimous in their belief that God "is neither body, ghost, corpse, form, flesh, blood, substance, nor accident and that He is devoid of color, taste, smell, tactual traits, heat, cold, moistness, dryness, height, width, or depth . . . and He is indivisible . . . and is not circumscribed by the place or subject to time. . . . He has always been the First, prior to all contingent things. . . . Sight cannot perceive Him . . . and the imagination cannot encompass Him, the only eternal Being."[24] The Mu'tazilites' negative theology ran counter to the divine attributes explicitly defined and even enumerated in the Holy Book (the Koran contains ninety-nine of His "names," such as the Omnipotent, the All-Knowing, the Merciful, and the like). The Mu'tazilites were aware of this discrepancy and endeavored to resolve it. Some of them declared that these attributes had merely metaphorical meaning while others reduced them to the "effects" derived from the divine entity and arising only in the context of particular realities.

The polemics surrounding the attributes of divine will and speech were especially fierce. The denial of such attributes had the most serious implications because it led to the acknowledgment of man's free will and the assertion of the Koran's creation (contrary to the thesis upholding the pre-existent nature of God's Word). Yet, the Mu'tazilites' arguments were so convincing that the creation of the Koran received official recognition in A.D. 827 under the reign of Caliph al-Ma'mūn.

By ascribing to God only a single, unitary act—that of bringing the previously nonexistent world into being from nothing—the Mu'tazilites dissociated God from current developments in the world. Thus it was natural for Mu'tazilites to be declared heretics by traditional theologians. As for the general course of development in Muslim spiritual culture, however, the Mu'tazilites played the role of forerunners to philosophy.

The First Principle of the "Oriental Peripatetics"

The Arab philosophers, among them al-Kindī (circa 800–870), al-Fārābī (870–950), Ibn Sīnā (980–1037), and Ibn Rushd (1126–1198), elaborated on the problem of the Beginning by drawing on the experience of Greek philosophers. Al-Kindī, the first in a vast array of Eastern peripatetics, made use of the theological term "God" along with purely philosophical terms in defining the Beginning. He called it the "First Principle," the "Eternal," and occasionally the "True Being." This Being (or the "One") could not have a cause other than originating in itself. It is immutable, indestructible, remaining forever in a state of eternal perfection. It stands above all existent things and has no analogy. It is free from multiplicity and devoid of relation to anything else. It is formless and immaterial.

That credit goes to al-Kindī for his cultivation of Greek philosophical ideas and the introduction of philosophical terminology into the Arabic lexicon is unquestionable. One should keep in mind, however, that his studies in philosophy and his preoccupation with the Greeks had no effect on his religiosity and his attitude toward such Islamic dogmas as the temporal creation of the world, the resurrection, the reality of divine providence, and the authority of a prophetic revelation. Later on, the "Oriental peripatetics" came to display greater consistency in their philosophical worldviews.

Al-Fārābī, the "second teacher" (after Aristotle), as he was called by the Arabs, defined the Beginning as "First Being": "This One or First is the First Cause of all things, it is perfect, necessary, self-sufficient, eternal, uncaused, immaterial without associate or contrary, and is not susceptible to being defined . . . the First possesses unity."[25] The great Islamic philosopher Avicenna, the European name for Ibn Sīnā, elaborated on the Beginning in the same spirit: "For everything derives from it, but does not share with it in anything, and it is the source of all things, without being any one of the things posterior to it."[26]

Atomism of the Kalām

The Koran forwards a mythological version of Creation, one virtually identical to that found in the Bible. Theism, with its belief in the transcendental nature of God the creator and his unremitting guidance, finds its manifestation in Muslim theology through its rigid dissociation of God from the world (God is the substance of the highest order whereas the created world is of a lower order). The mutakallimūn, proponents of Kalām, put forward an atomism as the ontological foundation of Muslim scholasticism, claiming that "the entire world (i.e., all bodies therein) is composed of tiny particles, too fine to be divided."[27] In contrast to the Greek atomists, the mutakallimūn insisted that the existence of these tiny indivisible particles was not "secure in the universe" for "God creates these substances constantly when He so wills,"[28] and that, although the natural order of things could not be acknowledged as infinite because of its substantial character (i.e., the existence of an infinite body or bodies, whose number is infinite, is impossible), the infinity of accidents was nevertheless partly justified.

Objects possess no permanent properties, for these are created by God every time anew and it is God who creates atoms and whatever accidents he pleases at one stroke. As soon as one accident is created, however, it disappears, because it does not endure longer than one instant, and God creates another of its kind, which also disappears in turn, "and so forth as long as God wills that sort of accident to endure."[29] When, say, a man moves a pen it is not he who moves it, for the motion in the pen and in the hand arises owing to the properties created by God. Hence, the mutakallimūn draw the following general conclusion: "There is no such thing as a body which has any sort of action at all; in the last analysis the only doer is God."[30]

"The Unity of Being" in Sufism

The theism of Muslim scholastics was offset by the mystical pantheism of the Sufis, which is most fully represented by Ibn ʿArabī (1165–1240), "the Apostle of Theosophic Mysticism" and "the Greatest Mystic of Arab Genius." It is his treatises, primarily *Fuṣuṣ al-ḥikam* (*Bezels of Divine Wisdom*), that evolved a concept later to be called *waḥdat al-wujūd* (the "Unity of Being"), which was to become a major trend in Ṣūfī thought.

The monistic principle of the Unity of Being was considered by Ibn ʿArabī from two angles that may be tentatively defined as the "cosmic" and the "phenomenal." The Unity of Being reveals itself at three levels: the Absolute, the Divine Names (archetypes), and the phenomenal world. Ibn ʿArabī defines the Being of the first level as the Absolute, God, and the Truth. This is the unique essential reality (*ḥaqīqa*), absolute perfection in which all existential realities are hidden.

If God is all, what then is the world in which we are living? It is merely the "shadow of God"? This shadow appears because God wanted to manifest himself and thus to "see His own essence." That wish is explained by the "sadness of primordial solitude," His suffering anguish from staying anonymous because no one ever mentions His Divine Names. The creation of the world is the effect of God's yearning to become "known."

As many other mystics, Ibn ʿArabī refers to the *qudsī* hadith (a sacred hadith: an utterance from the Muslim scriptures attributed not to the Prophet but to Allāh himself) stating that when the prophet David asked God why he had created the world God answered, "I was a hidden treasure, and I wanted to be known, so I created the world." Drawing on this hadith, the Ṣūfīs treat the origin of the world as God's wish to manifest Himself and His hidden essence. Yet God never manifests Himself completely, always "hiding" something of Himself away. He hides behind the veils of darkness, which are natural spirits, for the world is made up of both crude and subtle matter. (Vedānta, we recall, describes this "behavior" of God as *līlā*, "a divine play" during which the Absolute is shrouded in *māyā*.)

According to the adepts of the *waḥdat al-wujūd* system, the divine act of Creation is God's manifestation through the created world. Creation is a transition from the state of potentiality into the state of manifestation, that is, the process of realization of the unconditional Divine Being in the world of infinite potentialities.

God's manifestations (*al-tajallī*) are revealed in the following two ways: first, through the Divine Names of the Divine Being and, second, through concrete forms of Being in the physical world. These names, on the one hand, are identified exclusively with the named and, on the other hand, set the named apart in their particular meaning. Each name reveals a certain facet of the One, differing from all others in its essence. At the same time, the particular nature discloses the limitation of each Divine Name, its belonging to the category of multiplicity. The Divine Names are not only theological categories used to define the divine attributes but philosophical universals as well.

The Great Shaykh repeatedly stressed the specific reality of universals. To elucidate his point, he referred to the manner in which the universal values of humanity were unconditionally integrated, in his opinion, in each particular life of a human person. These universals devoid of diversity and multiplicity, though affecting individuals, remain purely intellectual realities.

The Divine Names are manifestations of God in the unmanifested "world of mystery" (*'ālam al-ghayb*) whereas the phenomenal world is a manifestation of the Divine Being in the "world of testimony" (*'ālam al-shahāda*). The True, Absolute Being is God alone; the world is a manifestation of His Essence. The term *waḥdat al-wujūd* implies both the transcendence and immanence of God in respect to the phenomenal world. Any denial of the world's resemblance to the Divine Being is decried by Ibn 'Arabī as "ignorance."[31] The consistent adherence to the principle of transcendence leads ultimately to dualism. As for the adepts of the monistic concept of *waḥdat al-wujūd*, they insisted "Thou art not Him; and yet thou art Him; thou wilt see Him in the essence of things."[32]

Although Ibn 'Arabī continually emphasizes the derivative nature of the world and its dependence on the Divine Being, he nonetheless points to the actuality of the world as a manifestation of the Divine Absolute, the realization of the necessary in the accidental: "God first created the world as something amorphous and without grace, comparable to a mirror not yet polished."[33] The "receptacle" derived from God contained an inexhaustible emanation of the Divine revelation. God's potentials for manifestation are infinite; hence the boundless diversity of our world:

Know the world from end to end is a mirror;
In each atom a hundred stars are concealed.
If you pierce the heart of a single drop of water,
From it will flow a hundred dear oceans;
If you look intently at each speck of dust,
In it you will see a thousand beings;
A gnat in its lines is like an elephant;
In name a drop of water resembles the Nile,
In the heart of a barley-corn is stored a hundred harvests,
Within a millet-seed a world exists.
In an insect's wing is an ocean of life,
A heaven is concealed in the pupil of an eye,
The core in the center of the heart is small,
Yet the Lord of both worlds will enter there.

(*Maḥmūd al-Shabīstarī, Rose-Garden*)

The inexhaustible infinity of forms in which the Divine Being goes on revealing himself is predetermined by the continuous, uninterrupted process of manifestation, a transition from the state of nonmanifestation in which God resides by pure chance into a concrete state of manifestation.

Thus, the multiplicity of things existing in the world is derivative and secondary in its relation to the One, or the Divine Being. All the above cited statements of Ibn 'Arabī clearly reveal Neoplatonic influences. In the latter case the Neoplatonic idea is apparently treated by the Great Shaykh in a way similar to that of the Neoplatonist Proclus (410–485), the last of the renowned ancient philosophers. According to the triad initiated by Proclus, the One resides within itself, then goes beyond itself, and finally returns to itself. In the *waḥdat al-wujūd* system, the Divine Being, with neither name nor attributes, having manifested itself in the phenomenal world, perpetually strives to "return" to its primordial state: the entire reality from beginning to end is derived from God alone and it is to Him that it returns.

The mystical pantheism of Sufism, outlined above, was opposed primarily to the theism of Muslim theology, although it also differed from the ontology of the Arab peripatetics.

The Doctrine of Emanation

Beginning with al-Fārābī, Arab peripatetics developed the Neoplatonic doctrine of "emanation." Al-Fārābī believed that the First Being provided a kind of emanation of its being into the beings of other things.[34] He presented a systematic hierarchy of emanations, which was heretical from the viewpoint of Islam, though quite reminiscent of the one advanced by Proclus.

According to al-Fārābī, the First Being gives rise to the being of the Second, which is also an absolutely incorporeal substance (the First Intellect). It is capable of conceiving both its own essence and the First Being. By virtue of its conceiving something from the First Being, it inevitably generates the being of the Third, which is also incorporeal intellect aware of its substance. This gives rise to the sphere of fixed stars. This process of emanating one being, or intellect, from another goes on successively up to the generation of the tenth intellect, along with the respective spheres of Saturn, Jupiter, Mars, the sun, Venus, Mercury, and the moon.

The being of the lunar sphere precedes the Eleventh Being arising from it, the last of those beings that need no material basis for their existence, constituted wholly by intellects and conceivable objects of intellection. Next follows the hierarchy of sublunar beings, either natural or accidental. These include fire, air, water, earth, minerals, plants, animals, and finally, the human being. Human beings complete the cosmic hierarchy.

The ideas propounded by al-Fārābī were further developed and systematized by Ibn Sīnā (Avicenna), who described the origin of the universe as a perpetual process, or "emanation" from the One (the First, the Essential Being). According to Ibn Sīnā,

> The First Being produces a certain intellectual substance, which is truly created. It generates another intellect and a celestial body. Under this intellect the celestial bodies become perfected, and it ends with a certain intellect which no longer gives rise to any celestial body. . . . The matter of the elementary world should have originated in the latter intellect, while the celestial bodies might have assisted in so doing. This was insufficient, however, for securing its emergence until it was combined with a certain form. . . . The intellect underlying this world generates the vegetative, animal, and intelligent souls. The intelligent soul completes the successive being of intellectual substances. The intelligent soul needs perfection by means of bodily organs and its relationship with the highest beings.[35]

Al-Ghazālī's Refutation of the Philosophers

The ideas of philosophers and any other trespassers of the Islamic theological worldview were refuted by al-Ghazālī (1058–1111). It is no suprise that one of his major treatises was entitled the *Collapse of the Philosophers* (*Tahāfut al-falāsifa*).[36] Al-Ghazālī warned true believers of the dangers inherent in the "sixteen metaphysical" and the "four physical" postulates of the philosophers. Their allegations concerning the eternity of the world was treated as the most "harmful" of these concepts. Al-Ghazālī insisted on the notion that the world was created by God's will at a specific point in time.

Al-Ghazālī's criticism delivered a staggering blow. It failed, however, to erase peripateticism from the minds of Muslims. Quite the reverse, his criticisms perhaps provoked the emergence of the greatest follower of Aristotle in the Islamic world. This was Ibn Rushd, or Averroës, as he was later called by the medieval Latin authors.

Ibn Rushd (Averroes)

We shall discuss Ibn Rushd in greater detail below, but for now let us assess his views on the issues under immediate consideration. In his "Grand Commentary" on Aristotle's *Metaphysics,* Ibn Rushd evaluates the most popular contemporary theories pertaining to the origins of the world. The first one is religious, creationistic, according to which God creates the world from nothing. Its antithesis is *al-kumūn* (meaning literally "staying in a hidden form"), a theory according to which "creation" constitutes an act of "imparting forms" implanted by the active intellect into material bodies (Ibn Rushd ranks al-Fārābī and Ibn Sīnā among the adherents of this view). The third idea was that developed by Aristotle himself, which Ibn Rushd believes to be "the least dubious and the most adequate to the nature of being" and which he himself shares.

According to Ibn Rushd, "creation is the transformation of potential into actual being";[37] it is an act of the Omnipotent "doer" or agent. Creation can be correlated with the Omnipotent only accidentally but not essentially.[38] He who rejects matter, Ibn Rushd writes, presupposes that the agent's act is related primarily and essentially with Nonbeing. But it is not so. For "there are two essential fundamental principles underlying the origin and destruction of things, namely: matter and form, and one accidental principle—nonbeing, which is a prerequisite for the appearance of something, for when the arising thing begins its existence, its nonbeing disappears, and when it is destroyed, its nonbeing appears."[39]

Ibn Rushd criticized the Arab peripatetics, Ibn Sīnā in particular, for their distorted interpretation of Aristotle's ideas. Specifically, Ibn Rushd deemed it fallacious to assume that an essence was logically pre-existent and could be defined regardless of the Being or Nonbeing of its "bearer." He argued instead that an essence could be apprehended and defined only if it actually existed. Ibn Rushd surmised that Ibn Sīnā's erroneous judgment was due to his confusing two meanings of Being: the real, or "ontological," on the one hand, and the "conceptual" on the other, for only the latter could be comprehended and defined.

Neither did Ibn Rushd share Ibn Sīnā's opinion that the existence of matter was manifest in metaphysics rather than in mundane physics, and the Being of nature was not self-evident but in need of verification. Ibn Rushd challenged

Ibn Sīnā's statement that a demonstration of the ultimate material cause and the "prime mover"[40] was a matter of metaphysics rather than physics. On the contrary, he believed that a metaphysician obtained knowledge about the existence of the ultimate causes of the world primarily from the physicist, not the other way around.

The multiplicity of views on the nature, constitution, and operation of the universe demonstrated in India, China, and the Islamic world justifies our prudence toward efforts to reduce different trends of thought in any of those cultures to the "Tradition." Highly respected scholars have, no doubt, made a number of assertions with which one could be quite sympathetic and hence easily agree. Some claim that philosophy in China originates, from the earliest period, in a view of the natural realm as chaotic, dangerous, and largely inscrutable. A later view that remained dominant through subsequent Chinese history is that philosophy arose from a belief in a well-ordered and manageable world, inclined toward human good and open to human understanding.[41]

No less plausible appears an opinion concerning the Indian world outlook: God's mind does not play a role of creating out of nothing. "If creation out of nothing, and so creation in the strict sense, has no place in Indian thought, that . . . determines some very central features not only of the Indian cosmogonics, but also of the metaphysical notions of God, substance, time, and negation."[42]

And at last, there is widespread consideration of Islamic ontology as both theocentric and cosmic, because its main tenet—*tawḥīd* ("Unity of Being")—necessitates at the same time the cosmic unity of all beings and their absolute dependence upon Allah.

Yet, it is preferable to avoid such generalizations. First, because they have been challenged not only "externally" by some foreign scholars, but, what is more essential, "internally" as well by Indian, Chinese, and Muslim thinkers through the course of history in those cultures. Second, it goes against the main purpose of this book: to present Eastern traditions (as much as a limited scope of the introductory course permits) in their diversity, thus prompting both teachers and students to reflect on and discuss the essence of the presented texts and to make their own independent conclusions rather than follow any normative approach.

FURTHER READING

Indian Tradition

Chakrabarti, A. "Metaphysics in India." In *A Companion of Metaphysics,* ed. Jaegwon Kim and Ernest Sosa. Oxford: Blackwell, 1955.

Larson, G. *India's Agony over Religion.* Albany: SUNY Press, 1995.

Potter, K., ed. *Indian Metaphysics and Epistemology.* Princeton, N. J.: Princeton University Press, 1980.

Chinese Tradition

Graham, A. C. *Disputers of the Tao: Philosophical Argument in Ancient China.* La Salle: Open Court, 1989.

Hall, D., and R. T. Ames. *Thinking Through Confucius.* Albany: SUNY Press, 1987.

Hansen, Ch. "Metaphysics in China." In *A Companion to Metaphysics,* ed. Jaegwon Kim and Ernest Sosa. Oxford: Blackwell, 1995.

Rosemont, H., Jr., ed. "Exploration in Early Chinese Cosmology." *Journal of the American Academy of Religious Studies.* Thematic Issue 50, 2. Atlanta: Scholars Press.

Islamic Tradition

Davidson, H. A. *Proofs for Eternity, Creation and the Existence of God in Medieval Islamic and Jewish Philosophy.* Oxford: Oxford University Press, 1987.

Shehadi, F. *Metaphysics in Islamic Philosophy.* Delmar: Caravan Books, 1982.

Wolfson, H. A. *The Philosophy of the Kalām.* Cambridge: Harvard University Press, 1976.

NOTES

1. *The Principal Upaniṣads.* Ed. with introd., text, trans., and notes by Radhakrishnan. S. London: George Allen & Unwin Ltd., 1953, pp. 449, 457.

2. Ibid., p. 232.

3. Ṣaṅkara. "Commentary on Brahmasūtra" (II. 1. 14). Isaeva, N. *Shankara and Indian Philosophy.* Albany: SUNY Press, 1993.

4. Ibid., II. 1. 17.

5. Ibid., II. 3. 17.

6. In the texts of Sāṃkhya and Vedānta, *buddhi* implies "intellect" (Cf. *manas,* meaning "mind" or "intelligence").

7. Ṣaṅkara. "Commentary on Brahmasūtra" (II. 3. 17).

8. Ibid., II. 3. 40.

9. Ṣaṅkara. "Commentary on Iṣapaniṣad." (IV). Isaeva, N. Op. cit.

10. Meister Eckhart. *Lateinische Werke.* Stuttgart: Band 5, Seite 42, No. I.

11. *The Tao. The Great Luminant. Essays from Huai Nan Tzu.* Trans. Evan Morgan. London: Kegan Paul, Trench, Trubner & Co., 1933, p. 3.

12. Ibid., p. 3.

13. Ibid., p. 4.

14. Lao-tzu. *Tao Te Ching. A Source Book in Chinese Philosophy.* Translated and compiled by Wing-Tsit Chan. Princeton, N.J.: Princeton University Press, 1963, p. 157.

15. "Selections from Remarks on Certain Trigrams." Ibid. p. 269.

16. Ibid.

17. See A. Kobzev, *The Symbols and Numbers Teaching in Classical Chinese Philosophy.* Moscow: Vostochnaya literatura, 1994.

18. Tung Chung-Shu. *Ch'un-ch'iu fan-lu.* (*Luxuriant Gems of the "Spring and Autumn Annals"*). *A Source Book in Chinese Philosophy,* p. 284.

19. *Chi* is variously translated as "breath," "energy," and "air." It designates the continuous psychophysical sea of energies that ceaselessly flow.

20. Ibid., p. 348.

21. *Mo Tzu: Basic Writings.* Trans. Burton Watson. New York: Columbia University Press, 1966, pp. 88–89.

22. Ibid., p. 80.

23. Wang Ch'ung. Lun-heng ("Balanced Inquiries"). *A Source Book in Chinese Philosophy,* pp. 297–98.

24. Cited from M. Fakhry, *A History of Islamic Philosophy.* New York: Columbia University Press; London: Longman, 1983, p. 57.

25. Ibid., p. 117.

26. Ibid., p. 154.

27. Maimonides, M. *Maaseh Bereshit* (The Act of Creation). RAMBAM. Readings in the Philosophy of Moses Maimonides. Selected and translated with introduction and commentary by Lenn E. Goodman. New York: The Viking Press, 1976, p. 127.

28. Ibid., p. 128.

29. Ibid., p. 132.

30. Ibid., p. 133.

31. Muhyi-d-din Ibn Arabī. *The Wisdom of the Prophets (Fuṣuṣ al-ḥikam).* Transl. by Angela Culme-Seymour. Aldsworth, Gloucesteshire, 1975, p. 32.

32. Ibid., p. 34.

33. Ibid., p. 9.

34. See M. Fakhry, *A History of Islamic Philosophy,* pp. 118–19.

35. Ibn Sīnā. "Books of Remarks and Admonitions." *Collected Philosophical Works.* Moscow: Nauka, 1980, p. 351.

36. *Tahāfut* literally means "inconsistency," "unsteadiness," "wavering." However, al-Ghazālī's treatise is traditionally known as *Collapse of the Philosophers.*

37. Ibn Rushd. "The Incoherence of the Incoherence." *Collected Works of the Mid-Eastern Thinkers.* Moscow: Vostochnaya literatura, 1961, p. 489.

38. Ibid., p. 498.

39. Ibid.

40. The "prime mover" is Aristotle's notion of a first cause, the first movement giving rise to all subsequent movements.

41. See P. J. Ivanhoe, "Human Beings and Nature in Traditional Chinese Thought." In *A Companion to World Philosophies.* Ed. Eliot Deutsch and Ron Bontekoe, Oxford: Blackwell, 1997, p. 155.

42. Mohanty, J. N. "The Idea of the Good in Indian Thought." *A Companion to World Philosophies,* p. 248.

3

Human Nature

HUMAN NATURE IN INDIAN TRADITION

G. W. F. Hegel contended that "Man . . . has not been posited" in India, because on his reading they viewed human individuals exclusively as a transitory manifestation of the Absolute and, therefore, devoid of self-value. Hegel's views have received wide currency in the history of philosophy. But how valid is his judgment? Is it not tinged with a touch of Eurocentrism? Perhaps such an assessment comes from an insufficient understanding of Indian traditions, and a failure to adequately interpret it.

Brahman–*ātman*

The first thing that "baffles" a Western person reared in the spirit of the Enlightenment is the seeming nondetachment of human beings in the Indian tradition from the world of all other living creatures. Indeed, in the Vedic texts (whose authority is acknowledged by all Brahmanic schools) the human being is often named *paśu*, a domestic animal listed among cows, horses, goats, and sheep (a list that sometimes includes camels, dogs, and donkeys). The same ancient texts, however, place the human being apart from all other animals, even comparing him or her to Indra (the supreme deity) in the world of living creatures. Though one of the most widespread synonyms for the word "man" in Ancient Hindu texts is *manusya*, a derivative from the verb "to think," some of those texts point out that the access to knowledge is not an exclusively human ability: "True, humans are knowledgeable, but they are not the only ones; for even birds and beasts all have knowledge of some sort."[1] The unique status that the sacred texts attribute to a human being is his or her exclusive right to conduct rituals and make sacrifices, thereby recognizing the particular bond between the human and the divine.

The select status of human beings is due to their ability to think. Yet, the most fundamental distinction between the human being and the rest of the world is the fact that they represent the fullest manifestation of *Ātman*, or the supreme "Ego." *Aitareya-āraṇyaka* (2.3.2) contains the following lines:

> [I]n herbs and trees sap only is seen, but thought (*citta*) in animated beings.
> Among animated beings again the self develops gradually, for in some sap (blood) is seen (as well as thought), but in others thought is not seen.
> And in man again the self develops gradually, for he is most endowed with knowledge. He says what he has known, he sees what he has known. He knows what is to happen tomorrow, he knows heaven and hell. By means of the mortal he desires the immortal—thus is he endowed.[2]

The fundamental difference between human beings and animals lies in the former's capacity to follow the dharma, or the "moral law."

According to the Indian tradition, the relationship between Brahman-*Ātman* and the *ātman* as an individual "self" is essentially founded on the principle of nonduality. The most revealing statement in this respect belongs to Śaṅkara:

> [T]he existence of Brahman is known on the ground of its being the self of everyone. For everyone is conscious of the existence of his or her self, and never thinks "I am not." If the existence of the self were not known, everyone would think "I am not." And this self (of whose existence all are conscious) is Brahman.[3]

Because of the nondual bond between the individual self and the Self, the Brahman-*ātman* present in all, every individual is *essentially* identified with all others.

The Moral Law of Dharma

The human being is predestined to play a special role as an agent for the world order. As mentioned above, according to the conventional idea predominating in India, the world was created in order to realize the moral law of dharma. Although dharma is a salient concept in Indian culture, its interpretation is far from unequivocal. Generally speaking, the matter at issue involves the cosmogonic processes viewed not as related to the arbitrary rule of gods, nor to natural mechanical causes, but rather to moral principles—or to be more precise, to the moral state of the creatures inhabiting the cosmos. According to the epic cosmology of the Indians, the "decline" of dharma at the end of each cosmic cycle leads to *pralaya*, a period of "cosmic night" during which the world disintegrates while souls reap the fruits of their past actions.

One should not draw hasty conclusions from the above, however, and assign the exclusive role of nature's "king" to human beings alone. First, there are quite a lot of Hindu, Buddhist, and Jainist texts recognizing the involvement of not only human beings but also of animals in the maintenance of dharma. Besides, one should keep in mind that people themselves in the Hindu tradition enjoy different "rights" regarding their participation in the dharmic process.

According to the Vedic tradition, humans acquire the knowledge of dharma, the rules of conducting rituals and making sacrifices through their reliance on the Vedas. Not everyone is entitled to access to the Vedas, however. People are divided into four *varṇas*, falling in turn into a multitude of castes. (Lokāyata was the only Indian philosophical school that traditionally rejected the caste-based system and the doctrines of karma and *saṃsāra*. Ājīvika recognized *saṃsāra* to a certain extent but without karma. Buddhists and some other unorthodox trends also renounced caste discriminations.)

In conformity with the Vedas, Brahmā in the beginning assigned "their several names, actions, and conditions to all created beings, even according to the words of the Veda" (1:21).[4] In other words, Brahmā assigned them to different castes. According to the Vedic myths, Puruṣa, having a thousand heads, a thousand eyes, a thousand legs, and the like, thus representing a certain macro- and microcosmic model of the cosmos and of humankind at the same time, procreated the moon from his spirit, the sun from his eyes, and the wind from his breath; the priests, brahmans, appeared from the lips of Puruṣa; *kṣatriyas*, the class of warriors, from his hands; *vaiśyas*, the tradesmen, from his hips; and finally, *śūdras*, all the rest of people, from his feet (pariahs, "the untouchables," stand outside this caste system). Only members of the first three *varṇas* were regarded as "twice-born," that is, those who had passed the principal rituals to gain access to the reading and studying of the Vedas. *śūdras* are prescribed to serve the members of the higher castes, brahmans first among them. Accordingly, "no collection of wealth must be made by a *śūdra*, even though he be able to do so; for a *śūdra* who has acquired wealth, gives pains to brahmans" (10:129).[5]

The transition from one caste to another is impossible during one's lifetime. The ideal behavior implies a strict observance of the caste's corresponding code of conduct (*varṇāśramadharma*), which could secure a higher social status only during a future birth. The karmic determinism is absolute:

> Of Brahmans, of *Kṣatriyas*, and *Vaiśyas* as also of *Śūdras*, O Conqueror of the foe (Arjuna), the activities are distinguished, in accordance with the qualities born of their nature.

> Devoted each to his own duty man attains perfection. How one, devoted to one's own duty, attains perfection, that do thou hear.
>
> Better is one's own law though imperfectly carried out than the law of another carried out perfectly. One does not incur sin when one does the duty ordained by one's own nature.[6]

The human being's involvement in the dharmic process, which is considered on the one hand "a mandate for dharma," singles him or her out from all the other living creatures. "Only man is open for the 'ought,'" we read, "regardless of what he has in common with the animals, he finds himself faced with norms and duties, i.e., dharma."[7] On the other hand, the *varṇāśrama-dharma* code regulates the standards of human life so rigidly that it leaves virtually no room for free choice, for a human being behaves not as an independent agent of morality but as an "actor" playing the role that has been assigned to him or her.

The following factor should also be taken into consideration. In addition to the castes, there exist other limitations on the human being's soteriological prerogatives. India is quite frequently regarded as the only country providing for salvation from the cycle of death and birth. For instance, *Viṣṇu Purāṇa* asserts: "Bhārata . . . is the only land of responsible action," whereas other regions are characterized as "areas of enjoyment."[8] It is also noteworthy that the terms *manu* and *manuṣya* are not used for defining every member of the human race, but only Aryans. This contrasts them with the rest of humanity, who are understood as *dāsa* or *dasyu*, that is, barbarians.

Life Negation and Life Affirmation

The normative or "communal" model as outlined above is oriented toward unconditional observance of the standards and rules of conduct designed to uphold a definite social structure. Under these conditions, the world- or life-affirming position turns out to be aimed at safeguarding the preordained. In this way, "life affirmation," strictly speaking, turns in fact into "life negation," for it restrains any volition and action going beyond conventional standards, which eventually hampers progress. Max Weber thus wrote about the conservative effects of the caste-based system: "A ritual law in which every change of occupation, every change in work technique, could result in ritual degradation is certainly not capable of giving birth to economic and technical revolutions from within itself."[9]

At the same time, it would be an oversimplification to suggest that social conventions fully exclude an active attitude toward life. One should keep in mind, however, that such an attitude within the framework of the "normative" model in most cases has a social orientation: for its aim is to improve the surrounding world and the human environment. In this respect it may be valid to treat Indian conventionality as evidence of a certain optimistic approach toward the attainment of an ideal world order.

In contrast, the so-called individualistic model takes shape under the impact of objective conditions invoking a loss of hope in the possibility of salvation from suffering, evil, and injustice. (The case in point is a model typical of religious consciousness and, as a rule, predisposed toward mysticism.) The human being in this model is seeking peace and salvation as an ideal outside his or her environment. His or her endeavors are directed toward self-perfection in order to bring him or her closer to, and "merging" with, the ideal of a transcendental Absolute. It is in this way that he or she escapes from the surrounding world.

In India, the caste system sanctified by the holy Vedas so rigidly predetermined human life that it seemed to leave no hope for salvation from suffering other than through the rupture of *saṃsāra*, that is, a chain of rebirths, by transcending its confines. Salvation from the turmoil of being and suffering, from the cycle of new births and deaths dependent on preceding karma, is what the Indians call *mokṣa.*

Mokṣa and *Nirvāṇa*

The Indian texts offer various definitions of *mokṣa.* In contrast to most *darśanas,* which perceived the ultimate ideal primarily in a negative vein, merely as salvation from suffering, the Vedantists associated it with a positive term, *nirvāṇa.* The stance of Jainists and some Buddhists is also ambiguous, not infrequently shrouded in metaphorical definitions. For instance, a twelfth-century Jainist author compared salvation from *saṃsāra* with the breaking of a vessel-body imprisoning the soul striving for freedom, or *mokṣa.*

No less varied are the ways for attaining *mokṣa.* Some Shivaistic and Tantric sects believed that the salvation from bad karma and the attainment of *mokṣa* called for making sacrifices (not only of animals but of humans as well). Of course, such views were not widespread. The way to *mokṣa* usually lies through hard work toward self-perfection.

First and foremost, this involves one's compliance with conventional moral rules specified in the code of conduct, prescribed by the religion. (For Hindus, it is the "Laws of Manu" that took shape from the second century B.C. through the second century A.D.) Next follows the renunciation of worldly passions and temptations.

Perfection is understood as the ability to apprehend one's own "self" identical with *ātman.* The *Dhammapada* (one of the most popular Buddhist texts) portrays the *bhikṣu,* a beggar or monk, who has received full ordination of the Buddhist community, thus:

> That mendicant is said to be calmed who has a calmed body, a calmed speech, and a calmed mind, who is well established, who has rejected the baits of the world.
>
> Raise yourself by yourself, examine yourself by yourself. Thus guarded by yourself and attentive, you, mendicant, will live happy.
>
> For self is the lord of self; self is the refuge of self.[10]

Buddhism offers the most comprehensive way to lead an ascetic life in mystical quest. Being, or the empirical world, is viewed by the Buddhists as the eternal agitation of suffering. Therefore, it is not an outcome of a fall, sin, calling for redemption but infinite suffering of the true being. Being implies suffering, for these are identical to each other.

True Being breaks up into an infinite number of dharmas, each experiencing its own share of suffering. This share depends on one's karma, the sum total of an individual's actions during his or her past birth. This is due to the fact that each given, single life is linked with those preceding it, the latter being responsible for sufferings in the current life. It happens thus because any single life is nothing more than a temporary combination of eternal and infinite components, comparable to a ribbon interwoven during a particular period of time out of threads having neither beginning nor end. Therefore life is a particular pattern, whereas death means the falling of this pattern into pieces, the unraveling the threads and the intermingling of them into a new pattern.

To achieve salvation from suffering, one has to put an end to the process of thread interweaving, or, to use another favorite Buddhist metaphor, to break away from the tumultuous "ocean of being." The Way to Perfection is through an escape from the whirlwind of existence, and through one's subsequent conversion into a transparent "drop," free of any disturbance or muddiness. The saved ones are those who have managed to break away from the nebulous vortex of rebirth; they are called *bodhisattvas,* meaning literally "the enlightened ones." The bodhisattvas, nearing complete release on the "shore" of the raging ocean of existence, give up this blessing of their own free will and plunge back into the vortex to help others out of it.

The bodhisattvas include a few select, who are esteemed as the most perfect creatures and who, upon finally "reaching the shore," stay in eternal peace. These are buddhas (the "awakened ones"). Each buddha appears to have three "bodies": his own physical body, which has attained perfection; a second, mystical one as reflected in bodhisattvas; and finally the absolute body. Buddhas are reflected in the other bodhisattvas as guru, mentor, and ultimate representation of the ideals to be followed.

In providing guidance on the Path to Perfection, Buddhism instructs: "Give up what is before, give up what is behind, give up what is in the middle, passing to the farther shore of existence. When your mind is wholly freed you will not again return to birth and old age. . . . He who has reached the good, who is fearless, who is without craving and without sin, he has broken the thorns of existence, this body is his last."[11]

The ascent of the Path to Perfection finishes with the state of *nirvāṇa*. The notion of *nirvāṇa* was gradually specified and elaborated in greater detail along with the mounting influence of Gautama's teaching. Yet, in all probability owing to the very fact that it symbolizes an ideal goal, desirable but virtually inaccessible to all but a select few, if any, the notion of *nirvāṇa* has proved to be irreducible to a single, precise definition. The meaning of the word "*nirvāṇa*" is polyphonic, implying extinction, wane, nonexistence, and the like. Varied interpretations of the notion of *nirvāṇa* reflect more than the complexities involved in conveying the psychological state associated with it. The ambiguity of the "ultimate" goal carries a tremendous optimistic charge as well: the Way to Perfection is infinite, it stimulates all human energies regardless of any preconceived scope.

Moreover, the polysemantic character of this notion is evidence of the diverse functions attributed by society to the ascetic tradition. It reveals dissatisfaction with, and a challenge to, the existing social order; on the other hand, it may also signify humble resignation manifested in an "escape" from life. It reflects a pessimistic tendency regarding the possibility of changing the world for the better, but at the same time it is imbued with an optimistic belief in salvation to be achieved through unity with the Absolute.

World- and life-negation quite often turns out to convey solely a denial of the world of evil, but not a denial of life as such. On the contrary, perpetual striving for self-perfection and a relentless search for the Truth evince a genuine assertion of life as an eternally changing process, a flow of never-ending changes.

HUMAN NATURE IN CHINESE TRADITION

In their attempts to define the Chinese philosophical tradition as a whole, many scholars are inclined to characterize it as anthropomorphically oriented. Indeed, neither ontology nor cognitive problems occupy as conspicuous a place in the speculations and reflections of Chinese thinkers as does the subject matter of the human being.

How are Human Beings Distinguished from the Myriad Things?

The human being is but one of the "ten thousand things." At the same time, however, he or she is the most valuable among a myriad of mundane things. Referring to Confucius's maxim, "Of the creatures born from the refined essence of Heaven and Earth, none is more noble than man," Tung Chung-shu asserted that "Man receives the mandate from Heaven and is therefore superior to other creatures."[12]

What distinguishes the human being from all other creatures? The answer to this question is provided in the "Debates in the White Tiger Hall" (*Bohutong*), a text that formally established the orthodox doctrine of Confucianism during the later period of the Han Dynasty. The human being is a creature endowed by nature with the following five gifts: humanity, righteousness, propriety, wisdom, and truthfulness. *Jen,* meaning "humanity," is identical with *pujen,* or "not to be hard-hearted." It implies empathy and love for one's fellow human beings. *I,* standing for "righteousness," is identical with *i* denoting uprightness and duty. It means "to respond without any thought of gaining." *Li,* or "propriety," is identified with *li* meaning "to act," to follow one's path in search of self-perfection. *Chi,* or "wisdom," is related to *chi* meaning "to know," to have one's own vision and deep understanding, without entertaining delusions in apprehending the innermost and grasping the truth. *Hsing,* or "sincerity," is identical with *chen* standing for "truthfulness," meaning to give oneself wholly to a certain single goal, without deviating from one's course.[13]

One can readily see that the essential characteristics of the human being, as specified above, encompass virtually all the ethical principles underlying a human being's relationships with other members of the race. The Chinese philosophers seem to be exclusively interested in the human being as a social being and, therefore, preoccupied primarily with the matters of good and evil, predestination and free will, destiny and luck. Their answers to these issues were as diverse as those observable in the traditions of other cultures.

Good and Evil in Human Nature

According to legend, Confucius believed in the essential unity of all people, perceiving this in terms of the inherent goodness of human nature. (Some scholars, however, deduce from the maxim ascribed to Confucius, according to which people are close to one another in their nature but stand far apart in their habits, that human nature is neutral to good and evil.)

Mencius (fourth through the third centuries B.C.) was more unequivocal in characterizing human nature as inherently good. Stating that it is the intrinsic goodness that makes a common person and the sage "the same in kind," he wrote: "Humanity, righteousness, propriety, and wisdom are not drilled into us from outside. We originally have them with us."[14]

Mencius's ideas were challenged by Hsun Tzu (circa 313–238 B.C.), his principal adversary, who insisted that "human nature was evil and its goodness was nothing more than an artificial acquisition." Over the next two millennia, from Confucius to Wang Yang-Ming, Confucians put forward and substantiated virtually every possible solution to the correlation between human nature and the good and evil problem. The truly comprehensive manner in which all possible answers to this philosophical question was posed is good evidence of the continual development and gradual collation of positions within traditional Chinese philosophy. All possible solutions to the problems raised in ancient times were surveyed, in every possible combination.

The Emperor as Embodiment of Heaven's Will

The problem of good and evil has been closely associated with that of predestination and free will. Regarding this issue we also encounter a wide variety of contrasting views. Notions concerning the existence of Heaven's "plan" with respect to all beings, and humans in the first place, is quite typical of Confucianism. According to the *Ch'un-ch'iu fan-lu,* "the basic substance naturally endowed is called man's nature. Nature is the basic substance. . . . What is called the person is received from Heaven (*T'ien,* Nature). Heaven has its dual operation of *yin* and *yang* (passive and active cosmic forces), and the person also has his dual nature of humanity and greed. . . . We must know that without training, our nature endowed by Heaven cannot in the final analysis make [the feelings and desires] weak."[15] So it stands to reason that the basic substance in human nature is predestined by Heaven and, therefore, it is beyond human control. Yet, "It is the true character of Heaven that nature needs to be trained before coming good. Since Heaven has produced the nature of man which has the basic substance for good but which is unable to be good [by itself], therefore it sets up the Emperor to make it good. This is the will of Heaven. The people receive from Heaven a nature which cannot be good [by itself], and they turn to the King [or Emperor] to receive the training which completes their nature. It is the duty of the King [or Emperor] to obey the will of Heaven and to complete the nature of the people."[16]

The passage cited above graphically illustrates the traditional Confucian predisposition for (1) negating absolute fatalism; (2) recognizing not only the possibility, but even the necessity of human efforts and actions aimed at realizing man's innate potentials for goodness and perfection, and (3) asserting (and this reveals a purely Chinese feature) the Emperor's select "mandate" to realize man's good nature.

The Emperor embodies Heaven's will and, therefore, he is virtually omnipotent. It depends on him alone whether the potential for goodness with which man's nature is endowed will manifest itself or not. Human nature is compared (by Tung Chung-shu) to rice stalks and goodness to the rice. Rice comes out of the rice stalk but not all the stalks yield rice. The same happens to the human being. Not everyone reveals his or her innate potentials, in particular the potential for generating good. In both cases it involves certain actions and efforts. Heaven endowed human beings with the potential for goodness, but for making good on this potential he or she has to act in compliance with the rules of proper upbringing ordained by the Emperor.

The Emperor is the bedrock of the state, and respect for him is the foundation of its proper order. This respect rests on the distribution of functions among Heaven, Earth, and the Human Being. Heaven grants life, Earth nourishes it, and the Human Being governs all by means of rules and music, that is, through the corresponding ritual forms. The Emperor symbolizes the unity of the three prime movers: by performing sacrifices, he serves Heaven; by taking part in the ritual of a first plowing, he serves Earth; and by taking care of his people, their upbringing and enlightenment, he serves Human Beings. By providing his services for all three, the Emperor personifies father and mother to his subjects, which makes violence and punishment unnecessary because people follow him like children that obey their parents. This interpretation of the role assigned to the Emperor readily discloses the ideological underpinnings of the Chinese imperial regime.

From the Western viewpoint, the Chinese Empire represents a variety of "Oriental despotism" permeated with the spirit of totalitarianism. Hegel and the historians of philosophy who followed his line of thinking in interpreting the Eastern intellectual legacy[17] believe that the Chinese understanding of the self is characterized by "self-negation" and "impersonality," hence their definition of the Chinese model of the human being as that of the "hollow personality." Morality is thereby viewed as an object of legalization, wherein everything associated with internal subjective feelings must abide by an external organization.

According to widespread opinion,[18] the Chinese tradition rejects the "autonomy of personality," lacking the notion of a "discrete and isolated self." Quite probably, however, Western assessments carry the imprint of a stereotyped vision of this alien culture, one that fails to explain how it could be possible for Chinese civilization to hold on and flourish for several thousand years if it had indeed eliminated the principle of individuality.

Focus-Field Model of the Self

One plausible answer to the question posed above is provided by an American sinologist, Roger T. Ames, who attempts to overcome certain widespread

Western stereotypes regarding the East. Convinced that Chinese culture is characterized by a close interrelationship of personal, public, and political precepts, Ames extrapolates a personal precept, or in other words, "a model of the self," out of the model of political organization inherent in traditional Chinese society. In ancient times, China was understood to be divided into "five zones." The first, "central" zone was directly governed by the Emperor; the second zone included the appendage principalities; the third, so-called suppressed zone embraced the principalities conquered by the ruling dynasty; the fourth zone was inhabited by "barbarians" partly controlled by the center; and finally, the fifth, "wild" zone was occupied by the uncontrolled barbarians. As a whole, in the words of Ames, "the solar system of a centripetal harmony" predominated in the political structure of Chinese society.

A similar model operated in the social plane, one based on *li,* or "ritual." The Chinese differentiate between "absolute" rituals and those subject to temporal change. To the Chinese, "absolute rituals" are more than customs and social practices, for they have a cosmological basis. These rituals "are rooted in the nature of heaven. They are like the order and laws of heaven, how can they be changed?"[19] The hierarchy of all beings is one of such absolute rituals or principles. In short, the observance of rituals is aimed at keeping the world, society included, in a state of stability and harmony to be secured through "differentiation and integration."

The above-mentioned mechanism of "centripetal harmony" is also applicable to the Chinese concept of "self." In a certain sense, the self is akin to the cosmos, in which matter clusters around some focal points determined by a dominant mass each time adjacent masses accord it enough freedom. What is characteristic of astronomic space can be observed in the microcosmic domain as well. Established centers constitute a focus of the force field that emanates forces and in which they converge. The focal points thus shaped are further interconnected as a sum of focal points, which in their interaction set up a balancing centripetal focus striving to distribute the forces of its field symmetrically around its own focal point. An individual "self" is thereby one of the focal points whose interaction with all other "self-focuses" determines the structure of an entity, being arranged around what may be called a well-balanced focus. As Mencius used to say, "all the myriad things are here in myself" and "he who uses his heart and mind wholly, realizes himself and upon self-realization, realizes heaven."

Thus, the "self" turns out to be a particle of the common force field and simultaneously a focus structuring its own entity. Therefore, human and society interrelationships manifest not a tyranny and "totalitarian spirit" but a "collectivistic spirit,"[20] which is geared toward what is most beneficial both for individuals and for society at large.

The Sage of Taoism

The Chinese cultural tradition is characterized not only by a "normative," "collectivistic" model of the human being, but also by an "individualistic" model, which found its fullest expression in the Taoist tradition. In contrast to Confucianism, which viewed the human being primarily as a social being, the Taoists concentrated on the natural aspects of the human being first and foremost.

According to Taoism, the human being appears to be endowed with two natures. The natural in him is ingrained, created and determined by the universal Tao (and therefore it is true), and the other is artificial, generated and determined by passions intrinsic in the human ego (and therefore it is false). Drawing on this premise, the Taoists consider the human being to be ideal if he or she manages to make the true nature predominate over the false. "The sage-man learns of Heaven and follows nature. He should not be tied by convention nor enticed by the sophism of man. He looks to Heaven as father and Earth as mother: on *yin* and *yang* as the determining principles, and the four seasons as the fundamental periodicity. Heaven is in *repose* by purity. Earth is *stable* through *tranquility*. . . . The Repose, being boundless, forms the dwelling of the soul. The Unconditioned is the abode of the Tao. Hence, should it be sought from without it will be missed within; should it be held as being alone within, it will be lost without. . . ."[21]

The Taoists criticized the Confucians and Mohists, stating, "By plausible and specious theories, the orthodox was slandered and the multitude captivated. Confucian writers, too, set up their own schools of music and dances; and, by embroidering their talk with quotations from the Odes, they 'bought' fame and became renowned in the world. The system of ceremonies in imperial interviews or social intercourse became excessive; the fashions in dress became luxurious."[22] According to the Taoists, it was unworthy of a sage to make "outward adornment of benevolence and righteousness," for "the impressions conveyed by the senses of eye and ear" should have no influence on the sage, for he "cultivates the tao-method within" and he "moves in tune with the soul and spirit."[23]

The Taoists display utter indifference to the external approval of their behavior, other people's opinion thereof, and the conformity of their behavior to conventional rules and standards. They are inclined not only to ignore these altogether but to even despise them in the most defiant manner: "He (the True Man) is concerned with foundations, he protects the spirit that he may soar to the circumference of the Universe. Far and wide, at pleasure (or following his own volition) he soars beyond this 'world of dirt': and dwells in the sphere of *wu wei*,[24] spirit-action. . . . He harbors no scheme of cunning in his heart:

hence life and death are both great and dignified: they are alike. Though the firmament covers and the earth sustains all, yet he is not tied to them (but maintains an independence): the spirit is above the flux. . . . Such one as this is verily in harmony with his being, depending not on the sight of the eye or the hearing of the ear or on courage, he has his heart and purpose governed by the spirit within."[25]

One can easily see the resonance between the antinormative poignancy of Taoism and many tenets propounded by Buddhism. It is no wonder, therefore, that their subsequent encounter on Chinese soil gave birth to a common brainchild, namely *Ch'an* Buddhism,[26] whose ideal is to expose one's primordial nature, to behave unencumbered like a fish in water or a bird in the sky, to wander free like wind blowing wherever it will, without looking for any support or shelter.

PREDESTINATION AND FREE WILL IN ISLAM

The rigid norms inferred in the "communal" model of a virtuous person in Islamic culture are based on the fatalistic notions about the limitless dependence of all beings on the supreme Absolute. The predetermination of human destiny and behavior is asserted in numerous *ayats* of the Koran,[27] although the text also contains verses that could be considered a negation of blind fatalism.

The idea of fatalism was codified as a basis of the Islamic ethical system by Muslim theologians. In particular, it received its fullest and most conspicuous manifestation in the works of al-Ghazālī. In his treatise *Revival of the Religious Sciences,* he wrote: "The moon, sun, stars, earth stones, and all nature and creation are the instruments in the hands of the Lord, they are His agents and like unto the pen . . . in the hands of the Lord. The Lord says, 'it is not you that have thrown the handful of dust, it is I Who am the real Thrower thereof.' The real scribe is the Lord."[28]

Disputes and contentions among Muslims on the issue of predestination arose as early as the reign of the first caliphs. The inherent contradiction in this doctrine lay in its incompatibility with the principle of human responsibility for his or her actions. How could a person be responsible for his or her actions if they depend not on his or her volition but rather on the primordial and preordained plan of God? And how could the conception of Allāh the "Omnipotent" tally with the conception of His infinite goodness? If God is all-powerful, good and evil exist only because He has willed it so, and that means He is not absolutely good. If God is absolutely good, and evil comes from something beyond Him, it follows that He is not omnipotent and does not determine human destinies.

Absolute fatalism was called into question by the Qādiriyyah school (from the Arabic word *qadar* meaning "destiny," "fate"), the first "perplexed" and "squabbling" Muslims. According to the great medieval Islamic historian al-Shahrastānī (d. 1153), the essence of the Qādiriyyah lay "in their desire to find the cause of any thing, and this came from the essence of the first damned [i.e., Satan] because the latter was looking, first, for the cause of creation; second, for wisdom in religious duty, and third, for gains from worshipping Adam. . . ."[29] The Qādiriyyah endorsed the idea of the free will of human beings and their responsibility for their actions before Allāh.

The Mu'tazilah theologians also upheld the teaching of free will. As a matter of fact, the polemics between the adherents of absolute fatalism and the champions of at least a modicum of free will proceeded throughout the entire history of Islam, becoming especially acute in the nineteenth and twentieth centuries.

Al-Insān Al-Kāmil—The "Perfect Person"

For all the dissimilarities between Islam and Buddhism or Taoism, the "individualistic" model that evolved in these three traditions has some common features. Perfection of, say, the Buddhist bodhisattva and the Ṣūfī *al-insān al-kāmil* (the "Perfect Person") is determined not by comparing their merits with those of other people but by their relationship with the Absolute, the highest degree of their nearness to Buddha or Allāh, because the criterion of ideality lies outside or at least far above conventional standards (even if these have been sanctified by religion) and does not belong to the phenomenal world. The ideal is oriented toward the transcendental but realizable in the human "self."

Such a criterion becomes possible by transferring the emphasis away from the biological and social nature of the human being and redirecting it toward his or her supernatural, divine essence.

According to the Ṣūfī tradition, human beings have within themselves the "divine" and the "created" merged together in an unbreakable bond. In the Koran[30] God says: "O Iblis! What prevents thee from prostrating thyself to one whom I have created with My hands?"[31] The great shaykh, Ibn 'Arabī, interprets this *ayat* as evidence of the union, as early as Adam, of the following two forms: the "exterior," created of the world's realities, and the "interior," corresponding to "a sum total of the divine names and qualities."

The human being as a species is considered the most perfect in the universe. Any other being is a mere reflection of one of the numberless attributes of the Absolute, whereas human beings synthesize in themselves all the forms of God's manifestation, incorporating all existing realities of the world. In the *wahdat al-wujūd* system, the human being is viewed as a "microcosm," a kind of measure of the world at large, or the "macrocosm." Moreover, the human being represents an intermediate link between God and the world, predestined to secure the unity of cosmic and mundane being.

Ibn 'Arabī compares the human being to a bezel in the seal: he is a sign, a mark engraved on a seal with which God's treasury is guarded; thus, the human being is called the "Representative of God," whose creation he safeguards as one safeguards a treasury by a seal.

Drawing from the Koran,[32] where it says: "We did indeed offer the trust to Heaven and Earth and the Mountains, but they refused to undertake it, being afraid thereof: but man undertook it," the Ṣūfīs considered it proven that the human being was predestined to be the "Receptacle of the Divine Essence."

The Way to Perfection

In satisfaction of their supreme predestination, human beings should strive for self-perfection. For if the heart is like a mirror in which the Divine Light is reflected, this mirror has to be properly "polished" so that one might see in it God's image, with a view to making the reflection correspond to the reflected. It means that the mission of human existence is to perform one's highest duty, which is the calling for constant perfection.

To achieve this goal, it is not enough to merely follow the standards of conduct prescribed by society. A law is merely a "reference point" in the manifested world, but for those who have embarked on the Way to the temple of True Being, the role of "leading lights" is performed by saints.

The "Perfect Person" (*al-insān al-kāmil*) is the highest rank in the hierarchy of Ṣūfī saints. In contrast to Ibn 'Arabī, who regarded the "Perfect Person" mainly (and perhaps exclusively) as fulfilling a *metaphysical* function, as the key to the solution of philosophical problems such as that of the One and the Many, individuality and multiplicity, universals and particulars, and essences and phenomena, the later Ṣūfīs brought into the foreground the *religious* function of the "Perfect Person," as one who acts as an intermediary between the human being and God.

The incorporation of both the metaphysical and religious definitions of the "Perfect Person" allowed the principles of moral perfection to be shaped in accordance with the adept's own particular level of understanding. The majority of Ṣūfīs, common folk, and generally illiterate relied on the guidance and examples of saints. The lives and behavior of saints served as a model for common Ṣūfīs to imitate and follow. Blind and often thoughtless imitation sometimes made the adept a tool in the hands of deceitful and imperious men who knew how to force the humble and inexperienced adepts to submit to their will.

At the same time, the metaphysical interpretation of *al-insān al-kāmil* held substantial humanitarian potential. It was presupposed that human beings themselves, capable of becoming perfect on the way to self-cognition and apprehension of their own true selves, could and should serve as models of morality, an indicator of good and evil: "The ultimate aim and meaning of the Way is to reveal the Absolute in one's own self" (Ibn al-Fāriḍ).

Freedom of Will as God's Mercy

The concept of the "Perfect Person" runs counter to Islamic traditionalism at least in two respects. First, the notion of the human being as a haven of the divine and the possibility of one returning to one's true "self" through union with God led to the logical conclusion that God's presence was immanent in human nature, which is inconsistent with the theistic notion of God's absolute transcendence. Second, the very positing of the question about the individual's capacity to attain the level of *al-insān al-kāmil* carries a challenge to the tenet of fatalism.

The recognition of the complete predetermination of human actions would make embarking on the Way to Perfection meaningless, but that was the Ṣūfīs' key prerogative and the bedrock of their teaching and practice. Hence, their intention was to combine a notion of God's omnipotence with human free will.

According to Ibn 'Arabī, God's omnipotence implies that He is always the "giver," for God is the "treasurer of all possibilities." However, the Great Shaykh was far from recognizing necessity alone and excluding chance. He disparaged as intellectually feeble those thinkers who denied chance as such and accepted only absolute necessity (as a logical and ontological category). Ibn 'Arabī founded his acceptance of human free will on the assumption that human freedom was a "receptacle" of possibilities granted to the human being by God, a set of possibilities that one was able and obliged to realize by oneself: "From God comes only the effusion of the Being on thee (who art only pure possibility) whereas thine own judgment comes from thee. Then, praise only thyself and blame only thyself."[33]

Freedom of will is, therefore, qualified by God's mercy. What then is the point in the Almighty limiting the might of His own free will? The point is to submit human beings to a "test." Why should God test human beings? Could He not endow human beings only with virtues? He so willed in order to reveal the true righteousness of human beings for, as the ṣūfī poet Jalāl al-Dīn Rūmī says, "chastity is worth nothing unless it is tempted by lust." The main point, however, is not to test the human being to reveal his or her real worth. Evil and good are necessary to demonstrate the universal scope of the Absolute Being.

God is all, which means that He manifests Himself even in the qualities of imperfection and in the qualities deserving blame.

The idea that God, in order to be "known," manifests Himself in contrasting forms, when the dazzling Divine Light needs opposing darkness to be contemplated, is consonant with Neoplatonic views that affirm that the vitiation of things could not be discussed unless there were things that could be vitiated, nor could "evil" be spoken of unless there was "good."

Good and evil appear as objective manifestations of the paired divine attributes, mercy and retribution, ensuing from the Almighty's wish to manifest Himself. They are, in a certain sense, predetermined. To stop at that, however, would mean not only to acknowledge the natural presence of good and evil in the world but also to recognize the futility of our attempts to overcome evil. In such a case nothing would remain but to reconcile oneself with the existing evil and acknowledge the pointlessness of high ideals and the futility of all endeavors to attain personal perfection and social progress. Being aware of the adverse implications of such an approach, the Ṣūfīs sought to specify that, despite the objective existence of good and evil in the world, the human being was free to exercise volition.

Jalāl al-Dīn Rūmī compares the freedom of will to "capital" that brings profit to its owner who knows how to properly dispose of it, while the one who does not know how to make use of it or misuses it will be punished on doomsday. Nevertheless, the same Rūmī acknowledged that the dispute between the adherents of divine predetermination and their opponents could hardly be settled rationally and, therefore, it should be transferred from the sphere of reason to a sphere where "the heart reigns." Being totally absorbed in love for the Almighty, the human being becomes part of "the ocean," that is, the Absolute Reality, and therefore any action on the part of the human being is not his or her action alone but rather that of the "ocean." The overwhelming love for God changes the human being so much that the problem of free will appears null and void, for one feels oneself completely merged with the Absolute Being and becomes naturally aware of the perception: "I am God."

Manṣūr al-Ḥallāj ventured to utter this bold statement (for which he was sentenced to public execution in A.D. 922) because he had come to the following conclusion: "If the Spirit is my spirit, and my spirit is His Spirit, then what He wishes I wish, and what I wish He wishes." Rūmī reckons Ḥallāj's "I am God" as evidence of great humility rather than as an act of insolent pretension: "The man who says 'I am the servant of God' asserts that two exist, one himself and the other God. But he who says 'I am God' is saying, 'I am not, He is all, nothing has existence but God, I am pure nonentity, I am nothing."

According to Sufism, freedom of the will meant volition liberated from prescribed, normative standards, a volition in conformity with nothing but the individual's own choice. The criterion of morality, therefore, lay in one's personal judgment of what was good. Yet, the Ṣūfīs' free volition was limited and conditioned as only the few select were considered to be worthy and capable of making an independent judgment and choice whereas the majority were obliged to obey their sheikhs.

The right to a free judgment could only be secured upon advancement on the Way to Perfection. It had to be suffered for, and could be obtained only through "torments" in the unremitting quest for Truth. The ascent of the Way ends with *fanā'*, a state akin to the Buddhist *nirvāṇa.*

The "Virtuous Person" According to al-Fārābī

The notions of Islamic philosophers about what the human being is in principle and what the characteristics of a "perfect" or "virtuous" person are in particular took shape under the opposing influence of religious dogmatism and the considerable impact exerted by the Greek philosophers. By way of illustration, let us consider the views of al-Fārābī, one of the most impressive figures in the field of philosophical anthropology in the Muslim East.

Al-Fārābī regarded the human being as belonging to the fourth stage of being. The first instinct in human beings at birth is to be fed; it is then followed, in running succession, by the stimulation of sense faculties, the wishing for or rejection of sensations, imagination, and finally reasoning. By virtue of the power of reasoning, the human being perceives objects of intellection, distinguishes between beauty and ugliness, and masters the arts and sciences. This power of reasoning predominates over all the other faculties or abilities.[34]

Drawing on the findings of contemporary medicine, al-Fārābī describes in detail the functions of various organs of the human body, ranking the brain as second (after the heart) in its magnitude. It is noteworthy that al-Fārābī, contrary to the Islamic tradition of gender discrimination, asserts that men and women do not differ in their sensations, imagination, and intellect.

As soon as one has perceived the apprehensible objects of intellection, one becomes naturally predisposed for thinking over, reflecting, recollecting, striving for deductions, and expressing wishes. As al-Fārābī contends, "The craving for what is apprehensible is in general the volition. If it proceeds from a sensation or imagination, it is commonly called volition; but if it proceeds from the reflection or reasoning, it is generally defined as choice, which is inherent specifically in man."[35]

The realization of the first apprehensible objects of intellection is one's first accomplishment, being granted to one for the sole purpose of attaining one's supreme perfection, that is, "happiness." Al-Fārābī defines happiness as "the good sought after for itself," for it "consists in the human soul arriving at such perfection of being when it no longer needs matter for its subsistence, for it merges with a set of beings devoid of corporeity, and the substances separated from matter, and thereby existing eternally."[36] This definition of happiness is quite reminiscent of the one used to describe the state of a mystic arriving at the highest degree of perfection. However, al-Fārābī*'s* further discourse on the "city of virtue" and the life of its inhabitants reveals that for him the notion of happiness also had a quite distinct social import.

The leading theme of his *Treatise on the Opinions of the Inhabitants of the City of Virtue* is the social nature of the human being. As al-Fārābī writes, "none could achieve perfection for which he is predestined by nature unless he reunites with many other individuals helping one another, each providing for another some share of what is necessary for his subsistence."[37] The city of virtue, the ideal society, is destined to secure favorable conditions for free choice and will, which would make people happy.[38] On the contrary, the ignorant or "erring city" is the one "which expects to find happiness after the present life" and "whose inhabitants have never known happiness nor even suspected what it is to strive for it."[39]

Al-Fārābī compared the city of virtue to a healthy body with all of its organs performing their proper functions and acting in an integral harmony. He insisted on a certain hierarchy to be followed in society. The highest rank belongs to the chief who surpasses the rest of the citizens in his qualities and virtues. The first rank consists of the persons who come very near to the chief in their disposition and customs, each acting in accordance with the chief's intention. Next in the hierarchy are persons acting to meet the ends of the first rank. Then come persons acting to meet the ends of the preceding echelon. And so on, until the entire community is ranked correspondingly down to the lowest echelon, which is occupied by persons who, without being served themselves, provide services for others. These belong to the last and the lowest rank.[40]

The city of virtue could be headed only by a person who is by nature ready for governing and, second, has enough willpower to realize these innate abilities. Al-Fārābī believes that human beings mature into real personalities provided they assume their natural forms that are capable and willing to become active intellects. Initially, the human being is endowed with a passive intellect comparable to matter. At the next stage this intellect passes into active intellect, and the latter in turn gives rise to the acquired intellect. If the passive intellect is substance for the acquired intellect, the latter acts as matter for the active intellect. As al-Fārābī wrote, "What overflows from Allāh into the active intellect is poured by the latter into the passive intellect through mediation of the acquired intellect, and then into his power of imagination. And this man by virtue of what overflows to his passive intellect becomes a sage, philosopher, and the owner of a perfect intellect. And by virtue of what overflows into his power of imagination (he becomes) a prophet, a herald of the future, and narrator of the current particular events. . . . Such a man achieves the highest degree of human perfection and attains supreme happiness. His soul is perfect and united with the above-mentioned active intellect."[41] Only such a person, called the *'imām,* is entitled to govern the city of virtue.

Al-Fārābī's views of the human being and society reveal the undeniable influence of the Greeks: Aristotle, in his discourse on the human soul and its intrinsic forces and dispositions; Plato, in particular his notion of the ideal governing of the state; and the Neoplatonists, in expounding the process of "emanation," the effusion of various levels of being. At the same time, al-Fārābīs views reveal an urge to adapt the ideas of the Greek thinkers to the conditions of Muslim society and the Islamic tenets of the inseparable unity of sacred and secular powers and the ideal theocratic monarchy.

The Sociology of Ibn Khaldūn

Al-Fārābī is acclaimed as a precursor to Ibn Khaldūn (1332–1406), a thinker of such caliber that some historians consider him the founder of sociology, having anticipated the ideas of such later thinkers as Giambattista Vico, Auguste Comte, Niccolo Machiavelli, Adam Smith, and Herbert Spencer. Sometimes his thinking is considered a precursor to historical materialism, making him a "pre-Marxian Marxist" or the "Arabian Marx."

By the early fourteenth century, when philosophy and scholastic theology in the Muslim East seemed to have been completely defeated by the *Neo-Ḥanbalīs* (the most conservative branch of orthodox Islam), Ibn Khaldūn stood apart. His contributions to the legacy of Islamic philosophy are particularly impressive in two respects: first, by virtue of his extensive commentaries and critiques of the Arab peripatetic tradition, and second, through his pioneering philosophy of history. His principal work is *al-Muqaddimah* (*Prolegomena*), representing an introduction to his major treatise on history.

In the *Muqaddimah,* Ibn Khaldūn criticizes philosophers and comes to the conclusion that metaphysics has failed altogether to solve any problem pertaining to human destiny and salvation. In his opinion, the sole "fruitful" effect of metaphysics is its ability to "sharpen the mind" by cultivating a "habit for truthfulness" in people by means of its logical methods. He conceded that, despite their shortcomings, such methods were still the best known to date. Just the same, Ibn Khaldūn recommended that resort to these methods be made only after serious study in the religious sciences, in Koranic exegetics (*tafsīr*), and Muslim jurisprudence (*fiqh*) in particular.

Ibn Khaldūn's theory of history and civilization is a result of his generally positivistic approach, combined with the religious and even mystical inclinations of medieval thinking. Although asserting that the historical process was dependent on the will of God, Ibn Khaldūn constructed his theory of history by drawing on the empirical data of geography, climate, ecology, and culture, as well.

Ibn Khaldūn defined the orientation of his sociological constructs as that of a "social physics," following the contemporary model of physics based on Aristotelian ideas of nature. In his opinion, "this world with all the created things in it has a certain order and social construction. It shows nexuses between causes and things caused, combinations of some parts of creation with others, in a pattern that is both remarkable and endless."[42]

The human being is inseparably linked with nature. The greatest effect on human beings, he contends, is exerted by the temperature of the air, varying in each of the seven "climates." He proceeds according to a naturalistic line of thinking, one that can be traced back to the works of his predecessors, al-Fārābī and Ibn Rushd, as he explains the differences in people's mental features, culture, and social organization.

The human being is not only a natural creature, but also a political creature in the sense that "he cannot do without the social organization for which the philosophers use the technical term 'city' (*polis*)."[43] It is absolutely necessary for a human being to have the cooperation of his fellows in order to obtain food, nourishment, and protection. "Consequently, social organization is necessary to the human species. Without it, the existence of human beings would be incomplete."[44]

One major thesis advanced by Ibn Khaldūn is presented as follows: "It should be known that differences of condition among people are the result of the different ways in which they make their living."[45] Those who follow the ways of nature in making their living, by simply tilling the soil and breeding cattle, remain at a primitive stage of life, being unable to obtain anything exceeding their natural requirements. With the appearance of assets exceeding the elementary needs, human society passes from a primitive to a civilized stage. To Ibn Khaldūn's mind, the former stage is in fact much more wholesome than the latter, which inevitably leads to excess, inertia, stagnation, and eventual downfall.

Ibn Khaldūn believed that a dynasty (or any state) passes, as a rule, through the following five stages of development: (1) the "stage of consolidation," during which a monarchy is established by relying on the people's solid support; (2) the "stage of tyranny," during which a monarch monopolizes his power and loses touch with his compatriots; (3) the "stage of abuses," wherein the privileges granted those in power are misused; (4) the "stage of attempts," designed to appease the people's discontent; and finally (5) the "stage of decline," which heralds the breakdown of society.

Ibn Khaldūn 's deliberations over law-governed regularities in social development reveal the unambiguous influence of "The Brethren of Purity," a secret religio-philosophical society founded in Baṣra in the tenth century. They too advocated a cyclical notion of social development, whereby each state goes through a time of upsurge and a time of decline. These influential predecessors, however, were principally interested in the political aspects of this cyclical process, whereas Ibn Khaldūn stressed the interrelationship of political and economic factors, placing greater emphasis on the latter, on the conditions under which "people make their living."

In which way do Eastern notions of human being share commonality in being compared with Western ones? By "Western" we mean the approach dominant in the part of the world molded by the European Renaissance and the Enlightenment onward. (Though, of course, there had been premises for those movements rooted in the classical ideas of the Greeks and the Romans.) In fact, the very East-West "duality" became the object of discourse from the late eighteenth century.

That commonality in its turn has two aspects. One in reference to its nature, and another in reference to society. In the first case it seems that what unites the great variety of trends in such nonsimilar cultures as Indian, Chinese, and Muslim is their adherence to anthropocosmism in contrast to mainly secular Western anthropocentrism. It is no wonder, then, that leading philosophers with heterogeneous cultural backgrounds of the East sound so much in tune with each other in their criticism of the Western approach.

Let us consider just two quotations. The first is from Tu Weiming, one of the most distinguished contemporary philosophers (Director of the Harvard–Yenching Institute, Harvard University). "The human form of life envisioned by Confucius," says the Chinese scholar, "is anthropocosmic in the sense that there is implicit mutuality, constant communication, and dynamic interaction between the anthropological world and the cosmic order."[46]

Strikingly similar is what S. H. Nasr, the very prominent and modern Muslim thinker, writes in many of his books: that man is conceived in Islam not in his "titanic" and "promethean" nature, that is, one that rebels against the "will of heaven" in a heroic manner. On the contrary, he is leveled down in a sense to being the *'abd*, or servant, of Allāh, and his duty then "does not mean a selfish and blind conquest and domination of nature. It means living in harmony with nature."[47]

While the cosmic order understood in China and the Muslim world is not the same, their criticism of the Western approach demonstrates significant likeness. In Tu Weiming's words, "the Enlightenment faith in instrumental rationality, fueled by the Faustian drive to explore, know, subdue, and control," along with the modern developments in the Western mode of thinking, are "diametrically opposed to the Chinese habits of heart," and have "challenged all dimensions of the Sinic world."[48] As for S. H. Nasr, he has no doubt that "the perennial wisdom of various traditions and traditional knowledge lying at the heart of the authentic religions opposed to the whole enterprise of modern philosophy from the Renaissance onward."[49]

The second aspect of the commonality of the East in contrast to the West, as it has been said before, concerns the co-relation of the human being with society. Indeed, that contrast holds in a much broader context, for it is not limited only to the "East" and "West," it also holds between so-called traditional and post-traditional liberal societies. To make this standpoint clearer, let us consider just one component of that co-relation manifested in the notion of "Justice."

Some consider justice to belong to the set of so-called universal human values. However, the notion of justice is always enclosed within the framework of a particular value system. Traditional societies typically differ in their approach toward the ideal of justice from the approach taken by post-traditional societies in at least four respects.

First, before the emergence of Western liberal society, there were basically two types of moral prescriptions: one sanctioned by religion and the other by the local authority. Indian, Muslim, and Medieval Christian civilizations are characterized by the recognition of morality as a system of ethical norms prescribed by the corresponding religious belief. In the Islamic world, for example, the source of any law, including the moral law, is Allāh. Hence there is a rejection of any right to lawmaking by mere human beings and a demand that one strictly follow the law of Allāh, *Shari'ah.* As for an authoritarian moral system, the most vivid example of it one can find is perhaps provided by the dominant Confucian tradition in traditional Chinese society.

Second, the realization of justice in traditional societies usually refers not to the present but to the future, by which is meant the life after death, when we have passed from this mundane life. In Islam, justice will reign only at the Day of the Last Judgment, when God will treat each human in accordance with his or her sins and virtues. No human being or society, but God alone, is absolutely just:

> For those who do good is the best (reward) and more (thereto). Neither dust nor ignominy cometh near their faces. Such are rightful owners of the Garden; they will abide therein. And those who earn ill-deeds, (for them) requital of

> each ill-deed by the like thereof; and ignominy overtaketh them—They have no protector from Allāh—as if their faces had been covered with a cloak of darkest night. Such are rightful owners of the Fire; they will abide therein.[50]

According to the Indian tradition, after death, which is thought of as the death of the body, the transition is done in conformity with karma or deeds. It is in this way that justice is achieved.

Third, justice is related to a certain "collective" to which an individual belongs. That could be a caste, a community, a class or social stratum, a religious confession, and so on. For equal virtues or sins, different blessings or punishments could be expected. Thus, for example, when a *kṣatria* (a member of a caste of warriors) engages in violence or even kills on the battlefield, that is not only excused but considered a virtue. For those who belong to other castes, however, such behavior is considered to be criminal. In traditional society, where a "stratified labor division" (Max Weber's phrase) exists, an individual is expected to fulfill those functions that are prescribed as a result of his or her belonging to a particular social community. Here justice is measured on the basis of how successful an individual has been in following the prescribed behavior patterns of the social stratum to which he or she was assigned by birth. In this sense, it could be said that in the traditional society, justice has a tendency to be of an egalitarian nature.

The situation is quite different in the post-traditional society. Here the labor division is "functional," by which is meant that the place of an individual in the social stratification is determined by the function that he or she fulfills, and a change of that function can lead to a change in social status. Accordingly, here justice is measured strictly on the basis of the deeds of an individual; he or she carries personal responsibility for those deeds. It is not by chance that in English "justice" is defined as "reward or penalty as deserved." Similarly, in French "justice" means "acknowledgment and respect of the rights and dignity of everybody."

Fourth, justice is regarded only in terms of duty—which is to say, without any consideration of human "rights." It is significant that in Sanskrit there is no word that corresponds to "right." Similarly, the traditional Chinese ethical system presents a set of duties, rather than of rights.

The post-traditional or liberal society differs from the traditional one in all the above-mentioned respects. (1) The source of justice and the ultimate judge, ruling it, is the people itself, represented by the elected members of parliament and the courts. (2) Justice is thought of in terms of the categories of the present: it should be realized here and now, in this life. (3) Everyone should have an equal right to justice in full accordance with his or her own deeds. (4) Justice and the law are undivided.

The general notion of "human being" unavoidably determines the criteria used by him or her in the search for Truth.

FURTHER READINGS

Indian Tradition

Crawford, C. *The Evolution of Hindu Ethical Ideals.* Honolulu: University of Hawaii Press, 1982.

Hindery, R. *Comparative Ethics in Hindu and Buddhist Traditions.* New Delhi: Motilal Banarsidass, 1978.

Jaini, P. *The Jaina Path of Purification.* New Delhi: Motilal Banarsidass, 1979.

Motilal, B. K. *Logical and Ethical Issues of Religious Belief.* Calcutta: University of Calcutta, 1982.

Thakur, S. *Christian and Hindu Ethics.* London: George Allen and Unwin, 1969.

Chinese Tradition

Chad, H. "Classical Chinese Ethics." In *A Companion to Ethics,* ed. Peter Singer. Oxford: Blackwell, 1997.

Fingarette, H. *Confucius—The Secular as Sacred.* New York: Harper & Row, 1972.

Graham, A. *Later Mohist Logic, Ethics, and Science.* Hong Kong: Chinese University Press, 1978.

Hall, D., and R. T. Ames. *Thinking from the Han: Self, Truth, and Transcendence in Chinese and Western Culture.* Albany: SUNY Press, 1998.

Munro, J. *The Concept of Man in Early China.* Stanford: Stanford University Press, 1969.

Islamic Tradition

Fakhry, M. *Ethical Theories in Islam.* Leiden, N.Y.: E. J. Brill, 1991.

Hourani, G. *Reason and Tradition in Islamic Ethics.* Cambridge: Cambridge University Press, 1985.

Houvannisian, M., ed. *Ethics in Islam.* Malibu, Calif.: Undena Publications, 1985.

Khadduri, M. *The Islamic Conception of Justice.* Baltimore: Johns Hopkins University Press, 1984.

Stepaniants, M. *Sufi Wisdom.* Albany: SUNY Press, 1994.

NOTES

1. Cited from Chakrabarti, A. "Rationality in Indian Philosophy." *A Companion to World Philosophies.* Ed. by Eliot Deutsch and Ron Bontekoe. Oxford: Blackwell, 1999, p. 260.

2. Aitareya-Āraṇyaka. *The Sacred Books of the East: The Upaniṣads.* Trans. F. Max Muller. Vol. 1, Pt. 1. New Delhi: Motilal Banarsidass, 1988, p. 222.

3. Cited from Nakamura, N. *Ways of Thinking of Eastern Peoples. India-China-Tibet-Japan.* Honolulu: East-West Center Press, 1964, p. 99.

4. *The Laws of Manu.* Trans. G. Duhler. New Delhi: Motilal Banarsidass, 1988, p. 504.

5. Ibid., p. 430.

6. *The Bhagavad Gītā.* With an introductory essay, Sanskrit text, English translation, and notes by S. Radhakrishnan. London: George Allen & Unwin Ltd., 1967, 18: 41, 45, 47.

7. Halbfass, W. *Tradition and Reflection. Exploration in Indian Thought.* Albany: SUNY Press, 1991, p. 278.

8. Ibid., p. 273. "Bhārata" is another name for India in Sanskrit; it originates from the name of an ancient monarch.

9. Weber, M. *Essays in Sociology.* New York: Oxford University Press, 1974, p. 413.

10. *The Dhammapada,* 25:378–380. Ed. S. Radhakrishnan. London: Oxford University Press, 1968, pp. 175–76.

11. Ibid., 24:348, 351, p. 168.

12. Tung Chung-shu. *Ch'un ch'iu fan-lu* (*Luxuriant Gems of the "Spring and Autumn Annals"*). In *A Source Book in Chinese Philosophy.* Translated and compiled by Wing-Tsit Chan. Princeton, N.J.: Princeton University Press, 1972, p. 280.

13. Ibid., p. 247.

14. *The Book of Mencius* in *A Source Book in Chinese Philosophy,* p. 54.

15. Tung Chung-shu. *Ch'un ch'iu fan-lu,* pp. 273, 247.

16. Ibid., p. 276.

17. For example, D. Monroe, R. Edwards, M. Alwin, S. K. Young, and others.

18. That of Marcel Mauss and Herbert Fingarette, for instance.

19. See Kai-wing Chow. "Ritual, Cosmology, and Ontology: Chang Tsai's Moral Philosophy and Neo-Confucian Ethics." *Philosophy East & West,* vol. XLIIII, No. 2, April 1993, p. 216.

20. See R. Ames. "The Individual in Classical Confucianism ('Focus-Field' Model)." *God-Man-Society in Traditional Oriental Cultures.* Ed. M. Stepaniants. Moscow: Vostochnaya literatura, 1993, pp. 39–65.

21. *The Tao. The Great Luminant. Essays from Huai Nan Tzu.* Trans. Evan Morgan. London: Kegan Paul, Trench, Trubner & Co., 1933, p. 58–59.

22. Ibid., p. 47.

23. Ibid., p. 44.

24. The meaning of *wu wei* here involves "not doing" or "not being coercive."

25. Ibid., p. 65.

26. "Zen" in Japanese.

27. For instance, 6:134, 6:39, 7:188.

28. Al-Ghazālī. *Revival of the Religious Sciences (Ihya 'ulum al-din).* Trans. Bankey Behari. Franham, Surrey: Sufi Publishing Co. Ltd., 1972, p. 237.

29. Al-Shahrestānī. *The Book About Religions and Sects.* Trans. S. N. Prozorov. Pt. 1. Moscow: Vostochnaya literatura, 1984, p. 33.

30. Koran (38: 75).

31. "Iblis" is the Islamic equivalent of Satan, the fallen angel.

32. Koran (33: 72).

33. Ibn 'Arabī. *The Wisdom of the Prophets (Fuṣūṣ al-ḥikam).* Trans. Angela Culme-Seymour. Aldsworth: Beshara Publications, 1975, p. 175.

34. Al-Fārābī. *Idées des habitants de la cité vertueuse.* Trad. R. P. Jaussen, Youssef Harani, and J. Chlala. Le Cairo: L'Institut Francais d'archéologie Orientale. 1949, p. 56.

35. Ibid., p. 68.

36. Ibid., p. 68.

37. Ibid., p. 76.

38. Ibid., pp. 76–77.

39. Ibid., p. 86–87.

40. Ibid., p. 77.

41. Ibid., pp. 82–83.

42. Ibn Khaldūn. *The Muqaddimah. An Introduction to History.* Trans. Franz Rosenthal. In 3 vols. London: Routledge & Kegan Paul, 1958, vol. 1, p. 194.

43. Ibid., p. 89.

44. Ibid., p. 91.

45. Ibid., p. 249.

46. Tu Weiming. "Chinese Philosophy: A Synoptic View." *A Companion to World Philosophies.* Ed. Eliot Deutsch and Ron Bontekoe. Oxford: Blackwell, 1999, p. 7.

47. Nasr, S. H. *A Young Muslim's Guide to the Modern World.* Chicago: Kazi Publications, Inc., 1994, p. 38.

48. Tu Weiming. Op. cit., p. 22.

49. Nasr, S. H. Op. cit., p. 178.

50. Koran (X, 26–27).

4

In Search of the Truth

THE SEARCH FOR TRUTH IN INDIAN TRADITION

"External" versus "True" Knowledge

The "barometer" of rationality in classical Indian culture was based on the joint endeavors of the Sāṃkhya-Yoga and Nyāya-Vaiśeṣika schools. The ideal of rationality inherent in Indian Brahmanic philosophy took shape within these classical *darśanas.* This philosophy invariably differentiates between "external" and "true" knowledge:

> The senses, the mind, and the intellect are said to be its seat; enveloping Knowledge through these it (i.e., desire) deludes the embodied soul. (3:40)
>
> Thus, the Lord instructs Arjuna, the epic hero in the Bhagavadgītā, that: In this world, there is no purifier like Knowledge; he who has attained purity of heart through the practice of Karmayoga automatically realizes it in the self over the course of time. (4:38)

The above verses represent a formula of knowledge encoded in the classical Indian philosophical tradition in its Brahmanic version.

Pramāṇas

There are several sources of knowledge, or *pramāṇas,* three of which are the most significant. These are perception, inference, and *śabda-pramāṇa.* The first two need no special commentary because their meaning is quite obvious. They involve universally acknowledged sources of knowledge such as perception and deduction. According to the Yoga-Sūtras of Patañjali, the basic text of Sāṃkhya-Yoga, "Perception is that source of valid ideas when the mind-stuff has been affected by some external thing through the channel of the sense-organs.

This fluctuation is directly related to that [object], but, whereas the intended object . . . consists of a genus and a particular, [the fluctuation] is chiefly concerned with the ascertainment of the particular. . . . Inference is [that] fluctuation [of the mind-stuff] which refers to that relation which is present in things belonging to the same class as the subject-of-the-illation . . . and absent from things belonging to classes different [from that of the subject-of-the-illation]; and it is chiefly concerned with the ascertainment of the genus."[1]

Śabda-pramāṇa provides knowledge of that which is inaccessible to observation and deduction and related to extralogical realities. It presents evidence taken for granted. Sāṃkhya proclaims that there are three available sources of *śabda-pramāṇa*. These are: first (and foremost), the eternal, imperishable Vedas; second, the tradition of *smṛti*, embracing *dharmaśāstras*, *itihāsas*, and *purāṇas*; and third, the spiritual experience of the "perfect," "competent," and "passionless."

Some scholars point out that the understanding of *śabda-pramāṇa* sources in the classical Sāṃkhya-Yoga reveals the normative Hindu approach to the matter, as well as the models of thinking and antinomy inherent in the Hindu consciousness. At issue is the notorious contradiction between a striving for "orthodoxy" and an apparent relativism and pragmatism in their confessional affiliations. On the one hand, the Sāṃkhya followers emphasize the prime authority of *śruti* and *smṛti*, while on the other hand, they acknowledge the authority of any spiritual experience gathered by those who, in their opinion, are "passionless" and endowed with "supernatural" faculties.

One resorts to *śabda-pramāṇa* as a source of true knowledge when observation and reflection prove fruitless. The objects of *śabda-pramāṇa* are supersensible and logically undeducible. The most reliable way to bring them to cognition is by an "inward knowledge" that makes a distinction between *guṇas* and *purūṣa*, transforms one's consciousness and leads one to a state of utter "estrangement": "He whose understanding is unattached everywhere, who has subdued his self and from whom desire has fled—he comes through renunciation to the supreme state transcending all work."[2]

Estrangement and detachment attained through the psychological and physical practices of Yoga are supposed to help in attaining the supreme goal of knowledge, which in Brahmanic philosophy, with its explicit soteriological orientation, is salvation from *saṃsāra* through the union or identity with Brahman or *ātman*: "Even here (on earth) the created (the world) is overcome by those whose mind is established in equality. God is flawless and the same in all. Therefore are these (persons) established in God."[3]

The elevation to "true knowledge" starts with the precise knowledge of one's self. Then follows meditation, ending with the renunciation of all attachments and eventually the attainment of the state of "estrangement," freedom from all "bodily" things. Like a deer casting off its horns or a bird flying away from a tree falling into water, one comes to consummate one's true selfhood.

The enlightened one looks "undistressed" and "luminous" thanks to the acquired stability and peace of mind. As it is said in Yoga-Sūtras of Patañjali, "mind-stuff comes to a state of balance with regard to the feeling of personality and becomes waveless like the Great Sea; peaceful [and] infinite, the feeling of personality and nought beside. In regard to this it has been said: 'Pondering upon this self which is a mere atom, one is conscious in the same way as when one is conscious to the extent that one says "I am." ' "[4]

Brahmanic epistemology has been elaborated in Nyāya-Vaiśeṣika in still greater detail than Sāṃkhya-Yoga. In this case, in addition to the three aforementioned *pramāṇas*, there is a fourth: comparison. As for the second one, logical inference, it is divided into three classes, while the fourth class—verbal authority—in its turn breaks up into two classes depending on whether the objects of authoritative testimony are "visible" or "invisible." Furthermore, all the *pramāṇas* are subject to close scrutiny by criticizing actual and potential objections to their definition, and to the latters' refutation.

Buddhist Logic

Nyāya-Vaiśeṣika developed a theory of syllogism with five members (thesis, reason, example, application, and conclusion) that, in the words of Th. Stcherbatsky, represented "a theory of logical fallacies."[5] Because Nyāya-Vaiśeṣika logic obtained the status of a protoscientific discipline founded on a "realistic" ontology, it sharply contradicts prevailing Buddhist logic. The first Buddhist thinker to overthrow Nyāya-Vaiśeṣika logic was Nāgārjuna (circa fourth century A.D.), who ushered in the centuries-long polemics between the two basic trends in the Indian philosophical tradition: the "realistic" and the "idealistic."

Indian realistic ontology recognized the existence of the external world and hence the possibility of its cognition by individuals. "There are no innate ideas and no *a priori* principles. Everything comes into the cognizing individual from without. . . . Cognition . . . does not apprehend images, but it apprehends external reality, reality itself."[6]

The ontological tenets of Buddhism are diametrically opposed to this, denying the actuality of both Being and Nonbeing. According to Nāgārjuna, Buddha had taught to avoid extremes in theories of origin and destruction. Therefore, *nirvāṇa* is logically unrelated to either Being or Nonbeing. If *nirvāṇa* were twofold, Being *and* Nonbeing, salvation would have also involved Being and Nonbeing. But this is logically impossible. It is in the cessation of all perceptions and diverse mental manifestations wherein lies the divine blessing. Hence we have Buddha's refusal to discuss or answer any metaphysical questions, preferring to keep silent on such matters as these.

Paradoxical as it may seem, the Buddhists proved to be the most accomplished masters of dialectical logic, the methods of which they employed in polemics with their ideological opponents in India and, subsequently, in other regions where Buddhism came to enjoy wide currency.

THE SEARCH FOR TRUTH IN CHINESE TRADITION

Notwithstanding the geographical proximity of India and China, and the spreading of Buddhism into China as early as the first century A.D., the Indian philosophical tradition failed to have a tangible impact on Chinese spiritual culture. Buddhism proved powerless to change the Chinese indigenous mentality and type of reflection. The famed Great Wall of China remained for centuries not only a major monument of Chinese architecture, but also the most impressive symbol of China's isolation and uniqueness, which includes its own particular mentality.

Chinese Teaching on Symbols and Numbers

The Chinese model of reflection was primarily determined by a peculiar perception of the world, viewing the universe as a self-sufficient, self-regulated dynamic system with an immanent and intrinsic order. In contrast to the Greek and Indian traditions, the Chinese did not recognize the existence of an external force or principle distinguished for its perfection, objectiveness, universality, and constancy, a principle giving rise to this world and bringing order into it. Hence the absence of any differentiation between Being and Nonbeing, the ideal and the material, and of dual categorizations as such. Order (*li*) is immanent in its relation to a world governed by its own basic, self-organizing, and self-regulating principles. Therefore, one's mission is not to disclose the linear causal relationships obtaining among things but rather to apprehend the interdependence and correlative nature of all the "ten thousand things." Hence the singularity of the Chinese model of thinking and its peculiar mental strategy.

The correlative, associative thinking of the Chinese called for using a special methodology, namely, the symbolization of spatial and numerical structures, termed in Chinese *xiang shu zhi xue*, or "the teaching on symbols and numbers," defined by some sinologists as "numerology." The European analogy to Chinese numerology is the Pythagorean-Platonic arhythmology, or structurology, which is also based on the categories of symbols, or images, and numbers. In contrast to Europe, however, where the Aristotelian-Stoic logic prevailed over Pythagorean-Platonic numerology, in China it was the reverse insofar that Confucian-Taoist numerology overpowered the embryonic logical methods used by the Mohists, the "School of Names" (*ming tzu*), and partly by the Legalists (*fa tzu*).

Numerology is a formalized system composed of mathematical and mathematical-like objects interrelated by symbolic, associative, and aesthetic means. It was founded in China on three types of graphic signs: "symbols" of a geometric nature (trigrams and hexagrams); "numbers" in figures; and finally hieroglyphs denoting *yin-yang* and the five elements (*wu hsing*).

Despite its extreme formalization, numerology is nonetheless socially oriented. Some scholars surmise that the singular nature of major numerological systems is determined by the common, "human" factor. The basic numbers in the Chinese case are 2, 3, and 5 (because from their origin things have a two-, three-, or fivefold intrinsic nature): the "dual images" of *yin* and *yang* as the feminine and masculine principles; a system of "three movers"—Heaven, the Human Being, and Earth, with the human being in the center; and the five elements of "water, fire, wood, metal, and land," all of them in their primordial essence being the fundamental categories of objects involved in human economic and labor activity. (It is noteworthy that the same three numbers made the basis of computation practices in ancient Babylonia.)

The Chinese associate symbols and numbers with pneuma (*chi*) and objective things (*wu*). This is evident, among other things, from the treatise *Tso-chuan* (dating from the fifth through the fourth centuries B.C.), which states: "The birth of things gives rise to symbols; these are followed by reproduction; the latter give rise to numbers." Thus, virtually the entire cosmological system is presented in numerical form.

Numerology, which deals with symbols and numbers, could conceivably become a mediating link in the transition from empiricism to logic. This potential was never realized in China. One plausible explanation for this fact is the lack of developed forms of idealism in classical Chinese philosophy, which instead has no notion of a conceptual sphere or special kind of reality governed by its own logical laws.

The Principle of Harmony (*he*)

The predominant cultural disposition in China views the "ten thousand things" as a constantly interacting diversity oriented toward the maintenance of a harmonious unity. The idea of unity is symbolized, in particular, by the principle of *he*. It is interesting that, under obvious influence of Marxian precepts that establish the law-governed validity of the dialectical conflict of opposites, many Chinese and Russian sinologists today interpret *he* as the principle of attaining unity through confrontation.[7] The untenability of such interpretation, however, is quite apparent even for those trying to "get the gist" of classical Chinese texts in translation. As an illustration, let us consider one among numerous examples by turning to the record of a conversation between an emperor and one of his advisors. The advisor, explicating the essence of *he* to the Emperor says: "The unity underlying *he* may be compared to cooking a dish. Having water, fire, vinegar, pickled vegetables, salt, and plums near at hand, one starts cooking fish. Having boiled water on the firewood and mixing all the components, the cook adds, according to his taste, what is missing and takes away what is superfluous, thus attaining the *he* unity."[8]

Unity is to be achieved not through a clash of opposites, resolved or "removed" by synthesis in a new formation, but rather through harmonization, an equilibrium among all available elements of a multiplicity. Hence the peculiarly Chinese attitude toward any activity and the mind-set associated with it: to strive for harmony by cherishing the traditions of the ancients who once lived in harmony with the world.

Assimilation of the Tradition

This unity manifests itself in the special terms used in the Chinese language for defining cognitive activity. Three are the most essential: *hsüeh,* or "learning"; *ssu,* "contemplation" or "reflection"; and finally, *chih,* "to know," "to anticipate," or "to realize." The first means "learning" not in the customary European sense of obtaining knowledge through reflection, but in the traditionally Confucian sense of knowledge through the assimilation of a tradition and the resultant possession of relevant information. As Confucius says, "I do not forge new paths; with confidence I cherish the ancients."[9] The term *ssu* means contemplation. In some definite sense of the word it also means "reflection," that is, as the assimilation of tradition and its reapplication in the context of present-day life. Lastly, *chih* or "to know" is also associated with tradition. It implies "wisdom," or the knowledge that facilitates compliance with the sagacity of the ancients in the tradition. In short, all three terms imply an orientation not toward the cognition of what was previously unknown, not "innovation," but rather stress one's loyalty and adherence to the established world order. The most eloquent words on this matter belong to the great teacher himself, Confucius: "Reviewing the old as a means of realizing the new—such a person can be considered a teacher," and "There are probably those who can initiate new paths while still not understanding them, but I am not one of them. I learn much, select out of it what works well, and then follow it. I observe much, and remember it. This is a lower level of wisdom."[10]

In contrast to the Western tradition, which associates philosophy with perpetual skepticism and an unflagging search for the truth, the Chinese traditionally admonished doubt and emphasized instead its futility and, therefore, harmfulness. As Confucius instructs, "Listen broadly, set aside what you are unsure of."[11] One might say that in contrast to the Western-European proclivity "to query and to reason," the Chinese disposition is one "to learn first and foremost" or, as Confucius said, "repeatedly apply what you have learned."[12] Hence the goal of knowledge turns out to lie in cognizing not the truth but what is right and proper, that is, order. Right thinking implies the ability to classify. According to Ssu-ma Ch'ien, the founder of Chinese historical science, "it is through classification that one cognizes." According to Chinese traditionalists, to calculate and shape a geometric structure, to compile a table, to grade and to classify, these are enough to obtain sufficient knowledge, and in some cases, even to present it in its definitive form.

THE SEARCH FOR TRUTH IN ISLAMIC TRADITION

Compared to India or China, the types of reasoning inherent in the spiritual culture of the Islamic world appear to be nearest in character to those conventionally identified with Western culture. To account for this the following two factors should be duly considered: first, there are many common features between Islam and Christianity, two closely linked monotheistic religions, and second, there was a decisive influence exerted by the Greek philosophers on the formation of the philosophical tradition of Islam itself (*falsafa*).

The Koranic Notion of Knowledge

The texts of the Koran and the Sunna suggest that knowledge is viewed in Islam as one of the most essential cultural values. According to the Sunna, the Prophet Muḥammad says: "The search for knowledge is incumbent upon every Muslim," and "Knowledge is a light which God throws into the heart." Still, the key point is what the word "knowledge" implies in this case and what is regarded as its source.

As mentioned above, the Qādiriyyah were the first "perplexed" and "squabbling" Muslims whose debates with their opponents from among the Jabrites (from the Arabic *jabr* meaning "enforcement") denied man's freedom of choice and action and thereby ushered in reflection over the texts of the Koran and the Sunna. These disputations spurred the establishment of a dogmatic religious system and philosophy. The contention of the Qādiriyyah and Jabrites established a polemic atmosphere and pinpointed the first abstract problem, namely the freedom of will and predestination, providing a focal point for subsequent theological controversies.

This dispute has often been compared to that of the Pelagians and Augustinians. The similarity, however, is rather formal. True enough, the bone of contention was common, but the methods and devices used during these discourses differed fundamentally: the Qādiriyyah intellectual endeavors were directed not so much toward attaining the objective truth in disputation as toward invalidating the views of their opponents. Their criticisms were adverse and devastating rather than constructive and explicative. The case of the Qadariyya reveals only timid attempts to make the reasoning behind their own opinions convincing and well-grounded. It fell to the Mu'tazilites to be the first to employ in full measure the methods of explicative criticism.

The Mu'tazilite "Heresy"

The Mu'tazilites were the first in Islamic society to venture into discussing the ways of God and the nature of good and evil in rational terms. Their basic premise was that God was loath to anything that either contradicted reason or neglected people's welfare. While expositing the views of the Mu'tazilites, the distinguished Muslim historiographer, al-Shahrastānī (d. 1153) remarked: "They agreed that man was capable of his own independent actions, a creator of his own deeds—both good and bad, to be rewarded or punished in the hereafter according to what he is doing. . . . Good and loathsome things ought to be cognized by the mind."[13] Al-Shahrastānī blamed the Mu'tazilites for their "agreement with the philosophers," and "a lack of moderation in presenting the philosophical teachings," as well as for making theology look like a felony, an approach that was fraught, in his view, with neglect of the "golden age."

The Mu'tazilite "heresy" was denounced and for a time censured as a result of the shattering criticism launched on behalf of traditionalists, primarily Aḥmad Ibn Ḥanbal and his followers supported by the 'Abbāsid caliph al-Mutawakkil. Nevertheless, no repressions could stifle the irresistible urge for the rationalization of theological quests. Mu'tazilism had left an indelible imprint and paved the way for the Ash'arite school (named after Abū'l-Ḥasan al-Ash'arī, d. 935), which came to replace the primitive and short-sighted traditionalism of earlier Islamic theologians and exegetes.

The Ash'arites' doctrine was first presented in systematic form by Abū Bakr al-Baqillānī (d. 1013) in his treatise, *al-Tamhīd*, which opens with a discussion of the nature of knowledge or "science" (*'ilm*). *'Ilm* is defined by the author as "the knowledge of the object, as it really is." Science falls into two major categories: the eternal knowledge of God and the temporal knowledge of creatures capable of cognition such as humans, angels, jinn ("demons" or "spirits"), and so on. The latter, temporal knowledge is subdivided in turn into necessary, or intuitive, knowledge and discursive knowledge.

In contrast to discursive knowledge, necessary knowledge cannot be doubted. The Ash'arites, like the Mu'tazilites, recognized the validity of rational knowledge but they limited its framework. The Ash'arites took an anti-Mu'tazilite stand on two fundamental questions, namely, whether God could be known rationally, independently of revelation, and whether the knowledge of good and evil was possible prior to revelation.[14]

Al-Ghazālī's Synthesis

The Muslim tradition of theological rationality received its fullest and most consistent manifestation in the works of al-Ghazālī (d. 1111), whose treatise, *The Revival of the Religious Sciences,* is considered unrivaled in the whole of Muslim literature for its presentation of ideas pertaining to the problem of knowledge.[15] The treatise opens with a dictum ascribed to the Prophet Muḥammad, which reads: "The search for knowledge is incumbent upon every Muslim." Then follows al-Ghazālī's own understanding of the concept of "knowledge."

The author presents the four existing definitions of "intellect." First, it is "a faculty distinguishing man from all animals, by means of which man appears prepared for apprehending the perceivable sciences and knowledge, and for mastering the complex mental crafts." This mental ability, in al-Ghazālī's view, "is correlated with knowledge like an eye with vision, while the Koran and the Sunna are correlated with this ability in its attainment of knowledge like the light of the sun with eyesight."[16] Second, "intellect is the ability to acquire necessary knowledge such as the knowledge of the possibility of the possible and the impossibility of the impossible."[17] Third, intellect is the knowledge "derived from experience . . . the one who learns much from one's experience and life is called an intelligent person."[18] Finally, intellect is the ability to anticipate the consequences of one's actions and hence to exercise control over those leading to "transient enjoyment." Summing up all four definitions of intellect, it would be valid to assert that it is a gift granted by Allāh "to make people happy."[19] It is by virtue of this gift that people are capable of obtaining knowledge.

Al-Ghazālī is categorical in his assertion that "the final unquestionable conclusion is that . . . knowledge is divided into the Science of behavior and the Science of revelation."[20] As it turns out, the matter involves exclusively the knowledge of religious precepts and dogmas. As for metaphysical problems, these cannot be comprehended. For instance, human beings are "not obliged to discover . . . for themselves through contemplation, examination, and verification" the essence of the basic Koranic dogma: "There is no god save Allāh, and Muḥammad is His Prophet." In al-Ghazālī's opinion, "it is enough for [one] to believe in it, to get firmly convinced of it without any hesitation, doubt and mistrust, which is possible only through imitation, without examination and verification."[21] Human beings ought not deliberate on ritual precepts either, for their duty is merely to know them and follow them in daily life.

According to al-Ghazālī, human souls are endowed with faith by nature. However, people are divided into those "withdrawn and forgetting" and those "revoking it upon prolonged mediation." For it is said in the Koran:

> (Here is) a Book which
> We have sent down
> Unto thee, full of blessings,
> that they may meditate
> On its Signs, and that
> men of understanding may
> Receive admonition. (38:29)

What is at issue, therefore, is nothing but the knowledge of *faith,* in full conformity with the dictum ascribed to the Prophet Muḥammad: "Intelligent is he who has taken Allāh on faith, believing His prophets and acting in compliance with Him."

Al-Ghazālī reassessed the basic tenets of Muslim theology, Sufism, Ismā'īliyya, and *falāsifa,* indeed all the principal trends in Islamic thought. As for philosophy, his criticism was mainly leveled against Aristotle, al-Fārābī, and Ibn Sīnā. It is noteworthy that, while exposing the fallaciousness of philosophical method, al-Ghazālī himself nonetheless made wide use of philosophical techniques of refutation, often resorting to the devices of Greek logic. Hence, paradoxically enough, al-Ghazālī, the indubitable denouncer of philosophy, has made a weighty contribution to its development.

The motivating force behind his own search for truth was skepticism. It was so great that some scholars came to believe that he had reached the highest degree of intellectual skepticism and, by breaking the shackles of causality with the blade of dialectics some seven centuries before David Hume, al-Ghazālī proved that we knew neither cause nor effect but only the fact that one phenomenon followed another.[22] Some contend that, after al-Ghazālī, "Hume had nothing to add."[23]

In giving al-Ghazālī credit for his contributions to the development of Islamic philosophy, one should abstain from a modernist interpretation of the views expounded by this medieval theologian who, although recognizing the importance of intellect in cognizing the truth, nevertheless emphasized the presence of *dhawq* (literally "taste" or "spiritual insight"), regarding mystical intuition as the highest and most authentic source of knowledge. On the whole, one could say that al-Ghazālī made an attempt to criticize and at the same time "synthesize" all the current approaches to cognition. It was due to his efforts that Islamic theology came to be reconciled with Sufism, with the latter even being elevated to the rank of "divine science."

"Divine Science"

As mysticism, Sufism is naturally associated with irrationalism. "Mystic works of theosophic Ṣūfīs are full of criticism of 'rationalists' and of disparagement of reason over against intuition, and *give the impression* that the Ṣūfīs are the arch-enemies of philosophy."[24] Sufism, however, opposed not so much the rationality of philosophers as that of theologians.

Insisting on the transcendental nature of God, Muslim theology detaches human beings so far from God as to leave them no other way but to take Koranic "knowledge" for granted. As for the Ṣūfīs, despite their belief in the unknowability of God as the Absolute Truth, they nevertheless acknowledge the possibility of maximizing their "approximation" to it.

The Ṣūfī view of the human person as microcosm, recognizing individuals as astrolabical instruments for apprehending the Divine Essence, elevates the human being's status immeasurably as compared to that allotted the individual in Islamic theology, which associates the individual exclusively with the phenomenal world. It is human beings who were "entrusted" with the mission to safeguard the Divine Essence, and therefore they might be able to grasp the Absolute. Human "ignorance," however, is due to the fact that humans have "forgotten" their predestination and have looked for the treasure of Truth everywhere but within themselves.

In one of the parables in *Mathnawī,* a religio-philosophical poem by Jalāl al-Dīn Rūmī, the story is told of a Ṣūfī who went with his friend for a walk in a fine orchard, and instead of enjoying the beauties of nature, sat on the ground to take a nap. Answering to his friend's bewilderment over his lack of attention to "the marks of the Divine Mercy" around him, the Ṣūfī replied that one should look for these marks within one's own heart.[25]

The Ṣūfī way for attaining Truth through self-cognition might seem to contradict the often repeated bidding of Muslim mystics for self-renunciation and the forsaking of personal ego. As a matter of fact, there is no incongruity at all, for it is the phenomenal ego that should be mortified for the sake of perceiving the true, essential "self."

> Ruined the house for the sake of the golden treasure,
> and with that same treasure builds it better than before;
> Cut off the water and cleansed the river-bed, then caused
> drinking-water to flow in the river-bed.[26]

The "death" of the phenomenal ego opens the way to acquiring the essential knowledge, which makes no differentiation between subject and object and discloses the truth underlying the unity of being.

What are the means of cognition that human beings have at their disposal? The Ṣūfīs believe that the human intellect (*al-ʿaql*) plays a positive role in only a limited part of cognition. Its inferences are based on sensory experience whose evidence is extremely deceptive. One of Rūmī's parables relates this point in the story of the elephant placed inside a dark barn. The people in the barn tried to find out what it was by fumbling and groping. One grabbed the trunk and declared that it was a water pipe, another touched an ear and concluded it was a huge fan, a third stumbled at the elephant's legs and presumed them to be columns, a fourth felt its back and declared it was a large throne. The parable is meant to relate that the information supplied by our sense organs is superficial and false.

The Ṣūfīs also point to the static nature inherent in the cognitive faculty of intellect. The word for "intellect," *ʿaql*, they remind us, is derived from *ʿiqāl* (literally "shackles" or "hobbling"). As for reality itself, it rejects any limitations, being comparable to the incessant divine "breathing," that is, it is characterized by perpetual changeability.

The Ṣūfīs consider the heart, not the intellect, to be the main organ of cognition. As Ibn ʿArabī asserted, knowledge "belongs only to the heart, since reason comes from the world of delimitation."[27] With their urge to give up sober discursive reasoning and fall into "perplexity," the Ṣūfīs thereby set the human being free from any precepts imposed from without, setting their hopes instead in the forces of instinct, uninhibited and unconscious, and the unrestrained power of human imagination.

The Ṣūfīs often associate the process of acquiring knowledge with the state of intoxication that leads to ecstasy and distraction:

> The hand of mine eye gave me love's strong wine to drink,
> when my cup was the face of Her that transcendth beauty,
> And in my drunkenness, by means of a glance I caused
> my comrades to fancy that it was the quaffing of *their* wine
> that gladdened my inmost soul,
> Although mine eyes made me independent of my cup, and
> my inebriation was derived from her qualities, not from my wine; . . .
> My finding her (in my heart) effacing me, whilst my
> losing her brings me back to myself. . . .
> And my being oblivious (of myself) in Her caused me
> to lose my reason, so that I did not return to myself or
> follow any desire of mine in consequence of my thinking (that I existed). . . .

(So was I seeking Her within me) until there rose from me
to mine eye a gleam, and the splendor of my daybreak shone
forth and my darkness vanished.[28]

These verses by the Arabian mystical poet Ibn al-Fāriḍ render in a most graceful style the Ṣūfī concept of knowledge: the Truth can be attained only through personal experience. Authentic knowledge is acquired by a heart reproducing in its imagination the beloved object of God. This idea receives its fullest expression in the works of Ibn 'Arabī, who saw the principal function of imagination in a hypostatic treatment of incorporeal phenomena, such as dreams, revelations, and creativity.

According to the Ṣūfīs, imagination virtually *serves* intellect, for it carries out the role of an intermediary, presenting in abstract form the images arising from sensory perception before conveying them to the mind. By means of intellect, intuition, and imagination human beings are coming close to the attainment of truth. In principle, human cognitive abilities are inexhaustible and human beings need to improve them constantly, otherwise merely the forms of things will be open to them, while the essence of things will remain hidden from human comprehension.

Islamic mystics divide people into the intellectual elite, capable of acquiring esoteric knowledge, and the masses of common people. To the first class belong the prophets and saints, regarded as akin to the Universal Intellect. As for the common person who seeks to know the Truth, he or she should embark upon the path to perfection, and choose a sheikh for him- or herself to follow as a guide. In this way the influence of traditional theology becomes replaced by the institution of Ṣūfīs sheikhs. The practice of Ṣūfīs religious orders shows that the sheikhs, or leaders, became masters of unquestionable authority while their disciples (the Murīds) absolutely obeyed them as a rule. At the same time, Sufism readily recognizes persons possessing their "own light," that is, those who upon reaching perfection may free themselves from compliance with prescribed rules and standards.

The idea of gaining knowledge through self-perfection carries a strong humanistic message. The human being acquires self-value, with the best in one being regarded as a sum total of one's own efforts at self-realization. Knowledge and ethical perfection appear to be inseparably linked. The idea according to which "Each does not know of God except that which he infers from himself"[29] reflects the Ṣūfī concept of knowledge in the most clear-cut and capacious form. This idea highlights the fundamental difference between the Ṣūfī concept of knowledge and that of the Islamic scholastics. For the Ṣūfī, the impersonal truth is offset by a personal truth, corporateness by individualism, traditionalism by antitraditionalism, and theological ordinance by the spontaneity of intuitive insight. Even when the Ṣūfī views seem to coincide with those of orthodox theology, a closer look reveals their nonidentity.

True enough, the Ṣūfīs, who are likewise theologians, assert that "God is unknowable." In contrast to the agnosticism of Islamic theology, however, which implies that attempts to attain the Truth are futile, and thus it becomes necessary to comply with the letter of sacred texts and theological precepts, Sufism proclaims something quite different, namely that the recognition of the unknowability of the Absolute invalidates any and all dogma, calling instead for interminable quests and asserting thereby the infinite nature of the process of cognition. "Anguish after the hidden" is a cryptic Ṣūfī formula denoting the perpetual quest for Truth, with its underlying message being an unquenchable thirst for knowledge. This code of Sufism made it a potential ally of philosophers and allowed Ibn Sīnā to call the Ṣūfīs his "brothers in search of the truth" despite the skepticism that these mystics entertained toward the rationalism inherent in the philosophical method of cognition and the very different orientations of mystical and philosophical knowledge. For a Ṣūfī, knowledge opens a way to the communion with God, it is always singular, individual, and internalized. As for the knowledge sought after by a philosopher, it is oriented to the sphere of universal values, toward cognizing the surrounding world.

Falsafa

In contrast to other trends in Islamic thought, the followers of *falsafa* did not simply acknowledge the role of intellect in the cognitive process, but taught that intellect was the human being's supreme faculty and the measure of truth. It was Ibn Sīnā who became a "symbol of Greek philosophy" in the Muslim world. In a celebrated treatise, *Dānish Nāma* (*Book of Knowledge*), Ibn Sīnā calls logic a science of measure (in Farsi, *tarāzu*, literally meaning "balance" or "scales"), arguing that any knowledge not weighed on the scales of reason is not authentic and, therefore, cannot be treated as true knowledge.

Ibn Sīnā identifies the following three types of reasoning: syllogism, induction, and analogy, with syllogism regarded as the most authentic. He makes a detailed assessment of all types of reasoning before considering philosophical (called by him "intellectual") science, which he divides into two categories: speculative and practical, each then subdivided further into three sciences. Practical sciences include the science of public management (falling itself into two types: one concerned with the nature of religious laws, and the other with the nature of politics), the science of household management, and finally the science of self-appraisal.

Speculative sciences in turn are divided into the following three categories: first, metaphysics, the branch of philosophy that treats of first principles, that is, "the science of primordials of that which is beyond nature"; next, an "intermediate" science, mathematics; and finally, natural or "inferior" science. "Natural science is closer to man and most comprehensible to him, it contains however more uncertainties than other sciences. The subject-matter of this science is sensible matter,"[30] which is movable and changeable.

Ibn Sīnā's metaphysics concentrate on the description and definition of the "Necessary Existent." Ibn Sīnā writes, "the Necessary Existent is that being to Whom the being of all things is due, Which has endowed all things with the necessity of being."[31] Referring to the Koran, the philosopher recognizes the identity of the necessary existent as God the Creator. At the same time, the necessary existent is not merely an ontological notion; for Ibn Sīnā it is "absolute wisdom," something that gives rise to the hierarchy of all intellect.

Although recognizing the power of rational knowledge and asserting that the force of intellect and what might be perceived by it was infinite, Ibn Sīnā still acknowledged the existence of a domain inaccessible to rational comprehension, the sphere of mystical insight.

Averroism

Ibn Sīnā was sharply criticized for his inconsistencies by Ibn Rushd (also known as Averroes), the last of the great Muslim philosophers.

Ibn Rushd defined intellect as "nothing but the perception of things with their causes," believing that "in this it distinguishes itself from all the other faculties."[32] Intellect makes it possible to obtain "true knowledge," which is "the knowledge of a thing as it is in reality."[33]

Taking heed of the criticism leveled against philosophy on the part of theologians, Ibn Rushd justified its religious "legitimacy" and underscored that it was treated as "obligatory" and even "recommended by the Law."[34] He appealed to the authority of the Koran, in which a number of the *ayats,* in his opinion, summoned Muslims to apply intellectual reasoning in the apprehension and cognition of things. On these grounds he drew the following conclusion: "The Law (Religion), then, has urged us to have demonstrative knowledge of God the Exalted and all the things of his creation."[35] Ibn Rushd viewed such knowledge as a mental "instrument" that the believer should become able to use.

Ibn Rushd agreed that "intellectual reasoning" might come into conflict with certain phrases in the Holy Book. In such cases, one should not forfeit one's intellectual reasoning but rather one's literal understanding of the Koran. On this point, Ibn Rushd stated: "So we affirm definitely that whenever the conclusion of a demonstration is in conflict with the apparent meaning of Scripture, that apparent meaning admits of allegorical interpretation."[36]

Ibn Rushd protested against any attack on Muslim philosophers on the grounds that they were preoccupied with matters foreign to Islamic religious teachings. He revolted against cultural isolation and urged for the continuity of the search for truth: "Whenever we find in the works of our predecessors of former nations a theory about beings and a reflection on them conforming to what the conditions of demonstration require, we ought to study what they said about the matter and what they affirmed in their books. And we should accept from them gladly and gratefully whatever in these books accords with the truth, and draw attention to and warn against what does not accord with the truth, at the same time excusing them."[37]

Ibn Rushd not only "protected" philosophy but also ranked it higher than theology. He classified people in accordance with their cognitive abilities. According to his classification, the first group includes common people or the "masses," those "who are not interpreters [of Scripture] at all: these are the rhetorical class. They are the overwhelming mass. . . . Another class are those of some dialectical interpretation: these are the dialecticians, either by nature alone or by nature and habit. Another class are those whose interpretations are forwarded with certainty: these are the demonstrative class by nature and training, i.e. in the art of philosophy."[38] Thus, all people were divided into the categories of the masses, theologians, and philosophers, with the philosophers belonging to the "best class," selected by Allāh from among all the others.

Ibn Rushd believed, however, that the knowledge accessible to philosophers ought not be expressed to the masses incapable of allegorical interpretation nor set down in rhetorical or dialectical books. "As for the man who expresses these allegories to unqualified persons, he is an unbeliever on account of his summoning people to unbelief."[39] Allegorical interpretations are accessible only to the select few. The harm done by the "dialecticians" among theologians is due to the fact that "in the methods which they followed to establish their interpretations they neither went along with the masses nor with the elite; not with the masses, because their methods were more obscure than the methods common to the majority, and not with the elite, because if these methods are inspected they are found deficient in the conditions required for demonstrations, as will be understood after the slightest inspection by anyone acquainted with the conditions of demonstration."[40] Therefore, a theological discourse gives rise to varied interpretations of the Scriptures—dissension, heresy, and unbelief.

Philosophy is proclaimed by Ibn Rushd not to be an enemy of religion but, quite the opposite, "the friend and milk-sister of religion," opening a way "to the class of persons who have trodden the path of study and sought to know the truth."[41]

Ibn Rushd spared no effort in neutralizing the critics of philosophy and protecting it. He was so determined and convincing in his endeavors that his views spread far beyond the Islamic world. His thinking came to be known as "Averroism" and had substantial impact on the history of world philosophy. All of his major treatises were translated and commented on by the Jewish philosophers. Some of them heralded him as an unsurpassed commentator of Aristotle, while others from among his admirers regarded him as the greatest "interpreter" of the philosopher.

Later Ibn Rushd's views came to the attention of Europeans, who called him "Averroës." His commentaries on Aristotle's works gained wide popularity primarily with the university community in Paris (circa A.D. 1230), where at the time fierce debates ensued between those striving for the revision of Aristotelianism in the spirit of Catholicism and those in opposition to orthodox theology. While on a papal mission, Albert the Great, professor at the Theology Department of Paris University, wrote a treatise in 1256 which he entitled *On the Unity of Mind Against Averroes.* Fifteen years later, Thomas Aquinas, professor at the same department, came out with his own treatise entitled *On the Unity of Mind Against Averroists.*

Notwithstanding the attacks of Catholic theologians, the influence of Averroes's ideas could not be held in check. This fact urged Tampie, Bishop of Paris, jointly with a number of French theologians, not only to admonish but also to ban the "thirteen theses" attributed to Averroes (although most of them were actually proclaimed by Siger de Brabant, one of his followers). A similar document was adopted in 1277, this time censuring as many as 219 theses. Averroes's theses were also denounced by Gille de Rome and Raymond Lull at the close of the thirteenth century. In the course of three centuries, up to the beginning of the seventeenth century, Averroism was influential in Italy, especially at the Universities of Bologna and Padua.

Compared to Europe, the destiny of Averroism within the Islamic world is most striking and significant. Ibn Rushd's ideas, which encouraged rationalism and scientific knowledge, turned out to be doomed there, where theology was ultimately victorious over philosophy. How can one explain this decline of rationalistic trends in the Islamic East after three truly golden centuries of the flourishing of *falsafa* and natural sciences?

"ORIENTAL" MENTALITY

The perception of and reasons for the centuries-long "inertness" of cultural life outside the Western world has been a matter of heated debate. The conservation of ideological traditions is explained by the specific socio-economic and political organization in place, a system sometimes referred to as "the Asiatic mode of production," by a singular perception and vision of the world predetermined perhaps by climate, geography, and natural environment, by the particularities of linguistic structures, and the like. It cannot be excluded, however, that the "roots" of any intellectual quest, that is, the genesis of a theoretical worldview itself, may be an important factor in this dispute.

As Hegel wrote, "We are too apt to mould the ancient philosophers into our own forms of thought."[42] Let us take heed of this warning in our effort to apprehend what the particular features of an "Oriental" mentality are, and whether or not they really do exist.

Notions prevailing in the West conventionally distinguished the so-called Oriental type of thinking from the Western, pointing to the wide parameters of their difference. It is customary to assert, for example, that in the East, philosophy has never stood apart from religion, whereas in the West this detachment took place years ago; that Eastern spiritualism is opposed to Western naturalism; that the cardinal features of an "Oriental" mode of philosophical reflection are idealism, irrationalism, introversion, cosmocentrism, and pessimism, whereas in the West it is materialism, rationalism, extroversion, anthropocentrism, optimism, and the like.

In some cases such stereotypes follow a hierarchical principle according to which Western philosophical reasoning is considered to be superior to "Oriental" modes of thought. Under such an interpretation, the Indian tradition is looked down upon as incapable of scientific speculative thinking,[43] the Chinese described as "strikingly lacking in the creative power of imagination,"[44] while the Arabs are stated to be "utterly lacking in critical ability."[45]

On the other hand, it is the spirituality and mysticism allegedly ingrained in the Oriental mode of thinking that is sometimes treated as unambiguous evidence of its superiority over the Western modes of thought. Eastern thinkers, distinguished for their "spirituality," are, according to the eminent Orientalist Max Müller, "superior to most Western philosophers."[46]

Occasionally, the above stereotypes behave in an intercomplementary fashion. Hermann Hesse, for instance, a great admirer of "Oriental" philosophy, perceived in the "wisdom of the East and the West . . . not hostile, conflicting forces but the poles by which life swings in between."[47]

Although the above approach excludes unfair and abusive assessments of philosophical traditions, it seems equally dissatisfying by its polarization of East and West; and by underscoring only their differences, it fails to help in apprehending certain common features in the development of philosophical thought in separate nations, which renders each equally involved in the general history of human society at large.

Rejection of the stereotypes pertaining to the East and West does not necessarily imply the assertion of an all-around uniformity in the means and methods of philosophical reflection. The unique nature of these methods, and likewise of other cultural aspects, is absolutely clear. Yet, an adequate ascertainment of the wealth inherent in the legacy of philosophical reflection calls for giving up the narrow-minded and simplistic approach to separate philosophical traditions as lying "poles apart" and profits instead by taking the following factors into consideration.

The stereotyped appraisal of the Western mode of thought as primarily "rationalistic" was obviously prompted by trends in the development of European philosophical thought in modern times. But such a designation is undoubtedly inapplicable to, say, medieval philosophy in Europe. For the most part, the categorical judgment of the "Oriental" type of mentality as exclusively irrational arises from comparing Oriental philosophy in its current state with postmedieval Western philosophy. Having found no Cartesian trend in the East, some scholars are prone to drawing hasty conclusions according to which rationality is in principle alien to the "Oriental" mentality. As a matter of fact, the problem is not at all in the lack of rationalistic potentials as such, but in their insufficient realization in the East as compared to the West.

Any thinking person is apparently endowed with a certain degree of rationality, which makes this an integral element of spiritual culture of any nation. One can regard thinking as "rational" when it resorts to conceptual and logical categories. In this sense, theological, mystical, and theosophic concepts, rather than only philosophical or scientific theories, may be also qualified as "rational" to a certain extent.

Rationality per se is not at all identical with "rationalism." The latter involves a type of mentality characterized by the exclusive orientation to intellect as a solely authentic and potentially boundless source of knowledge. In consistent forms of rationalism, intellect comprises the foundation not only of epistemology but of ontology as well, with Intellect acting as God the Absolute, the origin of being and the universe. In contrast to that form of rationality inherent in the mentality of all civilized peoples, rationalism is undoubtedly not a universal but a rather exclusive phenomenon associated with a particular period of time and a certain level in cultural development.

This type of thinking is determined by and interrelated with a worldview, one with a distinct status given to the human being in the universe. As could be seen from chapter three, the Western concepts of human being differ principally from the Eastern ones by disengaging the human being from both cosmic and, in certain sense, rigid social order, thus making a person independent from the dictate of the larger order of which she or he is a part.

Acquirement of a "consistent subjectivity" means the primacy of self-fulfilment, and this has negative as well positive consequences. Charles Taylor points out that "community affiliation, the solidarities of birth, of marriage, of the family, of the polis, all take second place."[48] In his words, "the search for pure subjective expression makes life thin and insubstantial, and may ultimately undercut itself."[49] At the same time the primary moral value granted an individual human being gives to every person a certain dignity, rendering him or her more sovereign and much more confident in his or her abilities to succeed in many ways, including in the "construction" of our knowledge of the world.

FURTHER READING

Indian Tradition

Mohanty, J. N. *Reason and Tradition in Indian Thought: An Essay on the Nature of Indian Philosophical Thinking.* Oxford: Clarendon Press, 1992.

Motilal, B. K. *Perception: An Essay on Classical Indian Theories of Knowledge.* Oxford: Clarendon Press, 1986.

Potter, K., ed. *Encyclopaedia of Indian Philosophies.* Vol. II: *Indian Metaphysics and Epistemology. The Tradition of Nyāya-Vaiśeṣika up to Gangesa.* Princeton, N.J.: Princeton University Press, 1977.

Smart, N. *Doctrine and Argument in Indian Philosophy.* Leiden, N.Y.: E. J. Brill, 1992.

Chinese Tradition

Allinson, R. E., ed. *Understanding the Chinese Mind: The Philosophical Roots.* Hong Kong: Oxford University Press, 1989.

Graham, A. C. *Later Mohist Logic, Ethics, and Science.* Hong Kong: Chinese University Press, 1978.

Gua, A. S. *The Unity of Knowledge and Action: A Study in Wang Yang-ming's Moral Psychology.* Honolulu: University of Hawaii Press, 1982.

Hall, D., and R. T. Ames. *Thinking Through Confucius.* Albany: SUNY Press, 1987.

Hansen, Ch. *Language and Logic in Ancient China.* Ann Arbor: University of Michigan Press, 1983.

Islamic Tradition

Badawai, A. *Histoire de la philosophie en islam.* 2 vols. Paris: J. Vrin, 1972.

Chittick, W. *The Sufi Path of Knowledge: Ibn al-'Arabī's Metaphysics of Imagination.* Albany: SUNY Press, 1989.

Fakhry, M. "Rationality in Islamic Philosophy." In *A Companion to World Philosophies,* ed. Eliot Deutsch and Ron Bontekoe. Oxford: Blackwell, 1999.

Rozenthal, F. *Knowledge Triumphant: The Concept of Knowledge in Medieval Islam.* Leiden, N.Y.: E. J. Brill, 1970.

NOTES

1. Yoga-Sūtras of Patañjali. *The Yoga System of Patañjali or the Ancient Hindu Doctrine of Concentration of Mind.* Trans. James Haughton Woods. New Delhi: Motilal Banasidass, 1966, p. 20.

2. *The Bhagavad Gītā* (18:49). With an introductory essay, Sanskrit text, English translation, and notes by S. Radhakrishnana. London: George Allen & Unwin, Ltd., 1967.

3. Ibid., 5:19.

4. Yoga-Sūtras of Patañjali, p. 74.

5. Stcherbatsky, Th. *Buddhist Logic.* Vol. 1. New York: Dover Publications, Inc., 1962, p. 26.

6. Ibid., p. 24.

7. See L. S. Perelomov, *Confucius: Life, Teaching, Destiny.* Moscow: Vostochnaya literatura, 1993, pp. 34–37.

8. Ibid., p. 37.

9. *The Analects of Confucius: A Philosophical Translation.* By Roger T. Ames and Henry Rosemont, Jr. New York: Ballantine Books, 1998, p. 111.

10. *The Analects of Confucius* (2:11; 7:28), pp. 78, 117. This "lower level of wisdom" is next to innate knowledge.

11. *The Analects of Confucius* (2:18), p. 79.

12. *The Analects of Confucius* (1:1), p. 71.

13. Al-Shahrastānī. *The Book About Religions and Sects.* Moscow: Vostochnaya literatura, 1984, pp. 55–56.

14. See M. Fakhry, *A History of Islamic Philosophy.* New York: Columbia University Press, 1983, pp. 210–11.

15. Rosenthal, F. *Knowledge Triumphant: The Concept of Knowledge in Medieval Islam.* Leiden, N.Y.: E. J. Brill, 1970, p. 95.

16. Abū Ḥāmid al-Ghazālī. *Revival of the Religious Sciences (Ihyār'ʻrulūm al-din).* Trans. by Bankey Behari. Franham, Surrey: Sufi Publishing, 1972, pp. 92–93.

17. Ibid., p. 93.

18. Ibid., p. 94.

19. Ibid.

20. Ibid., p. 89.

21. Ibid.

22. See D. B. Macdonald, "The Life of al-Ghazālī." *Journal of the American Oriental Society.* New York–New Haven. Vol. 212, p. 1, 1899, p. 103.

23. See E. Rénan, *Averroes et êverroism.* Paris, 1903, p. 74.

24. Rahman, F. *Islam.* Chicago: The University of Chicago Press, 1966, p. 145. Italics added.

25. Rūmī, J. *Mathnawī.* Trans. and commentary by R. A. Nickolson in 8 vols. London: Luzac, 1925–40. Book 4, verses 4286–89.

26. Ibid., Book 2, p. 20.

27. Cited from W. Chittick, *Ibn al-'Arabī's Metaphysics of Imagination. The Sufi Path of Knowledge.* Albany: SUNY Press, 1989, p. 109.

28. Nicholson, R. *Studies in Islamic Mysticism.* New Delhi: Idarah, 1981, pp. 199, 200, 246–47.

29. Ibn 'Arabī. *The Wisdom of the Prophets (Fuṣuṣ al-ḥikam),* p. 13.

30. Avicenna. *Dānish Nāma.* Morewedge, P. *The Metaphysica of Avicenna* (Ibn Sīnā). New York: Columbia University Press, 1973, pp. 12–13.

31. Ibid., p. 70.

32. Averroes. *Tahāfut al-Tahāfut (The Incoherence of the Incoherence).* Trans. Simon Van Den Bergh. In 2 vols. Vol. 1. London: Luzac & Co., 1954, p. 319.

33. Ibid., p. 325.

34. Averroes. *On the Harmony of Religion and Philosophy.* Trans. George F. Howrani. London: Luzac & Co., 1961, p. 44.

35. Ibid., p. 45.

36. Ibid., p. 51.

37. Ibid., p. 48.

38. Averroes. "The Decisive Treatise Determining the Nature of the Connection between Religion and Philosophy." *Philosophy in the Middle Ages. The Christian, Islamic, and Jewish Traditions.* Ed. Arthur Human and James J. Walsh. Indianapolis: Hackett Publishing Company, 1987, p. 312.

39. Ibid., p. 313.

40. Ibid., p. 315.

41. Ibid., p. 316.

42. Hegel, G.W.F. *Hegel's Lectures on the History of Philosophy.* Vol. 1. Atlantic Highlands, N.J.: Humanities Press International, 1996, p. 44.

43. *General History of Philosophy* (in Russian). Ed. A. Vedensky and E. Radlov. In 2 vols. St. Petersburgh: Obschestvennaya polza, 1910. Vol. 2, p. 38.

44. Ibid., p. 43.

45. Ibid., p. 87.

46. Müller, M. F. *The Six Systems of Indian Philosophy.* Varanasi: The Chowkhamba Sanskrit Series Office, 1919, p. xiii.

47. Hesse, H. "Addressing My Japanese Readers." *East-West Studies. Translations. Publications.* Moscow: Vostochnaya literatura, 1982, p. 217.

48. Taylor, Ch. *Sources of the Self. The Making of the Modern Identity.* Cambridge: Harvard University Press, 1996, p. 507

49. Ibid., p. 511.

5

Tradition and Modernity

The initial departure from traditional types of thinking in the cultural areas contiguous with Indian, Chinese, and Islamic civilizations came as a result of sociocultural influence from without, rather than from an organic evolution of intellectual life at home.

The colonial "invasion" of the West shattered the deep-rooted bedrock of political and socioeconomic organization in Eastern societies, challenging the traditional ideals and values of indigenous cultures. The invasion proved to be both destructive and invigorating: it undermined the foundations of political despotism, the communal structure, and primitive domestic industry. At the same time, however, it awakened national self-awareness, giving rise to the search for ways to emerge from economic backwardness and spiritual stagnation and put an end to a protracted "medieval" stage of development.

Philosophical thought, a "spiritual quintessence" of the times, reflected these transformations and served to outline future trends in the historical development of these civilizations.

EASTERN "WESTERNIZERS"

The immediate response to the developments mentioned above was a rejection of indigenous cultural traditions, including philosophical traditions, viewing these as chiefly responsible for social backwardness and for the lack of spiritual motivation toward progress. A number of Eastern intellectuals tended toward an uncritical adoption of Western "spirituality" as the sole antidote to the contemporary decline and stagnation they faced.

In this respect, the most revealing stand is that taken by the Chinese intellectual Hu Shih (1891–1962), an influential leader of the "intellectual revolution" who openly called for the complete assimilation of Western ways of life. This

Chinese philosopher, enjoying wide popularity among the bourgeois intellectuals and students, severely disapproved of Eastern ways and enthusiastically acclaimed Western civilization. He called the former a "civilization of rickshaws" and the latter a "civilization of motor cars." In his view, the prime cause of this striking gap lay in the materialistic orientation of Eastern mentality, whereas Western mentality was inherently rationalistic. Hu Shih discerned the signs of this "materialistic" Eastern mentality in "the contentment with one's destiny," "subjection to the material environment," the inability and reluctance to change the environment by breaking away from the established confines, and an overall "sluggishness of mind and spirit." As for rationality, he interpreted it as "dissatisfaction," a creative activity giving an impetus to the development of philosophy and sciences and an unflagging search for novel objectives and approaches.

Hu Shih opposed any revolutionary shattering of social foundations, calling for achieving effective results through "ongoing, drop by drop, gradual reforms" based on the spiritual and moral revitalization of the human person. He advocated a "sound individualism" as the only way of securing freedom and prosperity for each and all, both the individual and the state. By Hu Shih's own account, his worldview took shape under the strong influence of Thomas Huxley's agnostic ideas and John Dewey's pragmatism. Quite a number of Eastern thinkers came under the influence of these two philosophers.

The orientation toward trends in Western philosophical thought was selective, depending on the priority interests of Eastern thinkers. Of primary interest were ideas justifying law-governed regularities in the evolutionary processes unfolding in nature and society, hence an immense interest in Charles Darwin and the Social-Darwinism of Herbert Spencer. The awareness of progressive advancement being possible only through overcoming inert dogmatism enhanced the appeal of Cartesian arguments (Rene Descartes) or, all the more popular, positivistic ideas (Auguste Comte). Their opposition to abstract thinking and contemplation led Eastern thinkers to pragmatism, which forwarded a program of "reconstruction in philosophy," transforming it into a method of solving vital problems (William James, John Dewey). Finally, the assertion that human beings are subjects of social transformation and perfection inspired interest in, and resonated with, philosophers who placed emphasis on the creative and volitional principles in human agency (Arthur Schopenhauer, Henri Bergson, and Friedrich Nietzsche).

This nihilistic attitude toward indigenous philosophical traditions, coupled with a faithful conversion to one or another Western philosophical system, was a trend most characteristic of the early twentieth century. It turned out, however, to be short-lived and failed to find wide support. Nonetheless, it gave rise to schools of "Chinese pragmatism," "Arabian Social-Darwinism," and the like.

EAST-WEST SYNTHESIS

The trend toward the exclusive recognition of Western ideas raised sharp public criticism in Eastern countries. According to Sarvepalli Radhakrishnan (1888–1975), one of the foremost Indian philosophers of the twentieth century, those who strove to imitate the West uprooted their own ancient civilization—exchanging, for the sake of the alleged prosperity and welfare of India, their allegiance toward India and her culture for one toward Britain, now the "spiritual mother," and Greece, the "spiritual grandmother." Such an attitude toward one's own culture, however, is disastrous: "As long as a society lives by its ideals, its tools and forms have meaning. If the faith fails, the society loses its guide and direction."[1] Hence it is more reasonable and preferable to build up life on the previously laid foundation of national culture, which does not exclude but, on the contrary, necessarily implies assimilation of the most valuable elements of Western civilization.

The methods of this assimilation may vary. In some cases it is realized through a synthesis of Western and Eastern ideas. Muhammad Mayan Sharif (d. 1965), one of the most authoritative Muslim thinkers of the twentieth century and the founder of the Pakistan Philosophical Congress, editor of such fundamental works as *A History of Muslim Philosophy*,[2] put forward an ontological theory of "dialectical monadism." It is based on the atomistic conceptions of Muslim scholastic theology. Following in the footsteps of the mutakallimūn, Sharif asserts that the entire universe and each body is composed of the tiniest indivisible substances, which he calls "monads." He assumes that there are three types of being: God as the ultimate being or reality, monads as spiritual essences, and the world of sensations in time and space. All things in the world, from an electron to a human being, are spiritual monads. Inasmuch as God is immanent in every monad, the monad is eternal, deathless, invisible, indivisible, and infinite in time and space. Its existence is determined by the divine will, although this divine will provides for each monad a certain degree of freedom, depending on its level in the scale of things.

In many respects Sharif's monadology is akin to that developed by Leibniz. The Pakistani philosopher, however, rejects the Leibnizian principle of the impregnability of monads, asserting that monads interact with and even interpenetrate one another. He also complements Leibniz's theory with a dialectical approach (obviously prompted by Hegel): monads are dialectical in nature. Within them the process of development occurs by triads "from self through the complementary, not-self, or rather not-yet self, to the final synthesis of both in a more developed self."[3]

Sharif's constructs are noteworthy because the ontological formula of Islamic scholasticism is expressed here in Western philosophical terms and notions, which allows one to view the Islamic tradition as fully blending with conventional philosophical standards. What is far more significant is Sharif's "dialectical" reappraisal of mutakallimūn atomistics, providing an ideological ground for the development of evolutionary process in all its manifestations, both natural and social.

Another example of a synthesis of Eastern and Western traditions is found in the work of Fung Yu-lan (1895–1990), the most distinguished among twentieth-century Chinese philosophers by virtue of his "Neo-Confucianism," the basic tenets of which can be interpreted as logical concepts. According to Fung Yu-lan, the "new rationalistic Confucianism" is based on the following four metaphysical "pillars": principle, material force, the Tao substance, and the Great Entity. Fung's concept of principle derives from the following proposition: "Since there are things, there should be some particular principles." A thing has to be based on some definite principle, although the latter is not necessarily actualized in a thing, belonging to the sphere of reality rather than actuality, and representing a purely formal concept.[4]

The concept of material force derives from the following proposition: "Since there is a principle, there should be a material force" by virtue of which a thing can exist. A material force does not belong to the actual world either, representing solely an existentialistic and purely formal concept.

Tao means "the universal process," the universe of "daily renovation" and perpetual transformation. Finally, the notion of the Great Entity, in which one is everything and everything is one, is also a formal concept. The Great Entity is a general name for everything, corresponding to the Absolute in Western philosophy.

As a matter of fact, Fung Yu-lan made an attempt to "translate" the principal tenets of his Neo-Confucianism into a positivistic vocabulary. But as a result, Neo-Confucianism, a philosophy of immanent order, was virtually replaced by a philosophy of transcendent order.

THE IMPACT OF THE PROTESTANT PARADIGM

The assimilation of Western experience by the East proceeded through a paradigm that appears to find its correspondence in the West. The strongest influence on Eastern philosophical thought was exerted by a paradigm prevailing in Europe during the later Middle Ages, the period of transition from the feudal to the bourgeois form of a communal life and world outlook, which was similar to a pattern predominating the twentieth-century Eastern societies. Although this paradigm was actually similar, it was also quite different in many respects. As if making up for lost centuries, time in the East seemed to be pressing: the twentieth century in the East came to embrace simultaneously the signs of the Renaissance and Reformation in the West. It is partly due to the fact that the traditional modes of life were becoming outdated, not from within but falling down under the powerful impact of economic forces unleashed by capitalist monopolies. These alien forces, along with the awareness that the East was lagging behind Western standards of development and had to rapidly overcome this disastrous gap, stimulated a reassessment of the ethical motivation behind adaptation to this new situation and toward further advancement along capitalist lines of development. Under these circumstances, the Protestant paradigm acquired particular importance.

Just as the transition to capitalism in Europe in the sixteenth century was impossible without the Reformation—"the bourgeois religious revolution"—the breakdown of the medieval world structure in the East seemed feasible only through a radical change of the social role assigned to traditional religions and, therefore, through a reappraisal of the entire set of dogmatic tenets.

Similarly, just as the Reformation was striving to do away with religious alienation, to remove the division between the objective and the subjective, and to set Christians free from the mediation of the church and the clergy, the reformers of Eastern religions were trying to reappraise the relationship between the divine and the human, with a view toward bringing the believer "nearer" to God and thereby fostering the believer's "emancipation."

The reformative approach to the concept of God in Hinduism manifests itself primarily in its renunciation of idolatry, polytheism, and the attribution of anthropomorphic traits to deities. The Hindu reformers placed emphasis on the special status of the human being in the universe. Swāmi Vivekānanda (1863–1902), one of the most outstanding modern Indian thinkers and public figures, repeatedly reminded his readers of the divine nature of human beings. He once wrote: "Get rid, in the first place, of all these limited ideas and see God in every person—working through all hands, walking through all feet, and eating through every mouth. . . . I am not this limited little being, I am the universal. I am the life of all the sons of the past. I am the soul of Buddha, of Jesus, of Mohammed. . . . Stand up then; this is the highest worship. You are one with the universe. That only is humility—not crawling upon all fours and calling yourself a sinner."[5]

This Hindu reformer was looking forward to a time when each Indian would become self-confident and be rid of personal slavery. He appealed to his compatriots with the following words: "Do not be frightened. Awake, be up and doing. Do not stop until you have reached the goal."[6] It is noteworthy that Vivekānanda considered the main mission of the human being to lie in earthly work, rather than in leading an ascetic life and escaping from the world. Comparing the "real" with the "apparent" person, Vivekānanda wrote: "Man . . . is the greatest being that is in the universe, and this world of work the best place in it, because only herein is the greatest and the best chance for him to become perfect."[7]

The concept of God and man has been reappraised in the views of Muslim reformers in a similar, humanistic vein. Thus, Muhammad Iqbal (1873–1938), a poet-philosopher, wrote: "The world, in all its details, from the mechanical movement of what we call the atom of matter to the free movement of thought in the human ego, is the self-revelation of the 'Great I Am'."[8] The world achieves its highest level in the human being alone. Therefore, Iqbal concludes: "That is why the Koran declares the Ultimate Ego to be nearer to man than his own neck-vein." Further on he stresses that man "possesses a much higher degree of reality than the things around him. . . . Of all the creations of God he alone is capable of consciously participating in the creative life of his Maker."[9]

The reformative approach provides grounds for a novel treatment of the human being's role in the universe, more in line with the spirit of the times. Recognition of human free will to a certain degree not only justified the self-dependence of human efforts aimed at transforming earthly life but also elevated these responsibilities to the level of moral, religious duties. The reformers' ethics were based not on an escape from the world and a search for individual salvation but on an active attitude to, and personal involvement in, the transformation of a society according to a new set of humanistic principles.

The key concepts of Hinduism and Buddhism, such as karma, *māyā, nirvāṇa, mukti,* and others, came to be revised. The Hindu enlighteners, Rammohan Roy and Debendranath Tagore, rejected these notions altogether as logically ungrounded. Buddhist reformers (U Otama, U Lun, and U Timisara) believed that the efforts undertaken to attain *nirvāṇa* could be justified only upon the emancipation from mundane slavery.

To be concerned exclusively with one's personal salvation is in principle regarded as sinful. The supreme ethical duty is to take care of others, something realizable through the liberation movements current at the time. According to Aurobindo Ghose (1872–1950), who has radically transformed the most influential of the classical Indian religio-philosophical schools into "political Vedantism," the word "nationalism" itself is "a religion granted by God," the nation is the "embodiment of a Divine principle," and the love of one's motherland is identical to the worship of God. "A ruler of the souls," as he was called by Jawaharlal Nehru, Aurobindo Ghose tried to synthesize in his teaching the Yogic methods employed in various trends of Indian religio-philosophical thought with the intention of using the "integral Yoga" for transforming human nature and society at large.

Aurobindo Ghose viewed culture as a universal means for people's education, for culture constitutes "the hard core of civilization, its heart." Human history testifies to a one-sided mode of development because each civilization so far has focused on a single element of culture: religion in the Ancient Orient, morality in Sparta, art in Europe during the Renaissance, and science in modern Western society. Therefore, it is necessary to transcend the limitations of such a unilateral approach to culture through a harmonious synthesis of cultural elements, which is feasible with the aid of an "integral Yoga." This fosters the mental, spiritual, and supraliminal transformation of the human being. By means of Karma-Yoga, Jñāna-Yoga and Bhakti-Yoga, one can purify respectively one's will, mind, and emotions, achieving a "breakthrough" from the empirical ego to the spiritual "self." The fourth yoga, the so-called Yoga of Perfection, depends exclusively on God's mercy (the human being has simply to "step aside" and allow God to do what He wills) and enables one to attain supraliminal consciousness. In contrast to Śaṅkara and Mādhava, the greatest authorities of the Middle Ages, Aurobindo attached particular importance to Karma-Yoga, which involves volitional activity, with its supreme principle: dharma, an intuitively perceivable code of conduct, one that provides for the optimal combination of interests of the individual and society. Aurobindo stressed the social aspect of dharma, regarding Karma-Yoga as an effective means in the struggle for national liberation, for it cultivates selflessness and martyrdom and instills confidence in justice and the ultimate triumph of the anticolonial movement.

Emancipated thinking is essential for an individual's creative activity. The plea for the right to independent judgment free from any dogma is a key issue in the Eastern reformation. The vital importance attached in the East to the problem of correlating faith and knowledge, religion and science, is quite justifiable, taking into consideration that the backwardness of the countries in this particular region was largely due to the negative attitude of the ruling religious dogma toward rational knowledge, the development of natural sciences, and technological progress. As Jamāl al-Dīn Afghānī (1834–1905), a Muslim reformer and the ideologue of Pan-Islamism, acknowledged himself, it is Islam that "bears all the blame" for the decline of Arab civilization. "Wherever it penetrated, it sought to choke science, and was assiduously encouraged in this by [its own] despotism."[10] Such admissions were also made by other Islamic reformers inclined to bring the blame for the backwardness of the Muslim world to bear not on traditional religion as such but on its dogmatic interpretation. Hence, they saw their task as validating the compatibility of faith and knowledge and verifying that a "true" religion was not an enemy but an ally of scientific progress.

Pravas Jivan Chaudhuri (1916–1961), a pioneering figure in "the philosophy of science" in independent India, a physicist by education, rejected the opposition of science and religion, believing that the purpose and implications of science did not differ in principle from the religious article of faith that God was the Creator of the world. The implications of this tenet, that is, the presence of harmony and expediency in nature, provides evidence for the existence of a supernatural, transcendental agent—a universal or cosmic mind conventionally defined as "God." Using Vedantic terminology, Chaudhuri characterized mental activity as *līlā*, or an "interplay," giving rise to the wealth and diversity of the phenomenal world and at the same time keeping it secure from chaos. Science is designed to identify and describe the relevance of the cosmic mind; reasoning may be based only on the idea of a cosmic spirit as a major hypothesis for explaining our particular experiences in cognizing the world.

Following the Vedantic line of reasoning, Samporan Singh, a contemporary Indian philosopher, affirms that religion should be "moulded" with philosophy and science into a new universal worldview. This type of symbiosis is required because objective science offers merely a transient flash of the truth whereas religion surmises the truth in its totality.

This same tendency to differentiate between the spheres of science and religion can be discerned in the views of Seyyed Hossein Nasr (born 1933), the leading Muslim philosopher of today. Upon graduating from the physics department at the Massachusetts Institute of Technology and later from Harvard University, Nasr held the posts of rector at Teheran University and director of the Shah Academy of Sciences on the eve of the anti-Shah revolution in Iran. His theory of the synthesis of science and religion was influenced by the objective conditions of his time and place. The Shah's regime was vigorously carrying out reforms designed to update the national economy. This was certainly to involve a wide use of technological know-how and modern experimental and theoretical knowledge. The Shah and his associates, however, strove also to retain the religious foundations of the Iranian monarchy. Thus, the task was to elevate Iran to the level of modern world economies, and at the same time keep the traditional underpinnings of indigenous society intact.

In his attempt to synthesize science and religion, Nasr was also guided by the desire to make use of the achievements of technological progress, bypassing its pernicious side effects. Nasr chides moderns (and by this he means Westerners) for their "ignorant attitude" toward nature and their worship of rationalism. The latter implies "a secular vision of nature in which there is no place left for God."[11] He believes that such a rationalism fails to take into consideration the sacred aspect of nature, its dependence on the Almighty, and orients human beings toward the utilization and exploitation of nature according to their own selfish interests.

In his theory of the synthesis of science and religion, Nasr appeals to Sufism, deducing the ontological grounds for the existence of science and religion from the idea that it is the human being, by nature, that occupies a middle position between heaven and earth, the "absolute" and "relative" realities.[12] From the state of a "detachment from God," the human being is striving to return to a state of nearness to him, which manifests itself in the search for the Eternal and the Absolute. This search is realized through "intellectual intuition," which implies the faculty of gaining an insight, an instantaneous and immediate perception, of transcendental knowledge in one's soul. Intellectual intuition is potentially inherent in everyone, but it is only wholly actualized in prophets and mystics. Although intellect is a natural faculty of human beings, they are capable of using it only through divine revelation: religion creates a "niche" and provides the adequate orientations and dispositions to progress, allowing human beings to fulfill their intellectual potentials.

Human residence in the empirical world does indeed create needs that can be satisfied through knowledge of the mundane world. Thus other cognitive faculties, namely senses and reason, are set into action. In Nasr's opinion, reason can interpret the data of sensory experience in two possible ways: as factual and naturalistic or as symbolic. Hence, there are two types of sciences, each differing in quality: the "natural" and the "cosmological" sciences. Natural sciences deal with the empirical nature of things, which is characterized by multiple and eternally changing materiality. Cosmology studies the supernatural, which is eternal and immutable. According to Nasr's classification of the types of knowledge, metaphysics belongs to the highest category; cosmology is located at the intermediary level, and the natural sciences are reduced to the lowest category. This last type of science studies things in their own material relationships. Being metaphysically limited, it is not preoccupied with the evaluation of deeper, extramaterial causes underlying the origin and existence of the natural world. Because the object of natural sciences (the phenomenal world) represents the reflected image of God, the natural sciences are nothing but a reflection of metaphysics, which is the knowledge of Divine Reality.

Cosmological sciences, for their content, draw on the same sensory experience as natural sciences, but through the superimposition of metaphysical coordinates upon the data supplied by the senses they disclose the hidden meaning of natural phenomena. Making use of the *ta'wīl* allegorical method applied by the Ṣūfīs in their interpretations of the Koran, Nasr tries to translate the conceptual vocabulary of science into the language of religious symbols. In the final analysis, Nasr fails to remove the dichotomy of science and religion, but his system validates the autonomous existence of scientific knowledge in a society regulated by religious principles. Such reformative approaches reveal the social need to employ the achievements of modern science, although this employment remains essentially utilitarian, confined exclusively to the sphere of material production.

The ontological, epistemological, and ethical ideas reappraised in this reformative spirit are invariably marked by their social orientations. Prior to the attainment of political sovereignty, however, there was virtually no clear-cut idea about what kind of social structure was most desirable. One thing was obvious: the stagnant economic and political organization of traditional society had to be radically changed. But in what direction? This acute question challenged all newly independent nations faced with a choice between the two most influential models of social and economic development currently operating in the world: the capitalist and the socialist. Many of these nations opted for a third variety combining elements of both—hence, the generation of theories advocating a "third way of development" and various kinds of "religious socialism." These theories placed emphasis on those traditional institutions and values that seemed adequate to secure the bourgeois mode of development, at the same time leveling off the adverse effects inherent in capitalism. The principle of establishing a monastic *saṅgha* or "community" was used as a model for social organization in countries where Buddhism was prevalent; the revised content of such Hindu concepts as *dāna*, *yajña*, and *tapas* was used in India to justify the movement of *bhūdān* (donation of land); in the case of Islam, *zakāt* (tax payments for the benefit of the poor), the ban on collecting *ribā* (capital interest), and Sharī'ah rules of inheritance were interpreted as "pillars" of the Islamic socioeconomic system, restraining the potential abuses of property transactions.

"EASTERN SOCIALISM"

Even in cases when one of the two global economic models was unconditionally embraced, it inevitably carried an imprint of national character, often radically transforming and distorting the chosen ideal. Maoism in China and, to a still greater extent, *Jucheism* in North Korea are the most revealing examples in this respect.

The latter, according to Kim Il Sung, its principal theorist, constituted "fresh advances in revolutionary theory," proclaimed as a creative development of Marxism-Leninism. Etymologically, the word *juche* derives from the combination of two characters, one meaning "master" and the other "body," fused to imply "subject." The advocates of *juche* believe that their interpretation of the concept of "subject" signifies a new approach to one of the basic questions of philosophy, which is formulated in the following way: "Who is ruler of this world?" Their reply: "Man is the master of everything, he determines everything" or "Man is the creature *ruling* the world."[13] In practice, these ideas presupposed "reliance on one's own forces" to be manifested in adhering to "independent politics, self-sufficient economy, and national self-defense."[14]

Since its emergence, in theory and practice the Korean revolutionary movement carried the potentials for giving rise to *Jucheism*. In North Korea, a socialist revolution was aimed at emancipating the population from the oppression of feudal and foreign rule, the goal of both social and national liberation. Under these conditions the masses could be mobilized for political activity and selfless devotion to the revolution by cultivating the idea that it was completely up to them to make themselves happy, for their own destiny and that of the motherland depended solely on their efforts. The key to an earthly paradise seemed to have been discovered: just be self-confident, exercise your will power and perseverance in the attainment of a set of objectives, and you are sure to win. However, in real life everything proves to be much more complicated, for one false step not infrequently turns self-confidence into self-elevation and ideological convictions into dogmatism. This step was taken in the 1960s, when the term *juche* was coined and turned into an object of theoretical speculation. It was prompted by the developments in the USSR, namely: the denunciation of the personality cult around Stalin and the liberalization of social life. Peculiar interpretations of such politically neutral notions as "subject" and "singularity" became the main obstacles to the spread of the ideological "thaw."

The *juche* ideas were proclaimed as "the sole guidelines" in the policies of the North Korean government, which qualified itself as "the most advanced revolutionary power in the world."[15] The program for future action was formulated in the following way: "Communism is the people's government plus three revolutions. The communist paradise can be built up if the people's government is consolidated without fail, and three revolutions—ideological, technological, and cultural—are consistently carried out."[16] It is noteworthy that out of the three revolutions the top priority was given to the ideological: "While carrying out the three revolutions . . . we should consistently follow the principle according to which the ideological revolution *takes the lead* over all of our endeavors."[17]

Thus, the "subject" is a master of all things and everything depends on one's own decision; in turn, however, this is predetermined by the level of one's own revolutionary consciousness. Hence, the logical conclusion: total ideological compliance is necessary. This brainwashing made it possible to justify the regime of barracklike communism, an inflexible rule of the leader's personality cult, complete national isolation, and unreasonable claims for possessing the absolute truth in matters of world politics.

The North Korean experience is one among numerous examples of how the application of "alien" models, either socialist or capitalist, entails the resistance of "Eastern realities," overcome in most cases by the establishment of political dictatorship. In some cases, it involves the dictatorship of one party and a cult of personality; in others, military dictatorship; still in others, absolute monarchy, and the like. Yet, in the long run, even the strongest power turns out to be incapable of securing a successful "transplant." The postwar history of Eastern countries provides many cases of "graft rejection." The most illustrative example is the anti-Shah revolution in Iran.

RELIGIOUS FUNDAMENTALISM

The reformative approach was subjected to criticism by an ideological trend conventionally called "revivalism," or "fundamentalism." Its social basis is quite wide, ranging from legions of the middle class, to petty bourgeoisie, to tradesmen, to young people in general. The credo of fundamentalism is associated with a militant nationalism hostile to cultural nihilism and any attempts to adopt alien models. Revivalism entails the notion that a nation's "salvation" will occur through a return to the "golden age" when Buddhism, Hinduism, Confucianism, and Islam manifested themselves in their "pure" form. However, this purity is treated in the most diverse ways. Plurality of opinion among the advocates of revivalism is as wide as the ideological deviations inherently present in the middle class itself, ranging from the most conservative (oriented toward a return to the Middle Ages) all the way to the most extreme leftist views.

The upsurge of revivalistic trends (for example, the "Muslim Brothers" movement and Khomeinism in the Muslim countries, and "Jana Sangh" in India) is not indicative of a failure of reformist efforts because the multifold phenomenon of fundamentalism can hardly be reduced to its antireformist variety alone. The expansion of revivalism testifies not to the end of the reformation process but, quite on the contrary, to its beginning, this time not as an elitist undertaking (as it has been so far) but as a large-scale movement for a radical transformation of traditional society.

The fruitless experiments aimed at "overtaking capitalism" or oriented toward "installed socialism" revealed that any model of society, no matter how ideal it may be, would be distorted and prove lifeless if transplanted onto unprepared and all the more vulnerable soil. Even if according to the conceptions and goals of the revolution the ideological processes in the East in some cases resembled developments in Europe at the dawn of the modern age, these processes can hardly be viewed as "reformation" in the full sense of the word. To make reforms workable here, it is necessary to identify the internal impulses of development and set them into action.

THE JAPANESE "MIRACLE"

In this respect, the most instructive example is the Japanese economic "miracle" accomplished largely because the ethical motivations of capitalism had been fortified by an independent reappraisal of indigenous cultural traditions. The Japanese deviated from the well-trodden Western path of stimulating enterprise by material incentives and cultivating individualism. The Japanese cultural tradition, comprising a synthesis of Confucianism, Shintoism, and Buddhism, is averse to the idea of a human being treated as "the king of nature" or having any value outside the social community. This explains the logical underpinnings of an ideology developed in Japan to fulfill functions similar to those of Protestantism in the West.

Japan's ascent on the capitalist road of development, speeded by the violent "discovery" of that country by the Europeans in 1853, was preceded by a period that saw the progression of an ideology espoused by the new urban strata—forerunners of the Japanese bourgeoisie. The teaching of *shingaku* (literally, "teaching on the heart"), which was developed by Ishida Baigan (1684–1744), provided the philosophical grounds for the adaptation of a traditional society to the bourgeois mode of living.

According to Baigan's teaching on the human individual, every person is one of the "ten thousand things" essentially united with Heaven and Earth. People are essentially equal, for each "represents a unique tiny universe" and each is capable of achieving the state of "sagehood." In conformity with the "heavenly principle," every individual is predestined for some definite vocation (the Japanese *shyokubun* is akin to the Indian caste system). The individual realizes oneself through a particular occupational activity that is indispensable for the state; one is therefore regarded as part and parcel of a single social organism. In contrast to customary notions prevailing earlier in Japan, the followers of *shingaku* regard as equally important all social functions, recognizing no difference between the "path of tradesmen" and the "path of the Samurai," the latter having been formerly regarded as superior in the social hierarchy. Tradesmen have their own duty, no less important in its social magnitude than that of the warrior, and that is to meet consumers' needs, thereby contributing to "the content of the people's heart." Loyalty to one's duty presupposes a thorough knowledge of and an unflagging pursuit of perfection in one's vocational pursuit, as well as the virtues of diligence, honesty, prudence, and saving. The greatest sign of filial disrespect is the ruin of a paternal home. Thrift in those having an "individualistic" heart, that is, those showing concern solely about their own interests, is assessed as greedy and self-serving and, therefore, it is "overt," for an individualistic heart is prone to be deceptive in its perception of the "self" in relation to the world at large. In order to be authentic, prudence must proceed from the "primeval heart" undistorted by individualistic perception.

The *shingaku* and other reform-oriented Japanese teachings have remained loyal to the Confucian concept of the "self" viewed exclusively in terms of social functions and obligations. An individual remains at the crux of his or her potential as long as these are realized in a social community, and personal success depends on the degree of efficiency in fulfilling a particular social function. At the same time, these teachings uphold the Zen Buddhist and Shintoist notions of the unity of the human being with nature. The philosophy of the Japanese analogy to Protestantism rests on the principles of maintaining "harmony," presupposing mutual confidence and care for one another, which together in turn guarantees justice, or humaneness. Thus corporate ethics rather than individualism, in this case, act as an impetus for the capitalization of society.

The Japanese example demonstrates that it is feasible for an indigenous variety of the reformation paradigm to succeed in transforming a traditional society into a bourgeois society.

GANDHI'S "NONVIOLENT CIVILIZATION"

Of course, it cannot be overlooked that other Eastern nations opted for different paradigms in structuring their reforms. Quests in this direction are still under way in fact. The latest claims for opening up novel civilizational horizons have been associated with such disparate personalities as Mua'mmar Muḥammad Qadhāfī, extravagant leader of the Libyan Jamahirya and founder of the "Third World Theory," and Mahatma Gandhi, the apostle of nonviolence. Paradoxical as it may seem, for all the cultural, ideological, and political differences in their positions, the initiators of these "new" theories have something in common, namely the spirit of revivalism. It is certain archaic features inherent in these views that cause their critics to censure and reject them outright and with haste as simpleminded and outdated. The ideology of the European Reformation, however, also represented a step back, but simultaneously a "comeback" at a new level, a new turn of the historical spiral. Is this not true? Clearly, Gandhi's "nonviolent civilization" is far from a literal recurrence of the past, offering a certain vision, no matter how utopian it may seem, of a future ideal for the world.

Mahātma (literally "the great soul," as his compatriots used to call him) based his ideal of civilization on the universal principle of nonviolence. He treated violence as evidence of the wild origins of the human species and nonharming (*ahiṃsā*) as a sign of its divine essence. *Ahiṃsā* is synonymous with the Truth or God; it involves the soul and the means toward its full realization. Gandhi acknowledged that the ideal of nonviolence as such is not very original. As an "eternal truth" it could be traced back to the commandments of the holy scriptures. The problem, however, lay in consummating this commandment, in establishing it as the standard rule of individual and social being. Mahatma regarded his own life as the story of "Experiments with the Truth," that is, experiments in nonviolence. Gandhi carried out an unprecedented experiment by applying something called *Sātyagraha*, a nonviolent method in the struggle for national independence. He also nurtured the project of *Rāmaraj*, that is, the establishment of "the Divine Kingdom on Earth" (Rāma is the incarnation of Viṣṇu), based on the *universal* triumph of the nonviolence principle. There is virtually no room in this kingdom for machinery production, described by Gandhi as "killing man's harmony with nature," like "a snakehole which may contain from one to a hundred snakes." These "snakes" consist of large cities destroying villages, the slavery of workers, the exploitation of female labor, unemployment, dissipation, unbelief in God, mechanical transportation devices hazardous to the public health, and so on.[18] He urged people to give up machinery and take up the spinning-wheel as a symbol of handicrafts; to turn from centralized production and urban development to decentralized, local models of development based on the revival of villages and rural communities; from exploitation he urged the turn to "trusteeship" in human relationships; from bourgeois democracy he advocated the transformation to a nonviolent political structure called *swaraj*, conceived as "a confederation of free and willingly interacting" villages, each representing a kind of state enjoying all requisite powers and governed by a *pañcāyat* (a council of five members); from the separation of religion and politics he urged their mandatory unity, for any political action should be ethical and, therefore, sanctified by religion; last, to end wars and conflagration between nations he advocated the institution of a world union of free nations, with "the law of love" reigning supreme in international affairs.

Gandhi himself took a sober approach toward the prospects of instituting a "nonviolent civilization." Two years before his violent death, he wrote: "I may be taunted with the retort that this is all utopian and, therefore, not with a single thought. If Euclid's point, though incapable of being drawn by human agency, has an imperishable value, my picture has its own for mankind to live."[19]

For all its utopian nature, Gandhi's project reveals the "sores" of industrial civilization, its critical spirit exerts a sobering effect on those seeking to overcome socioeconomic backwardness and prevents them from blindly imitating alien social models. Besides, Gandhi's criticism may be found constructive by those who, even if residing in a prospering country, are nevertheless aware of the necessity to strive for perfection and move ahead in order to set up a better world to live in, not only for a few "select" nations, but for the entire human community.

The East is currently at a crossroads. The future of our whole planet depends on the choice it is to make. Should the Western-style reformation paradigm prevail in the East, Hegel's prediction that the spiritual-intellectual development of Europe is the teleological end of mankind at large will largely become true. Expectations of such a limited, Eurocentric monologue with the East, however, as predominant as it was in the first half of the twentieth century, seems now to be giving way to increasing expectations for long-term and, perhaps, perpetual East-West dialogue. This inspires hope that cultural accomplishments in all of their diversity, East and West, will be cherished and saved for posterity.

FURTHER READING

Cooper, D. E. *World Philosophies. An Historical Introduction* (Chapter 9. "Recent Non-Western Philosophies"). Oxford: Blackwell, 1996.

Indian Tradition

Gupta, B. "The Contemporary Indian Situation." In *A Companion to World Philosophies,* ed. Eliot Deutsch and Ron Bontekoe. Oxford: Blackwell, 1999.

Mohanty, J. N. "Philosophy in India, 1967–73." In *Review of Metaphysics,* vol. 28, N1, 1974.

Murty, K. S., and K. R. Rao, eds. *Current Trends in Indian Philosophy.* Waltair, India: Andhra University, 1972.

Rama Rao Pappu, S. S., and R. Puligandla, eds. *The Indian Philosophy: Past and Future.* Delhi: Motilal Banarsidass, 1982.

Chinese Tradition

Ames, R. T. "Contemporary Chinese Philosophy." In *A Companion to World Philosophies.* Oxford: Blackwell, 1997.

Hua Shiping. *Scientism and Humanism: Two Cultures in Post-Mao China (1978–1989).* Albany: SUNY Press, 1995.

Shi Yanping. "Developments in Chinese Philosophies Over the Last Ten Years." In *Philosophy East and West,* vol. 43, N1, 1993.

Islamic Tradition

Enayat, H. *Modern Islamic Political Thought.* London: Macmillan, 1982.

Nasr, S. H. *Traditional Islam in the Modern World.* London: Kegan Paul International, 1987.

Rahman, F. "Islam and Modernity." *Transformation of an Intellectual Tradition.* Chicago: Chicago University Press, 1982.

Stepaniants, M. "Contemporary Islamic Thought." In *A Companion to World Philosophies.* Oxford: Blackwell, 1997.

NOTES

1. *Radhakrishnan Reader. An Anthology.* General Editors K. M. Munshi and R. R. Diwakar. Bombay: Bharatya Vidya Bhavan, 1988, p. 418.

2. *A History of Muslim Philosophy.* Ed. M. M. Sharif. In 2 vols. Wiesbaden: O. Harrassowitz, 1963–66.

3. Sharif, M. M. "Dialectical Monadism." *The Contemporary Indian Philosophy.* Ed. S. Radhakrishnan. London: Allen & Unwin, 1952, p. 585.

4. Chan, Wing-tsit. "Chinese Philosophy." *The Encyclopedia of Philosophy.* In 3 vols. Ed. P. Edwards. New York: Macmillan, 1967, vol. 2, p. 95.

5. Swāmi Vivekānanda. "What is Religion?" *The Complete Works of Swāmi Vivekānanda.* In 2 vols. Calcutta: Advaita Ashrama, 1968, vol. 1, p. 341.

6. Swāmi Vivekānanda. "The Way to Blessedness." Ibid., vol. 2, p. 410.

7. Swāmi Vivekānanda. "Jñāna-Yoga." Ibid., vol. 2, p. 271.

8. Iqbal, M. *The Reconstruction of Religious Thought in Islam.* Lahore, Pakistan: Ashraf Press, 1962, p. 71.

9. Ibid., p. 72.

10. Afghani, Dj. *Réfutation des matérialistes.* Paris: Librarie Orientale, 1942, p. 184.

11. Nasr, S. H. *The Encounter of Man and Nature: The Spiritual Crisis of Modern Man.* London: Allen & Unwin, 1968, p. 20.

12. See Nasr, S. H. *Knowledge and the Sacred.* New York: Crossroad, 1981, p. 130.

13. Kim Il Sung. *On the Juche Ideas* (in Russian). Pyongyang: Izdatelstvo literatury na inostrannih yazikah, 1979, p. 14. Italics added.

14. Ibid., p. 51.

15. Kim Il Sung. *The Tasks of the People's Government to Transform the Entire Society on the Basis of Juche Ideas* (in Russian). Pyongyang: Izdatelstvo literatury na inostrannih yazikah, 1982, pp. 9–10.

16. Ibid., p. 3.

17. Ibid., p. 13. Italics added.

18. Gandhi, M. K. "Hind Swaraj." *The Collected Works of Mahatma Gandhi.* Vol. 10. Ahmedabad: Navajivan Publishing House, 1963, p. 59.

19. Gandhi, M. K. "Independence." *Nonviolence in Peace & War.* In 2 vols. Ahmedabad: Navajivan Publishing House, 1949, vol. 2, p. 112.

II

PRIMARY SOURCES

6

Indian Tradition

HINDU SACRED TEXTS

The corpus of Hindu sacred scriptures includes the four Vedas, taken in the broad sense of the word; that is, the four *Saṃhitās*—a collection of hymns, chants, sacrificial mantras, and magic spells (Ṛgveda, Sāmaveda, Yajurveda, and Atharvaveda), their corresponding *brāhmaṇas* (brahmanic explanations), *āraṇyakas* (forest texts, that is, religious writings composed by hermits living in the forests), and Upaniṣads (speculative elaborations on the Vedas in prose and verse).

The Upaniṣads (in Sanskrit, *upa* means "near," *ni* is "down," and *ṣad* is "sit"—"to sit down near to," that is, to sit at the feet of the guru) comprise the final portion of the revealed part of the Vedas. They are thus the end of the Veda (Vedānta). The classical philosophical school that bases its tenets on the authority of the Upaniṣads is therefore called Vedānta.

The first Upaniṣads were formulated prior to the rise of Buddhism. The genre, however, continued to be used up to the spread of Islam in India. There are over two hundred Upaniṣads, although the traditional number is one hundred and eight. Of the twelve most important or principal Upaniṣads, the Aitareya and Kauṣītaki belong to the Ṛgveda; the Chāndogya and Kena belong to the Sāmaveda; the Taittirīya, Kaṭha, Śvetāśvatara, Bṛhadāraṇyaka, and Iṣa belong to the Yajurveda; and the Praśna, Muṇḍaka, and Māṇḍūkya belong to the Atharvaveda. Hence each of the Upaniṣads relies on a particular Veda.

As speculative treatises, the Upaniṣads are mainly concerned with the nature of reality, and with the relation between the universe and the human being. The cosmic nature of the human self or soul, called *ātman*, is treated. Of fundamental importance to all Indian philosophy is the equation of *ātman* (the self) with Brahman (ultimate reality), summed up in the phrase *tat tvam asi*: "that art thou," or Brahman-*ātman.*

Not all scholars of Indian philosophy are of the opinion that the Upaniṣads should be treated as philosophical texts. However, even those who hesitate to rank them as such acknowledge the presence of philosophical reflections in at least some of the Upaniṣads. Below, one example of an undisputed philosophical reflection from Śvetāśvatara-Upaniṣad is provided.

The Bhagavad Gītā, or "Song of the Lord," is by far the best known religio-philosophical text in Sanskrit. This didactic poem forms the sixth book of the Indian epic poem, the *Mahābhārata.* The date of its composition is a widely discussed matter. Most probably, it has no definite author and slowly crystallized out of a "floating mass of oral tradition" over a very long period between the fifth century B.C. and the second century A.D. The text of the poem as it is known today came to be fixed only in the ninth century A.D. by Śaṅkara, its first commentator.

The Gītā is the "song" that the Lord Krishna (an incarnation of the Hindu god Viṣṇu) presented to Arjuna, an epic hero, in response to his request for guidance on the battlefield of the Kuruksetra, confronting the Kauravas' armies, which consisted of Arjuna's relatives and friends. Hence, against a very dramatic background the most vital questions are posed and answered: questions concerning the meaning of human existence and the duties of individuals, about the path leading to spiritual perfection and emancipation, and about the ways of true devotion and knowledge.

The Gītā should not be approached as if it is a systematic treatise. Its style of presentation is not rational or logical but literary, epic. One should also keep in mind that the "teaching" of Krishna here presents a certain synthesis of the most prominent philosophical trends of the time: Sāṃkhya, Yoga, and Vedānta.

The passage here selected from the Bhagavad Gītā, the seventh chapter, speaks about the Absolute hidden from us by *guṇas* (the three main components) of the material nature and about how to unite with the highest reality through knowledge (Jñāna-Yoga), devotion (Bhakti-Yoga) and meditation (Rāja-Yoga), the classic paths of Yoga.

From The Śvetāśvatara-Upaniṣad

Translated by R. E. Hume. Reprinted from A Source Book in Indian Philosophy. *Edited by S. Radhakrishnan and Charles Moore. Princeton, N.J.: Princeton University Press, 1957 (pp. 89–92).*

Conjectures Concerning the First Cause

1. What is the cause: *Brahman*? Whence are we born?
Whereby do we live? And on what are we established?
Overruled by whom, in pains and pleasures,
Do we live our various conditions, O ye theologians?
2. Time, or inherent nature, or necessity, or chance,
Or the elements, or a [female] womb, or a [male] person are to be considered [as the cause];
Not a combination of these, because of the existence of the self (*ātman*).
The self certainly is impotent over the cause of pleasure and pain.
3. Those who followed after meditation and abstraction (*yoga*)
Saw the self-power of God (*deva*) hidden in his own qualities.
He is the One who rules over all these causes,
From "time" to "the self."
6. In this which vitalizes all things, which appears in all things, the Great—
In this Brahmā-wheel the self flutters about,
Thinking that itself and the Actuator are different.
When favored by Him, it attains immortality. (I.1–3, 6)

The Saving Knowledge of the One Inclusive Brahman

7. This has been sung as the supreme *Brahman.*
In it there is a triad. It is the firm support, the Imperishable.
By knowing what is therein, *Brahman*-knowers
Become merged in *Brahman*, intent thereon, liberated from the womb [i.e., from rebirth].
10. What is perishable, is primary matter. What is immortal and imperishable, is Hara (the "Bearer," the self).
Over both the perishable and the self the One God rules.
By meditation upon Him, by union with Him, and by entering into His being
More and more, there is finally cessation from every illusion.
11. By knowing God there is a falling off of all fetters;
With distresses destroyed, there is cessation of birth and death.
By meditating upon Him there is a third stage at the dissolution of the body,
Even universal lordship; being absolute, his desire is satisfied.
12. That Eternal should be known as present in the self.
Truly there is nothing higher than that to be known.
When one recognizes the enjoyer, the object of enjoyment, and the universal Actuator,
All has been said. This is the threefold *Brahman.*

16. The Self (*Ātman*), which pervades all things
    As butter is contained in cream,
    Which is rooted in self-knowledge and austerity—
    This is *Brahman*, the highest mystic doctrine (*upaniṣad*)!
    This is *Brahman*, the highest mystic doctrine! (I.7, 10–12, 16)

Knowing the One Supreme Person Overcomes Death

7. Higher than this is *Brahman*. The Supreme, the Great,
   Hidden in all things, body by body,
   The One embracer of the universe—
   By knowing Him as Lord (*Iśā*) men become immortal.
8. I know this mighty Person
   Of the color of the sun, beyond darkness.
   Only by knowing Him does one pass over death.
   There is no other path for going there.
9. Than whom there is naught else higher,
   Than whom there is naught smaller, naught greater,
   The One stands like a tree established in heaven.
   By Him, the Person, this whole world is filled.
10. That which is beyond this world
    Is without form and without ill.
    They who know That, become immortal;
    But others go only to sorrow. (III.7–10)

The One God of the Manifold World

1. The One who, himself without color, by the manifold application of his power
   Distributes many colors in his hidden purpose,
   And into whom, its end and its beginning, the whole world dissolves—He is God (*deva*)!
   May he endow us with clear intellect!
9. Sacred poetry (*chandas*)—the sacrifices, the ceremonies, the ordinances,
   The past, the future, and what the Vedas declare—
   This whole world the illusion-maker (*māyin*) projects out of this [*Brahman*].
   And in it by illusion (*māyā*) the other is confined.
10. Now, one should know that Nature (*Prakṛti*) is illusion (*māyā*),
    And that the Mighty Lord (*maheśvara*) is the illusion-maker (*māyin*).
    This whole world is pervaded
    With beings that are parts of Him.

19. Not above, not across,
    Nor in the middle has one grasped Him.
    There is no likeness of Him
    Whose name is Great Glory.
20. His form is not to be beheld.
    No one soever sees Him with the eye.
    They who thus know Him with heart and mind
    As abiding in the heart become immortal. (IV.1, 9–10, 19–20)

Liberation through Knowledge of the One God

13. Him who is without beginning and without end, in the midst of confusion,
    The Creator of all, of manifold form,
    The One embracer of the universe—
    By knowing God one is released from all fetters. (V.13)

The One God, Creator and Lord, In and Over the World

1. Some sages discourse of inherent nature;
   Others likewise, of time. Deluded men!
   It is the greatness of God in the world
   By which this Brahmā-wheel is caused to revolve.
2. He by whom this whole world is constantly enveloped
   Is intelligent, the author of time, possessor of qualities, omniscient.
   Ruled o'er by Him, [his] work revolves—
   This which is regarded as earth, water, fire, air, and space!
9. Of Him there is no ruler in the world,
   Nor lord; nor is there any mark of Him. . . . (VI.1–2, 9)

From The Bhagavad Gītā

Translated by S. Radhakrishnan. Reprinted from A Source Book in Indian Philosophy. *Edited by S. Radhakrishnan and Charles Moore. Princeton, N.J.: Princeton University Press, 1957 (pp. 126–29).*

Chapter 7: God and the World

God is Nature and Spirit

The Blessed Lord said:

1. Hear then, O Pārtha (Arjuna), how, practicing *yoga*, with the mind clinging to Me, with Me as thy refuge, thou shalt know Me in full, without any doubt.

2. I will declare to thee in full this wisdom together with knowledge by knowing which there shall remain nothing more here left to be known.

3. Among thousands of men scarcely one strives for perfection, and of those who strive and succeed scarcely one knows Me in truth.

The Two Natures of the Lord

4. Earth, water, fire, air, ether, mind, and understanding, and self-sense—this is the eightfold division of My nature.

5. This is My lower nature. Know My other and higher nature which is the soul, by which this world is upheld, O Mighty-armed (Arjuna).

6. Know that all beings have their birth in this. I am the origin of all this world and its dissolution as well.

7. There is nothing whatever that is higher than I, O Winner of wealth (Arjuna). All that is here is strung on me as rows of gems on a string.

8. I am the taste in the waters, O Son of Kuntī (Arjuna). I am the light in the moon and the sun. I am the syllable *Aum* in all the Vedas. I am the sound in ether and manhood in men.

9. I am the pure fragrance in earth and brightness in fire. I am the life in all existences and the austerity in ascetics.

10. Know Me, O Pārtha (Arjuna), to be the eternal seed of all existences. I am the intelligence of the intelligent. I am the splendor of the splendid.

11. I am the strength of the strong, devoid of desire and passion. In beings am I the desire which is not contrary to law, O Lord of the Bhāratas (Arjuna).

12. And whatever states of being there may be, be they harmonious, passionate, slothful—know thou that they are all from Me alone. I am not in them; they are in Me.

The Modes of Nature Confuse Men

13. Deluded by these threefold modes of nature (*guṇas*) this whole world does not recognize Me who am above them and imperishable.

14. This divine *māyā* [power] of Mine, consisting of the modes, is hard to overcome. But those who take refuge in Me alone cross beyond it.

The State of Evildoers

15. The evildoers who are foolish, low in the human scale, whose minds are carried away by illusion and who partake of the nature of demons do not seek refuge in Me.

Different Kinds of Devotion

16. The virtuous ones who worship Me are of four kinds, the man in distress, the seeker for knowledge, the seeker for wealth, and the man of wisdom, O Lord of the Bhāratas (Arjuna).

17. Of these, the wise one, who is ever in constant union with the Divine, whose devotion is single-minded, is the best, for I am supremely dear to him and he is dear to Me.

18. Noble indeed are all these, but the sage, I hold, is verily Myself for, being perfectly harmonized, he resorts to Me alone as the highest goal.

19. At the end of many lives, the man of wisdom resorts to Me, knowing that Vāsudeva [the Supreme] is all that is. Such a great soul is very difficult to find.

Toleration

20. But those whose minds are distorted by desires resort to other gods, observing various rites, constrained by their own natures.

21. Whatever form any devotee with faith wishes to worship, I make that faith of his steady.

22. Endowed with that faith, he seeks the worship of such a one and from him he obtains his desires, the benefits being decreed by Me alone.

23. But temporary is the fruit gained by these men of small minds. The worshippers of the gods go to the gods but My devotees come to Me.

The Power of Ignorance

24. Men of no understanding think of Me, the unmanifest, as having manifestation, not knowing My higher nature, changeless and supreme.

25. Veiled by My creative power (*yogamāyā*), I am not revealed to all. This bewildered world knows Me not, the unborn, the unchanging.

26. I know the beings that are past, that are present, O Arjuna, and that are to come, but Me no one knows.

27. All beings are born deluded, O Bhārata (Arjuna), overcome by the dualities which arise from wish and hate, O Conqueror of the foe (Arjuna).

The Object of Knowledge

28. But those men of virtuous deeds in whom sin has come to an end [who have died to sin], freed from the delusion of dualities, worship Me steadfast in their vows.

29. Those who take refuge in Me and strive for deliverance from old age and death—they know the *Brahman* [or the Absolute] entire; they know the Self and all about action.

30. Those who know Me as the One that governs the material and the divine aspects, and all sacrifices—they, with their minds harmonized, have knowledge of Me even at the time of their departure from here.

This is the seventh chapter, entitled "The *Yoga* of Wisdom and Knowledge."

BUDDHIST PHILOSOPHY IN INDIA

One of the three "world" religions, Buddhism takes its name after the "buddha," or "awakened one," a person who has achieved enlightenment. The historical Buddha, the founder of the religion, who lived in the sixth century B.C., is not the first and only buddha. It is believed that six to thirteen buddhas preceded him.

The historical Buddha's given name was Siddhartha Gautama. He was the son of a prince of the Shakyas, whose kingdom was situated on the territory of present-day Nepal.

The core of Buddha's teaching is the doctrine of the Four Noble Truths.

1. All life is sorrowful.
2. Sorrow is due to craving.
3. Sorrow can be stopped by stopping the craving.
4. The stopping of craving can be attained by discipline and moral conduct.

These four truths are the common property of all schools of Buddhist thought.

The differences among Buddhist schools come primarily from their understanding of the ways in which enlightenment is achieved. Accordingly, there are in Buddhism three main trends, or yāna, "vehicles," which the adherents follow along the spiritual "journey" to enlightenment. The first is the Hīnayāna, or "lesser vehicle." It is called so because the number of those it allows to reach enlightenment is limited to a select few, these being *arhats*, or "saints," who succeed in "blowing out" as a lamp their personality, thus reaching the state of nirvāṇa. Hīnayāna Buddhism is currently the prevalent school in Ceylon, Burma, Thailand, Cambodia, and Laos. The followers of this school prefer to call it Theravāda, the "teaching of the elders."

The period between the first and the seventh centuries A.D. is marked by the emergence and spread of Mahāyāna Buddhism (the "greater vehicle"), with its two major currents: Mādhyamika and Yogācāra. Mahāyāna focuses on the ideal of the bodhisattva, who, unlike the arhat, turns back from nirvāṇa to help others attain that state. In contrast to the Hīnayāna the Mahāyāna Buddhism is also called the "southern canon" because it is currently found in such countries as China, Japan, and Vietnam.

After the seventh century, Buddhist Tantra developed, primarily in Tibet, and received the name of Vajrayāna (the "vehicle of the thunderbolt").

The total literature of Buddhism is immense. Each of the numerous sects has, in fact, its own version of sacred scriptures. Still, the basic ideas of Buddhism are summed up in the Tripiṭaka (the "three baskets") consisting accordingly of three parts, namely: Vinaya-piṭaka, Sūtta-piṭaka, and Abhidharma-piṭaka. The piṭaka contains accounts of the origin of the Buddhist order—saṇgha and the rules of conduct for its members. The second "basket" is made of the discourses attributed to the Buddha or his immediate disciples. The third part is a compendium (collection of seven writings) of Buddhist philosophy and psychology.

Buddhism presents threefold characterization of the nature of the world: sorrowful, transient, and soulless. Without grasping this truth nobody has chance for salvation. All things of the universe are classified into five components: form and matter (rūpa), sensations (vedana), perceptions (saññā), psychic dispositions (saṃkhārā), and consciousness (viññāna). The individual is made of a combination of the five components, which are never the same; the whole being of the individual is in a state of constant flux.

The selection below presents to the readers highly representative Hīnayāna Buddhism: *The Questions of King Milinda.* It is the only work composed by the Northern Buddhists (either in Sanskrit itself or in some North Indian Prakrit) that is regarded with reverence by the orthodox Buddhists of the southern schools. It consists of the discussion of a number points of Hīnayāna Buddhist doctrine between King Milinda and Nāgasena the Elder.

From *The Questions of King Milinda*

Translated by T. W. Rhys Davids. Reprinted from Sacred Books of the East. *Edited by F. Max Muller. Vol. 49. Delhi: Motilal Banarsidass Publishers, 1965.*

Book II. Chapter 3.

1. The king said: "What is the root, Nāgasena, of past time, and what of present, and what of future time?"

"Ignorance. By reason of Ignorance came the Confections, by reason of the Confections consciousness, by reason of consciousness name-and-form, by reason of name-and-form the six organs of sense, by reason of them contact, by reason of contact sensation, by reason of sensation thirst, by reason of thirst craving, by reason of craving becoming, by reason of becoming birth, by reason of birth old age and death, grief, lamentation, sorrow, pain, and despair. Thus is it that the ultimate point in the past of all this time is not apparent."

"You are ready, Nāgasena, in reply."

2. The king said: "You say that the ultimate point of time is not apparent. Give me an illustration of that."

"Suppose, O king, a man were to plant in the ground a tiny seed, and that it were to come up as a shoot, and in due course grow, develop, and mature until it produced a fruit. And then the man, taking a seed from that fruit, were again to plant it in the ground, and all should happen as before. Now would there be any end to this series?"

"Certainly not, Sir."

"Just so, O king, the ultimate point in the past of the whole of this time is not apparent."

"Give me a further illustration."

"The hen lays an egg. From the egg comes a hen. From the hen an egg. Is there any end to this series?"

"No."

"Just so, O king, the ultimate point in the past of the whole of this time is not apparent."

"Give me a further illustration."

Then the Elder drew a circle on the ground and asked the king: "Is there any end to this circle?"

"No, it has no end."

"Well, that is like those circles spoken of by the Blessed One. 'By reason of the eye and of forms there arises sight, when these three come together there is touch, by reason of touch sensation, by reason of sensation a longing [Tanhā, thirst], by reason of the longing action [Karma], and from action eye is once more produced.' Now is there any end to this series?"

"No."

Then setting out a precisely corresponding circle of each of the other organs of sense (of the ear, nose, tongue, body, and mind), he in each case put the same question. And the reply being always the same, he concluded:

"Just so, O king, the ultimate point of time in the past is not apparent."

"You are ready, Nāgasena, in reply."

3. The king said: "When you say that the ultimate point is not apparent, what do you mean by 'ultimate point'?"

"Of whatsoever time is past. It is the ultimate point of that, O king, that I speak of."

"But, if so, when you say that it is not apparent, do you mean to say that of everything? Is the ultimate point of everything unknown?"

"Partly so, and partly not."

"Then which is so, and which not?"

"Formerly, O king, everything in every form, everything in every mode, was ignorance. It is to us as if it were not. In reference to that the ultimate beginning is unknown. But that, which has not been, becomes; as soon as it has begun to become it dissolves away again. In reference to that the ultimate beginning is known."

"But, reverend Sir, if that which was not, becomes, and as soon as it has begun to become passes again away, then surely, being thus cut off at both ends, it must be entirely destroyed?"

"Nay, surely, O king, if it be thus cut off at both ends, can it not at both ends be made to grow again?"

"Yes, it might. But that is not my question. Could it grow again from the point at which it was cut off?"

"Certainly."

"Give me an illustration."

Then the Elder repeated the simile of the tree and the seed, and said that the Skandhas (the constituent elements of all life, organic and inorganic) were so many seeds, and the king confessed himself satisfied.

4. The king said: "Are there any Confections which are produced?"

"Certainly."

"Which are they?"

"Where there is an eye, and also forms, there is sight, where there is sight there is a contact through the eye, where there is contact through the eye there is a sensation, where there is sensation there is a longing, where there is longing there is a grasping, where there is grasping there is a becoming, where there is becoming there is birth, and at birth old age and death, grief, lamentation, pain, sorrow, and despair begin to be. Thus is the rise of the whole of this class of pain.—Where there is neither eye nor form there is no sight, where there is not sight there is no contact through the eye, where there is not contact there is no sensation, where there is not sensation there is no longing, where there is not longing there is no grasping, where there is not grasping there is no becoming, where there is not becoming there is no birth, and where there is not birth there is neither old age nor death nor grief, lamentation, pain, sorrow, and despair. Thus is the ending of all this class of pain."

"Very good, Nāgasena!"

5. The king said: "Are there any Confections (qualities) which spring into being without a gradual becoming?"

"No. They all have a gradual becoming."

"Give me an illustration."

"Now what do you think, great king? Did this house in which you are sitting spring suddenly into being?"

"Certainly not, Sir. There is nothing here which arose in that way. Each portion of it has had its gradual becoming—these beams had their becoming in the forest, and this clay in the earth, and by the moil and toil of women and of men was this house produced."

"Just so, great king, there is no Confection which has sprung into being without a gradual becoming. It is by a process of evolution that Confections come to be !"

"Give me a further illustration."

"They are like all kinds of trees and plants which, when set in the ground, grow, develop, and mature, and then yield their fruits and flowers. The trees do not spring into being without a becoming. It is by a process of evolution that they become what they are. Just so, great king, there is no Confection which has sprung into being without a gradual becoming. It is by a process of evolution that Confections come to be!"

"Give me a further illustration."

"They are like the pots of various kinds which a potter might form when he has dug up the clay out of the earth. The pots do not spring into being without a becoming. It is by a process of evolution that they become what they are. Just so, great king, there is no Confection which has sprung into being without a gradual becoming. It is by a process of evolution that Confections come to be!"

"Give me a further illustration."

"Suppose, O king, there were no bridge of metal on a mandolin, no leather, no hollow space, no frame, no neck, no strings, no bow, and no human effort or exertion, would there be music?"

"Certainly not, Sir."

"But if all these things were there, would not there be a sound?"

"Of course there would."

"Just so, great king, there is no Confection which has spring into being without a gradual becoming. It is by a process of evolution that Confections come to be!"

"Give me a further illustration."

"Suppose, O king, there were no fire-stick apparatus, no twirling-stick, and no cord for the twirling-stick, and no matrix, and no burnt rag for tinder, and no human effort and exertion, could there be fire by attrition?"

"Certainly not."

"But if all these conditions were present, then might not fire appear?"

"Yes, certainly."

"Just so, great king, there is no Confection which has sprung into being without a gradual becoming. It is by a process of evolution that Confections come to be!"

"Give me one more illustration."

"Suppose, O king, there were no burning glass, and no heat of the sun, and no dried cow-dung for tinder, could there be fire?"

"Certainly not."

"But where these things are present there fire might be struck, might it not?"

"Yes."

"Just so, great king, there is no Confection which has sprung into being without a gradual becoming. It is by a process of evolution that Confections come to be!"

"Give me another illustration."

"Suppose, O king, there were no looking-glass, and no light, and no face in front of it, would there appear an image?"

"No."

"But given these things, there might be a reflection?"

"Yes, Sir, there might."

"Just so, great king, there is no Confection which has sprung into being without a gradual becoming. It is by a process of evolution that Confections come to be!"

"Very good, Nāgasena!"

6. The king said: "Is there, Nāgasena, such a thing as the soul?"

"What is this, O king, the soul [Vedagu]?"

"The living principle within which sees forms through the eye, hears sounds through the ear, experiences tastes through the tongue, smells odors through the nose, feels touch through the body, and discerns things [conditions, "dhammā"] through the mind—just as we, sitting here in the palace, can look out of any window out of which we wish to look, the east window or the west, or the north or the south."

The Elder replied: "I will tell you about the five doors, great king. Listen, and give heed attentively. If the living principle within sees forms through the eye in the manner that you mention, choosing its window as it likes, can it not then see forms not only through the eye, but also through each of the other five organs of sense? And in like manner can it not then as well hear sounds, and experience taste, and smell odors, and feel touch, and discern conditions through each of the other five organs of sense, besides the one you have in each case specified?"

"No, Sir."

"Then these powers are not united one to another indiscriminately, the latter sense to the former organ, and so on. Now we, as we are seated here in the palace, with these windows all thrown open, and in full daylight, if we only stretch forth our heads, see all kinds of objects plainly. Can the living principle do the same when the doors of the eyes are thrown open? When the doors of the ear are thrown open, can it do so? Can it then not only hear sounds, but see sights, experience tastes, smell odors, feel touch, and discern conditions? And so with each of its windows?"

"No, Sir."

"Then these powers are not united one to another indiscriminately. Now again, great king, if Dinna here were to go outside and stand in the gateway, would you be aware that he had done so?"

"Yes, I should know it."

"And if the same Dinna were to come back again, and stand before you, would you be aware of his having done so?"

"Yes, I should know it."

"Well, great king, would the living principle within discern, in like manner, if anything possessing flavor were laid upon the tongue, its sourness, or its saltiness, or its acidity, or its pungency, or its astringency, or its sweetness?"

"Yes, it would know it."

"But when the flavor had passed into the stomach would it still discern these things?"

"Certainly not."

"Then these powers are not united one to the other indiscriminately. Now suppose, O king, a man were to have a hundred vessels of honey brought and poured into one trough, and then, having had another man's mouth closed over and tied up, were to have him cast into the trough full of honey. Would he know whether that into which he had been thrown was sweet or whether it was not?"

"No, Sir."

"But why not?"

"Because the honey could not get into his mouth."

"Then, great king, these powers are not united one to another indiscriminately."

"I am not capable of discussing with such a reasoner. Be pleased, Sir, to explain to me how the matter stands."

Then the Elder convinced Milinda the king with discourse drawn from the Abhidharma, saying: "It is by reason, O king, of the eye and of forms that sight arises, and those other conditions—contact, sensation, idea, thought, abstraction, sense of vitality, and attention—arise each simultaneously with its predecessor. And a similar succession of cause and effect arises when each of the other five organs of sense is brought into play. And so herein there is no such thing as soul (Vedagu)."

JAINISM

Jainism, the third most important religious tradition in India (after Brahmanism and Buddhism), refers to twenty-four tīrthankaras, teachers, also called jinas (the "conquerors"). The last of the tīrthankaras—Mahāvīra Vardhamāna, who was roughly contemporary of the Buddha—is considered to be the founder of Jainism.

Along with Buddhists and Cārvākas, Jains do not accept the authority of the Vedas. They strongly criticize the theistic position by rejecting Īśvara—God's role in the creation of the world. The philosophy of Jainism might be called a pluralistic realism because it affirms the plurality of substances that exist independently from consciousness.

The Jains try to reconcile the extreme positions of Vedāntism and Buddhism by formulating a concept of the relativity (anekāntatva) of everything that exists. According to Jainism, all definitions of reality are true from some particular point of view, in some certain sense. That is why any statement about reality should include a modal expression: syād, which means "maybe," "possibly," or "perhaps." This kind of logical relativism leads to a nonabsolutist metaphilosophical position: any philosophical school is respected in succeeding to grasp some aspects of the universe, any system of thought is believed to be true in a certain respect.

The most important categories of Jaina philosophy are jīva (soul) and ajīva (inanimate object); the relations between the two define all the rest. The jīvas are divided into perfect, liberated ones (siddha) and bound by saṃsāra; that is why these are called hellish ones (narakīya). By their nature all souls are eternal and omniscient. A soul is soiled by a kind of a fine matter, "karma," that attaches to it in accordance with its actions. The purification of a soul from karma, that is, the destruction of soiling, is called "nirjārā," and leads to liberation, "mokṣa." Liberation is attained through right belief, right knowledge, and right action. Being the school most committed to the value of life, Jainism particularly stresses the practice of noninjury, "*ahiṃsā*."

The selection presents the Jaina doctrine of *ahiṃsā* from *The Acaraṅga Sūtra.*

From the *Acaraṅga Sūtra*

Translated by Muni Mahendra Kumar. New Delhi: Today and Tomorrow's Printers and Publishers, 1981.

The True Doctrine: Non-Violence

1. I say—

   The *Arhats* (Venerable Ones) of the past, those of the present and the future narrate thus, discourse thus, proclaim thus, and asseverate thus:

   One should not injure, subjugate, enslave, torture, or kill any animal, living being, organism, or sentient being.

2. This Doctrine of Non-violence (viz. *Ahiṃsā-dharma*) is immaculate, immutable, and eternal.

   The Self-realized *Arhats*, having comprehended the world (of living beings), have propounded this (Doctrine).

3. (The *Arhats* have propounded the Doctrine of Non-violence for one and all, equally for)

   those who are intent on practicing it and those who are not;
   those who are desirous to practice it and those who are not;
   those who have eschewed violence and those who have not;
   those who are acquisitive and those who are not;
   those who are deeply engrossed in worldly ties and those who are not.

4. This Doctrine of *Ahiṃsā* is Truth. It is truly axiomatic. It is rightly enunciated here (i.e. in the Teachings of the *Arhats*).
5. Having accepted this (Great vow of Non-violence), one should neither vitiate it nor forsake it.

   Comprehending the true spirit of the Doctrine (one should practice it till one's last breath).
6. He should be dispassionate towards sensual objects.
7. He should refrain from worldly desires. [Annotation] The three main worldly desires are—craving for son, wealth, and longevity. A *sādhaka* should not cherish these as well as such other worldly desires.
8. How can one who is bereft of the knowledge of this (Doctrine of *Ahiṃsā*), have the knowledge of other (Doctrines)?
9. This (Doctrine of Non-violence) which is being expounded has been perceived, heard, deliberated upon, and thoroughly understood.
10. Those who resort to and remain engrossed in violence suffer (the miseries of) transmigration again and again.
11. O *Sādhaka*! You, who are endeavoring day and night; discern that those who are stupefied are outside the sphere of the Doctrine (of Non-violence). You should, therefore, be alert and always sedulous. . . .
20. Some put forth mutually . . . contradictory doctrines in the field (of philosophy).

    Some of them contend: "The following doctrine has been perceived, heard, reflected upon, thoroughly comprehended and scrutinized in all directions—upwards, downwards and lateral:

    'All animals, living beings, organisms and sentient creatures may be injured, governed, enslaved, tortured and killed.'

    "Know that there is no sin in committing violence."
21. This (approval of violence) is the doctrine of the ignoble ones.
22. Those who are Noble Ones assert thus: "O Protagonists of the doctrine of violence! Whatever you have perceived, heard, reflected upon, thoroughly comprehended and scrutinized in all directions—upwards, downwards and lateral, is fallacious, and hence, you say, speak, assert and preach: 'All animals, living beings, organisms and sentient creatures may be injured, governed, enslaved, tortured and killed: Know that there is no sin in committing violence.'
23. "We, on the other hand, say, speak, assert and preach: 'All animals, living beings, organisms and sentient creatures should not be injured, governed, enslaved, tortured and killed.' Know that it is non-violence which is (completely) free from sin."

24. This (approval of non-violence) is the doctrine of the Noble ones.
25. First, we shall ask (each philosopher) to enunciate his own doctrine and then put the following question to him: "O philosophers! Is suffering pleasing to you or painful?
26. "(If you say that suffering is pleasing to you, your answer is contradictory to what is self-evident. And if you, on the other hand, say that suffering is painful to you, then) your answer is valid. Then, we want to tell you that just as suffering is painful to you, in the same way it is painful, disquieting and terrifying to all animals, living beings, organisms and sentient beings."
122. Through observation and scrutiny find out for yourself that inquietude is distasteful to, highly terrifying and painful for all animals, all beings, all those throbbing with life and all souls. So do I say. . . .
123. (Being overwhelmed by grief), the creatures are scared from (all) directions and intermediate directions. . . .
124. See! Almost everywhere the passionate man are tormenting (mobile-beings).
125. (Each of the) mobile-beings has its own body to inhabit.
126. See! Every (ascetic who has ceased from causing violence to these beings), leads a life of self-discipline.
127. (And discern from them) those pseudo-monks who, despite professing, "We are mendicants," (act like householders i.e. cause violence to the mobile-beings).
131. Some monk either indulges himself in action causing violence to the mobile-beings through various kinds of weapons, makes others to cause violence to the mobile-beings, or approves of others causing violence to the mobile-beings.
132. Such an act of violence proves baneful for him, such an act of violence deprives him of enlightenment.
133. He (true ascetic), comprehending it (i.e. consequences of an act of violence), becomes vigilant over the practice of self-discipline.
134. Hearing from the Bhagavān Mahāvīra Himself or from the monks, one comes to know:—It (i.e. causing violence to the mobile-beings), in fact, is the knot of bondage,
   it, in fact, is the delusion,
   it, in fact, is the death,
   it, in fact, is the hell.
137. I say—Just as consciousness of a man born without any sense-organs (i.e. one who is blind, deaf, dumb, crippled, etc. from birth) is not manifest, the consciousness of the mobile-beings is also not manifest.

(Nevertheless) such a man (the one born organless) (experiences pain) when struck or cut with a weapon (so also do the mobile-beings).

138. (On simultaneously) cutting and severing with weapons, (all the following thirty-two anatomical features of a man, he suffers excruciating pain though he would not be able to express it): Foot, ankle, leg, knee, thigh, waist, belly, stomach, flank, back, bosom, heart, breast, shoulder, arm, hand, finger, nail, neck, chin, lip, tooth, tongue, palate, throat, temple, ear, nose, eye, brow, forehead and head. (So is the case with the mobile-being).
139. Man (experiences pain) when forced into unconsciousness or when he is deprived of life. (So do the mobile-beings).
143. Having discerned this, a sage should neither use any weapon causing violence to the mobile-being, nor cause others to use it nor approve of others using it.
144. He who discerns (i.e. comprehends and forswears) the actions that cause violence to the mobile-beings, can be regarded as a (true) ascetic (for a true ascetic is he) who has discerningly forsworn actions.

THE CĀRVĀKA (LOKĀYATA)

One of the most controversial thought systems in India is the Lokāyata (which can be translated as "prevalent in the world"), also known as Cārvāka (called so after the name of its teacher). In the beginning it did not directly oppose Brahmanism and its followers were considered to be the masters of dialectics in disputes among the brahmans. By the time of the Arthaśāstra (third century B.C.) it became a fully articulated philosophical system mentioned as the third after the Sāṃkhya and the Yoga schools. The Lokāyata became an openly secular trend of thought and joined Buddhism and Jainism as a "nāstika," an unorthodox philosophical school that did not recognize the authority of the Vedas. It is common to associate the Lokāyata with the atheistic and materialistic trends in Indian philosophy.

The original texts of the Cārvāka have not survived. One can judge them only through their exposition in different treatises, mostly those of their opponents. The vast majority of modern writings on the Lokāyata are reiterations of the main contents of the first chapter of Mādhāvācarya's *Sarva-Darśana-Saṃgraha.* That Advaita Vedāntist of the fourteenth century is best known for his compendium of Indian philosophy. The compendium discusses sixteen philosophical systems of which the Cārvāka forms the first chapter.

From *The Sarva-Darśana-Saṃgraha*

By Mādhavācarya. Translated by E. B. Cowell and A. E. Gough. Reprinted from Cārvāka/Lokāyata: An Anthology of Source Materials and Some Recent Studies. *Edited by D. Chattopadhyaya. New Delhi, 1994.*

THE CĀRVĀKA SYSTEM

[We have said in our preliminary invocation, "salutation to Śiva, the abode of eternal knowledge, the storehouse of supreme felicity,"] but how can we attribute to the Divine Being the giving of supreme felicity, when such a notion has been utterly abolished by Cārvāka, the crest-gem of the atheistical school, the follower of the doctrine of Bṛhaspati? The efforts of Cārvāka are indeed hard to be eradicated, for the majority of living beings hold by the current refrain—

> While life is yours, live joyously;
> None can escape Death's searching eye:
> When once this frame of ours they burn,
> How shall it ever again return?

The mass of men, in accordance with the Śāstras of policy and enjoyment, considering wealth and desire the only ends of man, and denying the existence of any object belonging to a future world, are found to follow only the doctrine of Cārvāka. Hence another name for that school is Lokāyata—a name well accordant with the thing signified.

In this school the four elements, earth, etc., are the original principles; from these alone, when transformed into the body, intelligence is produced, just as the inebriating power is developed from the mixing of certain ingredients, and when these are destroyed, intelligence at once perishes also. They quote the Śruti for this (*Bṛhad Āraṇy. Up.* ii. 4, 12), "Springing forth from these elements, itself solid knowledge, it is destroyed when they are destroyed—after death no intelligence remains." Therefore the soul is only the body distinguished by the attribute of intelligence, since there is no evidence for any soul distinct from the body, as such cannot be proved, since this school holds that perception is the only source of knowledge and does not allow inference, etc.

The only end of man is enjoyment produced by sensual pleasures. Nor may you say that such cannot be called the end of man as they are always mixed with some kind of pain, because it is our wisdom to enjoy pure pleasure as far as we can, and to avoid the pain which inevitably accompanies it; just as the man who desires fish takes the fish with their scales and bones, and having taken as many as he wants, desists; or just as the man who desires rice, takes the rice, straw and all, and having taken as much as he wants, desists. It is not therefore for us, through a fear of pain, to reject the pleasure which our nature instinctively recognizes as congenial. Men do not refrain from sowing rice, because forsooth there are wild animals to devour it; nor do they refuse to set the cooking-pots on the fire, because forsooth there are beggars to pester us for a share of the contents. If anyone were so timid as to forsake a visible pleasure, he would indeed be foolish like a beast, as has been said by the poet—

> The pleasure which arises to men from contact with sensible objects,
> Is to be relinquished as accompanied by pain—such is the reasoning of fools;
> The berries of paddy, rich with the finest white grains,
> What man, seeking his true interest, would fling away because these are covered with husk and dust.

If you object that if there be no such thing as happiness in a future world, then how should men of experienced wisdom engage in the *agnihotra* and other sacrifices, which can only be performed with great expenditure of money and bodily fatigue; your objection cannot be accepted as any proof to the contrary, since the *agnihotra*, etc., are only useful as means of livelihood, for the Veda is tainted by the three faults of untruth, self-contradiction, and tautology; then again, the impostors who call themselves Vaidic pundits are mutually destructive, as the authority of the *jñāna-kāṇḍa* is overthrown by those who maintain that of the *karma-kāṇḍa*, while those who maintain the authority of the *jñāna-kāṇḍa* reject that of the *karma-kāṇḍa*, and lastly, the three Vedas themselves are only the incoherent rhapsodies of knaves, and to this effect runs the popular saying—

> The Agnihotra, the three Vedas, the ascetic's three staves, and smearing oneself with ashes—
> Bṛhaspati says, these are but means of livelihood for those who have no manliness nor sense.

Hence it follows that there is no other Hell than mundane pain produced by purely mundane causes, as thorns, etc.; the only Supreme is the earthly monarch, whose existence is proved by all the world's eyesight; and the only Liberation is the dissolution of the body. By holding the doctrine that the soul is identical with the body, such phrases as "I am thin," "I am black," etc., are at once intelligible, as the attributes of thinness, etc., and self-consciousness will reside in the same subject (the body); like the use of the phrase "my body" is metaphorical, "the head of Rāhu" (Rāhu being really *all head*).

All this has been thus summed up—

> In this school there are four elements, earth, water, fire, and air; and from these four elements alone is intelligence produced—just like the intoxicating power from *kiṇva*, etc., mixed together; since in "I am fat," "I am lean," these attributes abide in the same subject,
>
> And since fatness, etc., reside only in the body, it alone is the soul, and no other,
>
> And such phrases as "my body" are only significant metaphorically.

"Be it so," says the opponent; "your wish would be gained if inference, etc., had no force of proof; but then they have this force, else, if they had not, then how, on perceiving smoke, should the thoughts of the intelligent immediately proceed to fire; or why, on hearing another say, 'there are fruits on the bank of the river,' do those who desire fruit proceed, at once, to the shore?"

All this, however, is only the inflation of the world of fancy.

Those who maintain the authority of inference accept the *sign* or middle term as the cause of knowledge, which middle term must be found in the minor and be itself invariably connected with the major. Now, this invariable connection must be a relation destitute of any condition accepted or disputed; and this connection does not possess its power of causing inference by virtue of its *existence*, as the eye, etc., are the cause of perception, but by virtue of its being *known*. What, then, is the means of this connection's being known?

We will first show that it is not *perception*. Now perception is held to be of two kinds, external and internal (i.e., as produced by the external senses, or by the inner sense, mind). The former is not the required means; for, although it is possible that the actual contact of the senses and the object will produce the knowledge of the particular object thus brought in contact, yet as there never can be such contact in the case of the past or the future, the universal proposition, which was to embrace the invariable connection of the middle and major terms in every case, becomes impossible to be known. Nor may you maintain that this knowledge of the universal proposition has the general class as its object, because if so, there might arise a doubt as to the existence of the invariable connection in this particular case (as, for instance, in this particular smoke as implying fire).

Nor is *internal perception* the means, since you cannot establish that the mind has any power to act independently towards an external object, since all allow that it is dependent on the external senses, as has been said by one of the logicians, "The eye, etc., have their objects as described; but mind externally is dependent on the others."

Nor can *inference* be the means of the knowledge of the universal proposition, since in the case of this inference we should also require another inference to establish it, and so on, and hence would arise the fallacy of an *ad infinitum* retrogression.

Nor can *testimony* be the means thereof, since we may either allege in reply, in accordance with the Vaiśeṣika doctrine of Kaṇāda, that this is included in the topic of inference; or else we may hold that this fresh proof of testimony is unable to leap over the old barrier that stopped the progress of inference, since it depends, itself, on the recognition of a *sign* in the form of the language used in the child's presence by the old man, and, moreover, there is no more reason for our believing another's word that smoke and fire are invariably connected, than for our receiving the *ipse dixit* of Manu, etc. (which, of course, we Cārvākas reject).

And again, if testimony were to be accepted as the only means of the knowledge of the universal proposition, then in the case of a man to whom the fact of the invariable connection between the middle and major terms had not been pointed out by another person, there could be no inference of one thing (as fire) on seeing another thing (as smoke); hence, on your own showing, the whole topic of inference for oneself would have to end in mere idle words.

Then again, *comparison*, etc., must be utterly rejected as the means of the knowledge of the universal proposition, since it is impossible that they can produce the knowledge of the unconditioned connection (i.e. the universal proposition), because their end is to produce the knowledge of quite another connection, *viz.,* the relation of a name to something so named.

Again, this same absence of a condition, which has been given as the definition of an invariable connection (i.e., a universal proposition), can itself never be known; since it is impossible to establish that all conditions must be objects of perception; and therefore, although the absence of perceptible things may be itself perceptible, the absence of non-perceptible things must be itself non-perceptible; and thus, since we must here, too, have recourse to inference, etc., we cannot leap over the obstacle which has already been planted to bar them. Again, we must accept as the definition of the condition, "it is that which is reciprocal or equipollent in extension with the major term, though not constantly accompanying the middle." These three distinguishing clauses, "not constantly accompanying the middle term," "constantly accompanying the major term," and "being constantly accompanied by it" (i.e., reciprocal), are needed in the full definition to stop, respectively, three such fallacious conditions, in the argument to prove the noneternity of sound, as "being produced," "the nature of a jar," and "not causing audition"; wherefore the definition holds—and again, it is established by the *śloka* of the great Doctor beginning *samāsama.*

But since the knowledge of the condition must here precede the knowledge of the condition's absence, it is only when there is the knowledge of the condition, that the knowledge of the universality of the proposition is possible; i.e., a knowledge in the form of such a connection between the middle term and major term as is distinguished by the absence of any such condition; and on the other hand, the knowledge of the condition depends upon the knowledge of the invariable connection. Thus we fasten on our opponents, as with adamantine glue, the thunderbolt-like fallacy of reasoning in a circle. Hence, by the impossibility of knowing the universality of a proposition, it becomes impossible to establish inference, etc.

The step which the mind takes from the knowledge of smoke, etc., to the knowledge of fire, etc., can be accounted for by its being based on a former perception, or by its being an error; and that in some cases, this step is justified by the result, is accidental, just like the coincidence of effects observed in the employment of gems, charms, drugs, etc.

From this, it follows that fate, etc., do not exist, since these can only be proved by inference. But an opponent will say, if you do not thus allow *adṛṣṭa* the various phenomena of the world become destitute of any cause. But we cannot accept this objection as valid, since these phenomena can all be produced spontaneously from the inherent nature of things. Thus it has been said—

The fire is hot, the water cold, refreshing and cool the breeze of morn;
By whom came this variety? From their own nature was it born.

And all this has been also said by Bṛhaspati—

There is no heaven, no final liberation, nor any soul in another world.

Nor do the actions of the four castes, orders, etc., produce any real effect.

The Agnihotra, the three Vedas, the ascetic's three staves, and smearing one's self with ashes,

Were made by Nature as the livelihood of those destitute of knowledge and manliness.

If a beast slain in the Jyotiṣṭoma rite will itself go to heaven,

Why then does not the sacrificer, forthwith, offer his own father?—

If the Śrāddha produces gratification to beings who are dead,

Then here, too, in the case of travelers when they start, it is needless to give provisions for the journey.

If beings in heaven are gratified by our offering the Śrāddha here,

Then why not give the food down below to those who are standing on the housetop?

While life remains, let a man live happily, let him feed on ghee even though he runs in debt;

> When once the body becomes ashes, how can it ever return again?
> If he who departs from the body goes to another world, How is it that he comes not back again, restless for love of his kindred?
> Hence it is only as a means of livelihood that Brahmans have established here
> All these ceremonies for the dead—there is no other fruit anywhere.
> The three authors of the Vedas were buffoons, knaves, and demons.
> All the well-known formulae of the pandits, *jarpharī, turpharī,* etc.
> And all the obscene rites for the queen commanded in the Aśvamedha,
> These were invented by buffoons, and so all the various kinds of presents to the priests,
> While the eating of flesh was similarly commanded by night-prowling demons.

Hence, in kindness to the mass of living beings must we fly for refuge to the doctrine of Cārvāka. Such is the pleasant consummation.

SĀṂKHYA-YOGA

Philosophical views in India are classified according to their orientation toward religious traditions. Those that recognize the authority of Hindu sacred texts have crystallized into six systems or "darśans," linked in three pairs: Yoga-Sāṃkhya, Nyāya-Vaiśeṣika and Mīmāṃsā-Vedānta. The first of each pair is focused on the practice leading to the ultimate aim, "mokṣa," or salvation. The second of each pair deals mostly with metaphysics.

Elements of Sāṃkhya are found in two Upaniṣads. The process of distinguishing itself and becoming an independent system with its own terminology and set of doctrines had been complete under the Gupta dynasty.

The name of "Sāṃkhya" derives from the root "khyāi" with the prefix "sam," hence meaning a "summing up," or "calculation." Interpretations of the term, however, vary. It is referred to as the idea of enumeration, or it is understood as "reasoning." The term might as well designate those who seek salvation by knowledge.

The basic problem of classical Sāṃkhya is suffering. The presence of *puruṣa* (the "conscious being") is responsible for suffering, for when *puruṣa* is in proximity to *prakṛti* ("nature") this leads to suffering. There is only one means for the elimination of suffering: intuitive discrimination of the "knowing one" and "knower," the manifested world and the unmanifested one. Sāṃkhya teaches us the means of correct knowledge, "pramāṇas."

The first extant work of Sāṃkhya is Īśvarakṛṣna's *Sāṃkhyakārikā* ("Memorial Verses on Sāṃkhya"), created perhaps in the third century A.D. It has become the standard and has remained the authoritative interpretation for many centuries. Other important works are the *Tattva-kumudi* ("Elucidation of Categories") of the ninth century A.D. and the commentary of Vijñāña Bhikṣu (sixteenth century A.D.).

Yoga means "yoke" in Sanskrit. In Hinduism yoga means harnessing oneself in order to seek union with God. There are different yogic paths to the knowledge of God, such as Karma-Yoga, or selfless action; Bhakti-Yoga, or devout love of God; Rāja-Yoga, which is the "royal yoga" of Patañjali; Kuṇḍalinī-Yoga of Tantrism; and Jñāna-Yoga, the path of abstract knowledge.

One of the leading texts of yoga is the Yoga Vasiṣṭha dated as early as the sixth or seventh century A.D. and as late as the fourteenth century. It consists of spiritual instructions given to Rāma by the sage Vasiṣṭha. It is to Vasiṣṭha to whom the seventh book of the Ṛgveda is attributed. Manu calls Vasiṣṭha one of the first sages. In the *Mahābhārata* his name is mentioned more than one hundred times. Śaṅkarācāria refers to Vasiṣṭha as the first sage of the Vedānta school.

The distinguishing characteristics of Yoga Vasiṣṭha is its emphasis on the doctrine of mind. Everything is Consciousness, including the material world. The world is nothing but the play of Consciousness. Yoga Vasiṣṭha teaches of the spiritual life that leads an individual to liberation by negating the reality of things as external to the mind.

From *Īśvarakṛṣṇa's Sāṃkhyakārikā*

Reprinted from Classical Sāṃkhya. An Interpretation of Its History and Meaning, *by Gerald James Larson. Dehli: Motilal Banarsidass, 1979.*

I. Because of the torment of the threefold suffering, (there arises) the desire to know the means of removing it. If (it is said that) this (desire—i.e., inquiry) is useless because perceptible (means of removal are available), (we say) no, since (perceptible means) are not final or abiding.

II. The revealed (or scriptural, means of removing the torment) are like the perceptible (—i.e., ultimately ineffective), for they are connected with impurity, destruction, and excess; a different and superior method is the (discriminative) knowledge of the manifest (*vyakta*), the unmanifest (*avyakta*), and the knowing one (or knower—i.e., *puruṣa*).

III. Primordial nature (*mūlaprakṛti*) is uncreated. The seven—the great one (*mahat*), etc.—are both created and creative. The sixteen are created. *Puruṣa* is neither created nor creative.

IV. The attainment of that which is to be proved (is) by means of correct knowledge. The accepted means of correct knowledge are three because (these three) comprehend all means of correct knowledge. These three means (are as follows:) (a) perception, (b) inference, (c) reliable authority.

V. Perception is the selective ascertainment of particular sense-objects. Inference, which is of three kinds, depends upon a characteristic mark (*liñga*) and that which bears the mark (*liñgi*). Reliable authority is reliable teaching.

VI. The understanding of things beyond the senses is by means of (or from) inference by analogy. That which is imperceptible and, therefore, beyond both perception and inference, is established by means of reliable authority.

VII. (Perception may be impossible due to the following:)
- (a) because something is too far away;
- (b) because something is too close;
- (c) because of an injured sense-organ;
- (d) because of inattention;
- (e) because of intervention (of an object between an organ and the object to be perceived);
- (f) because of suppression (i.e., seeing the sun but no planets);
- (g) because of intermixture with what is similar.

VIII. The non-perception (of *prakṛti*) is because of its subtlety—not because of its non-existence. Its apprehension is because of (or by means of) its effect. Its effect—the great one (*mahat*), etc.—is different from yet similar to *prakṛti.*

IX. The effect exists (before the operation of cause) (*sat kārya*):
- (a) because of the non-productivity of non-being;
- (b) because of the need for an (appropriate) material cause;
- (c) because of the impossibility of all things coming from all things;
- (d) because something can only produce what it is capable of producing;
- (e) because of the nature of the cause (or, because the effect is non-different from the cause).

X. The manifest (*vyakta*) is
- (a) caused;
- (b) finite;
- (c) non-pervasive;
- (d) active;

(e) plural;
(f) supported;
(g) emergent;
(h) composite;
(i) dependent;
the unmanifest (*avyakta*) is the opposite.

XI. (Both) the manifest and unmanifest are
(a) (characterized by the) three *guṇas* ("qualities" or "strands");
(b) undiscriminating;
(c) objective;
(d) general;
(e) non-conscious;
(f) productive; the *puruṣa* is the opposite of them, although similar.

XXII. From *prakṛti* (emerges) the great one (*mahat*); from that (comes) self-awareness (*ahaṇkāra*); from that (comes) the group of sixteen. Moreover, from five of the sixteen (come) the five gross elements.

XXV. From self-awareness (known as) *vaikṛta* ("modified") proceeds the group of eleven, characterized by *sattva* ("goodness" or "purity"); from self-awareness (known as) *bhūtādi* ("the origin of gross elements") proceed the five subtle elements (*tanmātras*), characterized by *tamas* ("darkness" or "delusion"); from self-awareness (known as) *taijasa* ("shining" or "passionate") both proceed.

XXVI. The sense organs (*buddhīndriyas*) ("organs of the *buddhi*" or "organs of ascertainment") are called eye, ear, nose, tongue, and skin. The organs of action (*karmendriyas*) are called voice, hands, feet, and organs of excretion and generation.

XXVII. The mind (*manas*) is of the nature of both; it is characterized by reflection (or synthesis or construction) and it is a sense because it is similar (to the senses). The variety of external things and the variety (of the organs) is because of the specific modifications (or transformations) of the *guṇas.*

XXVIII. The function of the five (sense organs)—(hearing) sound, etc.—(is) mere awareness (*ālocanamātra*). The function of the five (organs of action) (is) speech, grasping, walking, excretion, and orgasm.

XXIX. With respect to the specific characteristics of the three (i.e., of the *buddhi, ahaṅkāra,* and senses) each functions differently; the five vital breaths (or winds) (make up) their common function.

XXXIV. Of these, the five senses (*buddhīndriyas*) (function with) specific and non-specific (i.e., gross and subtle) objects. Speech only has sound as its object, but the remaining (organs of action) have all five as objects.

XXXVIII. The subtle elements (*tanmātras*) are non-specific. From these five (emerge) the five gross elements. These (gross elements) are considered (to be) specific, and are tranquil, turbulent, and delusive.

XXXIX. Subtle (bodies), (bodies) born of father and mother together with gross elements are the threefold kinds (of bodies). Of these the subtle (bodies) are constant; (bodies) born of father and mother are perishable.

XLI. As a picture (does) not (exist) without a support or as a shadow (does) not (exist) without a post, etc.; so, too, the instrument (*liñga* or *karaṇa*) does not exist supportless without that which is specific (i.e., a subtle body).

L. The nine complacencies are thought of (in two groups); four are internal, including nature, means, time, and destiny; and five are external due to the cessation or turning away from the objects of sense.

LIV. (In the) upper (world) (there is) a predominance of *sattva.* (In the) lower creation (there is) a predominance of *tamas.* In the middle (there is) a predominance of *rajas.* (This is so) from Brahmā down to a blade of grass.

LV. The *puruṣa,* which is consciousness, attains there the suffering made by decay and death; until deliverance of the subtle body; therefore, suffering is of the nature of things.

LVI. This creation, brought about by *prakṛti*—from the great one (*mahat*) down to the specific gross elements—(functions) for the sake of the release of each *puruṣa*; (this is done) for the sake of another, as if it were for her own (benefit).

From the Yoga Vasiṣṭha

Translated by Swami Venkatesananda. Reprinted from The Concise Yoga Vasiṣṭha. *Albany: State University of New York Press, 1984*

Vasiṣṭha: Mokṣa, liberation, or the realization of the infinite is not existence as an immobile creature! Liberation is attained when one arrives at the state of supreme peace after intelligent inquiry into the nature of the self and after this has brought about an inner awakening. Kaivalya or total freedom is the attainment of pure being after all mental conditioning is transcended consciously and after a thorough investigation. The wise ones say that one is established in pure being or Brahman only after one has investigated the nature of the truth as expounded in the scriptures, in the company of and with the help of enlightened sages.

As long as psychological limitation and conditioning remain in the heart, even in their subtle "seed" state, it should be regarded as the deep sleep state; it gives rise to rebirth, even if a state of tranquillity is experienced and even when the mind appears to be self-absorbed. It is an inert state and is the source of unhappiness. Such is the state of insentient and immobile objects like rocks. They are not free of self-limitation (vāsanā) but self-limitation is hidden and latent in them even as flowers are latent in seeds (which sprout, grow, and yield flowers) and pots in clay. Where the seed of vāsanā (self-limitation, conditioning, or tendency) exists, that state is like deep sleep; it is not perfection. When all vāsanā are destroyed and even the potentiality of the vāsanā does not exist, that state is known as the fourth (beyond waking, dream, and deep sleep) and transcendental state. It brings about perfection. Vāsanā, fire, debt, disease, enemy, friendship (or glue), hate, and poison—all these are bothersome even if a little residue is left after their removal.

On the other hand, if all the vāsanā have been completely removed, then one is established in the state of pure being; whether such a one is alive or not, he is not again afflicted by sorrow. The cit-śakti (energy-consciousness) lies in immobile creatures as latent vāsanā. It is this cit-śakti that determines the nature of each object; it is the fundamental characteristic of the very molecules of each object.

If this is not realized as ātma-śakti (the energy of the self or infinite consciousness), it creates the delusion of world-appearance; if it is realized as the truth, which is infinite consciousness, that realization destroys all sorrow. The non-seeing of this truth is known as avidyā or ignorance; such ignorance is the cause of the world-appearance, which is the source of all other phenomena. Even as the arising of the first thought disturbs sleep and ends it, the slightest awakening of inner intelligence destroy ignorance. When one approaches darkness with light in hand, wishing to behold it, the darkness vanishes; when the light of inquiry is turned on ignorance, ignorance disappears. When one begins to inquire: "What is 'I' in this body composed of blood, flesh, bone, etc.?" at once ignorance ceases to be. That which has a beginning has an end. When all things that have a beginning are ruled out, what remains is the truth, which is the cessation of avidyā or ignorance. You may regard it as something or as nothing: that is to be sought which *is* when ignorance has been dispelled. The sweetness one tastes is not experienced by another: listening to someone's description of the cessation of avidyā does not give rise to your enlightenment. Each one has to realize it. In short, avidyā is the belief that "There exists a reality which is not Brahman or cosmic consciousness"; when there is the certain knowledge that "This is indeed Brahman," avidyā ceases.

Again and again I repeat all this, O Rāma, for the sake of your spiritual awakening: realization of the self does not happen without such repetition (or spiritual practice). This ignorance, known as avidyā or ajñāna, has become dense by having been expressed and experienced by the senses in thousands of incarnations, within and outside this body. But self-knowledge is not within the reach of the senses. It arises when the senses and the mind, which is the sixth sense, cease.

O Rāma, live in this world firmly established in self-knowledge, even as king Janaka lives, having known what there is to be known. In his case the truth is realized all the time, whether he is active or not, whether he is awake or not. Lord Viṣṇu incarnates in this world and takes on embodiment fully established in this self-knowledge. Even so, lord Śiva remains established in self-knowledge, and lord Brahmā too is established in self-knowledge. Be established in self-knowledge, O Rāma, as they are.

Discourse on Brahman

Rāma: Lord, pray tell me: What is the nature of the self-knowledge in which all these great ones are established?

Vasiṣṭha: Rāma, you know this already, yet in order to make it abundantly clear you are asking about it again.

Whatever there is and whatever appears to be the world-jugglery, is but the pure Brahman or the absolute consciousness and nothing else. Consciousness is Brahman, the world is Brahman, all the elements are Brahman, I am Brahman, my enemy is Brahman, my friends and relatives are Brahman, Brahman is the three periods of time, for all these are rooted in Brahman. Even as the ocean appears to be expanded on account of the waves, Brahman seems to be expanded on account of the infinite variety of substances. Brahman apprehends Brahman, Brahman experiences or enjoys Brahman,

Brahman is made manifest in Brahman by the power of Brahman himself. Brahman is the form of my enemy who displeases me who am Brahman: when such is the case, who does what to another?

The modes of the mind, like attraction and repulsion and likes and dislikes, have been conjured up in imagination. They have been destroyed by the absence of thoughts. How then can they be magnified? When Brahman alone moves in all which is Brahman, and Brahman alone unfolds as Brahman in all, what is joy and what is sorrow? Brahman is satisfied with Brahman, Brahman is established in Brahman. There is neither "I" nor another!

All the objects in this world are Brahman. "I" am Brahman. Such being the case, both passion and dispassion, craving and aversion are but notions. Body is Brahman, death is Brahman, too: when they come together, as the real rope and the unreal imaginary snake come together, where is the cause of rejoicing when body experiences pleasure? When, on the surface of the calm ocean, waves appear to be agitated, the waves do not cease to be water! Even when Brahman appears to be agitated (in the world-appearance), its essence is unchanged and there is neither "I"-ness nor "you"-ness. When the whirlpool dies in the water, nothing is dead! When the death-Brahman overtakes the body-Brahman, nothing is lost.

Water is capable of being calm and of being agitated: even so Brahman can be quiescent and restless. Such is its nature. It is ignorance or delusion that divides the one into "This is sentient jīva"; and "This is sentient matter"; the wise ones do not hold such erroneous views. Hence, to the ignorant the world is full of sorrow; to the wise the same world is full of bliss, even as to the blind man the world is dark and to one who has good eyesight the world is full of light.

When the one Brahman alone pervades all, there is neither death nor a living person. The ripples play on the surface of the ocean; they are neither born nor do they die! Even so do the elements in this creation. "This is" and "This is not"—such deluded notions arise in the self. These notions are not really caused nor do they have a motivation, even as a crystal reflects different colored objects without a motivation.

The self remains itself even when the energies of the world throw up endless diversities on the surface of the ocean of consciousness. There are no independent entities in this world known as "body," etc. What is seen as the body and what are seen as notions, the objects of perception, the perishable and the imperishable, the thoughts and feelings and their meaning—all these are Brahman in Brahman, the infinite consciousness. There is duality only in the eyes of the deluded and ignorant. The mind, the intellect, the ego-sense, the cosmic root-elements, the senses, and all such diverse phenomena are Brahman only; pleasure and pain are illusions (they are words without substance). Even as a single sound produced amongst hills echoes and re-echoes into diversity, the one cosmic consciousness experiences multiplicity within itself, with the notions "This is I" and "This is mine," etc. The one cosmic consciousness sees diversity within itself even as a dreamer of diverse objects within himself.

When gold is not recognized as such, it gets mixed up with the earth; when Brahman is not thus recognized, the impurity of ignorance arises. The knower of Brahman declares that such a great one is himself the Lord and Brahman; in the case of the ignorant the non-recognition of the truth is known as ignorance. (Or, it is the opinion of the knowers of Brahman that the very same Lord or supreme being is regarded as ignorance in the ignorant.) When gold is recognized as such it "becomes" gold instantly; when Brahman is recognized as such it "becomes" Brahman instantly.

Being omnipotent, Brahman becomes whatever it considers itself to be without any motivation for doing so. The knowers of Brahman declare that Brahman is the Lord, the great being which is devoid of action, the doer and the instrument, devoid of causal motivation and of transformation or change.

When this truth is not realized, it arises as ignorance in the ignorant, but when it is realized, the ignorance is dispelled. When a relative is not recognized as such, he is known as a stranger; when the relative is recognized, the notion of stranger is instantly dispelled.

When one knows that duality is illusory appearance, there is realization of Brahman, the absolute. When one knows "This is not I," the unreality of the ego-sense is realized. From this arises true dispassion. "I am verily Brahman"—when this truth is realized the awareness of the truth arises in one, and all things are then merged in that awareness. When such notions as "I" and "you" are dispelled, the realization of the truth arises and one realizes that all this, whatever there is, is indeed Brahman.

What is the truth? "I have nothing to do with sorrow, with actions, with delusion or desire. I am at peace, free from sorrow. I am

Brahman"—such is the truth. "I am free from all defects, I am the all, I do not seek anything nor do I abandon anything, I am Brahman"—such is the truth. "I am blood, I am flesh, I am bone, I am body, I am consciousness. I am the mind also, I am Brahman"—such is the truth. "I am the firmament, I am space, I am the sun and the entire space, I am all things here, I am Brahman"—such is the truth. "I am a blade of grass, I am the earth, I am a tree-stump, I am the forest, I am the mountain and the oceans, I am the non-dual Brahman"—such is the truth. "I am the consciousness in which all things are strung and through whose power all beings engage themselves in all their activities; I am the essence of all things"—such is the truth.

This is certain: all things exist in Brahman, all things flow from it, all things are Brahman; it is omnipresent, it is the one self, it is the truth.

The truth which is omnipresent and which is pure consciousness devoid of objectivity is referred to variously as consciousness, self, Brahman, existence, truth, order, and also as pure knowledge. It is pure, and in its light all beings know their own self. I am the Brahman, which is pure consciousness after its own appearance as the mind, the intellect, the senses, and all other such notions have been negated. I am imperishable consciousness or Brahman, in whose light alone all the elements and the entire universe shine. I am the consciousness of Brahman, sparks from whom arise, continually radiating reflected consciousness throughout the universe. Even when seen by a pure mind, it is expressed in silence. Though it appears to be in contact with the ceaseless experiences of the ego-sense of countless beings who thus derive the delight that is of Brahman, yet it is beyond the reach of these and untouched by them. For though it is truly the ultimate source of all happiness and delight, it is of the nature of deep sleep (devoid of diversity), peaceful and pure. In subject-object relationship and the consequent experience of pleasure, the bliss of Brahman is infinitesimally experienced.

I am the eternal Brahman, free from the wrong notions of pleasure and pain and therefore pure; I am the consciousness in which there is true pure experiencing. I am that pure consciousness in which the pure intelligence functions without thought interference. I am that Brahman, which is the intelligent energy that functions in all the elements (earth, water, fire, etc.). I am pure consciousness, which manifests as the characteristic taste of the different fruits.

I am the changeless Brahman which is realized when both elation at having gained what one desires and depression at not having gained it, are transcended. When the sun shines and the objects of the world are seen in that light, I am the pure consciousness that is in the middle between these two, and which is the very self of the light and of the illumined object. I am that pure consciousness or Brahman which exists unbroken in the waking, dream, and deep sleep states, and which is therefore the fourth or the transcendental truth.

Even as the taste of the juice of sugarcane cultivated in a hundred fields is uniform and same, even so the consciousness indwelling all beings is the same—that consciousness I am. I am that conscious energy (cit-śakti) which is larger than the universe and yet subtler than the minutest atomic particle and therefore invisible. I am the consciousness that exists everywhere like butter in milk, and whose very nature is experiencing.

Even as ornaments made of gold are only gold, I am the pure consciousness in the body. I am the self that pervades all things within and without. I am that consciousness which reflects all experiences without itself undergoing any change, untouched by impurity.

I salute that consciousness which is the bestower of all the fruits of all thoughts, the light that shines in all luminaries, the supreme gain; that consciousness pervades all the limbs, ever awake and alert, vibrates constantly in all substances, and is ever homogeneous and undisturbed, as if it were in deep sleep though wide awake. That consciousness is the reality that bestows the individual characteristic on each and every substance in the universe, and though within all and so nearest to all, is far on account of its inaccessibility to the mind and the senses. Continuous and homogeneous in waking, dreaming, deep sleep, and in the fourth (transcendental) state of consciousness, it shines when all thoughts have ceased, when all excitements have ceased, and when all hate has ceased. That consciousness is devoid of desire and ego-sense and cannot be divided into parts.

I have attained that consciousness which is the indweller of all, and yet though all, is beyond diversity. It is the cosmic net in which the infinite number of beings are caught like birds; in it all these worlds manifest, though in fact nothing has ever happened. That consciousness is of the nature of being and non-being and the resting place of all that is good and divine. It plays the roles of all beings and it is the source of all affection and peace, though it is forever united and liberated. It is the life of all living beings, the uncreated nectar that cannot be stolen by anyone, the ever existent reality. That consciousness which is reflected in sense-experiences is yet devoid of them and cannot be experienced by them. In it all beings rejoice, though it itself is pure bliss beyond all joy—like the space, glorious yet devoid of all expansions and glory. Though seemingly it does all, it does nothing.

All this is "I" and all this is "mine." But I am not and I am not "other than I." I have realized this. Let this world be an illusion or substantial; I am free from the fever of distress.

Established in this realization of the truth, the great sages lived forever in peace and equanimity. They were free from psychological predisposition, and hence they did not seek or reject either life or death. They remained unshaken in their direct experience like another Meru-mountain. Yet they roamed the forests, islands, and cities, they traveled to the heavens as if they were angels or gods, they conquered their enemies, they ruled as emperors, and they engaged themselves in diverse activities in accordance with scriptural injunctions, as they realized that such was appropriate conduct. They enjoyed the pleasure of life; they visited pleasure gardens and were entertained by celestial damsels. They duly fulfilled the duties of the household life. They even engaged themselves in great wars and they retained their equanimity even in those disastrous situations where others would have lost their peace and balanced state of mind.

Their mind had fully entered the state of satva or divinity and was therefore utterly free from delusion, from egoistic notion ("I do this"), and from the desire for achievement—though they did not reject such achievement or the rewards for their actions. They did not indulge in vain exultation when they defeated their enemies, nor did they give way to despair and grief when they were defeated. They were engaged in natural activities, allowing all actions to proceed from them non-volitionally.

Follow their example, O Rāma. Let your personality (ego-sense) be egoless and let appropriate actions spontaneously proceed from you. For the infinite, indivisible consciousness alone is the truth; and it is that which has put on this appearance of diversity which is neither real nor unreal. Hence live completely unattached to anything here. Why do you grieve as if you are an ignoramus?

Rāma: Lord, by your grace I am fully awakened to the reality. My delusion has vanished. I shall do as you bid me to do. Surely, I rest peacefully in the state of one who is liberated even while living. Pray, Lord, tell me how one reaches the state of liberation by the restraint of the life-force (prāṇa) and by the annihilation of all self-limitations or psychological conditioning.

Vasiṣṭha: They call it yoga, which is the method by which this cycle of birth and death ceases. It is the utter transcendence of the mind and is of two types. Self-knowledge is one type, and restraint of the life-force is another. However, yoga has come to mean only the latter, yet both the methods lead to the same result. To some, self-knowledge through inquiry is difficult; to others yoga is difficult. But my conviction is that the path of inquiry is easy for all, because self-knowledge is the ever-present truth. I shall now describe to you the method of yoga.

NYĀYA

Nyāya ("correct" or "logic" in Sanskrit) is also sometimes called Tarkavidyā ("science of debate") or Vādavidyā ("science of discussion"). That science was developed in response to the argumentation of the Buddhists and the followers of other schools of thought, who did not accept the authority of the Vedas and criticized the Vedic tradition. The Nyāya differs from other classical darśanas by a systematic development of the method of investigation and argumentation in support of the validity of the sacred texts. The use of reason and argumentation in defense of revelation and tradition resulted in a far-reaching reinterpretation of the latter.

The basic text of this darśana—the *Nyāya-Sūtra*—is believed to be established by Gautama. Its adherents, known as Niyāyikas, reflect less on what we know than on how we know it. They are concerned mainly with the means of right cognition: perception, inference, analogical acquisition of vocabulary, and reliable testimony. That is why Vātsyāyana (about A.D. 400), whose commentary on the *Nyāya-Sūtra* is regarded as standard, calls Nyāya's method a "critical testing of the objects of knowledge by means of logical proof." The achievements of the Nyāya in the field of analytic and logical inquiry were so significant that the term "Nyāya" was also adopted by some other Indian schools (by the Mīmāṃsā or Viśiṣtadvaita, for example) as a general term for correct and methodically disciplined thought.

The selection below is a part of Nyāya-Bhāṣya, a commentary by Vātsyāyana from the *Nyāya-Sūtra.*

From *The Nyāya-Sūtra* with a Commentary by Vātsyāyana

Translated by Mrinalkanti Gangopadhyay. Calcutta: Indian Studies, 1982.

Sūtra 4: Perception is the knowledge resulting from sense-object contact [and which is] "not due to words," "invariably related" [to the object] and is "of a definite character." (i.1.4)

Bhāṣya: The knowledge which results from the contact of the sense with the object is called perception. (Objection) But, then, it is not so. [It results when] the self [*ātman*] comes in contact with the mind [*manas*], the mind with the sense and the sense with the object. (Answer) It [the *sūtra*] does not specify the cause as "it alone is the cause of perception." It rather states the special cause [of perception]. That which is the special cause of perceptual knowledge is stated here, but it does not exclude the cause common to the inferential and other forms of knowledge.

(Objection) But, then, the contact of the mind with the sense should be stated. (Answer) This [the contact of the mind with the sense] does not differ in the different cases of perceptual knowledge and as such, being alike [i.e., being a common cause like the contact of self with mind], is not mentioned.

There are as many "naming words" as there are objects. [Every object has a word standing for it.] By these [i.e., words] the objects are properly known. Usage depends on the proper knowledge of the object. Now, this knowledge of object resulting from sense-object contact assumes the form: "It is color" [*rūpa*] or "It is taste" [*rasa*]. The words like *rūpa* and *rasa* are names of objects. Pieces of knowledge are referred to by these, e.g., one knows that it is color or one knows that it is taste. [Such pieces of knowledge] being referred to by words naming these, there is the apprehension of considering them as but due to words. Therefore, [i.e., to remove such an apprehension] [Gautama] says, not due to words.

Knowledge on the part of those unaware of the relation between the word and its corresponding object [e.g., of the infant and the dumb] is not referred to by the words naming the objects. Even if the relation between the word and the corresponding object is known, there is the knowledge that this word is the name of this object [i.e., even for those who are aware of the relation between a word and its corresponding object, the knowledge of the object is not due to the word naming it]. When that object is known, the knowledge does not differ from the aforementioned knowledge of the object [i.e., of the infant and the dumb]. This knowledge of the object is but similar to that. But this knowledge of the object has no other word to name it, being conveyed by which [word] it can be subject to usage, because there is no usage with what is not properly known. . . . Therefore, the knowledge of the object resulting from sense-object contact is not due to words.

During the summer the flickering rays of the sun intermingled with the heat radiating from the surface of the earth come in contact with the eyes of a person at a distance. Due to this sense-object contact, there arises, in the rays of the sun, the knowledge this is water. Even such a knowledge may be taken for valid perceptual knowledge. Hence [Gautama] says, "invariably connected with the object." An erroneous perception is the perception of an object as something which it is not. A right perception is the perception of an object as it actually is.

Perceiving with eyes an object at a distance, a person cannot decide whether it is smoke or dust. But such an "indecisive knowledge" resulting from sense-object contact may be taken for perceptual knowledge. Hence [Gautama] says, "of a definite character." It cannot, however, be claimed that this indecisive knowledge is due only to the contact of self with mind [i.e., is not due to the contact of the sense with the object]. Indecisive knowledge [like this] arises only after one sees the object with the eyes. Just as the object perceived by the senses is eventually perceived by the mind, so also an object is indecisively apprehended by the mind after being indecisively apprehended by the senses. Doubt is only the "vacillating knowledge" with a drive for the perception of some unique character which is apprehended by mind after being apprehended by the sense, and not the previous one [i.e., not the indecisive knowledge which is apprehended by the mind alone after the termination of the function of the senses]. In all cases of perception the knower has the definite knowledge of an object through the sense, for persons with impaired sense-organs cannot have any "after-knowledge" [cognising the first, i.e., the knowledge due to sense-object contact].

(Objection) A separate definition of perception needs to be given [to cover the perceptions of] the self etc. and pleasure etc., because it [the perception of self or pleasure] is not due to sense-object contact. (Answer) Though mind is a sense, it is mentioned separately from the other senses because of its different nature. The other senses are "made of the elements" and have fixed objects. These become senses by virtue of their possessing [the respective] qualities. Mind, on the other hand, is not made of elements, has no fixed object [lit., having everything for its object] and it does not become a sense by virtue of its possessing the quality. As we shall later explain, in spite of the sense-object contact, its [i.e., of mind] connection or absence of connection is the cause why a number of perceptions do not simultaneously occur. Since mind also is a sense, no separate definition [for such perception] is called for. This is to be learnt from what is discussed in "the other system." The viewpoint of others, when not refuted, becomes one's own. . . . Here ends the explanation of perception.

Sūtra 5: Next [is discussed] inference, which is preceded by it [i.e., by perception], and is of three kinds, namely, *pūrvavat* [i.e., having the antecedent as the probans], *śeṣavat* [i.e., having the consequent as the probans] and *sāmanyatodṛṣṭa* [i.e., where the *vyāpti* is ascertained by general observation]. (i.1.5)

Bhāṣya: By the expression "preceded by it" is meant "the perception of the [invariable] relation between the probans and the probandum" as well as "the perception of the probans." By the perception of the invariably related probans and the probandum is meant the recollection of the probans. Through this recollection and the perception of the probans is inferred the object which at that time "is not directly cognized."

Now, *pūrvavat*: When the effect is inferred from its cause, e.g., from the rising cloud [it is inferred that] it will rain. *Śeṣavat:* When the cause is inferred from its effect. On perceiving the water of the river as different from what it was before, [and further perceiving] the fullness of the river and the swiftness of the current, it is inferred that there was rain. *Śāmanyatodṛṣṭa:* the perception of an object at some place which was previously seen somewhere else is due to its movement; so also that of the sun. Therefore [it is inferred that], though imperceptible, the sun has movement.

Alternatively. *Pūrvavat:* when an object not perceived at the moment is inferred through the perception of one of the two objects as they were previously perceived. As for example, fire from smoke. [Two objects were previously (*pūrva*) perceived as being invariably related. An object similar to one of these is now perceived. From this is inferred an object similar to the other, though the object thus inferred is not perceived now.]

Śeṣavat means . . . residual. It is the definite knowledge resting on the residual after the elimination of [certain] possible objects and because of the irrelevance in the cases of [still] other objects. As for example, by characterizing sound as existent and non-eternal, which are the common characteristics of substance, quality, and action, it is differentiated from universal, particularity, and inherence. When doubt arises whether it [sound] is a substance, quality, or action, [we eliminate as follows]. It is not substance, because it has only a single substance [as the inherent cause] and it is not action, because it is the cause of a subsequent sound. Then it is what is the residual and sound is proved to be a quality.

Śāmanyatodṛṣṭa: When the relation between the probans and the probandum being imperceptible, the probandum is known from a probans having the same nature with any other object. As for example, self from desire etc. Desire etc. are qualities. Qualities reside in substances. Therefore, that which is the substratum of these [i.e., desire etc.] is the self. . . .

Perception has for its object things present. Inference has for its object things both present and absent. Why? Because of its capacity for knowing objects belonging to the three times [i.e., past, present and future]. By inference one knows objects belonging to the three times. We infer: it will be, it is, and it was. By "absent" here is meant the past and the future [objects].

Next is *upamāna.*

Sūtra 6: Comparison is the instrument of the valid knowledge of an object derived through its similarity with another well-known object. (i.1.6.)

Bhāṣya: Comparison is "definite knowledge" of the "object sought to be definitely known" through its similarity with an object already well-known. (Example) "The *gavaya* [a wild cow without the dew-lap] is like the cow." (Objection) What is the function here of comparison as an instrument of valid knowledge? When one perceives its similarity with the cow, one knows the object by perception itself. (Answer) As Gautama says, the function of comparison is to impart knowledge of the relation of the name [with the corresponding object]. When the proposition conveying the comparison "the *gavaya* is like the cow" is employed, a person perceiving through sense-object contact an object having similarity with the cow learns "the relation between the naming word and the object denoted" in the following way: this object is denoted by the word *gavaya*. After the propositions conveying a comparison "the *mudgaparṇī* [a kind of herb] is like the *mudga*" and "the *māṣaparṇī* [another kind of herb] is like the *māṣa*" are employed, a person acquires the knowledge of the relation between the naming word and the object denoted and he collects the herbs for preparing medicines. Thus, many other things are to be known as the objects of comparison in everyday life.

Next is verbal testimony.

Sūtra 7: Verbal testimony is the communication from a "trustworthy person." (i.1.7)

Bhāṣya: A trustworthy person is the speaker who has the direct knowledge of an object and is motivated by the desire of communicating the object as directly known by him. . . . This definition [of a trustworthy person] is equally applicable to the seer, noble, and barbarian [*mleccha*—person without Vedic practices]. Thus the practice of everybody is carried on.

In this way, the activities of god, man, and animal are maintained with the help of these instruments of valid knowledge and not otherwise.

Sūtra 33: (Objection) There is doubt about the existence of the whole [i.e., the whole standing over and above the parts], because it [i.e., the whole] is "not yet proved." (ii.1.33)

Bhāṣya (Objection) It is yet to be proved that an entity [viz. the whole] distinct [from the parts themselves] is produced by the causes [i.e., the constituent parts]. That is, this has not yet been logically demonstrated. Thus, there is the knowledge of two contradictory assertions [viz. "the whole exists" and "the whole does not exist"] and from this knowledge of the contradictory assertions there results the doubt about the [existence of the] whole.

Sūtra 34: (Answer) If the existence of the whole is denied, then there can be no knowledge of anything. (ii.1.34)

Bhāṣya: (Answer) If the whole does not exist, everything will remain unknown. What is meant here by everything? Substance, quality, activity, universal, particularity, and inherence. But how [are we to understand that without admitting the whole everything remains unknown]? The [mere] assemblage of the atoms cannot be the object of visual sense, because the atoms are imperceptible. [In your view] there is no other entity in the form of the whole, which can be the object of the visual sense. But these substance, etc., are apprehended as the object of the visual sense. Therefore, they cannot be apprehended without having any real basis. But [substance, etc.] are perceived in the form: "this jar is black; is one; is big; is conjoined; is vibrating; is existing; and is made of earth." And [also in the form] "the quality, etc., exist." Therefore, from the perception of everything we observe that there is a distinct entity [known as the whole].

Sūtra 35: (Answer continued) Also from being gripped and pulled [is proved the existence of the whole as distinct from the aggregate of parts or atoms]. (ii.1.35)

Bhāṣya: (Answer) The whole is an entity distinct [from the aggregate of atoms, because things like the tree can be gripped and pulled].

[Vātsyāyana raises a possible objection against this argument and refutes it. The objection is:] The cause of being gripped and pulled is the collectivity [of the atoms]. Collectivity implies a distinct quality coexisting with conjunction and produced by viscosity and fluidity. [E.g., the quality produced] in the unbaked jar due to the conjunction of water and in the baked jar due to the conjunction of fire. Had [the peculiarity of being gripped and pulled] been due to the whole, then it would have been possible even in the case of a handful of dust, etc. [Further, in your view] in the cases of grass, pebble, and wood, lumped together with lac, there would have been no [possibility of being gripped and pulled] because in this case no distinct entity is produced. Now, what question are you going to put to those who deny the existence of the whole and, in defense of perception, admit the aggregate itself to be the object of perception?

(Answer) The question to be asked is: what exactly is the object of knowledge when it [i.e., the knowledge] takes the form "this is o*ne single* substance?" Does this knowledge of one single substance reveal one object or a multiplicity of objects? [If it is assumed that] it reveals one single substance, then the whole will be proved from the admission of a distinct entity [as the object of that perceptual knowledge].

[If it is assumed that] it reveals a multiplicity of objects, then the knowledge of one single substance cannot belong to such a multiplicity of objects. The self-contradictionary knowledge, viz. "this is a single substance" in respect of a multiplicity of objects is never observed.

Sūtra 36: (Objection) [In spite of there being nothing called the whole] we have the perception of the [aggregate of atoms] like [the perception of] the army or the forest. (Answer) This is not possible, because atoms are [intrinsically] imperceptible. (ii.1.36)

Bhāṣya: (Objection) Just as in the case of the army-units [viz. the elephant-riders, cavalry, charioteers, and infantry] and in the case of the forest-units [viz. the groups of trees constituting the forest], where the perception of individual differences is not possible due to distance, we have knowledge in the form: "this is one" [viz. "this is *an* army" and "this is *a* forest"]. Similarly, when the atoms are collected together and the individual difference of each is not perceived, we have the apprehension in the form: "this is a single object."

(Answer) The individual differences of the army-units and forest-units are not perceived from a distance because of the presence of some special cause; nevertheless the individual differences of these are perceived [in the absence of the specific cause preventing their perception]. For example, in the case of the forest, though the differences among the species are perceptible, these are not perceived as *palāśa* or *khadira* from a distance. Similarly, [in the case of the individual trees] though the movements [of leaves and branches] are perceptible, yet these are not perceived from a distance. Thus, there is "the wrong perception that this is one" only in objects [intrinsically] perceptible when their individual differences are not perceived [due to some specific cause, viz. distance]. But there can be no such wrong perception in the case of the atoms as: "this is one." Because the atoms are intrinsically imperceptible, [though the objector wrongly claims] that the individual differences of these are unperceived simply because of the presence of some specific cause.

The question being examined is: Is the aggregate of the atoms the real object of the "knowledge of oneness in a thing" or is it not so? [The objector may claim] that the army-units and the forest-units are nothing but aggregates of atoms. [Our answer is] that it is illogical to cite as an instance a phenomenon under investigation, "because it is yet to be proved." [The objector may claim], it is an observed fact. [We answer] No; because its object is to be critically established. Even though you consider that because of the non-awareness of individual differences, the army-units and forest-units are found to be apprehended as single units and that the observed fact cannot be denied—still the case is not so, because its [i.e., of the knowledge] object is to be critically established. The nature of the object of what is observed is being examined. [That is, the real implication of] "the knowledge of oneness in a thing" is being examined. The mere knowledge [of oneness in an object] cannot prove either of the alternatives, namely, that the object of that knowledge is an independent entity or that it is an aggregate of atoms.

> Again, because of the multiplicity of the atoms and moreover because of the absence of the knowledge of individual differences, their apprehension as one single entity is the knowledge of something as something else, like the knowledge of a person in a pillar. (Objection) So what? (Answer) Since the knowledge of something as something else [i.e., erroneous or secondary knowledge] presupposes a primary knowledge [i.e., the knowledge of something as it is = valid knowledge], it [i.e., the erroneous knowledge of something as something else] proves the existence of the primary knowledge. In the case of the knowledge of a person in a pillar, which is the primary knowledge? The knowledge of the person as the person; only when there is such a primary knowledge, there can be [the secondary or erroneous] knowledge of a person in a pillar from the apprehension of the similarity [of the pillar] with a person. Similarly, the [secondary or erroneous] knowledge of oneness in a multiplicity of objects [i.e., in the atoms] is possible from the apprehension of oneness only when there is the primary knowledge [of oneness]. But this primary knowledge is not possible [in the Buddhist view], because of the absurdity of the non-awareness of everything. Therefore, this perception of non-difference in the form "this is one," is actually a perception of a single object [i.e., of the whole].

VAIŚEṢIKA

Vaiśeṣika has its roots as early as the six century B.C. As a system it took shape about A.D. 100 thanks to Kaṇāda, the author of *Vaiśeṣika-Sūtra* ("Aphorisms on Vaiśeṣika").

The system takes its name from viśeṣa—"referring to the distinctions." Focusing mostly on the question "What is there?" the Vaiśeṣika develops both realistic and pluralistic views of the physical universe through its atomic theory. According to the latter, not only objects are constituted of atoms (aṇu), but there are also indivisible particles of space (pradeśa), time (kṣaṇa) and units of motion (samyoga-vibhaga).

No less prominent a feature of the Vaiśeṣika is its atomistic mode of thinking, which manifests itself in the forms of theoretical analysis and in the methods of interpretation. The Vaiśeṣika's interpretation of a phenomenon means reducing it to some set of indivisible units that are casually unrelated. By dividing the multiplicity of nature into six categories, "padārthas," the Vaiśeṣika has created, in fact, the very first genuine philosophical language in India. The six padārthas are dravya ("substance" or "matter"), guṇa ("quality" or "characteristic"), karma ("activity"), sāmānya ("universality"), viśeṣa ("distinctiveness"), and samavāya ("inherence," the relation between a whole and its parts, between substance and quality, and between the general and the particular).

The Vaiśeṣika existed for centuries as a distinct school of philosophy. With Udayana, who lived about A.D. 1000, it merged with the Nyāya school, and afterward the proponents were often called Niyāyikas.

From *The Vaiśeṣika Sūtras of Kaṇāda*

Translated by Nandalal Sinha. Reprinted from The Sacred Books of the Hindus, *Vol. VI. Panini: Allahabad, 1923.*

Book I, Chapter 1

1. Now, therefore, we shall explain *dharma* (righteousness).
2. *Dharma* (is) that from which (results) the accomplishment of exaltation and of the supreme good.
3. The authoritativeness of the Veda (arises from its) being the Word of God.
4. The Supreme Good (results) from the knowledge, produced by a particular *dharma*, of the essence of the [categories] substance, attribute, action, genus, species, and combination [inherence] by means of their resemblances and differences.
5. Earth, water, fire, air, ether, time, space, self (or soul), and mind (are) the only substances.
6. Attributes are color, taste, smell, and touch, numbers, measures, separateness, conjunction and disjunction, priority and posteriority, understandings, pleasure and pain, desire and aversion, and volitions.
7. Throwing upwards, throwing downwards, contraction, expansion, and motion are actions.
8. The resemblance of substance, attribute, and action lies in this that they are existent and non-eternal, have substance as their combinative cause, are effect as well as cause, and are both genus and species.
9. The resemblance of substance and attribute is the characteristic of being the originators of their class concepts.
10. Substances originate another substance, and attributes another attribute.
15. It possesses action and attribute, it is a combinative cause—such (is) the mark of substance.
16. Inhering in substance, not possessing attribute, not an independent cause in conjunctions and disjunctions—such is the mark of attribute.
17. Residing in one substance only, not possessing attribute, an independent cause of conjunctions and disjunctions—such is the mark of action.
20. Action is the common cause of conjunction, disjunction, and impetus.

21. Action is not the cause of substances.
22. (Action is not the cause of substance) because of its cessation.

Book I, Chapter 2

1. Non-existence of effect (follows) from the non-existence of cause.
2. But non-existence of cause (does) not (follow) from the non-existence of the effect.
3. The notions, genus, and species, are relative to the understanding.
4. Existence, being the cause of assimilation only, is only a genus.
5. Substantiality, and attribute-ness and action-ness are both genera and species.
6. (The statement of genus and species has been made) with the exception of the final species.
7. Existence is that to which are due the belief and usage, namely "(it is) existent," in respect of substance, attribute, and action.

Book II, Chapter 1

1. Earth possesses color, taste, smell, and touch.
2. Waters possess color, taste, and touch, and are fluid and viscid.
3. Fire possesses color and touch.
4. Air possesses touch.
5. These (characteristics) are not in ether.
27. By the method of elimination (sound) is the mark of ether.
29. The unity (of ether is explained) by (the explanation of the unity of) existence.
30. (Ether is one), because there is no difference in sound which is its mark, and because there exists no other distinguishing mark.
31. And individuality also belongs to ether, since individuality follows unity.

Book II, Chapter 2

2. Smell is established in earth.
4. Hotness (is the characteristic) of fire.
5. Coldness (is the characteristic) of water.
6. "Posteriority" in respect of that which is posterior, "simultaneous," "slow," "quick,"—such (cognitions) are the marks of time.
8. The unity (of time is explained), by (the explanation of the unity of) existence.
9. The name time is applicable to a cause, inasmuch as it does not exist in eternal substances and exists in non-eternal substances.
10. That which gives rise to such (cognition and usage) as "This (is remote, etc.) from this,"—(the same is) the mark of space.

11. The substantiality and eternality (of space are) explained by (the explanation of the substantiality and eternality of) air.
12. The unity (of space is explained) by (the explanation of the unity of) existence.

Book III, Chapter 1

1. The objects of the senses are universally known.
2. The universal experience of the objects of the senses is the mark of (the existence of an) object different from the senses and their [phenomenal] objects.
4. (The body or the senses cannot be the seat of perception), because there is no consciousness in the causes [i.e., the component parts, of the body].
19. And activity and inactivity, observed in one's own self, are the marks of (the existence of) other selves.

Book III, Chapter 2

1. The appearance and non-appearance of knowledge, on contact of the self with the senses and the objects are the marks (of the existence) of the mind.
3. From the non-simultaneity of volitions, and from the non-simultaneity of cognitions, (it follows that there is only) one (mind) (in each organism).
4. The ascending life-breath, the descending life-breath, the closing of the eye-lids, the opening of the eye-lids, life, the movement of the mind, and the affections of the other senses, and also pleasure, pain, desire, aversion, and volition are marks (of the existence) of the self.
6. [Objection:] There is no visible mark (of the existence of the self), because there being contact (of the senses with the body of Yajñadatta) perception does not arise (that this self is Yajñadatta).
7. And from a commonly-observed mark (there is) no (inference of anything in) particular.
8. Therefore (the self is) proved by revelation.
9. [Answer:] (The proof of the existence of the self is not solely) from revelation, because of the non-application of the word "I" (to other designates or objects).
10. If (there are) such sensuous observations (or perceptions) as "I am Devadatta," "I am Yajñadatta," (then there is no need of inference).
11. As in the case of other percepts, so, if the self, which is grasped by perception, is also accompanied with, or comes at the top of, marks (from which it can be inferred), then, by means of confirmation, the intuition becomes fastened to one and only one object.

14. Because the intuition "I" exists in one's own self, and because it does not exist otherwhere, therefore the intuition has the individual self as the object of perception.
18. (The self is) not proved (only) by revelation, since, (as ether is proved by sound, so) (the self is) proved in particular by the innate as well as the sensible cognition in the form of "I," accompanied by the invariable divergence (of such cognition from all other things), as is the case with sound.

Book IV, Chapter 1

1. The eternal is that which is existent and uncaused.
2. The effect is the mark (of the existence) of the ultimate atom.
5. (It is) an error (to suppose that the ultimate atom is not eternal).
21. Space, time, and also ether are inactive, because of their difference from that which possesses activity.
23. (The relation) of the inactive [i.e., attribute and action] (to substance), is combination [inherence], (which is) independent of actions.

Book VII, Chapter 1

2. The color, taste, smell, and touch of earth, water, fire, and air, are also non-eternal, on account of the non-eternality of their substrata.
22. Ether, in consequence of its vast expansion, is infinitely large. So also is the self.
23. In consequence of non-existence of universal expansion, mind is atomic or infinitely small.
24. By attributes, space is explained (to be all-pervading).
25. Time (is the name given) to (a specific, or a universal) cause. (Hence, in either case it is all-pervading.)

Book VII, Chapter 2

9. Conjunction is produced by action of any one of two things, is produced by action of both, and is produced by conjunction, also.
10. By this disjunction is explained.
21. The prior and the posterior (are produced by two objects) lying in the same direction, existing at the same time, and being near and remote.
22. (Temporal priority and temporal posteriority are said, by suggestion, to arise respectively) from priority of the cause and from posteriority of the effect.
26. That is combination [inherence] by virtue of which (arises the intuition) in the form of "This is here," with regard to [subject and attribute].

Book VIII, Chapter 1

2. Among substances, the self, the mind, and others are not objects of perception.
4. Substance is the cause of the production of cognition, where attributes and actions are in contact (with the senses).
6. (Cognition which is produced) in respect of substance, attributes and action, (is) dependent upon genus and species.

Book VIII, Chapter 2

5. By reason of (its) predominance, and of possession of smell, earth is the material cause of the olfactory sense.
6. In like manner, water, fire, and air (are the material causes of the sense-organs of taste, color, and touch), inasmuch as there is no difference in the taste, color, and touch (which they respectively possess, from what they respectively apprehend).

Book IX, Chapter 1

1. In consequence of the non-application of action and attribute (to it), (an effect is) non-existent prior (to its production).
3. (The existent is) a different object (from the non-existent), inasmuch as action and attribute cannot be predicated on the non-existent.
5. And that which is a different non-existent from these, is (absolutely) non-existent.
9. That which has not been produced, does not exist;—this is a [tautological] proposition.
11. Perceptual cognition of the self (results) from a particular conjunction of the self and the mind in the self.

Book IX, Chapter 2

6. Reminiscence (results) from a particular conjunction between the soul and the mind and also from impression or latency.
10. False knowledge (arises) from imperfection of the senses and from imperfection of impression.
11. That (i.e., *avidyā*) is imperfect knowledge.
12. (Cognition) free from imperfection, is (called) *vidyā* or scientific knowledge.
13. Cognition of advanced sages, as also vision of the Perfected Ones, (results) from *dharma* or merits.

VEDĀNTA-MĪMĀṂSĀ

Of all the Indian systems of thought, the Vedāntic philosophy seems to be the most closely connected to the religion of Hinduism. The term *Vedānta* is compounded of "veda" and "anta," that is, "the end." Thus, Vedānta means the end of the Vedas, its conclusion as contained in the Upaniṣads. Vedānta emerged later than other *darśanas*, after India had experienced both Buddhist and Jaina challenges and was turning back toward Brahmanist religion.

Vedānta is often grouped with Mīmāṃsā, and in this case it is named as Uttara-Mīmāṃsā or later Mīmāṃsā. In contrast to Pūrva-Mīmāṃsā, or first Mīmāṃsā, Vedānta teaches not about ritual rules and laws, but about the integral sense of the Vedic revelation. Philosophic trends within Vedānta vary greatly. Three of them are of the most importance: Advaita-Vedānta (nondualism), whose major teachers were Gauḍapāda, Śaṇkara, Padmapāda, Sureśvara, and Vidyāraṇya; Viśiṣṭādvaita-Vedānta (qualified nondualism), whose main figure was Rāmānuja; and Dvaita-Vedānta (dualistic Vedānta), which referred primarily to Madhva.

Vedānta is Brahman-centered philosophy because its main preoccupation is with the nature of ultimate reality, "Brahman," and its relation to the manifested world. The basis of the philosophy of Vedānta makes up Vedānta-Sūtra or Brahma-Sūtra, which is dated older than the Bhagavad Gītā (most probably between 400 B.C. and A.D. 200). The author of Brahma-Sūtra, either Bādarāyaṇa or Vyāsa, summarized the insights concerning Brahman, the Absolute, and the *ātman*, the inner self of each person. Brahma-Sūtra has numerous commentaries. The selection below is from the commentary (bhāṣya) made by Śaṅkara, the founder of Vedānta as a religious and philosophical school. His authority among Hindus is so high that many of them believe that he was one of the avatāras of God Śiva. The selection is the introduction to the commentary, from Brahma, and Sūtra-Bhāṣya of Śri Śaṅkaracarya.

From Brahma-Sūtra-Bhāṣya of Śaṅkara

Translated by Swami Gambhirananda. Calcutta: Advaita Ashrama, 1965.

Introduction: It being an established fact that the object and the subject, that are fit to be the contents of the concepts "you" and "we" (respectively), and are by nature as contradictory as light and darkness, cannot logically have any identity, it follows that their attributes can have it still less. Accordingly, the superimposition of the object, referable through the concept "you," and its attributes on the subject that is conscious by nature and is referable through the concept "we" (should be impossible), and contrariwise the superimposition of the subject and its attributes on the object should be impossible. Nevertheless, owing to an absence of discrimination between these attributes, as also between substances, which are absolutely disparate, there continues a natural human behavior based on self-identification in the form of "I am this" or "This is mine."

This behavior has for its material cause an unreal nescience and man resorts to it by mixing up reality with unreality as a result of superimposing the things themselves or their attributes on each other.

If it be asked, "What is it that is called superimposition?"—the answer is: It is an awareness, similar in nature to memory, that arises on a different (foreign) basis as a result of some past experience. With regard to this, some say that it consists in the superimposition of the attributes of one thing on another. But others assert that wherever a superimposition on anything occurs, there is in evidence only a confusion arising from the absence of discrimination between them. Others say that the superimposition of anything on any other substratum consists in fancying some opposite attributes on that very basis. From every point of view, however, there is no difference as regards the appearance of one thing as something else. And in accord with this, we find in common experience that the nacre appears as silver, and a single moon appears as two.

Opponent: How, again, can there be any superimposition of any object or its attributes on the (inmost) Self that is opposed to the non-Self and is never an object (of the senses and mind)? For everybody superimposes something else on what is perceived by him in front; and you assert that the Self is opposed to the non-Self and is not referable (objectively) by the concept "you."

The answer (of the *Vedāntin*) is: The Self is not absolutely beyond apprehension, because It is apprehended as the content of the concept "I," and because the Self, opposed to the non-Self, is well known in the world as an immediately perceived (i.e., self-revealing) entity. Nor is there any rule that something has to be superimposed on something else that is directly perceived through the senses; for boys superimpose the ideas of surface (i.e., concavity) and dirt on space (i.e., sky) that is not an object of sense-perception. Hence there is nothing impossible in superimposing the non-Self on the Self that is opposed to it.

This superimposition, that is of this nature, is considered by the learned to be *avidyā*, nescience. And the ascertainment of the nature of the real entity by separating the superimposed thing from it is called *vidyā* (illumination). This being so, whenever there is a superimposition of one thing on another, the locus is not affected in any way either by the merits or demerits of the thing superimposed. All forms of worldly and Vedic behavior that are connected with valid means of knowledge and objects of knowledge start by taking for granted this mutual superimposition of the Self and non-Self, known as nescience; and so do all the scriptures dealing with injunction, prohibition, or emancipation.

Opponent: How, again, can the means of valid knowledge, such as direct perception as well as the scriptures, have as their locus a cognizer who is subject to nescience?

The (*Vedāntin's*) answer is: Since a man without self-identification with the body, mind, senses, etc., cannot become a cognizer, and as such, the means of knowledge cannot function for him; since perception and other activities (of a man) are not possible without accepting the senses, etc. (as his own); since the senses cannot function without (the body as) a basis; since nobody engages in any activity with a body that has not the idea of the Self superimposed on it; since the unrelated Self cannot become a cognizer unless there are all these (mutual superimposition of the Self and the body and their attributes on each other); and since the means of knowledge cannot function unless there is a cognizership; therefore it follows that the means of knowledge, such as direct perception as well as the scriptures, must have a man as their locus who is subject to nescience.

Moreover, there is no difference (of the learned) from the animals (in regard to empirical behavior). Just as animals and others turn away from sound etc. when these appear to be unfavorable after their ears etc. come in contact with them, and they move towards these when they are favorable; and just as by noticing a man approaching them with a raised stick, they begin to run away thinking, "This one wants to hurt me," and they approach another carrying green grass in his hands, similarly even the wise are repelled by the presence of strong, uproarious people with evil looks and upraised swords, and are attracted by men of opposite nature. Therefore the behavior of men with regard to the means and objects of knowledge is similar to that of animals. And it is a familiar fact that the animals use their means of perception etc. without discrimination (between the body and the Self). From this fact of similarity, the conclusion can be drawn that so far as empirical behavior is concerned, the use of the means of perception by the wise is similar to that of lower animals, (it being a result of superimposition). Of course, it is a fact that a man acting intelligently does not acquire the competence for scriptural duties unless he has a knowledge of the relationship of his soul with the next world. Still (a knowledge of) the absolute Reality, that is the Self, is not a prerequisite for such a competence; for It (i.e., Reality) has no relevance here, and It is opposed to such competence, inasmuch as It is beyond hunger and thirst, free from such differentiation as Brahman, Kṣatriya, etc., and is not subject to birth and death. And the scriptures, which are operative before the dawn of the real knowledge of the Self, cannot transgress the limits of their dependence on people groping in ignorance. To illustrate the point: Such scriptural injunction as "A Brahman shall perform a sacrifice" can become effective only by taking for granted various kinds of superimposition of caste, stage of life, age, condition, etc. And we said that superimposition means the cognition of something as some other thing. Thus in accordance as one's wife, children, or other relatives are hale and hearty with all their limbs intact, or as they suffer from the loss of those limbs, one thinks, "I myself am hale and hearty" or "I myself am injured"; thus one superimposes external characteristics on the Self. Similarly one superimposes the characteristics of the body when one has such ideas as "I am fat," "I am thin," "I am fair," "I stay," "I go," or "I scale." So also one superimposes the attributes of the senses and organs when one thinks, "I am dumb," "I have lost one eye," "I am a eunuch," "I am deaf," or "I am blind." Similarly one superimposes the attributes of the internal organ, such as desire, will, doubt, perseverance, etc. In the same way, one first superimposes the internal organ, possessed of the idea of ego, on the Self, the witness of all the manifestations of that organ; then by an opposite process, one superimposes on the internal organ etc. that Self which is opposed to the non-Self and which is the witness of everything. Thus occurs this superimposition that has neither beginning nor end but flows on eternally, that appears as the manifested universe and its apprehension, that conjures up agentship and enjoyership, and that is perceived by all persons. In order to eradicate this source of evil and in order to acquire the knowledge of the unity of the Self, is begun a discussion (after the study) of all the Upaniṣads. We shall show in this discussion about the nature of the embodied soul, that this is the purport of all the Upaniṣads.

MODERN INDIAN PHILOSOPHY

The Indian renaissance and Hindu reformation of the nineteenth and early twentieth centuries was personified best for India and, in particular, for the world beyond its borders, by Swāmi Vivekānanda (1863–1902). The most important disciple of Rāmakrishna, Vivekānanda founded in 1887 with a group of monk-disciples the Rāmakrishna Order and later the Rāmakrishna Mission.

The man who is called a great pathfinder, a prophet of a new resurgent India, was not a philosopher in a strict sense of this word. Being rather a religious reformer, Vivekānanda nevertheless made a great impact on modern Indian philosophy.

Though Vivekānanda said about himself: "I am Śaṅkara," his adherence to the philosophy of the Vedānta is neo-Vedāntic for sure. His teaching was referred to as "practical Vedānta" because it aimed at the spiritual regeneration of the individuals and the society as a whole.

Vivekānanda's main works were dedicated to the yogic paths, including Jñāna-Yoga, Rāja-Yoga, Karma-Yoga, and Bhakti-Yoga, exposing his concept of "practical Vedānta." The latter means, first, the removal of any prohibitions or limitations in learning the teaching of the Vedānta and its sacred sources: the Vedas and the Upaniṣads. He strongly opposes caste discrimination in this matter. Second, the wisdom of the Vedānta is to be popularized by the language understandable to the masses. Third, there should not be any gap between the teaching and everyday behavior of its adherents.

The great popularizer of the Vedānta to the West, Vivekānanda believed that the latter could make the foundation for the universal religion promoting peaceful coexistence and progress for all the people of the world. As to his own people, he called his compatriots to spiritual regeneration through faith in themselves. The text below, called *The Common Bases of Hinduism,* might pass on to the readers the spirit of the teachings of the great Swāmi.

From Vivekānanda

The Common Bases of Hinduism *by Vivekānanda. Reprinted from* The Complete Works of Swāmi Vivekānanda. *8 vols. Calcutta: Advaita Ashrama, 1989, vol. III*

This is the land which is held to be the holiest even in holy *Aryavarta*; this is the *Brahmavarta* of which our great Manu speaks. This is the land from whence arose that mighty aspiration after the Spirit, ay, which in times to come, as history shows, is to deluge the world. This is the land where, like its mighty rivers, spiritual aspirations have arisen and joined their strength, till they traveled over the length and breadth of the world and declared themselves with a voice of thunder. This is the land which had first to bear the brunt of all inroads and invasions into India; this heroic land had first to bare its bosom to every onslaught of the outer barbarians into *Aryavarta.* This is the land which, after all its sufferings, has not yet entirely lost its glory and its strength. Here it was that in later times the gentle *Nanak* preached his marvelous love for the world. Here it was that his broad heart was opened and his arms outstretched to embrace the whole world, not only of Hindus, but of Mohammedans too. Here it was that one of the last and one of the most glorious heroes of our race, Guru Govind Singh, after shedding his blood and that of his dearest and nearest for the cause of religion, even when deserted by those for whom this blood was shed, retired into the South to die like a wounded lion struck to the heart, without a word against his country, without a single word of murmur.

Here, in this ancient land of ours, children of the land of five rivers, I stand before you, not as a teacher, for I know very little to teach, but as one who has come from the east to exchange words of greeting with the brothers of the west, to compare notes. Here am I, not to find out differences that exist among us, but to find where we agree. Here am I trying to understand on what ground we may always remain brothers, upon what foundations the voice that has spoken from eternity may become stronger and stronger as it grows. Here am I trying to propose to you something of constructive work and not destructive. For criticism the days are past, and we are waiting for constructive work. The world needs, at times, criticisms even fierce ones; but that is only for a time, and the work for eternity is progress and construction, and not criticism and destruction. For the last hundred years or so, there has been a flood of criticism all over this land of ours, where the full play of Western science has been let loose upon all the dark spots, and as a result the corners and the holes have become much more prominent than anything else. Naturally enough there arose mighty intellects all over the land, great and glorious, with the love of truth and justice in their hearts, with the love of their country, and above all, in intense love for their religion and their God; and because these mighty souls felt so deeply, because they loved so deeply, they criticized everything they thought was wrong. Glory unto these mighty spirits of the past! They have done so much good; but the voice of the present day is coming to us, telling, "Enough!" There has been enough of criticism, there has been enough of fault-finding, the time has come for us to gather all our scattered forces, to concentrate them into one focus, and through that, to lead the nation on its onward march, which for centuries almost has been stopped. The house has been cleansed; let it be inhabited anew. The road has been cleared. March ahead, children of the Aryans!

Gentlemen, this is the motive that brings me before you, and at the start I may declare to you that I belong to no party and no sect. They are all great and glorious to me, I love them all, and all my life I have been attempting to find what is good and true in them. Therefore, it is my proposal tonight to bring before you points where we are agreed, to find out, if we can, a ground of agreement; and if through the grace of the Lord such a state of things be possible, let us take it up, and from theory carry it out into practice. We are Hindus. I do not use the word Hindu in any bad sense at all, nor do I agree with those that think there is any bad meaning in it. In old times, it simply meant people who lived on the other side of the Indus: today a good many among those who hate us may have put a bad interpretation upon it, but names are nothing. Upon us depends whether the name Hindu will stand for everything that is glorious, everything that is spiritual, or whether it will remain a name of opprobrium, one designating the downtrodden, the worthless, the heathen. If at present the word Hindu means anything bad, never mind: by our action let us be ready to show that this is the highest word that any language can invent. It has been one of the principles of my life not to be ashamed of my own ancestors. I am one of the proudest men ever born, but let me tell you frankly, it is not for myself, but on account of my ancestry. The more I have studied the past, the more I have looked back, more and more has this pride come to me, and it has given me the strength and courage of conviction, raised me up from the dust of the earth, and set me working out that great plan laid out by those great ancestors of ours. Children of those ancient Aryans, through the grace of the Lord may you have the same pride, may that faith in your ancestors come into your blood, may it become a part and parcel of your lives, may it work towards the salvation of the world!

Before trying to find out the precise point where we are all agreed, the common ground of our national life, one thing we must remember. Just as there is an individuality in every man, so there is a national individuality. As one man differs from another in certain particulars, in certain characteristics of his own, so one race differs from another in certain peculiar characteristics; and just as it is the mission of every man to fulfill a certain purpose in the economy of nature, just as there is a particular line set out for him by his own past *Karma*, so it is with nations—each nation has a destiny to fulfill, each nation has a message to deliver, each nation has a mission to accomplish. Therefore, from the very start, we must have to understand the mission of our own race, the destiny it has to fulfill, the place it has to occupy in the march of nations, the note which it has to contribute to the harmony of races. In our country, when children, we hear stories how some serpents have jewels in their heads, and whatever one may do with the serpent, so long as the jewel is there, the serpent cannot be killed. We hear stories of giants and ogres who had souls living in certain little birds, and so long as the bird was safe, there was no power on earth to kill these giants; you might hack them to pieces, or do what you liked to them, the giants could not die. So with nations, there is a certain point where the life of a nation centers, where lies the nationality of the nation, and until that is touched, the nation cannot die. In the light of this we can understand the most marvelous phenomenon that the history of the world has ever known. Wave after wave of barbarian conquest has rolled over this devoted land of ours. "Allah Ho Akbar!" has rent the skies for hundreds of years, and no Hindu knew what moment would be his last. This is the most suffering and the most subjugated of all the historic lands of the world. Yet we still stand practically the same race, ready to face difficulties again and again if necessary; and not only so, of late there have been signs that we are not only strong, but ready to go out, for the sign of life is expansion.

We find today that our ideas and thoughts are no more cooped up within the bounds of India, but whether we will it or not, they are marching outside, filtering into the literature of nations, taking their place among nations, and in some, even getting a commanding dictatorial position. Behind this we find the explanation that the great contribution to the sum total of the world's progress from India is the greatest, the noblest, the sublimest theme that can occupy the mind of man—it is philosophy and spirituality. Our ancestors tried many other things; they, like other nations, first went to bring out the secrets of external nature as we all know, and with their gigantic brains that marvelous race could have done miracles in that line of which the world could have been proud for ever. But they gave it up for something higher, something better rings out from the pages of the Vedas: "That science is the greatest which makes us know Him who never changes!" The science of nature, changeful, evanescent, the world of death, of woe, of misery, may be great, great indeed; but the science of Him who changes not, the Blissful One, where alone is peace, where alone is life eternal, where alone is perfection, where alone all misery ceases—that, according to our ancestors, was the sublimest science of all. After all, sciences that can give us only bread and clothes and power over our fellowmen, sciences that can teach us only how to conquer our fellow-beings, to rule over them, which teach the strong to domineer over the weak—those they could have discovered if they willed. But praise be unto the Lord, they caught at once the other side, which was grander, infinitely higher, infinitely more blissful, till it has become the national characteristic, till it has come down to us, inherited from father to son for thousands of years, till it has become a part and parcel of us, till it tingles in every drop of blood that runs through our veins, till it has become our second nature, till the name of religion and Hindu have become one. This is the national characteristic, and this cannot be touched. Barbarians with sword and fire, barbarians bringing barbarous religions, not one of them could touch the core, not one could touch the "jewel," not one had the power to kill the "bird" which the soul of the race inhabited. This, therefore, is the vitality of the race, and so long as that remains, there is no power under the sun that can kill the race. All the tortures and miseries of the world will pass over without hurting us, and we shall come out of the flames like *Prahlada*, so long as we hold on to this grandest of all our inheritances, spirituality. If a Hindu is not spiritual I do not call him a Hindu. In other countries a man may be political first, and then he may have a little religion, but here in India the first and the foremost duty of our lives is to be spiritual first, and then, if there is time, let other things come. Bearing this in mind we shall be in a better position to understand why, for our national welfare, we must first seek out at the present day all the spiritual forces of the race, as was done in days of yore and will be done in all times to come. National union in India must be a gathering up of its scattered spiritual forces. A nation in India must be a union of those whose hearts beat to the same spiritual tune.

There have been sects enough in this country. There are sects enough, and there will be enough in the future, because this has been the peculiarity of our religion that in abstract principles so much latitude has been given that, although afterwards so much detail has been worked out, all these details are the working out of principles, broad as the skies above our heads, eternal as nature herself. Sects, therefore, as a matter of course, must exist here, but what need not exist is sectarian quarrel. Sects must be, but sectarianism need not. The world would not be the better for sectarianism, but the world cannot move on without having sects. One set of men cannot do everything. The almost infinite mass of energy in the world cannot be managed by a small number of people. Here, at once we see the necessity that forced this division of labor upon us—the division into sects. For the use of spiritual forces let there be sects; but is there any need that we should quarrel when our most ancient books declare that this differentiation is only apparent, that in spite of all these differences there is a thread of harmony, that beautiful unity, running through them all? Our most ancient books have declared: "That which exists is One; sages call Him by various names." Therefore, if there are these sectarian struggles, if there are these fights among the different sects, if there is jealousy and hatred between the different sects in India, the land where all sects have always been honored, it is a shame on us who dare to call ourselves the descendants of those fathers.

There are certain great principles in which, I think, we—whether Vaishnavas, Shaivas, *Shaktas*, or *Ganpatyas*, whether belonging to the ancient Vedantists or the modern ones, whether belonging to the old rigid sects or the modern reformed ones—are all one, and whoever calls himself a Hindu, believes in these principles. Of course there is a difference in the interpretation, in the explanation of these principles, and that difference should be there, and it should be allowed, for our standard is not to bind every man down to our position. It would be a sin to force every man to work out our own interpretation of things, and to live by our own methods. Perhaps all who are here will agree on the First point that we believe the Vedas to be the eternal teachings of the secrets of religion. We all believe that this holy literature is without beginning and without end, coeval with nature, which is without beginning and without end; and that all our religious differences, all our religious struggles must end when we stand in the presence of that holy book; we are all agreed that this is the last court of appeal in all our spiritual differences. We may take different points of view as to what the Vedas are. There may be one sect which regards one portion as more sacred than another, but that matters little so long as we say that we are all brothers in the Vedas, that out of these venerable, eternal, marvelous books has come everything that we possess today, good, holy, and pure. Well, therefore, if we believe in all this, let this principle first of all be preached broadcast throughout the length and breadth of the land. If this be true, let the Vedas have that prominence which they always deserve, and which we all believe in. First, then, the Vedas. The second point we all believe in is God, the creating, the preserving power of the whole universe, and unto whom it periodically returns to come out at other periods and manifest this wonderful phenomenon, called the universe. We may differ as to our conception of God. One may believe in a God who is entirely personal, another may believe in a God who is personal and yet not human, and yet another may believe in a God who is entirely impersonal, and all may get their support from the Vedas. Still we are all believers in God; that is to say, that man who does not believe in a most marvelous Infinite Power from which everything has come, in which everything lives, and to which everything has come, and to which everything must in the end return, cannot be called a Hindu. If that be so, let us try to preach that idea all over the land. Preach whatever conception you have to give, there is no difference, we are not going to fight over it, but preach God; that is all we want. One idea may be better than another, but, mind you, not one of them is bad. One is good, another is better, and again another may be the best, but the word bad does not enter the category of our religion. Therefore, may the Lord bless them all who preach the name of God in whatever form they like! The more He is preached, the better for this race. Let our children be brought up in this idea, let this idea enter the homes of the poorest and the lowest, as well as of the richest and the highest—the idea of the name of God.

The third idea that I will present before you is that, unlike all other races of the world, we do not believe that this world was created only so many thousand years ago, and is going to be destroyed eternally on a certain day. Nor do we believe that the human soul has been created along with this universe just out of nothing. Here is another point I think we are all able to agree upon. We believe in nature being without beginning and without end; only at psychological periods this gross material of the outer universe goes back to its finer state, thus to remain for a certain period, again to be projected outside to manifest all this infinite panorama we call nature. This wave like motion was going on even before time began, through eternity, and will remain for an infinite period of time.

Next, all Hindus believe that man is not only a gross material body; not only that within this there is the finer body, the mind, but there is something yet greater—for the body changes and so does the mind—something beyond, the *Ātman*—I cannot translate the word to you for any translation will be wrong—that there is something beyond even this fine body, which is the *Ātman* of man, which has neither beginning nor end, which knows not what death is. And then this peculiar idea, different from that of all other races of men, that this *Ātman* inhabits body after body until there is no more interest for it to continue to do so, and it becomes free, not to be born again, I refer to the theory of *Saṃsāra* and the theory of eternal souls taught by our *Śāstras.* This is another point where we all agree, whatever sect we may belong to. There may be differences as to the relation between the soul and God. According to one sect the soul may be eternally different from God, according to another it may be a spark of that infinite fire, yet again according to others it may be one with that Infinite. It does not matter what our interpretation is, so long as we hold on to the one basic belief that the soul is infinite, that this soul was never created, and therefore will never die, that it had to pass and evolve into various bodies, till it attained perfection in the human one—in that we are all agreed. And then comes the most differentiating, the grandest, and the most wonderful discovery in the realms of spirituality that has ever been made. Some of you, perhaps, who have been studying Western thought, may have observed already that there is another radical difference severing at one stroke all that is Western from all that is Eastern. It is this that we hold, whether we are *Shaktas,* Sauras, or Vaishnavas, even whether we are Baudhas or Jainas, we all hold in India that the soul is by its nature pure and perfect, infinite in power and blessed. Only, according to the dualist, this natural blissfulness of the soul has become contracted by past bad work, and through the grace of God it is again going to open out and show its perfection; while according to the monist, even this idea of contraction is a partial mistake, it is the veil of *Māyā* that causes us to think the soul has lost its powers, but the powers are there fully manifest. Whatever the difference may be, we come to the central core, and there is at once an irreconcilable difference between all that is Western and Eastern. The Eastern is looking inward for all that is great and good. When we worship, we close our eyes and try to find God within. The Western is looking up outside for his God. To the Western their religious books have been inspired, while with us our books have been expired; breath-like they came, the breath of God, out of the hearts of sages they sprang, the *Mantra-drashtas.*

This is one great point to understand, and, my friends, my brethren, let me tell you, this is the one point we shall have to insist upon in the future. For I am firmly convinced, and I beg you to understand this one fame—no good comes out of the man who day and night thinks he is nobody. If a man, day and night, thinks he is miserable, low, and nothing, nothing he becomes. If you say yea yea, "I am, I am," so shall you be; and if you say "I am not," think that you are not, and day and night meditate upon the fact that you are nothing, ay, nothing shall you be. That is the great fact which you ought to remember. We are the children of the Almighty, we are sparks of the infinite, divine fire.

How can we be nothings? We are everything, ready to do everything, we can do everything and man must do everything. This faith in themselves was in the hearts of our ancestors, this faith in themselves was the motive power that pushed them forward and forward in the march of civilization; and if there has been degeneration, if there has been defect, mark my words, you will find that degradation to have started on the day our people lost this faith in themselves. Losing faith in one's self means losing faith in God. Do you believe in that infinite, good Providence working in and through you? If you believe that this Omnipresent One, the *Antaryamin*, is present in every atom, is through and through, *Ota-prota*, as the Sanskrit word goes, penetrating your body, mind and soul, how can you lose heart? I may be a little dribble of water, and you may be a mountain-high wave. Never mind! The infinite ocean is the background of me as well as of you. Mine also is that infinite ocean of life, of power, of spirituality, as well as yours. I am already joined—from my very birth, from the very fact of my life—I am in Yoga with that infinite life and infinite goodness and infinite power, as you are, mountain-high though you may be. Therefore, my brethren, teach this life-saving, great, ennobling, grand doctrine to your children, even from their very birth. You need not teach them Advaitism; teach them Dvaitism, or any "ism" you please, but we have seen that this is the common "ism" all through India; this marvelous doctrine of the soul, the perfection of the soul, is commonly believed in by all sects. As says our great philosopher Kapila, if purity has not been the nature of the soul, it can never attain purity afterwards, for anything that was not perfect by nature, even if it attained to perfection, that perfection would go away again. If impurity is the nature of man, then man will have to remain impure, even though he may be pure for five minutes. The time will come when this purity will wash out, pass away, and the old natural impurity will have its sway once more. Therefore, say all our philosophers, good is our nature, perfection is our nature, not imperfection, not impurity—and we should remember that. Remember the beautiful example of the great sage who, when he was dying, asked his mind to remember all his mighty deeds and all his mighty thoughts. There you do not find that he was teaching his mind to remember all his weaknesses and all his follies. Follies there are, weakness there must be, but remember your real nature always—that is the only way to cure the weakness, that is the only way to cure the follies.

It seems that these few points are common among all the various religious sects in India, and perhaps in the future, upon this common platform, conservative and liberal religionists, old type and new type, may shake hands. Above all, there is another thing to remember, which I am sorry we forget from time to time, that religion, in India, means realization and nothing short of that. "Believe in the doctrine, and you are safe," can never be taught to us, for we do not believe in that. You are what you make yourselves. You are by the grace of God and your own exertions, what you are. Believing in certain theories and doctrines will not help you much. The mighty word that came out from the sky of spirituality in India was *Anubhuti*, realization, and ours are the only books which declare again and again: "The Lord is to be *seen*." Bold, brave words indeed, but true to their very core; every sound, every vibration is true. Religion is to be realized, not only heard; it is not in learning some doctrine like a parrot. Neither is it mere intellectual assent—that is nothing; but it must come into us. Ay, and therefore the greatest proof that we have of the existence of a God is not because our reason says so, but because God has been seen by the ancients as well as by the moderns. We believe in the soul not only because there are good reasons to prove its existence, but, above all, because there have been in the past thousands in India, there are still many who have realized, and there will be thousands in the future who will realize and see their own souls. And there is no salvation for man until he sees God, realizes his own soul. Therefore, above all, let us understand this, and the more we understand it the less we shall have of sectarianism in India, for it is only that man who has realized God and seen Him, who is religious. In him the knots have been cut asunder, in him alone the doubts have subsided; he alone has become free from the fruits of action who has been Him who is nearest of the near and farthest of the far. Ay, we often mistake mere prattle for religious truth, mere intellectual perorations for great spiritual realization, and then comes sectarianism, then comes fight. If we once understand that this realization is the only religion, we shall look into our own hearts and find how far we are towards realizing the truths of religion. Then we shall understand that we ourselves are groping in darkness, and are leading others to grope in the same darkness, then we shall cease from sectarianism, quarrel, and fight. Ask a man who wants to start a sectarian fight, "Have you seen God? Have you seen the *Ātman*? If you have not, what right have you to preach His name—you walking in darkness trying to lead me into the same darkness—the blind leading the blind, and both falling into the ditch?"

Therefore, take more thought before you go and do not find fault with others. Let them follow their own path to realization so long as they struggle to see truth in their own hearts; and when the broad, naked truth will be seen, then they will find that wonderful blissfulness which marvelously enough has been testified to by every seer in India, by every one who has realized the truth. Then words of love alone will come out of that heart, for it has already been touched by Him who is the essence of Love Himself. Then and then alone, all sectarian quarrels will cease, and we shall be in a position to understand, to bring to our hearts, to embrace, to intensely love the very word Hindu and every one who bears that name. Mark me, then and then alone you are a Hindu when the very name sends through you a galvanic shock of strength. Then and then alone you are a Hindu when every man who bears the name, from any country, speaking our language or any other language, becomes at once the nearest and the dearest to you. Then and then alone you are a Hindu when the distress of anyone bearing that name comes to your heart and makes you feel as if your own son were in distress. Then and then alone you are a Hindu when you will be ready to bear everything for them, like the great example I have quoted at the beginning of this lecture, of your great Guru Govind Singh. Driven out from this country, fighting against its oppressors, after having shed his own blood for the defense of the Hindu religion, after having seen his children killed on the battlefield—ay, this example of the great Guru, left even by those for whose sake he was shedding his blood and the blood of his own nearest and dearest—he, the wounded lion, retired from the field calmly to die in the South, but not a word of curse escaped his lips against those who had ungratefully forsaken him! Mark me, every one of you will have to be a Govind Singh, if you want to do good to your country. You may see thousands of defects in your country-men, but mark their Hindu blood. They are the first Gods you will have to worship even if they do everything to hurt you, even if every one of them send out a curse to you, you send out to them words of love. If they drive you out, retire to die in silence like that mighty lion, Govind Singh. Such a man is worthy of the name of Hindu; such an ideal ought to be before us always. All our hatchets let us bury; send out this grand current of love all round.

Let them talk of India's regeneration as they like. Let me tell you as one who has been working—at least trying to work—all his life, that there is no regeneration for India until you be spiritual. Not only so, but upon it depends the welfare of the whole world. For I must tell you frankly that the very foundations of Western civilization have been shaken to their base. The mightiest buildings, if built upon the loose sand foundations of materialism, must come to grief one day, must totter to their destruction some day. The history of the world is our witness. Nation after nation has arisen and based its greatness upon materialism, declaring man was all matter. Ay, in Western language, a man gives up the ghost, but in our language a man gives up his body. The Western man is a body first, and then he has a soul; with us a man is a soul and spirit, and he has a body. Therein lies a world of difference. All such civilizations, therefore, as have been based upon such sand foundations as material comfort and all that, have disappeared one after another, after short lives, from the face of the world; but the civilization of India and the other nations that have stood at India's feet to listen and learn, namely, Japan and China, live even to the present day, and there are signs even of revival among them. Their lives are like that of the Phoenix, a thousand times destroyed, but ready to spring up again more glorious. But a materialistic civilization once dashed down, never can come up again; that building once thrown down is broken into pieces once for all. Therefore have patience and wait, the future is in store for us.

Do not be in a hurry, do not go out to imitate anybody else. This is another great lesson we have to remember; imitation is not civilization. I may deck myself out in a Rāja's dress, but will that make me a Rāja? An ass in a lion's skin never makes a lion. Imitation, cowardly imitation, never makes for progress. It is verily the sign of awful degradation in a man. Ay, when a man has begun to hate himself, then the last blow has come. When a man has begun to be ashamed of his ancestors, the end has come. Here am I, one of the least of the Hindu race, yet proud of my race, proud of my ancestors. I am proud to call myself a Hindu, I am proud that I am one of your unworthy servants. I am proud that I am a countryman of yours, you the descendants of the sages, you the descendants of the most glorious *rishis* the world ever saw. Therefore, have faith in yourselves, be proud of your ancestors, instead of being ashamed of them. And do not imitate, do not imitate! Whenever you are under the thumb of others, you lose your own independence. If you are working, even in spiritual things, at the dictation of others, slowly you lose all faculty, even of thought. Bring out through your own exertions what you have, but do not imitate, yet take what is good from others. We have to learn from others. You put the seed in the ground, and give it plenty of earth, and air, and water to feed upon; when the seed grows into the plant and into a gigantic tree, does it become the earth, does it become the air, or does it become the water? It becomes the mighty plant, the mighty tree, after its own nature, having absorbed everything that was given to it. Let that be your position. We have indeed many things to learn from others, yea, that man who refuses to learn is already dead. Declares our Manu: "Take the jewel of a woman for your wife, though she be of inferior descent. Learn supreme knowledge with service even from the man of low birth; and even from the *Chandala*, learn by serving him the way to salvation." Learn everything that is good from others, but bring it in, and in your own way absorb it; do not become others. Do not be dragged away out of this Indian life; do not for a moment think that it would be better for India if all the Indians dressed, ate, and behaved like another race. You know the difficulty of giving up a habit of a few years. The Lord knows how many thousands of years are in your blood; this national specialized life has been flowing in one way, the Lord knows for how many thousands of years; and do you mean to say that that mighty stream, which has nearly reached its ocean, can go back to the snows of its Himalayas again? That is impossible! The struggle to do so would only break it. Therefore, make way for the life-current of the nation. Take away the blocks that bar the way to the progress of this mighty river, cleanse its path, clear the channel, and out it will rush by its own natural impulse, and the nation will go on careering and progressing.

These are the lines which I beg to suggest to you for spiritual work in India. There are many other great problems which, for want of time, I cannot bring before you this night. For instance, there is the wonderful question of caste. I have been studying this question, its pros and cons, all my life; I have studied it in nearly every province in India. I have mixed with people of all castes in nearly every part of the country, and I am too bewildered in my own mind to grasp even the very significance of it. The more I try to study it, the more I get bewildered. Still at last I find that a little glimmer of light is before me, I begin to feel its significance just now. Then there is the other great problem about eating and drinking. That is a great problem indeed. It is not so useless a thing as we generally think. I have come to the conclusion that the insistence which we make now about eating and drinking is most curious and is just going against what the *Śāstras* required, that is to say, we come to grief by neglecting the proper purity of the food we eat and drink; we have lost the true spirit of it.

There are several other questions which I want to bring before you and show how these problems can be solved, how to work out the ideas; but unfortunately the meeting could not come to order until very late, and I do not wish to detain you any longer now. I will, therefore, keep my ideas about caste and other things for a future occasion.

Now, one word more and I will finish about these spiritual ideas. Religion for a long time has come to be static in India. What we want is to make it dynamic. I want it to be brought into the life of everybody. Religion, as it always has been in the past, must enter the palaces of kings as well as the homes of the poorest peasants in the land. Religion, the common inheritance, the universal birthright of the race, must be brought free to the door of everybody. Religion in India must be made as free and as easy of access as is God's air. And this is the kind of work we have to bring about in India, but not by getting up little sects and fighting on points of difference. Let us preach where we all agree and leave the differences to remedy themselves. As I have said to the Indian people again and again, if there is the darkness of centuries in a room and we go into the room and begin to cry, "Oh, it is dark, it is dark!," will the darkness go? Bring in the light and the darkness will vanish at once. This is the secret of reforming men. Suggest to them higher things; believe in man first. Why start with the belief that man is degraded and degenerated? I have never failed in my faith in man in any case, even taking him at his worst. Wherever I had faith in man, though at first the prospect was not always bright, yet it triumphed in the long run. Have faith in man, whether he appears to you to be a very learned one or a most ignorant one. Have faith in man, whether he appears to be an angel or the very devil himself. Have faith in man first, and then having faith in him, believe that if there are defects in him, if he makes mistakes, if he embraces the crudest and the vilest doctrines, believe that it is not from his real nature that they come, but from the want of higher ideals. If a man goes towards what is false, it is because he cannot get what is true. Therefore the only method of correcting what is false is by supplying him with what is true. Do this, and let him compare. You give him the truth, and there your work is done. Let him compare it in his own mind with what he has already in him; and, mark my words, if you have really given him the truth, the false must vanish, light must dispel darkness, and truth will bring the good out. This is the way if you want to reform the country spiritually; this is the way, and not fighting, not even telling people that what they are doing is bad. Put the good before them, see how eagerly they take it, see how the divine that never dies, that is always living in the human, comes up awakened and stretches out its hand for all that is good, and all that is glorious.

May He who is the Creator, the Preserver, and the Protector of our race, the God of our forefathers, whether called by the name of Viṣṇu, or Śiva, or Shakti, or Ganapati, whether He is worshipped as Saguna or as Nirguna, whether He is worshipped as personal or as impersonal, may He whom our forefathers knew and addressed by the words, "That which exists is One; sages call Him by various names"—may He enter into us with His mighty love; may He shower His blessings on us, may He make us understand each other, may He make us work for each other with real love, with intense love for truth, and may not the least desire for our own personal fame, our own personal prestige, our own personal advantage, enter into this great work of the spiritual regeneration of India!

7

Chinese Tradition

CONFUCIANISM

In the original name of this teaching (*tzu*—literally, "teaching of the school of intellectuals"), which can truly be said to have molded Chinese civilization, the name of the man who founded it—Confucius—is not mentioned. This can be explained by Confucius's stand expressed in his own words: "I transmit but do not create. I believe in and love the ancients." Grand Master K'ung (K'ung Fu-Tzu is the real name of Confucius) saw his mission as one of preserving and transmitting ancient culture, therefore he was mainly engaged in editing and commenting upon such classics as *Chih Ching* and *Chu Ching.*

Confucius was born in 551 B.C. in the small state of Lu to a noble but poor family. Summarizing his own life, the grand master said: "At fifteen my mind was set on learning. At thirty my character had been formed. At forty I had no more perplexities. At fifty I knew the Mandate of Heaven. At sixty I was at ease whatever I heard. At seventy I could follow my heart's desire without transgressing moral principles" (*Analects,* 2:4).

Confucius was a self-educated man. In his twenties he worked as a granary keeper and a supervisor of flocks. Later on he served as a government consultant. Confucius did not stay long in that position. At the age of thirty he opened the first private school in China, thus becoming the first professional teacher in Chinese history. According to the records of the historians, Confucius had three thousand pupils, seventy-two of whom mastered the "six arts."

In his fifties Confucius tried to make political career. He served as a magistrate, an assistant minister of public works, and minister of justice. Soon he became disappointed with politics and left it to go back to teaching. Confucius died at the age of seventy-three.

There is some controversy over whether or not Confucius is actually the author of the *Ch'un-ch'iu fan-lu* (*Spring and Autumn Annals*), the editor of other ancient classics, and commentator on the *Book of Changes.* Practically all scholars accept the *Analects* or *Lun yü* to be the most reliable source of the grand master's teachings.

The central concepts of Confucian teaching are *li* and *jen. Li* stresses proper conduct, that is, "ritual action." "If you do not learn the Rituals," says Confucius, "you will not have the means to take a stance." *Jen* means the self-making, self-transformation, self-perfection through which an individual becomes an exemplary or authoritative person—*chun-tzu.*[1] There are five attitudes (respect, tolerance, living up to one's word, diligence, and generosity) that lead an individual to the state of an exemplary person.

Confucius gave Chinese philosophy its humanistic foundation. In his vision, the true perfect man is the one who follows the golden middle way, who "wishing to establish his own character, also helps others to be prominent." In other words, he brings in harmony aspects of self and society. The Confucian ideal is the harmony of the perfect individual and a well-ordered society based on the mutual moral obligations of the five human relations, those between ruler and minister, father and son, elder brother and younger brother, husband and wife, and one friend and another.

From Confucius

Reprinted from The Analects of Confucius: A Philosophical Translation. *Translated by Roger T. Ames and Henry Rosemont, Jr. New York: Ballantine Books, 1998.*

2.8 Zixia asked about filial conduct (*xiao*). The Master replied: "It all lies in showing the proper countenance. As for the young contributing their energies when there is work to be done, and deferring to their elders when there is wine and food to be had—how can merely doing this be considered being filial?"

2.9 The Master said: "I can speak with Yan Hui for an entire day without his raising an objection, as though he were slow. But when he has withdrawn and I examine what he says and does on his own, it illustrates perfectly what I have been saying. Indeed, there is nothing slow about Yan Hui!"

2.10 The Master said: "Watch their actions, observe their motives, examine wherein they dwell content; won't you know what kind of person they are? Won't you know what kind of person they are?"

2.11 The Master said: "Reviewing the old as a means of realizing the new—such a person can be considered a teacher."

2.12 The Master said: "Exemplary persons (*junzi*) are not mere vessels."

2.13 Zigong asked about exemplary persons (*junzi*). The Master replied: "They first accomplish what they are going to say, and only then say it."

2.14 The Master said: "Exemplary persons (*junzi*) associating openly with others are not partisan; petty persons being partisan do not associate openly with others."

2.15 The Master said: "Learning without due reflection leads to perplexity; reflection without learning leads to perilous circumstances."

2.16 The Master said: "To become accomplished in some heterodox doctrine will bring nothing but harm."

2.17 The Master said: "Zilu, shall I teach you what wisdom (*zhi*) means?" To know (*zhi*) what you know and know what you do not know—this then is wisdom."

2.18 Zizhang was studying in order to take office. The Master said: "If you listen broadly, set aside what you are unsure of, and speak cautiously on the rest, you will make few errors; if you look broadly, set aside what is perilous, and act cautiously on the rest, you will have few regrets. To speak with few errors and to act with few regrets is the substance of taking office."

13.2 Zhonggong was serving as steward in the House of Ji, and asked about governing effectively (*zheng*). The Master said to him, "Set an example yourself for those in office, pardon minor offenses, and promote those with superior character (*xian*) and ability."

"How do you recognize those with superior character and ability in order to promote them?" Zhonggong asked.

The Master replied, "Promote those that you do recognize with the confidence that others will not spurn those that you do not."

13.4 Fan Chi wanted to learn to farm. "A farmer would serve you better," said the Master. He wanted to learn to grow vegetables. "A vegetable grower would serve you better," said the Master. When Fan Chi had left, the Master said, "This Fan Chi is certainly a petty person! If their superiors cherished the observance of ritual propriety (*li*), none among the common people would dare be disrespectful; if their superiors cherished appropriate conduct (*yi*), none among the common people would dare be disobedient; if their superiors cherished making good on their word (*xin*), none among the common people would dare be duplicitous. This being the case, the common people from all quarters would flock here with babies strapped to their backs. What need is there to talk of farming?"

15.17 The Master said, "Those who would get together all day long and, occupying themselves with witty remarks, never once get to the topic of appropriate conduct (*yi*)—such persons are hard to deal with."

15.18 The Master said, "Having a sense of appropriate conduct (*yi*) as one's basic disposition (*zhi*), developing it in observing ritual propriety (*li*), expressing it with modesty, and consummating it in making good on one's word (*xin*): this then is an exemplary person (*junzi*)."

15.19 The Master said, "Exemplary persons (*junzi*) are distressed by their own lack of ability, not by the failure of others to acknowledge them."

15.20 The Master said, "Exemplary persons (*junzi*) despise the thought of ending their days without having established a name."

15.21 The Master said, "Exemplary persons (*junzi*) make demands on themselves, while petty persons make demands on others."

15.22 The Master said, "Exemplary persons (*junzi*) are self-possessed but not contentious; they gather together with others, but do not form cliques."

15.23 The Master said, "Exemplary persons (*junzi*) do not promote others because of what they say, nor do they reject what is said because of who says it."

16.4 Confucius said, "Having three kinds of friends will be a source of personal improvement; having three other kinds of friends will be a source of personal injury. One stands to be improved by friends who are true, who make good on their word, and who are broadly informed; one stands to be injured by friends who are ingratiating, who feign compliance, and who are glib talkers."

16.5 Confucius said, "Finding enjoyment in three kinds of activities will be a source of personal improvement; finding enjoyment in three other kinds of activities will be a source of personal injury. One stands to be improved by the enjoyment found in attuning oneself to the rhythms of ritual propriety (*li*) and music (*yue*), by the enjoyment found in talking about what others do well (*shan*), and by the enjoyment found in having a circle of many friends of superior character (*xian*); one stands to be injured by finding enjoyment in being arrogant, by finding enjoyment in dissolute diversions, and by finding enjoyment in the easy life."

16.6 Confucius said, "There are three mistakes that are easily made in attendance on one's lord: to speak first without waiting for the lord to speak is called being rash; to not speak when you should speak up is called holding back; to speak up without taking into account the lord's countenance is called being blind."

16.7 Confucius said, "Exemplary persons (*junzi*) have three kinds of conduct that they guard against: when young and vigorous, they guard against licentiousness; in their prime when their vigor is at its height, they guard against conflict; in their old age when their vigor is declining, they guard against acquisitiveness."

16.8 Confucius said, "Exemplary persons (*junzi*) hold three things in awe: the propensities of *tian* (*tianming*), persons in high station, and the words of the sages (*shengren*). Petty persons, knowing nothing of the propensities of *tian*, do not hold it in awe; they are unduly familiar with persons in high station, and ridicule the words of the sages."

16.9 Confucius said, "Knowledge (*zhi*) acquired through a natural propensity for it is its highest level; knowledge acquired through study is the next highest; something learned in response to difficulties encountered is again the next highest. But those among the common people who do not learn even when vexed with difficulties—they are at the bottom of the heap."

16.10 Confucius said, "Exemplary persons (*junzi*) always keep nine things in mind: in looking they think about clarity, in hearing they think about acuity, in countenance they think about cordiality, in bearing and attitude they think about deference, in speaking they think about doing their utmost (*zhong*), in conducting affairs they think about due respect, in entertaining doubts they think about the proper questions to ask, in anger they think about regret, in sight of gain they think about appropriate conduct (*yi*)."

17.8 The Master said, "Zilu, have you heard of the six flaws that can accompany the six desirable qualities of character?"

"No, I have not," replied Zilu.

"Sit down," said the Master, "and I'll tell you about them. The flaw in being fond of acting authoritatively (*ren*) without equal regard for learning is that you will be easily duped; the flaw in being fond of acting wisely (*zhi*) without equal regard for learning is that it leads to self-indulgence; the flaw in being fond of making good on one's word (*xin*) without equal regard for learning is that it leads one into harm's way; the flaw in being fond of candor without equal regard for learning is that it leads to rudeness; the flaw in being fond of boldness without equal regard for learning is that it leads to unruliness; the flaw in being fond of firmness without equal regard for learning is that it leads to rashness."

17.9 The Master said, "My young friends, why don't any of you study the *Songs*? Reciting the *Songs* can arouse your sensibilities, strengthen your powers of observation, enhance your ability to get on with others, and sharpen your critical skills. Close at hand it enables you to serve your father, and away at court it enables you to serve your lord. It instills in you a broad vocabulary for making distinctions in the world around you."

MENCIUS

The greatest ancient disciple of Confucius was Mencius, originally called Meng Tzu (about 372–289 B.C.). He is titled in the official Confucian literature as second in wisdom (after Confucius).

Mencius was born in the same province as Confucius, modern Shantung. He was a pupil of the grandson of Confucius. Like Confucius, he traveled a lot to offer his service and advice to rulers. Like Confucius, Mencius was a great professional teacher. His talks with students are collected in the *Book of Men-*

cius, which is recognized as the most important part of the Confucian orthodoxy and, along with Confucius's *Analects, The Great Learning*, and *The Doctrine of the Mean* (the last two are believed to be the works of Confucius' pupils or his grandson, Tzu Ssu), is included in the "Four Books," which formed the basis of the Chinese service examinations for about six centuries.

Though Mencius's teachings were derived from Confucius, his views differ in some very important respects. The greatest difference between Mencius and Confucius is in their understanding of human nature. Mencius argues that human nature is originally and essentially good, possessing the "Four Beginnings": humanity (*jen*), righteousness (*yi*), propriety (*li*), and wisdom or the innate knowledge.

Mencius's doctrine of innate knowledge influenced tremendously the further development of Confucianism. He considered "heart" to be the main organ of knowledge, superior to the sense organs, and placed great emphasis on conscience and moral intuition.

The core of Mencius's political theory is the idea of "humane government." He treated justice as the primary political virtue and understood it in terms of respect for the rights of others.

From Mencius

From Mencius. *Translated with an introduction by D. C. Lau. Harmondsworth: Penguin Books, 1970.*

Book II. Part A

6. Mencius said, "No man is devoid of a heart sensitive to the suffering of others. Such a sensitive heart was possessed by the Former Kings and this manifested itself in compassionate government. With such a sensitive heart behind compassionate government, it was as easy to rule the Empire as rolling it on your palm.

"My reason for saying that no man is devoid of a heart sensitive to the suffering of others is this. Suppose a man were, all of a sudden, to see a young child on the verge of falling into a well. He would certainly be moved to compassion, not because he wanted to get in the good graces of the parents, nor because he wished to win the praise of his fellow villagers or friends, nor yet because he disliked the cry of the child. From this it can be seen that whoever is devoid of the heart of compassion is not human, whoever is devoid of the heart of shame is not human, whoever is devoid of the heart of courtesy and modesty is not human, and whoever is devoid of the heart of right and wrong is not human. The heart of compassion is the germ of benevolence; the heart of shame, of dutifulness; the heart of courtesy and modesty, of observance of the rites; the heart of right and wrong, of wisdom. Man has these four germs just as he has four limbs. For a man possessing these four germs to deny his own potentialities is for him to cripple himself; for him to deny the potentialities of his prince is for him to cripple his prince. If a man is able to develop all these four germs that he possesses, it will be like a fire starting up or a spring coming through. When these are fully developed, he can take under his protection the whole realm within the Four Seas, but if he fails to develop them, he will not be able even to serve his parents."

7. Mencius said, "Is the maker of arrows really more unfeeling than the maker of armor? He is afraid lest he should fail to harm people, whereas the maker of armor is afraid lest he should fail to protect them. The case is similar with the sorcerer-doctor and the coffin-maker. For this reason one cannot be too careful in the choice of one's calling.

"Confucius said, 'The best neighborhood is where benevolence is to be found. Not to live in such a neighborhood when one has the choice cannot by any means be considered wise.'[2] Benevolence is the high honor bestowed by Heaven and the peaceful abode of man. Not to be benevolent when nothing stands in the way is to show a lack of wisdom. A man neither benevolent nor wise, devoid of courtesy and dutifulness, is a slave. A slave ashamed of serving is like a maker of bows ashamed of making bows, or a maker of arrows ashamed of making arrows. If one is ashamed, there is no better remedy than to practice benevolence. Benevolence is like archery: an archer makes sure his stance is correct before letting fly the arrow, and if he fails to hit the mark, he does not hold it against his victor. He simply seeks the cause within himself."

8. Mencius said, "When anyone told him that he had made a mistake, Tzu-lu was delighted. When he heard a fine saying, Yü bowed low before the speaker. The Great Shun went even further. He was ever ready to fall into line with others, giving up his own ways for theirs, and glad to take from others that by which he could do good. From the time he was a farmer, a potter, and a fisherman to the time he became Emperor, there was nothing he did that he did not take from others. To take from others that by which one can do good is to help them do good. Hence there is nothing more important to a gentleman than helping others do good."

9. Mencius said, "Po Yi would serve only the right prince and befriend only the right man. He would not take his place at the court of an evil man, nor would he converse with him. For him to do so would be like sitting in mud and pitch wearing a court cap and gown. He pushed his dislike for evil to the extent that,

if a fellow-villager in his company had his cap awry, he would walk away without even a backward look, as if afraid of being defiled. Hence even when a feudal lord made advances in the politest language, he would repel them. He repelled them simply because it was beneath him to go to the feudal lord.

"Liu Hsia Hui, on the other hand, was not ashamed of a prince with a tarnished reputation, neither did he disdain a modest post. When in office, he did not conceal his own talent, and always acted in accordance with the Way. When he was passed over he harbored no grudge, nor was he distressed even in straitened circumstances. That is why he said,[3] 'You are you and I am I. Even if you were to be stark naked by my side, how could you defile me?' Consequently, he was in no hurry to take himself away, and looked perfectly at ease in the other man's company, and would stay when pressed. He stayed when pressed, simply because it was beneath him to insist on leaving."

Mencius added, "Po Yi was too straight-laced; Liu Hsia Hui was not dignified enough. A gentleman would follow neither extreme."

Book II. Part B

1. Mencius said, "Heaven's favorable weather is less important than Earth's advantageous terrain, and Earth's advantageous terrain is less important than human unity. Suppose you laid siege to a city with inner walls measuring, on each side, three *li* and outer walls measuring seven *li*, and you failed to take it. Now in the course of the siege, there must have been, at one time or another, favorable weather, and in spite of that you failed to take the city. This shows that favorable weather is less important than advantageous terrain. Sometimes a city has to be abandoned in spite of the height of its walls and depth of its moat, the quality of arms and abundance of food supplies. This shows that advantageous terrain is less important than human unity.

"Hence it is said, It is not by boundaries that the people are confined, it is not by difficult terrain that a state is rendered secure, and it is not by superiority of arms that the Empire is kept in awe. One who has the Way will have many to support him; one who has not the Way will have few to support him. In extreme cases, the latter will find even his own flesh and blood turning against him while the former will have the whole Empire at his behest. Hence either a gentleman does not go to war or else he is sure of victory, for he will have the whole Empire at his behest, while his opponent will have even his own flesh and blood turning against him."

2. Mencius was about to go to court to see the King when a messenger came from the King with the message, "I was to have come to see you, but I am suffering from a chill and cannot be exposed to the wind. In the morning I shall,

however, be holding court. I wonder if I shall have the opportunity of seeing you then." To this Mencius replied, "Unfortunately, I too am ill and shall be unable to come to court."

The next day, Mencius went on a visit of condolence to the Tung-kuo family. Kung-sun Ch'ou said, "Yesterday you excused yourself on the ground of illness, yet today you go on a visit of condolence. This is, perhaps, ill-advised."

"I was ill yesterday, but I am recovered today. Why should I not go on a visit of condolence?"

The King sent someone to inquire after Mencius' illness; and a doctor came. Meng Chung-tzu in reply to the inquiry said, "Yesterday when the King's summons came, Mencius was ill and was unable to go to court. Today he is somewhat better and has hastened to court. But I am not sure if, in his condition, he will get there."

Then several men were sent to waylay Mencius with the message, "Do not, under any circumstances, come home but go straight to court."

Mencius was forced to go and spend the night with the Ching-ch'ou family.

"Within the family," said Ching Tzu, "the relationship between father and son is the most important, while outside, it is that between prince and subject. The former exemplifies love, the latter respect. I have seen the King show you respect, but I have yet to see you show the King respect."

"What a thing to say! No one in Ch'i talks to the King about benevolence and rightness. Do you think it is because they do not think these beautiful? It is simply because, in their hearts, they say to themselves something to this effect, 'How can we talk to *him* about benevolence and rightness?' There is nothing more lacking in respect than that. I have never dared put before the King anything short of the way of Yao and Shun. That is why no man from Ch'i respects the King as much as I."

"No," said Ching Tzu. "That is not what I had in mind. According to the rites, 'When summoned by one's father, one should not answer, I am coming. When summoned by one's prince, one should not wait for the horses to be harnessed.' You were, in the first instance, about to go to court, but on being summoned by the King you changed your mind. This would seem to be contrary to the rites."

"Is that what you meant? Tseng Tzu said, 'The wealth of Chin and Ch'u cannot be rivalled. They may have their wealth, but I have my benevolence; they may have their exalted rank, but I have my integrity. In what way do I suffer in the comparison?' If this is not right, Tseng Tzu would not have said it. It must be a possible way of looking at the matter. There are three things which are acknowledged by the world to be exalted: rank, age, and virtue. At court, rank is supreme; in the village, age; but for assisting the world and ruling over the people it is virtue. How can a man, on the strength of the possession of one of these, treat the other two with condescension? Hence a prince who is to achieve great things must have subjects he does not summon. If he wants to consult them, he goes to them. If he does not honor virtue and delight in the Way in such a manner, he is not worthy of being helped towards the achievement of great things. Take the case of Yi Yin. T'ang had him first as a tutor and only afterwards did he treat him as a minister. As a result, T'ang was able to become a true King without much effort. Again, take the case of Kuan Chung. Duke Huan treated him in exactly the same way and, as a result, was able to become a leader of the feudal lords without much effort. Today there are many states, all equal in size and virtue, none being able to dominate the others. This is simply because the rulers are given to employing those they can teach rather than those from whom they can learn. T'ang did not dare summon Yi Yin, nor did Duke Huan dare summon Kuan Chung. Even Kuan Chung could not be summoned, much less someone who would not be a Kuan Chung."

3. Duke Wen of T'eng asked about government.

"The business of the people," said Mencius, "must be attended to without delay. The *Book of Odes* says,

> In the day time they go for grass;
> At night they make it into ropes.
> They hasten to repair the roof,
> Then they begin sowing the crops.

This is the way of the common people. Those with constant means of support will have constant hearts, while those without constant means will not have constant hearts. Lacking constant hearts, they will go astray and get into excesses, stopping at nothing. To punish them after they have fallen foul of the law is to set a trap for the people. How can a benevolent man in authority allow himself to set a trap for the people? Hence a good ruler is always respectful and thrifty, courteous and humble, and takes from the people no more than is prescribed. Yang Hu said, 'If one's aim is wealth one cannot be benevolent; if one's aim is benevolence one cannot be wealthy.'

"In the Hsia Dynasty, each family was given fifty *mu* of land, and the *'kung'* method of taxation was used; in the Yin, each family was given seventy *mu* and the *'chu'* method was used; in the Chou, each family was given a hundred *mu* and the *'ch'e'* method was used. In fact, all three amounted to a taxation of one in ten. *'Ch'e'* means 'commonly practiced'; *'chu'* means 'to lend help.' Lung Tzu said, 'In administering land, there is no better method than *chu* and no worse than *kung*.' With the *kung* method, the payment due is calculated on the average yield over a number of years. In good years when rice is so plentiful that it goes to waste, the people are no more heavily taxed, though this would mean no hardship; while in bad years, when there is not enough to spare for fertilizing the fields, the full quota is insisted upon. If he who is father and mother to the people makes it necessary for them to borrow because they do not get enough to minister to the needs of their parents in spite of having toiled incessantly all the year round, and causes the old and young to be abandoned in the gutter, wherein is he father and mother to the people?

"Hereditary emolument as a matter of fact is already practised in T'eng.

"The *Book of Odes* says,

> The rain falls on our public land,
> And so also on our private land.

There is 'public land' only when *chu* is practiced. From this we see that even the Chou practiced *chu*.

"'*Hsiang*,' '*hsü*,' '*hsüeh*' and '*hsiao*' were set up for the purpose of education. '*Hsiang*' means 'rearing,' '*hsiao*' means 'teaching' and '*hsü*' means 'archery.' In the Hsia Dynasty it was called '*hsiao*,' in the Yin '*hsü*' and in the Chou '*hsiang*,' while '*hsüeh*' was a name common to all the Three Dynasties. They all serve to make the people understand human relationships. When it is clear that those in authority understand human relationships, the people will be affectionate. Should a true King arise, he is certain to take this as his model. Thus he who practices this will be tutor to a true King.

"The *Book of Odes* says,

> Though Chou is an old state,
> Its Mandate is new.

This refers to King Wen. If you can put heart into your practice you would also be able to renew your state."

The Duke sent Pi Chan to ask about the well-field system.

"Your prince," said Mencius, "is going to practice benevolent government and has chosen you for this mission. You must do your best. Benevolent government must begin with land demarcation. When boundaries are not properly drawn, the division of land according to the well-field system and the yield of grain used for paying officials cannot be equitable. For this reason, despotic rulers and corrupt officials always neglect the boundaries. Once the boundaries are correctly fixed, there will be no difficulty in settling the distribution of land and the determination of emolument.

"T'eng is limited in territory. Nevertheless, there will be men in authority and there will be the common people. Without the former, there would be none to rule over the latter; without the latter, there would be none to support the former. I suggest that in the country the tax should be one in nine, using the method of *chu*, but in the capital it should be one in ten, to be levied in kind. From Ministers downwards, every official should have fifty *mu* of land for sacrificial purposes. In ordinary households, every extra man is to be given another twenty-five *mu*. Neither in burying the dead, nor in changing his abode, does a man go beyond the confines of his village. If those who own land within each *ching* befriend one another both at home and abroad, help each other to keep watch, and succor each other in illness, they will live in love and harmony. A *ching* is a piece of land measuring one *li* square, and each *ching* consists of 900 *mu*. Of these, the central plot of 100 *mu* belongs to the state, while the other eight plots of 100 *mu* each are held by eight families who share the duty of caring for the plot owned by the state. Only when they have done this duty dare they turn to their own affairs. This is what sets the common people apart.

"This is a rough outline. As for embellishments, I leave them to your prince and yourself."

4. There was a man by the name of Hsü Hsing who preached the teachings of Shen Nung. He came to T'eng from Ch'u, went up to the gate and told Duke Wen, "I, a man from distant parts, have heard that you, my lord, practice benevolent government. I wish to be given a place to live and become one of your subjects."

The Duke gave him a place.

His followers, numbering several score, all wore unwoven hemp, and lived by making sandals and mats.

Ch'en Hsiang and his brother Hsin, both followers of Ch'en Liang, came to T'eng from Sung, carrying plows on their backs. "We have heard," said they, "that you, my lord, practice the government of the sages. In that case you must yourself be a sage. We wish to be the subjects of a sage."

Ch'en Hsiang met Hsü Hsing and was delighted with his teachings, so he abjured what he had learned before and became a follower of Hsü Hsing.

Ch'en Hsiang saw Mencius and cited the words of Hsü Hsing. "The prince of T'eng is a truly good and wise ruler. However, he has never been taught the Way. To earn his keep a good and wise ruler shares the work of tilling the land with his people. He rules while cooking his own meals. Now T'eng has granaries and treasuries. This is for the prince to inflict hardship on the people in order to keep himself. How can he be a good and wise prince?"

"Does Hsü Tzu only eat grain he has grown himself?" asked Mencius.

"Yes."

"Does Hsü Tzu only wear cloth he has woven himself?"

"No. He wears unwoven hemp."

"Does Hsü Tzu wear a cap?"

"Yes."

"What kind of cap does he wear?"

"Plain raw silk."

"Does he weave it himself?"

"No. He trades grain for it."

"Why does Hsü Tzu not weave it himself?"

"Because it interferes with his work in the fields."

"Does Hsü Tzu use an iron pot and an earthenware steamer for cooking rice and iron implements for plowing the fields?"

"Yes."

"Does he make them himself?"

"No. He trades grain for them."

"To trade grain for implements is not to inflict hardship on the potter and the blacksmith. The potter and the blacksmith, for their part, also trade their wares for grain. In doing this, surely they are not inflicting hardship on the farmer either. Why does Hsü Tzu not be a potter and a blacksmith as well so that he can get everything he needs from his own house? Why does he indulge in such multifarious trading with men who practice the hundred crafts? Why does Hsü Tzu put up with so much bother?"

"It is naturally impossible to combine the work of tilling the land with that of a hundred different crafts."

"Now, is ruling the Empire such an exception that it can be combined with the work of tilling the land? There are affairs of great men, and there are affairs of small men. Moreover, it is necessary for each man to use the products of all the hundred crafts. If everyone must make everything he uses, the Empire will be led along the path of incessant toil. Hence it is said, 'There are those who use their minds and there are those who use their muscles. The former rule; the latter are ruled. Those who rule are supported by those who are ruled.' This is a principle accepted by the whole Empire."

TAOISM

The second in importance among the classical school of Chinese philosophy, Taoism derives its name from *Tao*, a central notion in Chinese culture. In

Confucianism and other non-Taoist trends of thought, *Tao* means a system of moral truth. In Taoism it is one, eternal, nameless, spontaneous, that which is the beginning of all things and the way in which they exist. When *Tao* is possessed by an individual thing, it becomes its virtue (*te*). Tao is the basis of the ideal life of the individual as well as of the society ruled by the ideal type of government. As a way of life it means simplicity, spontaneity, nonaction—letting nature take its own course.

Taoist philosophy is summed up at its best in two classics: the *Lao Tzu* (or *Tao Te Ching*) and the *Chuang Tzu*. The author of the first is believed to be Lao Tzu, in fact, the founder of Taoism, who lived in the sixth century B.C. Though *Tao Te Ching* is the smallest in size among the Chinese classics (about 5,250 characters), it has been commented on more than any other. There is a great controversy concerning Lao Tzu, whether it is a private name, a family name, or the title (literally meaning "an Old Philosopher").

The second Taoist classic, mentioned above, is named after its author Chuang Tzu (about 399–295 B.C.) who gave to Taoism a mystical turn. In *Chuang Tzu* the Tao is absolutely transcendental. Its dynamic nature reveals itself in the constant flux, thus making all things identical. At the same time, *Chuang Tzu*, in comparison with *Lao Tzu*, makes stronger emphasis on the individual, on particularity, by affirming that everything follows its own nature.

Chuang Tzu differs from Confucianism more than Lao Tzu. As Chu Hsi, the leading Neo-Confucianist, will say later on: "Lao Tzu still wanted to do something, but Chuang Tzu did not want to do anything at all." While Confucianism called people to develop their own nature and to participate in the creativity of Nature, Chuang Tzu insisted on the necessity of nourishing one's nature and enjoying Nature. Chuang Tzu's approach to learning also sharply differed from that of Confucianism. There is no wonder then that Chuang Tzu was strongly criticized by Confucianists. Still, its influence has been very significant, in particular on the emergence of Zen Buddhism, on the transformation of Confucianism into Neo-Confucianism, and on the development of Chinese poetry and arts.

From Lao Tzu

From The Lao Tzu (Tao Te Ching). *Reprinted from* A Source Book in Chinese Philosophy. *Translated by Wing-Tsit Chan. Princeton, N.J.: Princeton University Press, 1963.*

32. Tao is eternal and has no name.
    Though its simplicity seems insignificant, none in the world can master it.

If kings and barons would hold on to it, all things would submit to them spontaneously.
Heaven and earth unite to drip sweet dew.
Without the command of men, it drips evenly over all.
As soon as there were regulations and institutions, there were names (differentiation of things).
As soon as there are names, know that it is time to stop.
It is by knowing when to stop that one can be free from danger.
Analogically, Tao in the world (where everything is embraced by it), may be compared to rivers and streams running into the sea.

33. He who knows others is wise;
He who knows himself is enlightened.
He who conquers others has physical strength.
He who conquers himself is strong.
He who is contented is rich.
He who acts with vigor has will.
He who does not lose his place (with Tao) will endure.
He who dies but does not really perish enjoys long life.

34. The Great Tao flows everywhere.
It may go left or right.
All things depend on it for life, and it does not turn away from them.
It accomplishes its task, but does not claim credit for it.
It clothes and feeds all things but does not claim to be master over them.
Always without desires, it may be called The Small.
All things come to it and it does not master them; it may be called The Great.
Therefore (the sage) never strives himself for the great, and thereby the great is achieved.

35. Hold fast to the great form (Tao),
And all the world will come.
They come and will encounter no harm;
But enjoy comfort, peace, and health.
When there are music and dainties,
Passing strangers will stay.
But the words uttered by Tao,
How insipid and tasteless!
We look at Tao; it is imperceptible.

We listen to it; it is inaudible.
We use it; it is inexhaustible.

36. In order to contract,
 It is necessary first to expand.
In order to weaken,
 It is necessary first to strengthen.
In order to destroy,
 It is necessary first to promote.
In order to grasp,
 It is necessary first to give.
This is called subtle light.
The weak and the tender overcome the hard and the strong.
Fish should not be taken away from water.
And sharp weapons of the state should not be displayed to the people.

37. Tao invariably takes no action, and yet there is nothing left undone.
If kings and barons can keep it, all things will transform spontaneously.
If, after transformation, they should desire to be active,
I would restrain them with simplicity, which has no name.
Simplicity, which has no name, is free of desires.
Being free of desires, it is tranquil.
And the world will be at peace of its own accord.

38. The man of superior virtue is not (conscious of) his virtue,
And in this way he really possesses virtue.
The man of inferior virtue never loses (sight of) his virtue,
And in this way he loses his virtue.
The man of superior virtue takes no action, but has no ulterior motive to do so.
The man of inferior virtue takes action, and has an ulterior motive to do so.
The man of superior humanity takes action, but has no ulterior motive to do so.
The man of superior righteousness takes action, and has an ulterior motive to do so.
The man of superior propriety takes action,
And when people do not respond to it, he will stretch his arms and force it on them.
Therefore, only when Tao is lost does the doctrine of virtue arise.
When virtue is lost, only then does the doctrine of humanity arise.

When humanity is lost, only then does the doctrine of righteousness arise.
When righteousness is lost, only then does the doctrine of propriety arise.
Now, propriety is a superficial expression of loyalty and faithfulness, and the beginning of disorder.
Those who are the first to know have the flowers (appearance) of Tao but are the beginning of ignorance.
For this reason the great man dwells in the thick (substantial), and does not rest with the thin (superficial).
He dwells in the fruit (reality), and does not rest with the flower (appearance).
Therefore he rejects the one, and accepts the other.

39. Of old those that obtained the One:
Heaven obtained the One and became clear.
Earth obtained the One and became tranquil.
The spiritual beings obtained the One and became divine.
The valley obtained the One and became full.
The myriad things obtained the One and lived and grew.
Kings and barons obtained the One and became rulers of the empire.
What made them so is the One.
If heaven had not thus become clear,
It would soon crack.
If the earth had not thus become tranquil,
It would soon be shaken.
If the spiritual beings had not thus become divine,
They would soon wither away.
If the valley had not thus become full,
It would soon become exhausted.
If the myriad things had not thus lived and grown,
They would soon become extinct.
If kings and barons had not thus become honorable and high in position,
They would soon fall.
Therefore humble station is the basis of honor.
The low is the foundation of the high.
For this reason kings and barons call themselves the orphaned, the lonely ones, the unworthy.
Is this not regarding humble station as the basis of honor?
Is it not?

Therefore enumerate all the parts of a chariot as you may, and you still have no chariot.
Rather than jingle like the jade,
Rumble like the rocks.

40. Reversion is the action of Tao.
Weakness is the function of Tao.
All things in the world come from being.
And being comes from non-being.

41. When the highest type of men hear Tao,
They diligently practice it.
When the average type of men hear Tao,
They half believe in it.
When the lowest type of men hear Tao,
They laugh heartily at it.
If they did not laugh at it, it would not be Tao.
Therefore there is the established saying:
The Tao which is bright appears to be dark.
The Tao which goes forward appears to fall backward.
The Tao which is level appears uneven.
Great virtue appears like a valley (hollow).
Great purity appears like disgrace.
Far-reaching virtue appears as if insufficient.
Solid virtue appears as if unsteady.
True substance appears to be changeable.
The great square has no corners.
The great implement (or talent) is slow to finish (or mature).
Great music sounds faint.
Great form has no shape.
Tao is hidden and nameless.
Yet it is Tao alone that skillfully provides for all and brings them to perfection.

42. Tao produced the One.
The One produced the two.
The two produced the three.
And the three produced the ten thousand things.
The ten thousand things carry the *yin* and embrace the *yang*, and through the blending of the material force (*ch'i*) they achieve harmony.

People hate to be the orphaned, the lonely ones, and the unworthy.
And yet kings and lords call themselves by these names.
Therefore it is often the case that things gain by losing and lose by gaining.
What others have taught, I teach also:
"Violent and fierce people do not die a natural death."
I shall make this the father (basis or starting point) of my teaching.

43. The softest things in the world overcome the hardest things in the world.
Non-being penetrates that in which there is no space.
Through this I know the advantage of taking no action.
Few in the world can understand teaching without words and the advantage of taking no action.

44. Which does one love more, fame or one's own life?
Which is more valuable, one's own life or wealth?
Which is worse, gain or loss?
Therefore he who has lavish desires will spend extravagantly.
He who hoards most will lose heavily.
He who is contented suffers no disgrace.
He who knows when to stop is free from danger.
Therefore he can long endure.

45. What is most perfect seems to be incomplete;
But its utility is unimpaired.
What is most full seems to be empty;
But its usefulness is inexhaustible.
What is most straight seems to be crooked.
The greatest skills seems to be clumsy.
The greatest eloquence seems to stutter.

71. To know that you do not know is the best.
To pretend to know when you do not know is a disease.
Only when one recognizes this disease as a disease can one be free from the disease.
The sage is free from the disease.
Because he recognizes this disease to be disease, he is free from it.

72. When the people do not fear what is dreadful,
Then what is greatly dreadful will descend on them.

Do not reduce the living space of their dwellings.
Do not oppress their lives.
It is because you do not oppress them that they are not oppressed.
Therefore the sage knows himself but does not show himself.
He loves himself but does not exalt himself.
Therefore he rejects the one but accepts the other.

73. He who is brave in daring will be killed.
He who is brave in not daring will live.
Of these two, one is advantageous and one is harmful.
Who knows why Heaven dislikes what it dislikes?
Even the sage considers it a difficult question.
The Way of Heaven does not compete, and yet it skillfully achieves victory.
It does not speak, and yet it skillfully responds to things.
It comes to you without your invitation.
It is not anxious about things and yet it plans well.
Heaven's net is indeed vast.
Though its meshes are wide, it misses nothing.

From Chuang Tzu

From The Chuang Tzu. *Reprinted from* A Source Book in Chinese Philosophy. *Translated by Wing-Tsit Chan. Princeton, N.J.: Princeton University Press, 1963.*

C. Additional Selections

*1. **The Nature and Reality of Tao*** In the great beginning, there was non-being. It had neither being nor name. The One originates from it; it has oneness but not yet physical form. When things obtain it and come into existence, that is called virtue (which gives them their individual character). That which is formless is divided [into *yin* and *yang*], and from the very beginning going on with out interruption is called destiny (*ming*, fate). Through movement and rest it produces all things. When things are produced in accordance with the principle (*li*) of life, there is physical form. When the physical form embodies and preserves the spirit so that all activities follow their own specific principles, that is nature. By cultivating one's nature one will return to virtue. When virtue is perfect, one will be one with the beginning. Being one with the beginning, one becomes vacuous (*hsü*, receptive to all), and being vacuous, one becomes great. One will then be united with the sound and breath of things. When one is united with the sound and breath of things, one is then united with the universe. This unity is intimate and seems to be stupid and foolish. This is called profound and secret virtue, this is complete harmony. (ch. 12, NHCC, 5:8b–9b)

2. Tao Everywhere Tung-kuo Tzu asked Chuang Tzu, "What is called Tao—where is it?"

"It is everywhere," replied Chuang Tzu.

Tung-kuo Tzu said, "It will not do unless you are more specific."

"It is in the ant," said Chuang Tzu.

"Why go so low down?"

"It is in the weeds."

"Why even lower?"

"It is in a potsherd."

"Why still lower?"

"It is in the excrement and urine," said Chuang Tzu. Tung-kuo gave no response.

"Sir," said Chuang Tzu. "Your question does not touch the essential. When inspector Huo asked the superintendent of markets about the fatness of pigs, the tests were always made in parts less and less likely to be fat. Do not insist on any particular thing. Nothing escapes from Tao. Such is perfect Tao, and so is great speech. The three, Complete, Entire, and All, differ in name but are the same in actuality. They all designate (*chih*, mark) the One." (ch. 22, NHCC, 7:49a–50a)

3. Constant Flux "Is the sky revolving around? Is the earth remaining still? Are the sun and the moon pursuing each other? Who prescribes this? Who directs this? Who has the leisure to push them to go on? Is there perhaps some mechanical arrangement so that they cannot help moving? Or is it perhaps that they keep revolving and cannot stop themselves? Do clouds cause the rain or does the rain cause the clouds? Who makes them rise and sends them down? Who has the leisure and delights in promoting such things? The wind rises from the north. It now blows east and now west, and now it whirls upward. Who is sucking and blowing it alternately? Who has the leisure to shake it about like this? Please tell me why?"

Wu-hsien waved to him and said, "Come, let me tell you. There are in nature the six ultimates and five constancies. When rulers follow them there will be order. When they disobey them, there will be calamity." (ch. 14, NHCC, 5:35a–36a)

4. Evolution All species have originative or moving power (*chi*). When they obtain water, they become small organisms like silk. In a place bordering water and land, they become lichens. Thriving on the bank, they become moss. On the fertile soil they become weeds. The roots of these weeds become worms, and their leaves become butterflies. Suddenly the butterfly is transformed into an insect, which is born under the stove (for its heat), and which has the appearance of having its skin shed. Its name is call *chü-t'o*. After a thousand days, *chü-t'o* becomes a bird called *kan-yü–ku*. This spittle of the *kan-yü–ku* becomes an insect called *ssu-mi*. The *ssu-mi* becomes a wine fly, which produces the insect called *i-lu*. The insect *huang-k'uang* produces the insect called *chiu-yu*. Mosquitoes come from the rotten insects called *huan*. The plant *yang-hsi* paired with bamboo which for a long time has had no shoot, produces the insect called *ch'ing-ning*. The *ch'ing-ning* produces the insect called *ch'eng*, *ch'eng* produces the horse, and the horse produces men. Man again goes back into the originative process of Nature. All things come from the originative process of Nature and return to the originative process of Nature. (ch. 18, NHCC, 6:36a–b)

*5. **Tao as Transformation and One*** Although the universe is vast, its transformation is uniform. Although the myriad things are many, their order is one. Although people are numerous, their ruler is the sovereign. The sovereign traces his origin to virtue (*te*, individual and essential character), and attains his perfection in Nature. Therefore it is said that in the cases of sovereigns of high antiquity, no [unnatural] action (*wu-wei*) was undertaken and the empire was in order. That was because of their natural virtue. When speech is seen through the point of Tao, the name of the sovereign of the world becomes correct. When functions and ranks are seen through Tao, the distinction between the ruler and the minister becomes clear. When ability is seen through Tao, the offices of the empire become regulated. When all things in general are seen through Tao, the response of things to each other becomes complete. Therefore it is virtue that penetrates Heaven and Earth, and it is Tao that operates in all things. Government by the ruler means human affairs, and when ability is applied to creative activities, it means skill. Skill is commanded by human affairs, human affairs are commanded by the distinction of functions, distinction is commanded by virtue, virtue is commanded by Tao, and Tao is commanded by Nature. Therefore it is said that ancient rulers of empires had no [selfish] desires and the empire enjoyed sufficiency. They undertook no [unnatural] action and all things were transformed. They were deep and tranquil and all their people were calm. The *Record* says, "When one is identified with the One, all things will be complete with him. When he reaches the point of having no subjective feelings, spiritual beings will submit to him."

The Grand Master said, "Tao covers and supports all things. How overflowingly great! The ruler should cast away his [selfish] mind. To act without taking an [unnatural] action means Nature. To speak without any action means virtue. To love people and benefit all things means humanity (*jen*). To identify with all without each losing his own identity means greatness. To behave without purposely showing any superiority means broadness. To possess an infinite variety means richness. Therefore to adhere to virtue is called discipline. To realize virtue means strength. To be in accord with Tao means completeness. And not to yield to material things is called perfection. If a superior man understands these ten points, he surely makes up his mind and all the world will come to him like rushing water." (ch. 12, NHCC, 5:1a–3a)

THE MOHIST SCHOOL

Historically, the ancient period of Chinese philosophy (until 221 B.C.) is often called the time of the "Hundred Schools." The most prominent among them were the Confucians, the Taoists, the Mohists, the Logicians, the Yin Yang school, and the Legalists. Eventually only the first two schools maintained their influence, being joined by Buddhism after the tenth century. In the very early period, however, it was the Mohists who presented the main opposition to the Confucians.

The Mohist school derives its name from the founder—Mo Tzu (about 468–376 B.C.). Mohist views diametrically oppose Confucianism. While the latter based its ethics on the concept of humanity (*jen*) and argued that the good life was valuable in itself, the main ethical category for the Mohists was righteousness (*yi*) interpreted in a very utilitarian way: morality is what brings benefit, what maximizes the good.

Of all the ancient Chinese thinkers only the Mohists placed ethics on a religious foundation by directly linking righteousness or justice to the will of Heaven. The followers of Mo Tzu differed from the Confucians in their approach to human relations. The first propagated the doctrine of universal love in contrast to the Confucian notion of love with distinction: our attitude toward the other people depends on who we are, who they are, and how they relate to us. The Mohist concept of universal love presupposed their strong condemnation of war.

Besides ethical teachings, the Mohists developed a specific epistemology, a system of definition and argumentation. However, philosophically Mohism lacked a certain profoundness and hence maintained its importance only temporarily. It practically disappeared from the intellectual scene after the third century B.C. Interest in Mohism appeared once again in modern times, most probably because of its pragmatic, utilitarian spirit and its resemblance to Christian beliefs in the will of God and universal love.

From Mo Tzu

Universal Love. *Reprinted from* Basic Writings of Mo Tzu, Hsün Tzu, and Han Fei Tzu. *Translated by Burton Watson. New York: Columbia University Press, 1964.*

Part III (Section 16)

Mo Tzu said: It is the business of the benevolent man to try to promote what is beneficial to the world and to eliminate what is harmful. Now at the present time, what brings the greatest harm to the world? Great states attacking small ones, great families overthrowing small ones, the strong oppressing the weak, the many harrying the few, the cunning deceiving the stupid, the eminent lording it over the humble—these are harmful to the world. So too are rulers who are not generous, ministers who are not loyal, fathers who are without kindness, and sons who are unfilial, as well as those mean men who, with weapons, knives, poison, fire, and water, seek to injure and undo each other.

When we inquire into the cause of these various harms, what do we find has produced them? Do they come about from loving others and trying to benefit them? Surely not! They come rather from hating others and trying to injure them. And when we set out to classify and describe those men who hate and injure others, shall we say that their actions are motivated by universality or partiality? Surely we must answer, by partiality, and it is this partiality in their dealings with one another that gives rise to all the great harms in the world. Therefore we know that partiality is wrong.

Mo Tzu said: Whoever criticizes others must have some alternative to offer them. To criticize and yet offer no alternative is like trying to stop flood with flood or put out fire with fire. It will surely have no effect. Therefore Mo Tzu said: Partiality should be replaced by universality.

But how can partiality be replaced by universality? If men were to regard the states of others as they regard their own, then who would raise up his state to attack the state of another? It would be like attacking his own. If men were to regard the cities of others as they regard their own, then who would raise up his city to attack the city of another? It would be like attacking his own. If men were to regard the families of others as they regard their own, then who would raise up his family to overthrow that of another? It would be like overthrowing his own. Now when states and cities do not attack and make war on each other and families and individuals do not overthrow or injure one another, is this a harm or a benefit to the world? Surely it is a benefit.

When we inquire into the cause of such benefits, what do we find has produced them? Do they come about from hating others and trying to injure them? Surely not! They come rather from loving others and trying to benefit them. And when we set out to classify and describe those men who love and benefit others, shall we say that their actions are motivated by partiality or by universality? Surely we must answer, by universality, and it is this universality in their dealings with one another that gives rise to all the great benefits in the world. Therefore Mo Tzu has said that universality is right.

I have said previously that it is the business of the benevolent man to try to promote what is beneficial to the world and to eliminate what is harmful. Now I have demonstrated that universality is the source of all the great benefits in the world and partiality is the source of all the great harm. It is for this reason that Mo Tzu has said that partiality is wrong and universality is right.

Now if we seek to benefit the world by taking universality as our standard, those with sharp ears and clear eyes will see and hear for others, those with sturdy limbs will work for others, and those with a knowledge of the Way will endeavor to teach others. Those who are old and without wives or children will find means of support and be able to live out their days; the young and orphaned who have no parents will find someone to care for them and look after their needs. When all these benefits may be secured merely by taking universality as our standard, I cannot understand how the men of the world can hear about this doctrine of universality and still criticize it!

And yet the men of the world continue to criticize it, saying, "It may be a good thing, but how can it be put to use?"

Mo Tzu said: If it cannot be put to use, even I would criticize it. But how can there be a good thing that still cannot be put to use? Let us try considering both sides of the question. Suppose there are two men, one of them holding to partiality, the other to universality. The believer in partiality says, "How could I possibly regard my friend the same as myself, or my friend's father the same as my own?" Because he views his friend in this way, he will not feed him when he is hungry, clothe him when he is cold, nourish him when he is sick, or bury him when he dies. Such are the words of the partial man, and such his actions. But the words and actions of the universal-minded man are not like these. He will say, "I have heard that the truly superior man of the world regards his friend the same as himself, and his friend's father the same as his own. Only if he does this can he be considered a truly superior man." Because he views his friend in this way, he will feed him when he is hungry, clothe him when he is cold, nourish him when he is sick, and bury him when he dies. Such are the words and actions of the universal-minded man.

So the words of these two men disagree and their actions are diametrically opposed. Yet let us suppose that both of them are determined to carry out their words in action, so that word and deed agree like the two parts of a tally and nothing they say is not put into action. Then let us venture to inquire further. Suppose that here is a broad plain, a vast wilderness, and a man is buckling on his armor and donning his helmet to set out for the field of battle, where the fortunes of life and death are unknown; or he is setting out in his lord's name upon a distant mission to Pa or Yüeh, Ch'i or Ching, and his return is uncertain. Now let us ask,[4] to whom would he entrust the support of his parents and the care of his wife and children? Would it be to the universal-minded man, or to the partial man? It seems to me that, on occasions like these, there are no fools in the world. Though one may disapprove of universality himself, he would surely think it best to entrust his family to the universal-minded man. Thus people condemn universality in words but adopt it in practice, and word and deed belie each other. I cannot understand how the men of the world can hear about this doctrine of universality and still criticize it!

And yet the men of the world continue to criticize, saying, "Such a principle may be all right as a basis in choosing among ordinary men, but it cannot be used in selecting a ruler."

Let us try considering both sides of the question. Suppose there are two rulers, one of them holding to universality, the other to partiality. The partial ruler says, "How could I possibly regard my countless subjects the same as I regard myself? That would be completely at variance with human nature! Man's life on earth is as brief as the passing of a team of horses glimpsed through a crack in the wall." Because he views his subjects in this way, he will not feed them when they are hungry, clothe them when they are cold, nourish them when they are sick, or bury them when they die. Such are the words of the partial ruler, and such his actions. But the words and actions of the universal-minded ruler are not like these. He will say, "I have heard that the truly enlightened ruler must think of his subjects first, and of himself last. Only then can he be considered a truly enlightened ruler." Because he views his subjects in this way, he will feed them when they are hungry, clothe them when they are cold, nourish them when they are sick, and bury them when they die. Such are the words and actions of the universal-minded ruler.

So the words of these two rulers disagree and their actions are diametrically opposed. Yet let us suppose that both of them speak in good faith and are determined to carry out their words in action, so that word and deed agree like the two parts of a tally and nothing they say is not put into action. Then let us venture to inquire further. Suppose this year there is plague and disease, many of the people are suffering from hardship and hunger, and the corpses of countless victims lie tumbled in the ditches. If the people could choose between these two types of ruler, which would they follow? It seems to me that, on occasions like this, there are no fools in the world. Though one may disapprove of universality himself, he would surely think it best to follow the universal-minded ruler. Thus people condemn universality in words but adopt it in practice, and word and deed belie each other. I cannot understand how the men of the world can hear about this doctrine of universality and still criticize it!

And yet the men of the world continue to criticize, saying, "This doctrine of universality is benevolent and righteous. And yet how can it be carried out? As we see it, one can no more put it into practice than one can pick up Mount T'ai and leap over a river with it! Thus universality is only something to be longed for, not something that can be put into practice."

Mo Tzu said: As for picking up Mount T'ai and leaping over rivers with it, no one from ancient times to the present, from the beginning of mankind to now, has ever succeeded in doing that! But universal love and mutual aid were actually practiced by four sage kings of antiquity. How do we know that they practiced these?

Mo Tzu said: I did not live at the same time as they did, nor have I in person heard their voices or seen their faces. Yet I know it because of what is written on the bamboo and silk that has been handed down to posterity, what is engraved on metal and stone, and what is inscribed on bowls and basins.

The "Great Oath" says: "King Wen was like the sun or moon, shedding his bright light in the four quarters and over the western land."[5] That is to say, the universal love of King Wen was so broad that it embraced the whole world, as the universal light of the sun and the moon shines upon the whole world without partiality. Such was the universality of King Wen, and the universality which Mo Tzu has been telling you about is patterned after that of King Wen.

Not only the "Great Oath" but the "Oath of Yü"[6] also expresses this idea. Yü said: "All you teeming multitudes, listen to my words! It is not that I, the little child, would dare to act in a disorderly way. But this ruler of the Miao, with his unyielding ways, deserves Heaven's punishment. So I shall lead you, the lords of the various states, to conquer the ruler of the Miao." When Yü went to conquer the ruler of the Miao, it was not that he sought to increase his wealth or eminence, to win fortune or blessing, or to delight his ears and eyes. It was only that he sought to promote what was beneficial to the world and to eliminate what was harmful. Such was the universality of Yü, and the universality which Mo Tzu has been telling you about is patterned after that of Yü.

And not only the "Oath of Yü" but the "Speech of T'ang"[7] also expresses this idea. T'ang said: "I, the little child, Lü, dare to sacrifice a dark beast and make this announcement to the Heavenly Lord above, saying, 'Now Heaven has sent a great drought and it has fallen upon me, Lü. But I do not know what fault I have committed against high or low. If there is good, I dare not conceal it; if there is evil, I dare not pardon it. Judgment resides with the mind of God. If the myriad regions have any fault, may it rest upon my person; but if I have any fault, may it not extend to the myriad regions.'" This shows that, though T'ang was honored as the Son of Heaven and possessed all the riches of the world, he did not hesitate to offer himself as a sacrifice in his prayers and entreaties to the Lord on High and the spirits. Such was the universality of T'ang, and the universality which Mo Tzu has been telling you about is patterned after that of T'ang.

This idea is expressed not only in the "Speech of T'ang" but in the odes of Chou as well. In the odes of Chou it says:

> Broad, broad is the way of the king,
> Neither partial nor partisan.
> Fair, fair is the way of the king,
> Neither partisan nor partial.
>
> It is straight like an arrow,
> Smooth like a whetstone.
> The superior man treads it;
> The small man looks upon it.[8]

So what I have been speaking about is no mere theory of action. In ancient times, when Kings Wen and Wu administered the government and assigned each person his just share, they rewarded the worthy and punished the wicked without showing any favoritism toward their own kin or brothers. Such was the universality of Kings Wen and Wu, and the universality which Mo Tzu has been telling you about is patterned after that of Wen and Wu. I cannot understand how the men of the world can hear about this doctrine of universality and still criticize it!

And yet the men of the world continue to criticize, saying, "If one takes no thought for what is beneficial or harmful to one's parents, how can one be called filial?"

Mo Tzu said: Let us examine for a moment the way in which a filial son plans for the welfare of his parents. When a filial son plans for his parents, does he wish others to love and benefit them, or does he wish others to hate and injure them? It stands to reason that he wishes others to love and benefit his parents. Now if I am a filial son, how do I go about accomplishing this? Do I first make it a point to love and benefit other men's parents, so that they in return will love and benefit my parents? Or do I first make it a point to hate and injure other men's parents, so that they in return will love and benefit my parents? Obviously, I must first make it a point to love and benefit other men's parents, so that they in return will love and benefit my parents. So if all of us are to be filial sons, can we set about it any other way than by first making a point of loving and benefiting other men's parents? And are we to suppose that the filial sons of the world are all too stupid to be capable of doing what is right?

Let us examine further. Among the books of the former kings, in the "Greater Odes" of the *Book of Odes,* it says:

> There are no words that are not answered,
> No kindness that is not requited.
> Throw me a peach,
> I'll requite you a plum.[9]

The meaning is that one who loves will be loved by others, and one who hates will be hated by others. So I cannot understand how the men of the world can hear about this doctrine of universality and still criticize it!

Do they believe that it is too difficult to carry out? Yet there are much more difficult things that have been carried out. In the past King Ling of the state of Ching loved slender waists. During his reign, the people of Ching ate no more than one meal a day, until they were too weak to stand up without a cane, or to walk without leaning against the wall. Now reducing one's diet is a difficult thing to do, and yet people did it because it pleased King Ling. So within the space of a single generation the ways of the people can be changed, for they will strive to ingratiate themselves with their superiors.

Again in the past King Kou-chien of Yüeh admired bravery and for three years trained his soldiers and subjects to be brave. But he was not sure whether they had understood the true meaning of bravery, and so he set fire to his warships and then sounded the drum to advance. The soldiers trampled each other down in their haste to go forward, and countless numbers of them perished in the fire and water. At that time, even though he ceased to drum them forward, they did not retreat. The soldiers of Yüeh were truly astonishing. Now consigning one's body to the flames is a difficult thing to do, and yet they did it because it pleased the king of Yüeh. So within the space of a single generation the ways of the people can be changed, for they will strive to ingratiate themselves with their superiors.

Duke Wen of Chin liked coarse clothing, and so during his reign the men of the state of Chin wore robes of coarse cloth, wraps of sheepskin, hats of plain silk, and big rough shoes, whether they were appearing before the duke in the inner chamber or walking about in the outer halls of the court. Now bringing oneself to wear coarse clothing is a difficult thing to do, and yet people did it because it pleased Duke Wen. So within the space of a single generation the ways of the people can be changed, for they will strive to ingratiate themselves with their superiors.

To reduce one's diet, consign one's body to the flames, or wear coarse clothing are among the most difficult things in the world to do. And yet people will do them because they know their superiors will be pleased. So within the space of a single generation the ways of the people can be changed. Why? Because they will strive to ingratiate themselves with their superiors.

Now universal love and mutual benefit are both profitable and easy beyond all measure. The only trouble, as I see it, is that no ruler takes any delight in them. If the rulers really delighted in them, promoted them with rewards and praise, and prevented neglect of them by punishments, then I believe that people would turn to universal love and mutual benefit as naturally as fire turns upward or water turns downward, and nothing in the world could stop them.

The principle of universality is the way of the sage kings, the means of bringing safety to the rulers and officials and of assuring ample food and clothing to the people. Therefore the superior man can do no better than to examine it carefully and strive to put it into practice. If he does, then as a ruler he will be generous, as a subject loyal, as a father kind, as a son filial, as an older brother comradely, and as a younger brother respectful. So if the superior man wishes to be a generous ruler, a loyal subject, a kind father, a filial son, a comradely older brother, and a respectful younger brother, he must put into practice this principle of universality. It is the way of the sage kings and a great benefit to the people.

CHINESE BUDDHISM

Chinese Buddhism is one of the three most imortant trends of thought in the history of Chinese philosophy. The earliest record of Buddhism in China is 2 B.C. For the first several centuries, it existed here in the form of popular beliefs and practices. The translations of the Buddhist scriptures into Chinese, which started in the middle of the second century, stimulated the development of Buddhist teachings in China.

In the very beginning, Buddhism was taken as one of the forms of Taoism. There was a widespread belief that Buddhism had emerged in India as the result of the enlightenment brought to the barbarous Indians by Lao-tzu from China. In translations of the Buddhist texts it was common to use mainly Taoist terms.

However, by the third century the differences between the Chinese traditions and the Buddhist views became quite vivid. The controversy and discussions concentrated mainly around the problems of being and nonbeing. By the sixth century, two out of seven Buddhist schools existing in China were schools of nonbeing while the five others were of being. That sharp division did not exist too long and was replaced by a synthetic approach that asserted itself in three distinctly Chinese schools of Buddhism: the T'ien-t'ai (Heavenly Terrace), Hua-yen (Flower Splendor) and Ch'an (Meditation) schools.

The name Ch'an (derived from the Sanskrit dhyana—meditation—and known in Japanese as zen) is considered to be, more than any other school, a Chinese invention. According to Suzuki, it is in Ch'an that "the Chinese mind completely asserted itself, in a sense, in opposition to the Indian mind."

There are two main schools in Ch'an Buddhism: the Northern school and the Southern school. The first one is associated with Shen-hsiu, the second with Hui-neng and Shen-hui. Those Ch'an masters lived during the end of the sixth century and the beginning of the seventh century. According to both schools, the Buddha-nature resides in everyone; hence, all can become Buddhas. However, the two schools differ in their methods of reaching enlightenment. The Northern school affirms gradual enlightenment, the Southern school sudden enlightenment.

This difference derives from diverse concepts of pure mind. The Northern school starts with the premise that pure mind can be achieved after erroneous thoughts are eliminated and the mind is returned to a state of absolute quietude and undisturbedness. The Southern school rejects the possibility of mind's split into two parts; it affirms the unity of everything, including the mind. Enlightenment can be reached by gradual purification or perfection of mind, according to the former. The latter suggested unconventional techniques for reaching enlightenment, like koan—a question with an illogical answer—or the even more puzzling technique of shouting and beating. Those methods were believed to be helpful in grasping the truth that is mysterious, irrational, and, hence, paradoxical.

Ch'an Buddhism exercised a profound influence on the further development of Chinese philosophy. It brought into existence a doctrine of seriousness (ching) in Neo-Confucianism and made a great impact on such philosophers as the great Wang Yang-ming.

From I-Hsüan

From The Recorded Conversations of Zen Master I-Hsüan. *Reprinted from* A Source Book in Chinese Philosophy. *Translated by Wing-Tsit Chan. Princeton, N.J.: Princeton University Press, 1963.*

C. The Recorded Conversations of Zen Master I-Hsüan

1. The Prefect, Policy Advisor Wang, and other officials requested the Master to Lecture. The Master ascended the hall and said, "Today it is only because I, a humble monk, reluctantly accommodate human feelings that I sit on this chair. If one is restricted to one's heritage in expounding the fundamental understanding [of salvation], one really cannot say anything and would have nothing to stand on. However, because of the honorable general advisor's strong request today, how can the fundamental doctrines be concealed? Are there any talented men or fighting generals to hurl their banners and unfold their strategy right now? Show it to the group!"

A monk asked, "What is the basic idea of the Law preached by the Buddha?" Thereupon the Master shouted at him. The monk paid reverence. The Master said, "The Master and the monk can argue all right."

Question: "Master, whose tune are you singing? Whose tradition are you perpetuating?"

The Master said, "When I was a disciple of Huang-po, I asked him three times and I was beaten three times."

As the monk hesitated about what to say, the Master shouted at him and then beat him, saying, "Don't nail a stick into empty space."

2. The Master ascended the hall and said, "Over a lump of reddish flesh there sits a pure man who transcends and is no longer attached to any class of Buddhas or sentient beings. He comes in and out of your sense organs all the time. If you are not yet clear about it, look, look!"

At that point a monk came forward and asked, "What is a pure man who does not belong to any class of Buddhas or sentient beings?" The Master came right down from his chair and, taking hold of the monk, exclaimed, "Speak! Speak!" As the monk deliberated what to say, the Master let him go, saying, "What dried human excrement-removing stick is the pure man who does not belong to any class of Buddhas or sentient beings!" Thereupon he returned to his room. (TSD, 47:496)

3. The Master ascended the hall. A monk asked, "What is the basic idea of the Law preached by the Buddha?" The Master lifted up his swatter. The monk shouted, and the Master beat him.

[The monk asked again], "What is the basic idea of the Law preached by the Buddha?" The Master again lifted up his swatter. The monk shouted, and the Master shouted also. As the monk hesitated about what to say, the Master beat him.

Thereupon the Master said, "Listen, men. Those who pursue after the Law will not escape from death. I was in my late Master Huang-po's place for twenty years. Three times I asked him about the basic idea of the Law preached by the

Buddha and three times he bestowed upon me the staff. I felt I was struck only by a dried stalk. Now I wish to have a real beating. Who can do it to me?"

One monk came out of the group and said, "I can do it."

The Master picked up the staff to give him. As he was about to take it over, the Master beat him. (TSD, 47:496–97)

4. The Master ascended the hall and said, "A man stands on top of a cliff, with no possibility of rising any further. Another man stands at the crossroad, neither facing nor backing anything. Who is in the front and who is in the back? Don't be like VimalakÓrti (who was famous for his purity), and don't be like Great Gentleman Fu (who benefited others). Take care of yourselves." (TSD, 47:497)

5. The Master told the congregation: "Seekers of the Way. In Buddhism no effort is necessary. All one has to do is to do nothing, except to move his bowels, urinate, put on his clothing, eat his meals, and lie down if he is tired. The stupid will laugh at him, but the wise one will understand. An ancient person said, 'One who makes effort externally is surely a fool.'" (TSD, 47:498)

6. Question: "What is meant by the mind's not being different at different times?"

The Master answered, "As you deliberated to ask the question, your mind has already become different. Therefore the nature and character of dharmas have become differentiated. Seekers of the Way, do not make any mistake. All mundane and supramundane dharmas have no nature of their own. Nor have they the nature to be produced [by causes]. They have only the name Emptiness, but even the name is empty. Why do you take this useless name as real? You are greatly mistaken! . . . If you seek after the Buddha, you will be taken over by the devil of the Buddha, and if you seek after the patriarch, you will be taken over by the devil of the patriarch. If you seek after anything, you will always suffer. It is better not to do anything. Some unworthy priests tell their disciples that the Buddha is the ultimate, and that he went through three infinitely long periods, fulfilled his practice, and then achieved Buddhahood. Seekers of the Way, if you say that the Buddha is the ultimate, why did he die lying down sidewise in the forest in Kuúinagara after having lived for eighty years? Where is he now? . . . Those who truly seek after the Law will have no use for the Buddha. They will have no use for the bodhisattvas or arhats. And they will have no use for any excellence in the Three Worlds (of desires, matter, and pure spirit). They will be distinctly free and not bound by material things. Heaven and earth may turn upside down but I shall have no more uncertainty. The Buddhas of the ten cardinal directions may appear before me and I shall not feel happy for a single moment. The three paths (of fire, blood, and swords) to hell may suddenly appear, but I shall not be afraid for a single moment. Why? Because I know that all dharmas are devoid of characters.

They exist when there is transformation [in the mind] and cease to exist when there is no transformation. The Three Worlds are but the mind, and all dharmas are consciousness only. Therefore [they are all] dreams, illusions, and flowers in the air. What is the use of grasping and seizing them? . . .

"Seekers of the Way, if you want to achieve the understanding according to the Law, don't be deceived by others and turn to [your thoughts] internally or [objects] externally. Kill anything that you happen on. Kill the Buddha if you happen to meet him. Kill a patriarch or an arhat if you happen to meet him. Kill your parents or relatives if you happen to meet them. Only then can you be free, not bound by material things, and absolutely free and at ease. . . . I have no trick to give people. I merely cure disease and set people free. . . . My views are few. I merely put on clothing and eat meals as usual, and pass my time without doing anything. You people coming from the various directions have all made up your minds to seek the Buddha, seek the Law, seek emancipation, and seek to leave the Three Worlds. Crazy people! If you want to leave the Three Worlds, where can you go? 'Buddha' and 'patriarchs' are terms of praise and also bondage. Do you want to know where the Three Worlds are? They are right in your mind which is now listening to the Law." (TSD, 47:499–500)

7. Ma-ku came to participate in a session. As he arranged his seating cushion, he asked, "Which face of the twelve-face Kuan-yin faces the proper direction?"

The Master got down from the rope chair. With one hand he took away Ma-ku's cushion and with the other he held Ma-ku, saying, "Which direction does the twelve-face Kuan-yin face?"

Ma-ku turned around and was about to sit in the rope chair. The Master picked up the staff and beat him. Ma-ku having grasped the staff, the two dragged each other into the room.

8. The Master asked a monk: "Sometimes a shout is like the sacred sword of the Diamond King. Sometimes a shout is like a golden-haired lion squatting on the ground. Sometimes a shout is like a rod or a piece of grass [used to attract fish]. And sometimes a shout is like one which does not function as a shout at all. How do you know which one to use?"

As the monk was deliberating what to say, the Master shouted. (TSD, 47:504)

9. When the Master was among Huang-po's congregation, his conduct was very pure. The senior monk said with a sigh, "Although he is young, he is different from the rest!" He then asked, "Sir, how long have you been here?"

The Master said, "Three years."

The senior monk said, "Have you ever gone to the head monk (Huang-po) and asked him questions?"

The Master said, "I have not. I wouldn't know what to ask."

The senior monk said, "Why don't you go and ask the head monk what the basic idea of the Law preached by the Buddha clearly is?"

The Master went and asked the question. But before he finished, Huang-po beat him. When he came back, the senior monk asked him how the conversation went. The Master said, "Before I finished my question, he already had beaten me. I don't understand." The senior monk told him to go and ask again.

The Master did and Huang-po beat him again. In this way he asked three times and got beaten three times. . . . Huang-po said, "If you go to Ta-yü's place, he will tell you why."

The Master went to Ta-yü, who asked him, "Where have you come from?"

The Master said, "I am from Huang-po's place."

Ta-yü said, "What did Huang-po have to say?"

The Master said, "I asked three times about the basic idea of the Law preached by the Buddha and I was beaten three times. I don't know if I was mistaken."

Ta-yü said, "Old kindly Huang-po has been so earnest with you and you still came here to ask if you were mistaken!"

As soon as the Master heard this, he understood and said, "After all, there is not much in Huang-po's Buddhism." (TSD, 47:504)

NEO-CONFUCIANISM

Neo-Confucianism—a term of Western origin—is used to name those revised and transformed Confucian teachings that were systematized in the eleventh century. In a broader sense, Neo-Confucianism embraces all the Confucians from the eleventh century up to today.

Chou Tun-i (1017–1073) is called the pioneer of Neo-Confucianism. He assimilated the teaching of Confucius with some elements of Taoism and Buddhism (in particular, of Ch'an Buddhism) and based his entire philosophy on the *Book of Changes.*

Those who followed Chou Tun-i later on were divided in many schools. The two of most importance were the Ch'eng-Chu School and the Lu-Wang School. The first was named after two brothers, Ch'eng Hao (1032–1085) and Ch'eng I (1033–1107), and Chu Hsi (1130–1200). The contribution of the last in the development of Chinese philosophy was so great that the relation of Chu Hsi to Confucius was often compared with that of Thomas Aquinas to Aristotle in the West. His influence on Chinese thought ranks after Confucius, Mencius, Lao Tzu, and Chuang Tzu.

Chu Hsi standardized the *Analects, The Great Learning, The Doctrine of the Mean,* and the *Book of Mencius* as the "Four Books" that served as the basis of civil service examinations in China from 1313 to 1905. He formulated the six major concepts that characterize Neo-Confucianism up to this time: the Great Ultimate, principle (*li*), material force (*ch'i*), the nature, the investigation of things, and humanity.

The Great Ultimate is understood by him as "the principle of heaven and earth and the myriad things." There is only one Great Ultimate, yet each of the myriad things possesses it in its entirety, like the moon is one in the sky but its light is scattered upon everything.

The Great Ultimate involves both principle and material force. The former is incorporeal, eternal, and unchanging. It is the essence of things. The latter is corporeal, transitory, and changeable. It constitutes the substance of things.

The principle of a thing or of an individual is his or her very nature. There are two kinds of nature. One is original, that is, unmoved and perfectly good. The other is physical, in which principle is mixed with material force. The original nature is the substance, the physical is a function. The original nature is identified with the universal moral mind, the physical nature with the human mind. Every human being has a mind that is in its essence identical with the mind of the universe. This makes knowledge, including moral knowledge, possible. The knowledge comes through the investigation of things.

In his doctrine of the investigation of things, Chu Hsi considered seriousness (*ching*) as the prerequisite for true knowledge. He advocated deductive and inductive methods, objective observation, and intuitive understanding as the means of getting the true knowledge.

According to Chu Hsi, in the mind of an individual there are four moral qualities—namely, *jen*, righteousness, propriety, and wisdom. *Jen* is the most important one, since it embraces them all. Chu Hsi views *jen* as "the character of the mind" and "the principle of love" thus giving substance and function equal importance.

Chu Hsi's thought dominated Chinese philosophy for more than three centuries, until Wang Yang-Ming (1472–1529) introduced the so-called dynamic philosophy.

Because Chu Hsi's interpretation of Confucianism had been made orthodox, it in time lost its vitality. Wang Yang-Ming tried to return to Confucianism a dynamic vitality. He accepted many of Chu Hsi's ideas; however, he opposed the rationalism of his predecessor. Both thinkers used the phrase "investigation of things" (*ko-wu*), but Chu Hsi interpreted it as the rational and objective investigation of things, while Wang Yang-Ming understood it morally rather than intellectually. He affirmed that to investigate things means to eliminate evil, what is incorrect in the mind, so to preserve the correctness of its original substance.

Wang's main contributions to Chinese philosophy were the doctrine of the extension of the innate knowledge of the good and the doctrine of the unity of knowledge and action.

Wang Yang-Ming's teachings had a great impact not only in China, but also in Japan. Its dynamism appealed as well to a number of modern thinkers.

From Chu Hsi

Reprinted from A Source Book in Chinese Philosophy. *Translated by Wing-Tsit Chan. Princeton, N.J.: Princeton University Press, 1963.*

8. The Mind, the Nature, and the Feelings

85. The nature is comparable to the Great Ultimate, and the mind to *yin* and *yang*. The Great Ultimate exists only in the *yin* and *yang*, and cannot be separated from them. In the final analysis, however, the Great Ultimate is the Great Ultimate and *yin* and *yang* are *yin* and *yang*. So it is with nature and mind. They are one and yet two, two and yet one, so to speak. Philosopher Han Yü (768–824) described nature as humanity, righteousness, propriety, wisdom, and faithfulness and the feelings as pleasure, anger, sorrow, and joy. This is an advance over other philosophers on the problem of human nature. As to his division of human nature into three grades (superior, medium, and inferior), he has only explained material force but not nature. (45:1a)

86. Although nature is a vacuity, it consists of concrete principles. Although the mind is a distinct entity, it is vacuous, and therefore embraces all principles. This truth will be apprehended only when people examine it for themselves. (45:2a)

87. Nature consists of principles embraced in the mind, and the mind is where these principles are united. (45:2a)

88. Nature is principle. The mind is its embracement and reservoir, and issues it forth into operation. (45:2a)

89. Some time ago I read statements by Wu-feng (Hu Hung, 1100–1155) in which he spoke of the mind only in contrast to nature, leaving the feelings unaccounted for. Later when I read Heng-ch'ü's (Chang Tsai's) doctrine that "the mind commands man's nature and feelings," I realized that it was a great contribution. Only then did I find a satisfactory account of the feelings. His doctrine agrees with that of Mencius. In the words of Mencius, "the feeling of commiseration is the beginning of humanity." Now humanity is nature, and commiseration is feeling. In this, the mind can be seen through the feelings. He further said, "Humanity, righteousness, propriety, and wisdom are rooted in the mind." In this, the mind is seen through nature. For the mind embraces

both nature and the feelings. Nature is substance and feelings are function. (45:3a-b)

90. Nature is the state before activity begins, the feelings are the state when activity has started, and the mind includes both of these states. For nature is the mind before it is aroused, while feelings are the mind after it is aroused, as is expressed in [Chang Tsai's] saying, "The mind commands man's nature and feelings." Desire emanates from feelings. The mind is comparable to water, nature is comparable to the tranquillity of still water, feeling is comparable to the flow of water, and desire is comparable to its waves. Just as there are good and bad waves, so there are good desires, such as when "I want humanity," and bad desires which rush out like wild and violent waves. When bad desires are substantial, they will destroy the Principle of Heaven, as water bursts a dam and damages everything. When Mencius said that "feelings enable people to do good," he meant that the correct feelings flowing from our nature are originally all good. (45:4a)

91. The mind means master. It is master whether in the state of activity or in the state of tranquillity. It is not true that in the state of tranquillity there is no need of a master and there is a master only when the state becomes one of activity. By master is meant an all-pervading control and command existing in the mind by itself. The mind unites and apprehends nature and the feelings, but it is not united with them as a vague entity without any distinction. (45:4a-b)

92. In his reply to Heng-ch'ü's dictum that "nature in the state of calmness cannot be without activity," Ming-tao's (Ch'eng Hao's) idea is that we should not hate things and events nor chase after them. Nowadays people who hate things avoid them completely, and who chase after them are continuously lured away by them. The best thing is neither to shun away from things nor to drift with them, but to face and respond to them in various ways. For Heng-ch'ü's idea was to cut ourselves from the external world and achieve calmness internally, whereas Ming-tao's idea was that the internal and the external must be harmonized and unified. If (as Ming-tao said) that nature is calm "whether it is in a state of activity or in a state of tranquillity," then in our response to things we will naturally not be bound by them. If nature can be calmed only in a state of tranquillity, I am afraid that in time of activity it will be tempted and carried away by external things. (45:11b–12a)

93. *Question:* Is it correct to suppose that sages never show any anger?

Answer: How can they never show anger? When they ought to be angry, they will show it in their countenances. But if one has to punish someone for his crime and purposely smiles, that would be wrong.

Question: In that case, does it not show some feeling of wrath?

Answer: When Heaven is angry, thunder is also aroused. When sage-emperor Shun executed the four cruel criminals, he must have been angry at that time.

When one becomes angry at the right time, he will be acting in the proper degree. When the matter is over, anger disappears, and none of it will be retained. (45:14b–15a)

94. *Question:* "How can desires be checked? Simply by thought. In learning there is nothing more important than thought. Only thought can check desires." Someone said that if thought is not correct, it will not be adequate to check desires. Instead, it will create trouble. How about "having no depraved thoughts"?

Answer: Thoughts that are not correct are merely desires. If we think through the right and wrong, and the ought and ought-not of a thing, in accordance with its principle, then our thought will surely be correct. (45:19b)

9. Jen

95. Whenever and wherever humanity (*jen*) flows and operates, righteousness will fully be righteousness and propriety and wisdom will fully be propriety and wisdom. It is like the ten thousand things being stored and preserved. There is not a moment of cessation in such an operation for in all of these things there is the spirit of life. Take for example such things as seeds of grain or the peach and apricot kernels. When sown, they will grow. They are not dead things. For this reason they are called *jen* (the word *jen* meaning both kernel and humanity). This shows that *jen* implies the spirit of life. (47:3a)

96. *Jen* is spontaneous, altruism (*shu*) is cultivated. *Jen* is natural, altruism is by effort. *Jen* is uncalculating and has nothing in view, altruism is calculating and has an object in view. (47:6a–b)

97. *Jen* is the principle of love, and impartiality is the principle of *jen*. Therefore, if there is impartiality, there is *jen*, and if there is *jen*, there is love. (47:6b)

98. *Question:* Master Ch'eng Hao said, "'Seriousness is to straighten the internal life and righteousness is to square the external life.' This means *jen*." How can these be sufficient to be regarded as *jen*?

Answer: These two are *jen*. Wherever selfish desires can be entirely eliminated and the Principle of Nature freely operates, there is *jen*. For example, if one can "study extensively," be "steadfast in one's purpose," "inquire earnestly," and "reflect on things at hand (that is, what one can put into practice)," then "humanity (*jen*) consists in these." "To master oneself and return to propriety" is also *jen*. "When you go abroad, behave to everyone as if you were receiving a great guest. Employ the people as if you were assisting at a great sacrifice"—this is also *jen*. To "be respectful in private life, be serious in handling affairs, and be loyal in dealing with others"—these are also *jen*. All these depend on what path you follow. Once you have entered that path, exert effort until the limit is reached—all this is *jen*. (47:14b)

99. "When one makes impartiality the substance of his person, that is *jen*." *Jen* is the principle originally inherent in man's mind. With impartiality, there is *jen*. With partiality, there is no *jen*. But impartiality as such should not be equated with *jen*. It must be made man's substance before it becomes *jen*. Impartiality, altruism, and love are all descriptions of *jen*. Impartiality is antecedent to *jen*, altruism and love are subsequent. This is so because impartiality makes *jen* possible, and *jen* makes love and altruism possible. (47:19b–20a)

10. Principle (Li) *and Material Force* (Ch'i)

100. In the universe there has never been any material force without principle or principle without material force. (49:1a)

101. *Question:* Which exists first, principle or material force?

Answer: Principle has never been separated from material force. However, principle "exists before physical form [and is therefore without it]" whereas material force "exists after physical form [and is therefore with it]." Hence when spoken of as being before or after physical form, is there not the difference of priority and posteriority? Principle has no physical form, but material force is coarse and contains impurities. (49:1a–b)

102. Fundamentally principle and material force cannot be spoken of as prior or posterior. But if we must trace their origin, we are obliged to say that principle is prior. However, principle is not a separate entity. It exists right in material force. Without material force, principle would have nothing to adhere to. As material force, there are the Agents (or Elements) of Metal, Wood, Water, and Fire. As principle, there are humanity, righteousness, propriety, and wisdom. (49:1b)

103. Question about the relation between principle and material force.

Answer: I-ch'uan (Ch'eng I) expressed it very well when he said that principle is one but its manifestations are many. When heaven, earth, and the myriad things are spoken of together, there is only one principle. As applied to man, however, there is in each individual a particular principle. (49:1b)

104. *Question:* What are the evidences that principle is in material force?

Answer: For example, there is order in the complicated interfusion of the *yin* and the *yang* and of the Five Agents. Principle is there. If material force does not consolidate and integrate, principle would have nothing to attach itself to. (49:2b)

105. *Question:* May we say that before heaven and earth existed there was first of all principle?

Answer: Before heaven and earth existed, there was after all only principle. As there is this principle, therefore there are heaven and earth. If there were no principle, there would also be no heaven and earth, no man, no things, and in fact, no containing or sustaining (of things by heaven and earth) to speak of. As there is principle, there is therefore material force to operate everywhere and nourish and develop all things.

Question: Is it principle that nourishes and develops all things?

Answer: As there is this principle, therefore there is this material force operating, nourishing, and developing. Principle itself has neither physical form nor body. (49:3a–b)

106. K'o-chi asked: When the creative process disposes of things, is it the end once a thing is gone, or is there a principle by which a thing that is gone may return?

Answer: It is the end once a thing is gone. How can there be material force that has disintegrated and yet integrates once more? (49:3b–4a)

107. *Question:* "The Lord on High has conferred even on the inferior people a moral sense." "When Heaven is about to confer a great responsibility on any man. . . ." "Heaven, to protect the common people, made for them rulers." "Heaven, in the production of things, is sure to be bountiful to them, according to their natural capacity." "On the good-doer, the Lord on High sends down all blessings, and on the evil-doer, He sends down all miseries." "When Heaven is about to send calamities to the world, it will always first produce abnormal people as a measure of their magnitude." In passages like these, does it mean that Heaven has no personal consciousness and the passages are merely deductions from principle?

Answer: These passages have the same meaning. It is simply that principle operates this way. (49:4a)

108. Principle attaches to material force and thus operates. (49:4b)

109. Throughout the universe there are both principle and material force. Principle refers to the Way, which exists before physical form [and is without it] and is the root from which all things are produced. Material force refers to material objects, which exists after physical form [and is with it]; it is the instrument by which things are produced. Therefore in the production of man and things, they must be endowed with principle before they have their nature, and they must be endowed with material force before they have physical form. (49:5b)

110. What are called principle and material force are certainly two different entities. But considered from the standpoint of things, the two entities are merged one with the other and cannot be separated with each in a different place. However, this does not destroy the fact that the two entities are each an entity in itself. When considered from the standpoint of principle, before things existed, their principles of being had already existed. Only their principles existed, however, but not yet the things themselves. Whenever one stud-

ies these aspects, one should clearly recognize and distinguish them, and consider both principle and material force from the beginning to the end, and then one will be free from error. (49:5b–6a)

111. There is principle before there can be material force. But it is only when there is material force that principle finds a place to settle. This is the process by which all things are produced, whether large as heaven and earth or small as ants. Why should we worry that in the creative process of Heaven and Earth, endowment may be wanting? Fundamentally, principle cannot be interpreted in the senses of existence or nonexistence. Before Heaven and Earth came into being, it already was as it is. (49:6a)

112. Considering the fact that all things come from one source, we see that their principle is the same but their material force different. Looking at their various substances, we see that their material force is similar but their principle utterly different. The difference in material force is due to the inequality of its purity or impurity, whereas the difference in principle is due to its completeness or partiality. If you will please examine thoroughly, there should be no further doubt. (49:7a)

113. The nature of man and things is nothing but principle and cannot be spoken of in terms of integration and disintegration. That which integrates to produce life and disintegrates to produce death is only material force. What we called the spirit, the heavenly and earthly aspects of the soul (*hun-p'o*), and consciousness are all effects of material force. Therefore when material force is integrated, there are these effects. When it is disintegrated, there are no more. As to principle, fundamentally it does not exist or cease to exist because of such integration or disintegration. As there is a certain principle, there is the material force corresponding to it, and as this material force integrates in a particular instance, its principle is also endowed in that instance. (49:8a)

11. The Great Ultimate

114. The Great Ultimate is nothing other than principle. (49:8b)

115. *Question:* The Great Ultimate is not a thing existing in a chaotic state before the formation of heaven and earth, but a general name for the principles of heaven and earth and the myriad things. Is that correct?

Answer: The Great Ultimate is merely the principle of heaven and earth and the myriad things. With respect to heaven and earth, there is the Great Ultimate in them. With respect to the myriad things, there is the Great Ultimate in each and every one of them. Before heaven and earth existed, there was assuredly this principle. It is the principle that "through movement generates the *yang*." It is also this principle that "through tranquillity generates the *yin*." (49:8b–9a)

116. *Question:* [You said,] "Principle is a single, concrete entity, and the myriad things partake it as their substance. Hence each of the myriad things possesses in it a Great Ultimate." According to this theory, does the Great Ultimate not split up into parts?

Answer: Fundamentally there is only one Great Ultimate, yet each of the myriad things has been endowed with it and each in itself possesses the Great Ultimate in its entirety. This is similar to the fact that there is only one moon in the sky but when its light is scattered upon rivers and lakes, it can be seen everywhere. It cannot be said that the moon has been split. (49:10b–11a)

117. The Great Ultimate has neither spatial restriction nor physical form or body. There is no spot where it may be placed. When it is considered in the state before activity begins, this state is nothing but tranquillity. Now activity, tranquillity, *yin,* and *yang* all exist only after physical form [and are with it]. However, activity is after all the activity of the Great Ultimate and tranquillity is also its tranquillity, although activity and tranquillity themselves are not the Great Ultimate. This is why Master Chou Tun-i only spoke of that state as Non-ultimate. While the state before activity begins cannot be spoken of as the Great Ultimate, nevertheless the principles of pleasure, anger, sorrow, and joy are already inherent in it. Pleasure and joy belong to *yang* and anger and sorrow belong to *yin.* In the initial stage the four are not manifested, but their principles are already there. As contrasted with the state after activity begins, it may be called the Great Ultimate. But still it is difficult to say. All this is but a vague description. The truth must be personally realized by each individual himself. (49:11a-b)

From Wang Yang-Ming

Inquiry on The Great Learning. *Reprinted from* Instructions for Practical Living and Other Neo-Confucian Writings by Wang Yang-Ming. *Translated by Wing-Tsit Chan. New York: Columbia University Press, 1964.*

Question: The *Great Learning* was considered by a former scholar as the learning of the great man. I venture to ask why the learning of the great man should consist in "manifesting the clear character."

Master Wang said: The great man regards Heaven, Earth, and the myriad things as one body. He regards the world as one family and the country as one person. As to those who make a cleavage between objects and distinguish between the self and others, they are small men. That the great man can regard Heaven, Earth, and the myriad things as one body is not because he deliberately wants to do so, but because it is natural to the humane nature of his mind that he do so. Forming one body with Heaven, Earth, and the myriad things is not only true of the great man. Even the mind of the small man is no different. Only he himself makes it small. Therefore when he sees a child about to fall into a well, he cannot help a feeling of alarm and commiseration. This shows that his humanity forms one body with the child. It may be objected that the child belongs to the same species. Again, when he observes the pitiful cries and frightened appearance of birds and animals about to be slaughtered, he cannot help feeling an "inability to bear" their suffering. This shows that his humanity forms one body with birds and animals. It may be objected that birds and animals are sentient beings as he is. But when he sees plants broken and destroyed, he cannot help a feeling of pity. This shows that his humanity forms one body with plants. It may be said that plants are living things as he is. Yet, even when he sees tiles and stones shattered and crushed, he cannot help a feeling of regret. This shows that his humanity forms one body with tiles and stones. This means that even the mind of the small man necessarily has the humanity that forms one body with all. Such a mind is rooted in his Heaven-endowed nature, and is naturally intelligent, clear, and not beclouded. For this reason it is called the "clear character." Although the mind of the small man is divided and narrow, yet his humanity that forms one body can remain free from darkness to this degree. This is due to the fact that his mind has not yet been aroused by desires and obscured by selfishness. When it is aroused by desires and obscured by selfishness, compelled by greed for gain and fear of harm, and stirred by anger, he will destroy things, kill members of his own species, and will do everything. In extreme cases he will even slaughter his own brothers, and the humanity that forms one body will disappear completely. Hence, if it is not obscured by selfish desires, even the mind of the small man has the humanity that forms one body with all as does the mind of the great man. As soon as it is obscured by selfish desires, even the mind of the great man will be divided and narrow like that of the small man. Thus the learning of the great man consists entirely in getting rid of the obscuration of selfish desires in order by his own efforts to make manifest his clear character, so as to restore the condition of forming one body with Heaven, Earth, and the myriad things, a condition that is originally so, that is all. It is not that outside of the original substance something can be added.

Question: Why, then, does the learning of the great man consist in loving the people?

Answer: To manifest the clear character is to bring about the substance of the state of forming one body with Heaven, Earth, and the myriad things, whereas loving the people is to put into universal operation the function of the state of forming one body. Hence manifesting the clear character consists in loving the people, and loving the people is the way to manifest the clear character. Therefore, only when I love my father, the fathers of others, and the fathers of all men can my humanity really form one body with my father, the fathers of others, and the fathers of all men. When it truly forms one body with them, then the clear character of filial piety will be manifested. Only when I love my brother, the brothers of others, and the brothers of all men can my humanity really form one body with my brother, the brothers of others, and the brothers of all men. When it truly forms one body with them, then the clear character of brotherly respect will be manifested. Everything from ruler, minister, husband, wife, and friends to mountains, rivers, spiritual beings, birds, animals, and plants should be truly loved in order to realize my humanity that forms one body with them, and then my clear character will be completely manifested, and I will really form one body with Heaven, Earth, and the myriad things. This is what is meant by "manifesting the clear character throughout the world." This is what is meant by "regulation of the family," "ordering the state," and "bringing peace to the world." This is what is meant by "full development of one's nature."

Question: Then why does the learning of the great man consist in "abiding in the highest good"?

Answer: The highest good is the ultimate principle of manifesting character and loving people. The nature endowed in us by Heaven is pure and perfect. The fact that it is intelligent, clear, and not beclouded is evidence of the emanation and revelation of the highest good. It is the original substance of the clear character which is called innate knowledge of the good. As the highest good emanates and reveals itself, we will consider right as right and wrong as wrong. Things of greater or less importance and situations of grave or light character will be responded to as they act upon us. In all our changes and movements, we will stick to no particular point, but possess in ourselves the mean that is perfectly natural. This is the ultimate of the normal nature of man and the principle of things. There can be no consideration of adding or subtracting anything to or from it. Such a suggestion reveals selfish ideas and shallow cunning, and cannot be said to be the highest good. Naturally, how can anyone who does not watch over himself carefully when alone, and who has no refinement and singleness of mind, attain to such a state of perfection? Later generations fail to realize that the highest good is inherent in their own minds, but exercise their selfish ideas and cunning and grope for it outside their minds, believing that every event and every object has its own peculiar definite principle. For this reason the law of right and wrong is obscured; the mind becomes concerned with fragmentary and isolated details and broken pieces; the selfish desires of man become rampant and the Principle of Nature is at an end. And thus the learning of manifesting character and loving people is everywhere thrown into confusion. In the past there have, of course, been people who wanted to manifest their clear character. But simply because they did not know how to abide in the highest good, but instead drove their own minds toward something too lofty, they thereby lost them in illusions, emptiness, and quietness, having nothing to do with the work of the family, the state, and the world. Such are the followers of Buddhism and Taoism. There have, of course, been those who wanted to love their people. Yet simply because they did not know how to abide in the highest good, but instead sank their own minds in base and trifling things, they thereby lost them in scheming strategy and cunning techniques, having neither the sincerity of humanity nor that of commiseration. Such are the followers of the Five Despots and the pursuers of success and profit. All of these defects are due to a failure to know how to abide in the highest good. Therefore abiding in the highest good is to manifesting character and loving people as the carpenter's square and compass are to the square and the circle, or rule and measure to length, or balances and scales to weight. If the square and the circle do not abide by the compass and the carpenter's square, their standard will be wrong; if length does not abide by the rule and measure, its adjustment will be lost; if weight does not abide by the balances, its exactness will be gone; and if manifesting clear character and loving people do not abide by the highest good, their foundation will disappear. Therefore, abiding in the highest good so as to love people and manifest the clear character is what is meant by the learning of the great man.

Question: "Only after knowing what to abide in can one be calm. Only after having been calm can one be tranquil. Only after having achieved tranquillity can one have peaceful repose. Only after having peaceful repose can one begin to deliberate. Only after deliberation can the end be attained." How do you explain this?

Answer: People fail to realize that the highest good is in their minds and seek it outside. As they believe that everything or every event has its own definite principle, they search for the highest good in individual things. Consequently, the mind becomes fragmentary, isolated, broken into pieces; mixed and confused, it has no definite direction. Once it is realized that the highest good is in the mind and does not depend on any search outside, then the mind will have definite direction and there will be no danger of its becoming fragmentary, isolated, broken into pieces, mixed, or confused. When there is no such danger, the mind will not be erroneously perturbed but will be tranquil. Not being erroneously perturbed but being tranquil, it will be leisurely and at ease in its daily functioning and will attain peaceful repose. Being in peaceful repose, whenever a thought arises or an event acts upon it, the mind with its innate knowledge will thoroughly sift and carefully examine whether or not the thought or event is in accord with the highest good, and thus the mind can deliberate. With deliberation, every decision will be excellent and every act will be proper, and in this way the highest good will be attained.

Question: "Things have their roots and their branches." A former scholar considered manifesting the clear character as the root (or fundamental) and renovating the people as the branch (or secondary), and thought that they are two things opposing each other as internal and external. "Affairs have their beginnings and their ends." The former scholar considered knowing what to abide in as the beginning and the attainment of the highest good as the end, both being one thing in harmonious continuity. According to you, "renovating the people" (*hsin-min*) should be read as "loving the people" (*ch'in-min*). If so, isn't the theory of root and branches in some respect incorrect?

Answer: The theory of beginnings and ends is in general right. Even if we read "renovating the people" as "loving the people" and say that manifesting the character is the root and loving the people is the branches, it is not incorrect. The main thing is that root and branches should not be distinguished as two different things. The trunk of the tree is called the root, and the twigs are called the branches. It is precisely because the tree is one that its parts can be called root and branches. If they are said to be two different things, then since they are two distinct objects, how can we speak of them as root and branches of the same thing? Since the idea of renovating the people is different from that of loving the people, obviously the task of manifesting the character and that of loving the people are two different things. If it is realized that manifesting the clear character is to love the people and loving the people is to manifest the clear character, how can they be split in two? What the former scholar said is due to his failure to realize that manifesting the character and loving the people are basically one thing. Instead, he believed them to be two different things and consequently, although he knew that root and branches should be one, yet he could not help splitting them in two.

Question: The passage from the phrase, "The ancients who wished to manifest their clear character throughout the world" to the clause, "first [order their state . . . regulate their families . . .] cultivate their personal lives," can be understood by your theory of manifesting the character and loving the people. May I ask what task, what procedure, and what effort are involved in the passage from "Those who wished to cultivate their personal lives would [first rectify their minds . . . make their will sincere . . . extend their knowledge]" to the clause, "the extension of knowledge consists in the investigation of things"?

Answer: This passage fully explains the task of manifesting the character, loving the people, and abiding in the highest good. The person, the mind, the will, knowledge, and things constitute the order followed in the task. While each of them has its own place, they are really one thing. Investigating, extending, being sincere, rectifying, and cultivating are the tasks performed in the procedure. Although each has its own name, they are really one affair. What is it that is called the person? It is the physical functioning of the mind. What is it that is called the mind? It is the clear and intelligent master of the person. What is meant by cultivating the personal life? It means to do good and get rid of evil. Can the body by itself do good and get rid of evil? The clear and intelligent master must desire to do good and get rid of evil before the body that functions physically can do so. Therefore he who wishes to cultivate his personal life must first rectify his mind.

Now the original substance of the mind is man's nature. Human nature being universally good, the original substance of the mind is correct. How is it that any effort is required to rectify the mind? The reason is that, while the original substance of the mind is originally correct, incorrectness enters when one's thoughts and will are in operation. Therefore he who wishes to rectify his mind must rectify it in connection with the operation of his thoughts and will. If, whenever a good thought arises, he really loves it as he loves beautiful colors, and whenever an evil thought arises, he really hates it as he hates bad odors, then his will will always be sincere and his mind can be rectified.

However, what arises from the will may be good or evil, and unless there is a way to make clear the distinction between good and evil, there will be a confusion of truth and untruth. In that case, even if one wants to make his will sincere, he cannot do so. Therefore he who wishes to make his will sincere must extend his knowledge. By extension is meant to reach the limit. The word "extension" is the same as that used in the saying, "Mourning is to be carried to the utmost degree of grief." In the *Book of Changes* it is said: "Knowing the utmost, one should reach it." "Knowing the utmost" means knowledge and "reaching it" means extension. The extension of knowledge is not what later scholars understand as enriching and widening knowledge. It is simply extending one's innate knowledge of the good to the utmost. This innate knowledge of the good is what Mencius meant when he said, "The sense of right and wrong is common to all men." The sense of right and wrong requires no deliberation to know, nor does it depend on learning to function. This is why it is called innate knowledge. It is my nature endowed by Heaven, the original substance of my mind, naturally intelligent, shining, clear, and understanding.

Whenever a thought or a wish arises, my mind's faculty of innate knowledge itself is always conscious of it. Whether it is good or evil, my mind's innate knowing faculty itself also knows it. It has nothing to do with others. Therefore, although an inferior man may have done all manner of evil, when he sees a superior man he will surely try to disguise this fact, concealing what is evil and displaying what is good in himself. This shows that innate knowledge of the good does not permit any self-deception. Now the only way to distinguish good and evil in order to make the will sincere is to extend to the utmost the knowledge of the innate faculty. Why is this? When [a good] thought or wish arises, the innate faculty of my mind already knows it to be good. Suppose I do not sincerely love it but instead turn away from it. I would then be regarding good as evil and obscuring my innate faculty which knows the good. When [an evil] thought or wish arises, the innate faculty of my mind already knows it to be evil. If I did not sincerely hate it but instead carried it out, I would be regarding evil as good and obscuring my innate faculty which knows evil. In such cases what is supposed to be knowledge is really ignorance. How then can the will be made sincere? If what the innate faculty knows to be good or evil is sincerely loved or hated, one's innate knowing faculty is not deceived and the will can be made sincere.

Now, when one sets out to extend his innate knowledge to the utmost, does this mean something illusory, hazy, in a vacuum, and unreal? No, it means something real. Therefore, the extension of knowledge must consist in the investigation of things. A thing is an event. For every emanation of the will there must be an event corresponding to it. The event to which the will is directed is a thing. To investigate is to rectify. It is to rectify that which is incorrect so it can return to its original correctness. To rectify that which is not correct is to get rid of evil, and to return to correctness is to do good. This is what is meant by investigation. The *Book of History* says, "He [Emperor Yao] investigated (*ko*) heaven above and earth below"; "[Emperor Shun] investigated (*ko*) in the temple of illustrious ancestors"; and "[The ruler] rectifies (*ko*) the evil of his heart." The word "investigation" (*ko*) in the phrase "the investigation of things" combines the two meanings.

If one sincerely loves the good known by the innate faculty but does not in reality do the good as he comes into contact with the thing to which the will is directed, it means that the thing has not been investigated and that the will to love the good is not yet sincere. If one sincerely hates the evil known by the innate faculty but does not in reality get rid of the evil as he comes into contact with the thing to which the will is directed, it means that the thing has not been investigated and that the will to hate evil is not sincere. If as we come into contact with the thing to which the will is directed, we really do the good and get rid of the evil to the utmost which is known by the innate faculty, then everything will be investigated and what is known by our innate faculty will not be deficient or obscured but will be extended to the utmost. Then the mind will be joyous in itself, happy and without regret, the functioning of the will will carry with it no self-deception, and sincerity may be said to have been attained. Therefore it is said, "When things are investigated, knowledge is extended; when knowledge is extended, the will becomes sincere; when the will is sincere, the mind is rectified; and when the mind is rectified, the personal life is cultivated." While the order of the tasks involves a sequence of first and last, in substance they are one and cannot be so separated. At the same time, while the order and the tasks cannot be separated into first and last, their function must be so refined as not to be wanting in the slightest degree. This is why the doctrine of investigation, extension, being sincere, and rectification is a correct exposition of the true heritage of Sage-Emperors Yao and Shun and why it coincides with Confucius' own ideas.

MODERN CHINESE PHILOSOPHY

The main trends in Chinese philosophy in the twentieth century resemble those in India and the Muslim world. The sharp criticism of the traditional philosophy and orientation toward the West could be clearly seen in the views of Hu Shih (1891–1962), a strong champion of the philosophy of pragmatism and a loyal follower of James and Dewey. Along with extensive philosophical importation from the West (Kant, Bergson, Descartes, Darwin, Hegel, Nietzsche, Schopenhauer, Marx) there was as well a strong tendency for the renewal of Buddhism and Confucianism. The most prominent representative of the reformative trend in modern Chinese philosophy, most probably, was Fung Yu-lan (1895–1990).

Fung Yu-lan studied first in China, then got his Ph.D. in philosophy from Columbia University (1924). After his return from America, Fung Yu-lan taught in different universities of China. In the early thirties he wrote *A History of Chinese Philosophy* in two volumes. In 1939 Fung published *Hsin li-hsüeh* (*The New Rational Philosophy*)—the most original Chinese philosophical work in the twentieth century.

The "new system" created by Fung is based on four metaphysical concepts: principle (*li*), material force (*ch'i*), the substance of *Tao*, and the Great Whole. The first two concepts are deduced from propositions developed in the Neo-Confucianism of Ch'eng I. The last two concepts bear the impact of Chu Hsi and Taoism.

The greatest innovation of Fung Yu-lan is in the conversion of Neo-Confucianism into logical (in fact, Western) concepts. Because of that very conversion he was criticized for rejecting the immanent character of Neo-Confucianism and replacing this with transcendentalism.

Fung Yu-lan advocated a synthesis of Western and Chinese philosophies. In the peculiarity of the former, he saw its pragmatic orientation, and in those of the latter, an emphasis on morality. According to Fung, in Western philosophy positivist methods dominate, while in Chinese philosophy, negativist methods; that is, the search for the Truth is strongly based on intuition.

Fung Yu-lan called for the creation of a universal philosophy of the future. In his view, the perfect metaphysical system should start with the positivist (that is, rationalist) method and end with the negative method (negativism is understood by him as agnosticism). He believed that the two methods complement each other and should create the philosophy of the future.

Under the pressure of the political situation in Communist China, Fung repudiated many points of his philosophy.

From Fung Yu-lan

Hsin li-hsüeh. *Reprinted from* A Source Book in Chinese Philosophy. *Translated by Wing-Tsit Chan. Princeton, N.J.: Princeton University Press, 1963.*

1. The World and Principle

What makes a thing square is the square. As explained before, the square can be real but not actual. If in fact there are no actual square things, the square is then not actual. But if in fact there are actual square things, they must have four corners. An actual square thing necessarily follows that which makes a square square; it cannot avoid this. From this we know that the square is real. Since the square is real but not actual, it belongs to the realm of pure reality. . . .

When we say "There is a square," we are making a formal affirmation about reality. The statement "There is a square" does not imply an actual square thing. Much less does it imply a particular actual square thing. Therefore the statement does not affirm anything about actuality, but merely makes a formal affirmation about reality. From the point of view of our acquisition of knowledge, we must in our experience see an actual square thing before we can say that there is a square. But since we have said that there is square, we see that even if in fact there is no actual square thing, we still can say there is a square. (pp. 27–28)

Chu Hsi regards principle as that by which actual things necessarily are what they are and the specific principle according to which they should be. Our idea of principle is the same. A square thing must follow the principle of the square before it can be square, and it must completely follow the principle of the square before it can be perfectly square. Whether a square thing is perfectly square depends on whether or not it follows the principle of the square completely. According to this reasoning, the principle of the square is the standard of all square things; it is the specific principle according to which they should be. The *Book of Odes* says, "Heaven produces the teeming multitude. As there are things, there are their specific principles." This was often quoted by the Neo-Confucianists of the Sung period. Ch'eng I-ch'uan said, "As there are things, there must be their specific principles. One thing necessarily has one principle." The principle of a class of things is the same as the specific principle of that class of things. We often say, "This square thing is more square or less square than the other square thing." In saying so we are following this standard. Without this standard no criticism is possible. Those who do not accept the existence of principle have overlooked this point. (p. 53)

Sung Neo-Confucianists also have the theory that the "principle is one but its manifestations are many," which Chu Hsi also held. But when he talked about principle being one and its manifestations being many, the principle he talked about is already different from the principle when he discussed it [as such]. In commenting on the *Western Inscription* by Chang Heng-ch'ü (Chang Tsai, 1020–1077), Chu Hsi said, "There is nothing in the entire realm of creatures that does not regard Heaven as the father and Earth as the mother. This means that the principle is one. . . . Each regards his parents as his own parents and his son as his own son. This being the case, how can principle not be manifested as many?" The principle referred to here concerns the realm of that which exists after physical form and is with it (*hsing-erh-hsia*). It makes an affirmation about actuality. According to this theory, among individual, actual things there are certain internal relations. But this is a question about actuality. To say that there must be relations [among them] is to make an affirmation about actuality.

In our system we can still say that "the principle is one but its manifestations are many." But when we say so, the principle we are talking about is still the principle when we discuss it as such. Let us first take things in a certain class. The things in this class all follow one principle. However, although they all follow the same principle, they each have their own individuality. From the point of view of things of this class being related within the class, we can say that their principle is one but its manifestations are many. As we said before, the principle of a class implies the principle of a general class. From the point of view of specific classes within a general class, all specific classes belong to the general class but at the same time possess that which makes them specific classes. The relation among the specific classes within the general class can also be stated in terms that the principle is one but its manifestations are many. . . .

This is our theory that the principle is one but its manifestations are many. This theory is presented in its logical aspect. It only makes an affirmation about reality. It does not imply that there are internal relations among actual things, and therefore does not make any affirmation about actuality. (pp. 60–62)

2. Principle and Material Force

There are two aspects in every actually existing thing, namely, its "what" and that on which it depends for its existence or to become actually what it is. For example, every round thing has two aspects. One is that "it is round." The other is that on which it depends for existence, that is, to become actually round. This "what" is the thing's essential element in the class to which it belongs and the thing's nature. The reason that it exists is the foundation of the thing's existence. Its "what" depends on the principle it follows. That on which it depends for existence is the material which actualizes the principle. . . .

Material is either relative or absolute. Relative material has the two aspects just described. Absolute material, on the other hand, has only one of these aspects, namely, that it can be material simple and pure. Take a building, for example. . . . Bricks and tiles are material for the building, but they are relative and not absolute material. Earth is material for bricks and tiles, but it is still relative and not absolute material, for it still possesses the two aspects described above. . . .

When the nature of the building is removed, it will cease to be a building but only bricks and tiles. When the nature of bricks and tiles is removed, they will cease to be bricks and tiles but only earth. The nature of earth can also be removed, *ad infinitum.* At the end there is the absolute material. This material is called matter in the philosophies of Plato and Aristotle. . . . Matter itself has no nature. Because it has no nature whatsoever, it is indescribable, inexplicable in speech, and unrealizable in thought. . . .

We call this material *ch'i* (material force). . . . In our system material force is entirely a logical concept. It is neither a principle nor an actual thing. An actual thing is that which is produced by what we call material force in accordance with principle. Those who hold the theory of principle and material force should talk about material force in this way. But in the history of Chinese philosophy, those who held the theory of principle and material force in the past never had such a clear view of material force. In Chang Tsai's philosophy, material force is entirely a scientific concept. If there is the material force which he talked about, it is a kind of an actual thing. This point will be taken up in detail later. Even what Ch'eng I and Chu Hsi called material force does not seem to be a completely logical concept. For instance, they often described material force as clear or turbid. The way we look at the matter, the material force that can be described as clear or turbid is no longer material force [as such] but material force in accordance with the principle of clearness or turbidity. When they talked about material force as clear or turbid, they did not make clear whether they were talking about material force itself or about material force achieving the principle of clearness or turbidity. (pp. 64–68)

We shall first discuss [Chu Hsi's statement], "There has never been any material force without principle." This can very easily be proved. When we said that [what Ch'eng I called] the material force of the true source has no nature whatsoever, we spoke entirely from the point of view of logic. From the point of view of fact, however, material force has at least the nature of existence. If not, it fundamentally does not exist. If material force does not exist, then there will not be any actual thing at all. If material force has the nature of existence, it means that it follows the principle of existence. Since it at least has to follow the principle of existence, therefore "There has never been any material force without principle." (Chu Hsi also said), "There has never been any principle without material force." This saying cannot be interpreted to mean that all principles are with material force, for if so, it would mean that all principles are actually exemplified and that there would be no principle which is only real but not actual. This statement merely says, "There must be some principles with material force," or "There has never been the time when all principles are without material force." This has been proved above, for at least the principle of existence is always followed by material force. (p. 75)

3. Tao, Substance and Function, and Universal Operation

What we call the material force of the true source is the Ultimate of Non-being, and the totality of all principles is the Great Ultimate. The process from the Ultimate of Non-being to the Great Ultimate is our world of actuality. We call this process "The Ultimate of Non-being and also the Great Ultimate." The Ultimate of Non-being, the Great Ultimate, and the Ultimate of Non-being-and-also-the-Great-Ultimate are, in other words, the material force of the true source, the totality of principle, and the entire process from material force to principle, respectively. Collectively speaking, they are called Tao (the Way). . . .

Why have Tao in addition to the Great Whole or the universe? Our answer is that when we talk about the Great Whole or the universe, we speak from the aspect of tranquillity of all things, whereas when we talk about Tao, we speak from the aspect of activity of all things. . . .

The principle followed by "fact" (which includes all facts) is the Great Ultimate in its totality, and the material force depended on by "fact" is the Ultimate of Non-being in its totality. (Actually the Ultimate of Non-being has no totality to speak of. We merely say so.) In the first chapter we said that according to the old theory (of Sung Neo-Confucianists), principle is substance while actual things that actualize principle are function. But according to the concept of "the Ultimate of Non-being and also the Great Ultimate," the Great Ultimate is substance and the "and also" is function. As all functions are included in this function, it is therefore (what Chu Hsi called) the total substance and great functioning. . . .

All things (meaning both things and events) go through the four stages of formation, flourish, decline, and destruction. Old things go out of existence this way and new things come into existence this way. This successive coming-into-existence and going-out-of-existence is the universal operation of the great functioning. The universal operation of the great functioning is also called the process of creation and transformation. The formation and flourish of things are creation, while their decline and destruction are transformation. The creation and transformation of all things are collectively called the process of creation and transformation. At the same time each thing or event is a process of creation and transformation. Since all things are each a process of creation and transformation, they are collectively called ten thousand transformations (all things). The term "transformation" may also involve both meanings of creation and transformation. Therefore the process is also called great transformation. The universal operation of the great transformation is the same as the universal operation of the great functioning. Our actual world is a universal operation. (pp. 97–100)

The *Lao Tzu* and the "Appended Remarks" of the *Book of Changes* have a common idea, that is, that when things reach their limit, they return to their origin. . . . According to the law of circular movement described above, things in the universe come into existence and go out of existence at all times. They are always in the process of change. This is the daily renewal of the substance of Tao.

The daily renewal of the substance of Tao can be seen from four points of view. . . . (1) We can, from the point of view of classes, see the production and extinction of their actual members. Looked at this way, the daily renewal of the substance of Tao is cyclical. (2) We can, from the point of view of principle, see whether its actual exemplification tends to be perfect or not. Looked at this way, the daily renewal of the substance of Tao is one of progress and retrogression. (3) We can, from the point of view of the universe, see the increase or decrease of classes which have members in the actual world. Looked at this way, the daily renewal of the substance of Tao is one of increase and decrease. (4) And we can, from the point of view of an individual entity, see the process of its movement from one class to another. Looked at this way, the daily renewal of the substance of Tao is one of transformation and penetration. (pp. 110–11)

4. Principle and the Nature

Principle is the moral nature of things. From one point of view, if the moral nature of things is perfectly good, then the physical nature of things is also good, for the physical nature of things is that by which things actually follow their principle. Their following may not be perfect, but since they are following the highest good, they should be good. They may be eighty percent good or seventy percent good or not very good, but we cannot say they are not good. . . .

If a thing can follow its principle perfectly, it can be said to have "investigated principle to the utmost." To get to the utmost of the principle which it follows means to develop its own nature fully. Therefore investigating principle to the utmost is the same as fully developing one's nature. According to the idea of destiny set forth in this chapter, investigating principle to the utmost and full development of one's nature are the same as getting to the point of fulfilling one's destiny. I-ch'uan (Ch'eng I) said, "The investigation of principle to the utmost, the full development of one's nature, and the fulfillment of destiny are only one thing. As principle is investigated to the utmost, one's nature is fully developed, and as soon as one's nature is fully developed, destiny is fulfilled." We also say the same. We further believe that this does not apply only to man but to things also. (pp. 134–36)

5. Serving Heaven and Jen *(Humanity)*

From the point of view of Heaven (*T'ien*, Nature), every class of things has its own principle. Its principle is also its ultimate. With reference to the things in this class, their ultimate is the highest good, and their physical nature is that by which they actually follow principle. It is "what issues [from the Way]" and "is good." From the point of view of Heaven, what things in a given class should do in the great process of "the Non-ultimate and also the Great Ultimate" is to follow their principle completely. To be able to do so is to develop their nature fully and to investigate their principle to the utmost. This point has been discussed in chapter four. There the investigation of things means the use of my knowing faculty to know the principle of things. Here the term has a different meaning; it means to direct my conduct to realize fully the principle I am following. To use my knowing faculty to know the principle of things enables me to transcend experience and be free from the restriction of experience. This is transcendence of and freedom from experience. To direct my conduct to realize fully the principle I am following enables me to transcend myself and be free from self-bondage. This is transcendence and freedom from the self.

From the point of view of Heaven, men are also a class, and what they should do in the process of "the Non-ultimate and also the Great Ultimate" is also to follow their principle completely. Shao K'ang-chieh (Shao Yung, 1011–1077) said, "The sage is the ultimate of man." By the ultimate of man is meant the perfect man, one who can fully develop the nature of man and investigate the principle of man to the utmost.

Mencius said, "The sage is the ultimate standard of human relations." Human relations means to carry on the social relations, and to carry out human relations means the social activities of men. We said in chapter four that man's nature is social and that his social life issues from his nature. Therefore the full development of our nature and our investigation of principle to the utmost must be carried out in society.

In social life man's most social conduct is moral conduct. We can approach moral conduct in two different ways, one from the point of view of society and the other from the point of view of Heaven. From the point of view of society, man's moral conduct consists in fulfilling one's social duty. From the point of view of Heaven, one's moral conduct consists in fulfilling his universal duty, that is, fulfilling the way of man. From this point of view, in doing something moral, one is serving Heaven. . . .

We said previously that viewing things from the point of view of Heaven gives us a sympathetic understanding of them. In the sphere where the self is transcended, sympathy toward things is also increasingly enlarged until the sphere of what Sung and Ming Neo-Confucianists called "forming one body with all things" is reached. They call this sphere that of *jen.*

The word *jen* has two meanings. One is moral, the *jen* (humanity) in the (Five Constant Virtues) of humanity, righteousness, propriety, wisdom, and faithfulness discussed in chapter five. The other meaning refers to the sphere we are discussing. Ch'eng Ming-tao (Ch'eng Hao, 1032–1085) said, "The man of *jen* forms one body with all things without any differentiation. Righteousness, propriety, wisdom, and faithfulness are all [expressions of] *jen.*" What he meant is this *jen.* In order to distinguish the two meanings, we shall call this *jen* "the great *jen.*" (pp. 300–304)

NOTES

1. Because different translators prefer different romanizations, the terms *jen* and *chun-zi* are represented as *ren* and *junzi* in the *Analects* selections that follow. All *Analects* selections employ the Pinyin romanization system. All remaining text and translation in this section employs the Wade-Giles system.

2. Cf. the *Analects* of Confucius, IV.I.

3. In place of "that is why he said," the parallel passage in v.b.I has the sentence "when he was with a fellow-villager he simply could not tear himself away." In the present passage, this sentence must have dropped out by mistake, as without it what follows becomes quite unintelligible.

4. The text at this point appears to be corrupt and a few words have been omitted in translation.

5. The "Great Oath," supposedly a speech by King Wu, the son of King Wen, was a section of the *Book of Documents.* It was lost long ago, and the text by that name included in the present *Book of Documents* is a forgery of the third century A.D., though it includes a passage much like the one quoted here by Mo Tzu.

6. A section of the *Book of Documents,* now lost.

7. A section of the *Book of Documents,* now lost. Almost the same quotation is found at the beginning of Book XX of the Confucian *Analects.*

8. The first four lines are now found, not in the *Book of Odes,* but in the *Hung fan* section of the *Book of Documents.* The last four lines are from the *Book of Odes, Hsiao ya* section, "Ta tung" (Mao text no. 203).

9. The first two lines are from the poem "Yi" (Mao text no. 256), in the "Greater Odes" or *Ta ya* section of the *Book of Odes.* The last two lines, though not found in exactly this form, bear a close resemblance to lines in the poem "Mu-kua" (Mao text no. 64), in the *Kuo feng* or "Airs from the States" section of the *Odes.*

8

Islamic Tradition

KALĀM

Kalām ("speech" in Arabic) is historically the first major trend in Islamic thought. It is a speculative discipline cultivated mainly in Mu'tazilite and Ash'arite circles.

The term "Kalām" originally signified theoretical, rational reasoning. The subject matter primarily concerned theological questions. In the very beginning Kalām had a predominantly oral character, developed mainly in disputes that started in Islam with the appearance of various religious groups (Khārijites, Murji'tes, Qādiriyyah, etc.), and also during disputes with spokesmen of non-Muslim creeds. However above all that were disputes among Mutakallimūn themselves. Later on it began to be used as the name of the speculative discipline developed by Mu'tazilites and Ash'arites.

Themes of an ontological and natural philosophical character, known as the "nice problems of Kalām," have a significant and frequently predominant place in the works of Mutakallimūn. A leading place in the "niceties" of Kalām belongs to the problem of the structure of physical bodies. The disputes about "indivisible particles" that developed among mutakallimūn themselves and between finitist Mutakallimūn and their opponents were a continuation of a corresponding discussion in antique thought.

These disputes had started in Kalām at the beginning of the ninth century. The Mu'tazilite, al-Naẓẓām and his successors taught the infinite divisibility of bodies. Al-'Allāf and some other Mu'tazilites objecting to them, defended a thesis of the existence of a limit to divisibility, of "indivisible particles." There was a similar divergence among Ash'arites, though the founder of the school, Abū'l Ḥasan al-Ash'arī (d. 935), firmly held atomistic views.

From Al-Ash'arī

Risāla fī'l Istiḥsān al-Khawḍ fī 'Ilm al-Kalām (A Vindication of the Science of Kalām). *Translated by Richard J. McCarthy, S. J.*

The Objection to Kalām

2. A certain group of men have made ignorance their capital. Finding reasoning and inquiry into religious belief too burdensome, they incline towards the easy way of servile sectarianism. They calumniate him who scrutinizes the basic dogmas of religion and accuse him of deviation. It is innovation and deviation, they claim, to engage in Kalām about motion and rest, body and accident, accidental modes and states, the atom and the leap, and the attributes of the Creator.

3. They assert that if that were a matter of guidance and rectitude, the Prophet and his Caliphs and his Companions would have discussed it. For, they say, the Prophet did not die until he had discussed and amply explained all needful religious matters. He left nothing to be said by anyone about the affairs of their religion needful to Muslims, and what brings them near to God and removes them far from His anger.

4. Since no Kalām on any of the subjects which we have mentioned has been related from the Prophet, we know that such Kalām is an innovation and such inquiry a deviation. For if it were good, the Prophet and his Companions would not have failed to discuss it. For the absence of such Kalām on the part of the Prophet and his Companions can be explained in only two ways: either they knew it and were silent about it; or they did not know it, nay, were ignorant of it. Now if they knew it and did not discuss it, then we also may be silent about it, as they were, and we may abstain from plunging into it, as they abstained. For if it were a part of religion, they could not have been silent about it. On the other hand, if they did not know it, then we may have the same ignorance of it. For if it were a part of religion, they would not have been ignorant of it. So according to both explanations such Kalām is an innovation and plunging into it is a deviation.

This is the summary of their argument for abstaining from reasoning about the basic dogmas of religion.

First Answer

5. There are three ways of answering that argument. The first is to turn the question against them by saying: It is also true that the Prophet never said: "If anyone should inquire into that and discuss it, regard him as a deviating innovator." So you are constrained to regard yourselves as deviating innovators,

since you have discussed something which the Prophet did not discuss, and you have accused of deviation him whom the Prophet did not so accuse.

Second Answer

6. The second answer is to say to them: Actually the Prophet was not ignorant of any item of the Kalām which you have mentioned concerning body and accident, motion and rest, atom and leap. It is true that he did not discuss every one of these points specifically; and the same is true of the jurisprudents and learned men among the Companions. Nevertheless, the basic principles of these things which you have mentioned specifically are present in the Qur'ān and the Sunna in general terms, not in detail.

7. Take motion and rest and the Kalām about them. Their basic principle is present in the Qur'ān, where they prove the affirmation of God's oneness; and so for union and separateness. In relating what His friend Abraham said in the story of the setting of the star and the sun and the moon and their being moved from place to place, God said what proves that his (Abraham's) Lord cannot be subject to any of that, and that one who is subject to setting and translation from place to place is not a divinity.

8. The Kalām on the basic principles of the profession of God's oneness is also taken from the Book. God said: "Were there divinities other than God in them, the heavens and the earth would be in disorder" (21. 22). This Kalām is a brief reminder of the proof that God is unique and peerless, and the Kalām of the Mutakallimūn, in which they argue to the divine unity from mutual hindrance and contention, simply goes back to this verse. God also said: "God has taken for Himself no son, and there is no other divinity with Him—else each divinity would have taken away what he had created, and some would have been superior to others" (23. 91/93). And so on until He said: "Or have they appointed for God partners who have created even as He has, so that creation is a puzzle to them?" (13. 16/17) The Kalām of the Mutakallimūn in which they argue to the unity of God, simply goes back to these verses which we have mentioned. And similarly, all the Kalām which treats in detail of the questions deriving from the basic dogmas of God's oneness and justice is simply taken from the Qur'ān.

9. Such is also the case with the Kalām on the possibility and the impossibility of the resurrection (of the body). This question had been disputed by intelligent Arabs and by others before them until they were amazed at the possibility of that and said: "What! When we have died and become dust? That is an incredible return!" (50. 3); and: "Never, never a hope of what you are promised!"(23. 36/38); and: "Who will quicken bones when they have decayed?" (36. 78); and God's words: "Does he promise you that when you shall have

died and become dust and bones you will be brought forth?" (23. 35/37) Apropos of such Kalām of theirs God put into the Qur'ān argument designed to confirm, from the viewpoint of reason, the possibility of the resurrection after death. Moreover, He taught and instructed His Prophet how to argue against their denial of the resurrection in two ways, according to the two groups of adversaries. For one group admitted the first creation, but denied the second, while the other group denied both on the ground that the world is eternal.

10. So against him who admitted the first creation God argued by saying: "Answer: He will quicken them who produced them a first time" (36. 79), and by saying: "It is He who gives life by a first creation, then restores it; and it is very easy for Him" (30. 27/26), and by His words: "As He first made you, you will return" (7. 29/28). By these verses He called their attention to the fact that he who is able to effect something without reference to a preexisting exemplar is all the more able to effect something which has already been produced. Indeed, the latter is easier for him, as you know from your own experience. But in the case of the Creator, it is not "easier" for Him to create one thing than to create another.

This, then, was the argument which God adduced against the group which admitted creation.

11. As for the group which denied both the first creation and the second, and maintained the eternity of the world, a doubt entered their minds simply because they said: "It is our experience that life is wet and hot, and death is cold and dry, akin to the nature of earth. How, then, can there be any amalgamation of life and earth and decayed bones, resulting in a sound creation, since two contraries do not combine?" For this reason, then, they denied the resurrection.

12. It is certainly true that two contraries do not combine in one substrate, or in one direction, or in what exists (already) in the substrate. But they can exist in two substrates by way of propinquity. So God argued against them by saying: "He who makes fire for you from the green tree—for lo you kindle fire from it" (36. 80). In saying that, God referred them to their own knowledge and experience of the emergence of fire from green trees, notwithstanding the heat and dryness of the former and the coldness and wetness of the latter. Again, God made the possibility of the first production a proof of the possibility of the last production, because it is a proof of the possibility of the propinquity of life to earth and decayed bones and of making it a sound creation—for He said: "Just as we created man a first time, so we shall restore him" (21. 104).

13. As for the discussion of the Mutakallimūn involving (the principle) that (the series of) things which begin to exist has a first member, and their refu-

tation of the Materialists who hold that there is no motion not preceded by a motion, and no day not preceded by a day, and the Kalām against him who holds that there is no atom which cannot be halved ad infinitum—we find the basis of that in the Sunna of God's Apostle. On a certain occasion he said: "There is no contagious disease and no bad omen." And a Bedouin said: "Then what is the matter with camels, flawless as gazelles, which mingle with scabby camels and become scabby?" And the Prophet said: "And who infected the first?" And the Bedouin was silent because of what he had made him understand by that rational argument. Likewise we say to him who claims that there is no motion not preceded by a motion: If that were the case, then not a single motion would ever have begun to be, because the (antecedently) limitless cannot begin to be.

14. Similarly, when a certain man said: "O Prophet of God! My wife has borne a black male child"—and he hinted that he would repudiate it—the Prophet said: "Have you any camels?" He replied: "Yes" The Prophet said: "What color are they?" He said: "Red." And the Apostle of God said: "Is there an ash-colored one among them?" He said: "Yes, there is an ash-colored one among them." The Prophet said: "And whence came that?" He said: "Perhaps a sweat spoiled it." And the Prophet said: "And perhaps a sweat spoiled your son." This, then, is the way in which God taught His Prophet to refer a thing to its kind and like, and it is our basis in all the judgments we make regarding the similar and the like.

15. We use that argument against him who holds that God resembles creatures and is a body by saying to him: If God resembled anything, He would have to resemble it either in all of its respects or in one of its respects. Now if He resembled it in all of its respects, He would of necessity be produced in all of His respects. And if He resembled it in one of its respects, He would of necessity be produced, like it, in that respect in which He resembled it. For every two like things are judged the same regarding that in which they are alike. But it is impossible for the produced to be eternal, and for the eternal to be produced. Indeed God has said: "There is nothing like Him" (42. 11/9), and He has said: "There is no one equal to Him" (112. 4).

16. The basis for declaring that the body has a limit, and that the atom cannot be divided (ad infinitum), is the statement of God: "And everything has been numbered by us in a clear archetype" (36. 12/11). Now one cannot number what has no limit, and the single thing cannot be divided (ad infinitum). For this would necessitate that they (endlessly) be two things—and God has declared that numbering applies to them both.

17. The basis for declaring that the act must be effected for the Producer of the world as He intends and chooses, and in the absence of any aversion for it

on His part, is the utterance of God: "Do you not then see what you eject? Is it you who create it? Or are we the creators?" (56. 58/59). And they could not affirm with proof that they created (it). Despite their desire to have a child, he would not come if God was unwilling that he should. Thus God called their attention to the fact the Creator is He from whom creatures proceed according to His intention.

18. The basis of our rational refutation of our adversary is taken from the Sunna of our Master, Muḥammad. I refer to the teaching he received from God when he met the fat rabbi and said to him: "I conjure thee by God, do you find in what God has revealed of the Torah that God detests the fat rabbi?" And the rabbi became angry at being thus reproached, and he said: "God has not sent down anything to a human being!" (6. 91). Then God said: "Say: Who sent down the Book which Moses brought as light and guidance for men? etc." (6. 91). So he quickly refuted him, because the Torah is a thing, and Moses a human being, and the rabbi admitted that God had sent down the Torah to Moses. And in a similar way he refuted the men who claimed that God had enjoined upon them that they should not believe an apostle until he should come to them with a sacrifice which fire would consume (3. 183/179). For God said: "Say: Apostles before me have already brought you evidences, and the very thing you have mentioned. Why, then, did you kill them, if you are truthful?" (3. 183/180). And by means of that he refuted them and argued against them.

19. Our basis in correcting the sophistry of our adversaries is taken from the words of God: "You and what you worship, apart from God, will be fuel for Gehenna. You are drawing near to it. If these false gods had been divinities, they would not have arrived at (Gehenna). All will be there eternally. There they will send forth groans, but they will not be heard" (21. 98/100). For when this verse came down, word of it reached 'Abdallāh b. al-Zubayr—a disputatious and contentious man—and he said: "I have as good as triumphed over Muḥammad and the Lord of the Ka'ba!" Then the Apostle of God came to him, and 'Abdallāh said: "O Muḥammad, do you not claim that Jesus and 'Uzair and the angels were worshipped?" And the Prophet was silent, not from confusion or the lack of anything to say, but from astonishment at 'Abdallāh's ignorance, because there is nothing in the verse which necessitates the entrance into it of Jesus and 'Uzair and the angels. For God said: "and what you worship"; but He did not say: "and everything which you worship, apart from God." But Ibn al-Zubayr simply wanted to argue speciously against the Prophet, in order to make his people think that he had argued against Muḥammad successfully. So God sent down the verse: "Those, indeed, who have already received from us the best (reward)"—i.e., those of them who are

worshipped—"are far removed from it (Gehenna)!" (21. 101). The Prophet then recited that verse, and thereupon they raised a great outcry to mask their confusion and their error, and they said: "Are our divinities better, or is he?"—i.e., Jesus. So God sent down the verses: "When the Son of Mary is proposed as an example, see how your people turn away from him. They ask: 'Are our divinities better, or is he?' They have proposed this example to you only out of disputatiousness. Truly they are a contentious people" (43. 57/58).

20. All the verses which we have mentioned, as well as many which we have not mentioned, are a basis and argument for us in our Kalām on what we mention in detail. It is true that no question was particularized in the Book and the Sunna, but that was because the particularization of questions involving rational principles did not take place in the days of the Prophet. However, (he and) the Companions did engage in Kalām of the sort which we have mentioned.

Third Answer

21. The third answer is that the Apostle of God did know these questions about which they have asked, and he was not ignorant of any detail involved in them. However, they did not occur in his time in such specific form that he should have, or should not have, discussed them—even though their basic principles were present in the Qur'ān and the Sunna. But whenever a question arose which was related to religion from the standpoint of the Law, men discussed it, and inquired into it, and disputed about it, and debated and argued. Such, for example, were the questions concerning the fraction of the inheritance to which grandmothers are entitled—which is one of the questions involving obligations—and other questions touching on legal determinations. Such, too, were the questions pertaining to what is unlawful, and to the effects of irrevocable divorce, and to . . . the questions concerning hard punishments and divorce. These questions, too numerous to mention, arose in their days, and in the case of each one of them there had come no explicit determination from the Prophet. For if he had given explicit instructions concerning all that, they would not have differed over those questions, and the difference would not have lasted until now.

22. But even though there was no explicit instruction of the Apostle of God regarding each one of these questions, they referred and likened each to something which had been determined explicitly by the Book of God, and the Sunna, and their own ijtihad. Such questions, then, which involved judgments on unprecedented secondary cases, they referred to those determinations of the Law which are derivative, and which are to be sought only along the line of revelation and apostolic tradition. But when new and specific questions

pertaining to the basic dogmas arise, every intelligent Muslim ought to refer judgment on them to the sum of principles accepted on the grounds of reason, sense experience, intuition, etc. For judgment on legal questions which belong to the category of the traditional is to be based on reference to legal principles which likewise belong to the category of the traditional. And judgment on questions involving the data of reason and the senses should be a matter of referring every such instance to (something within) its own category, without confounding the rational with the traditional, or the traditional with the rational. So if Kalām on the creation of the Qur'ān and on the atom and the leap, in these precise terms, had originated in the Prophet's time, he would have discussed and explained it, just as he explained and discussed all the specific questions which did originate in his time.

23. Then one should say: There is no sound tradition from the Prophet to the effect that the Qur'ān is uncreated or created. Why, then, do you hold that it is uncreated? They may say: Some of the Companions and the Followers held that. One should say to them: The Companion, or the Follower, is subject to the same constraint as you are, namely, that he is a deviating innovator for saying what the Apostle did not say. And another may say: I suspend my judgment on that, and I do not say created, nor do I say uncreated. To him one should say: Then you, in suspending your judgment on that, are a deviating innovator. For the Prophet did not say: "If this question should arise after my death, suspend your judgment on it, and say nothing." Nor did he say: "Regard as deviating and unbelieving him who affirms that it is created, or, him who denies that it is created."

24. Furthermore, tell us: If one were to say that God's knowledge is created, would you suspend your judgment on that, or not? If they say no, then say to them: Neither the Prophet nor his Companions said a word about that. And likewise, if someone were to say: Is this Lord of yours surfeited with food, or with drink, or is He clothed, or naked, or cold, or bilious, or damp, or a body, or an accident, or does He smell odors, or not smell them, or has He a nose, and a heart, and a liver, and a spleen, and does He make the pilgrimage every year, and does He ride horseback, or not, and is He grieved, or not—and other questions of that sort—you would have to refuse to answer him. For neither the Apostle of God nor his Companions ever discussed a single one of those points. Or you would not remain silent, and would explain by your Kalām that none of those things can be predicated of God, etc., etc., because of this argument, and that, etc.

25. Someone may say: I should be silent and answer him not a word, or, I should shun him, or, I should leave him, or, I should not greet him, or, I should not visit him if he fell sick, or, I should show no respect to his corpse

if he died. To him one should say: Then you would be bound to be, in all these ways which you have mentioned, a deviating innovator.

For the Apostle of God never said: "If anyone should ask about any of those things, refuse to answer him, or, do not greet him, or, leave him." Since he said nothing of the sort, you would be innovators if you did that.

26. Moreover, why have you not refused to answer him, who says that the Qur'ān is created? And why have you accused him of unbelief? There is no sound tradition from the Prophet on denying its creation and accusing of unbelief him who says that it is created. They may say: Because Aḥmad b. Ḥanbal denied that it is created and held that he who says that it is created should be accused of unbelief. One should say to them: And why did not Aḥmad keep silent about that instead of discussing it? They may say: Because 'Abbās al-Anbārī, and Wakī', and 'Abd al-Raḥmān b. Mahdī, and so-and-so, and so-and-so, said that the Qur'ān is uncreated, and that he who says that it is created is an unbeliever. One should say to them: And why did not they keep silent about what Muḥammad had not discussed? They may say: Because 'Amr b. Dīnār, and Sufyān b. 'Uyaina, and Ja'far b. Muḥammad, and so-and-so, and so-and-so, said that it is neither creating nor created. One should say to them: And why did not they refrain from saying this, since the Apostle of God did not say it?

27. And if they refer that back to the Companions, this is sheer obstinacy. For one may say to them: And why did not they refrain from saying that, since the Prophet did not discuss it, and did not say: "Call him who says it an unbeliever." They may say: The "ulama" simply must engage in Kalām on a new question, so that the ignorant may know how to judge the matter. One should say: This is the admission which we wanted you to make. Why, then, do you hinder (men from engaging in) Kalām? You use it yourselves when you want to; but when you are silenced (in a discussion), you say: We are forbidden to engage in Kalām. And when you want to, you blindly and unquestioningly follow your predecessors, without argument or explanation. This is willfulness and capriciousness!

28. Then one should say to them: The Prophet did not discuss vows and testamentary injunctions, or manumission, or the manner of reckoning the uninterrupted transmission of estates, nor did he compose a book about those things, as did Malik, and al-Thawrī, and al-Shāfi'ī, and Abu Ḥanīfa. Hence you are forced to admit that they were deviating innovators, since they did what the Prophet had not done, and said what he had not said explicitly, and composed what the Prophet had not composed, and said that those who maintain that the Qur'ān is created are to be called unbelievers, though the Prophet had not said that.

What we have said contains enough to satisfy any intelligent man who is not perversely stubborn. The work is ended—praise be to God, and His blessing be on our Master, Muḥammad, and his household, and his Companions!

ABŪ NAṢR AL-FĀRĀBĪ

Al-Fārābī, recognized as the father of the Islamic Aristotelians, was also called the "second teacher" (Aristotle being the first). He was born most probably in A.D. 870 in the town Fārāb on the Syr-Daryā river. His father held a high position in the Turkish army. Abū Naṣr received education first in Harran, and then in Baghdad. In 942 he moved to Alleppo. He served in the court of the Ḥamdānī ruler Saif al-Daula, and died in Damascus in 950.

Al-Fārābī wrote a vast number of treatises and commentaries. He was greatly influenced by Aristotle, Plato, and Neoplatonics. Though there is an opinion that al-Fārābī confused Arisotle's ideas with Platonic and Neoplatonic ones, it seems that it was not in fact a "confusion" but rather an attempt to reconcile Aristotle and Plato in solving some utilitarian purposes.

Two main metaphysical doctrines are ascribed to al-Fārābī: first, the distinction between possible and necessary; second, the distinction between essence and existence. In his metaphysics God is a being necessary through itself. In God essence and existence are identical. God is incorporeal, pure intellect, the creator of everything that exists.

To explain the origin of the world, al-Fārābī turns to the Neoplatonic doctrine of emanation. God contemplates Himself and from that issues forth an intellect that is the first emanation. From this intellect there emanate successively nine further intellects, the last of which is the so-called Agent Intellect. The latter one governs the whole sublunary sphere.

Within the framework of his philosophy of nature al-Fārābī develops the doctrine of intellect. As the faculty of the human soul to think, there is the intellect in potentiality. When the intellect abstracts the intelligible from substances within the material world, it becomes an intellect in actuality. Thinking the intelligible within itself, the intellect becomes the acquired intellect. Finally, as any change, thinking requires an efficient cause, there is the Agent Intellect, the lowest of the self-existent intellects.

In his political theory al-Fārābī follows primarily Plato. He looks at the human being as a social creature who attains happiness within the ideal state. It is in al-Fārābī's writings on politics that the philosophy and religion come into successful coexistence. It is quite significant that the founder of the ideal state is considered to be the prophet who has attained philosophical illumination and whose duty is to transmit philosophical truth to the masses in symbolic form. Thus the philosopher and the prophet become identical. Al-Fārābī elevates philosophy to the highest place, because it is believed to contain truth while religion contains its image.

Al-Fārābī is most famed for his works in the fields of ethics and politics such as *al-Madīnah al-Fāḍilah (On the Opinions of the Citizens of the Virtuous City), Fuṣūl al-madanī (Aphorisms of the Statesman),* and *Taḥṣīl al-sa'ādah (The Attainment of Happiness).* Taking Plato's *Republic* as a model, the second teacher developed a theory of the ideal state—al-madīnah al-fāḍilah.

From Al-Fārābī

Fuṣūl al-madanī (Aphorisms of the Statesman). *Edited and translated by D. M. Dunlop. Cambridge: Cambridge University Press, 1961.*

[22] The city and the household may be compared with the body of a man. Just as the body is composed of different parts of a determinate number, some more, some less excellent, adjacent to each other and graded, each doing a certain work, and there is combined from all their actions mutual help towards the perfection of the aim in the man's body, so the city and the household are each composed of different parts of a determinate number, some less, some more excellent, adjacent to each other and graded in different grades, each doing a certain work independently, and there is combined from their actions mutual help towards the perfection of the aim in the city or household, except that the household is part of a city and the households are in the city, so the aims are different. Yet there is combined from these different aims, when they are perfected and combined, mutual help towards the perfection of the aim of the city. This again may be compared with the body, since the head, breast, belly, back, arms, and legs are related to the body as the households of the city to the city. The work of each of the principal members is different from the work of the other, and the parts of each one of these principal members help one another by their different actions towards the perfection of the aim in that principal member. Then there is combined from the different aims of the principal members, when they are perfected, and from their different actions, mutual help towards the perfection of the aim of the whole body. And similarly the situation of the parts of the households with respect to the households and the situation of the households with respect to the city, so that all the parts of the city by their combination are useful to the city and useful for the continued existence of the one through the other, like the members of the body.

[23] As the doctor treats any sick member only in accordance with its relation to the whole body and the members adjacent to it and connected with it,

since he treats it with a cure by which he affords it health whereby the whole body benefits, and the members adjacent to it and connected with it benefit, so the ruler of the city must necessarily rule the affair of each part of the city, small, like one man, or great, like a household, and treat it and afford it good in relation to the whole city and each of the other parts of the city, by seeking to do what affords that part a good which does not harm the whole city nor any of its parts, but a good from which the city as a whole benefits, and each of its parts according to its degree of usefulness to the city. And just as when the doctor does not observe this, aims at providing health to a particular member and treats it without regard to the condition of the other members near it, or treats it with what is bad for all the other members, and affords it health but thereby does something which does not benefit the body as a whole nor the members adjacent to it and connected with it, that member is impaired, as well as the connected members, and the evil permeates the other members, till the whole body is corrupted, so the city also.

[24] It is not disallowed that there is a man who has power to produce the mean in actions and morals as far as he himself is concerned, just as it is not disallowed that a man has power to produce the mean and moderate as regards the food with which he alone is nourished. The latter is a medical action, and he has power over a part of the art of medicine. So he who produces the moderate as regards morals and actions, as far as he himself is concerned, does so because he has power over a part of the political art, except that he who has power to produce the moderate for a particular one of his members, when he is not careful that what he is producing is not prejudicial to the other parts of the body and it is not made useful to the whole body and to its parts, operates with a part of a corrupt medical art. Similarly the man who has power to produce the moderate for himself in particular, with reference to morals and actions, if in what he produces he does not seek the advantage of the city nor of the rest of its parts, not perceiving it, or perceiving it and not minding the disadvantage to them, operates with a part of a corrupt political art.

[25] The city is sometimes "indispensable" and sometimes ideal. The indispensable (or "minimum") city is that in which the mutual help of its members is restricted to attaining merely what is indispensable for the continuance of man, his livelihood, and the preservation of his life. The ideal city is that in which the inhabitants help each other towards the attainment of the most excellent of things by which are the true existence of man, his continuance, his livelihood and the preservation of his life. Some think that this most excellent thing is the enjoyment of pleasures. Others think that it is riches. Yet others think that it is the combination of both. But Socrates, Plato, and Aristotle

thought that man has two lives. The continuance of the first is due to nourishment and the other external things which we need today for our continued existence. It is our first life. The other is that of which the continuance is in its essence without its requiring for the continuance of its essence things external to it, but it is sufficient in itself for its continued preservation. It is the after-life. Man, according to them, has a first and a last perfection. The last results to us not in this life but in the after-life, when there has preceded it the first perfection in this life of ours.

The first perfection is that a man does the actions of all the virtues, not that he is merely endowed with a virtue without performing its actions, and the perfection consists in his acting, not in his acquiring the qualities by which the actions come, as the perfection of the secretary is that he performs the actions of writing, not that he acquires the art of writing, and the perfection of the doctor, that he performs the actions of medicine, not that he acquires the art of medicine merely, and similarly every art. This perfection affords us the last perfection, which is ultimate happiness, i.e., the absolute good. It is that which is chosen and desired for itself and is not chosen, at any time whatever, for the sake of anything else. All else is chosen for its use in the attainment of happiness. Everything is good when it is useful for the attainment of happiness, and whatever interferes with happiness in any way is bad. The ideal city according to them is that whose inhabitants help one another towards the attainment of the last perfection, i.e., ultimate happiness. Therefore its inhabitants in particular are endowed with virtues above the other cities, because in the city whose inhabitants aim at helping each other to attain riches and enjoy pleasures they do not need for the attainment of their end all the virtues, or rather perhaps do not need even a single one. That is because the harmony and justice which they may employ among themselves is not truly justice, but only something resembling justice, not being so, and similarly the other pseudo-virtues which they employ among themselves.

[26] Moderate, mean actions, measured in relation to the circumstances which attach to them must be, among other conditions, useful in attaining happiness, and he who produces them must make happiness the mark for his eyes. Then he must consider how he is to measure the actions so that they may be useful either to the people of the city as a whole or to single persons among them, in the attainment of happiness, just as the doctor makes health the mark for his eyes when he tries to produce the moderate in the foods and medicines with which he treats the body.

[27] The true king is he whose aim and purpose in the art by which he rules the cities are that he should afford himself and the rest of the people of the city true happiness, which is the end and aim of the kingly craft. It is quite

necessary that the king of the ideal cities should be the most perfect of them in happiness, since he is the cause of the happiness of the people of the city.

[28] Some think that the end and purpose in kingship and the rule of cities is greatness and honor and domination and commanding and forbidding and being obeyed and made much of and praised, and they choose honor for its own sake, not for anything else which they obtain by it. They make the actions by which they rule the cities actions by which they may attain this aim, and they make the laws of the city laws by which they may attain this aim from the people of the city. Some of them attain it by employing virtue towards the people of the city, doing good to them, bringing them to the good things which in the opinion of the people of the city are goods, preserving the good things for them and preferring them above themselves therein. They thus obtain great honor. These are chiefs of honor and the most excellent of chiefs. Others of them think that they merit honor on account of riches. They aim at being the richest of the people of the city and at being unique in wealth that they may obtain honor. Some of them think that honor is given for descent alone. Others seek to obtain it by forcing the people of the city, dominating over them, humiliating and frightening them.

Yet others of the rulers of cities think that the aim in the rule of cities is riches. They make their actions by which they rule the cities actions by which they may attain riches, and they make the laws of the people of the city, laws by which they may attain riches from the people of the city, and if they choose a good or do anything of that kind, they choose and do it that riches may accrue to them. It is well known that between the man who chooses riches that he may be honored for them and the man who chooses honor and the obedience of others that he may be wealthy and attain riches there is a great difference. The latter are called people of base headship.

Others of the rulers of cities think that the end in the rule of cities is the enjoyment of pleasures. Others again think that it is all these three, honor, riches, and pleasures, and they monopolize them and make the people of the city as it were their tools to obtain pleasures and riches. Not one of these was called king by the ancients.

[29] The king is king by the kingly craft, by the art of ruling cities and by the power to employ the kingly art, at whatever time he has come to be chief over a city, whether he is known for his art or is not known for it, whether he has found implements to use or not, whether he has found people to receive from him or not, whether he is obeyed or not, just as the doctor is doctor by the medical craft, whether men know him for it or not, whether artificial implements are ready for him or not, whether he has found people to serve him in carrying out his orders or not, whether he has met with sick persons to re-

ceive his words or not, and his medicine is not deficient if he has none of these things. Similarly the king is king by the craft and the power to employ the art, whether he rules over people or not, whether he is honored or not, whether he is rich or poor.

Some people think that they should not apply the name of king to him who possesses the kingly craft without his being obeyed and honored in a city. Others add to that riches, while others think to add rule by force, subjection, terrorizing, and fear. None of these belong to the essential conditions of kingship, but are things which may be useful to the kingly craft, and are thought on that account to be kingship.

IBN-SĪNĀ (AVICENNA)

The most renowned and influential philosopher of the Islamic West, Abū ëAlī al-Ḥusayn Ibn Sīnā (latinized as Avicenna), was born in the village of Afsan near Bukhara in 980. He passed his youth in Bukhara, capital of the Samanids' domain, then moved to Gurganj, Ray, Hamadhan, and Isfahan, occupying posts as a vizier and a physician of the local rulers. He died in Hamadhan in 1037.

Avicenna was a physician and a scientist, a man of the court and a philosopher. He was greatly influenced by the Greeks. Ibn Sīnā's philosophical system owes a lot to both Aristotle and Neoplatonism. Plato also shaped his political views, while Galen influenced Avicenna's psychology, and the Stoics, his logic. As for the Islamic philosophers, al-Fārābī inspired Ibn Sīnā more than anybody else.

The central thesis of Avicenna's metaphysics is the division of reality into Contingent Being and Necessary Being. Something is necessary if from the assumption of its nonexistence an impossibility will follow. While something contingent is possible, if no impossibility will follow, whether it is assumed to exist or not to exist. Necessary Being in its turn is subdivided into what is necessary through itself and what is necessary through another. God is the only Necessary Being through itself, existing without a cause. He is eternal, one, devoid of all multiplicity.

The world emanates from God as the consequence of His self-knowledge. Here Avicenna identifies creation with the Neoplatonic notion of emanation. In his description of the world, Ibn Sīnā uses Aristotelian terms, though not without some of his own modifications.

In developing the doctrine of the human soul, Avicenna combines Aristotelian and Platonic ideas. The soul is an individual, indivisible, immaterial substance that does not exist as an individual prior to the body. It is created with the body, not imposed on it. Avicenna denies bodily resurrection but insists on the soul's individual immortality.

Avicenna's theory of knowledge follows the views common to the Muslim Aristotelians in general. However, it is modified by a theory of "illumination." In some of his works, Ibn Sīnā expresses a great interest in and respect for mystical ways of attaining the Truth, a fact that prompts quite a few of Avicenna's interpreters to speak about his adherence to mysticism at the end of his life.

Avicenna follows al-Fārābī in the evaluation of the difference between religion and philosophy: religion gives the same truths as philosophy but in the symbolic language that the masses can understand.

Ibn Sīnā's *The Book of Healing* is the fullest exposition of the Islamic Aristotelians' philosophy. He also wrote less extensive encyclopedic works: *The Book of Salvation, The Book of Demonstrations and Affirmations,* and *The Book of Knowledge.* Avicenna's *Canon of Medicine* is considered to be a digest of the medical knowledge accumulated at that time.

Avicenna was criticized from different sides. Muslim theologians, al-Ghāzālī for example, attacked his views for being incompatible with Islamic teachings. The philosophers, like Averroës, charged him with inconsistency and a surrender to religious dogmatism on certain crucial philosophical points. Still, Ibn Sīnā for centuries remained the most respected among the Muslim philosophers in the world of Islam as well as beyond its borders.

From Ibn-Sīnā (Avicenna)

Dānish Nāma (The Book of Knowledge). *Translated by Parviz Morewedge in his* The Metaphysica of Avicenna (Ibn Sīnā). *New York: Columbia University Press, 1973.*

21. Finding That There Cannot Be a Multiplicity (Kathra) in the Necessary Existent

The Necessary Existent cannot contain a multiplicity as though it were composed of many elements, as a man's body consists of many parts. The Necessary Existent cannot have different kinds of parts, each standing by itself and forming a unit, such as wood and clay in a house. Nor can such parts be separate in idea (*maʿnā*) but not in essence (*dhāt*) in the manner matter and form are "separate" in natural bodies. Hence, the possibilities mentioned here are ruled out, for if any of them were accurate, then the Necessary Existent would have to be united with the causes as we explained before. Different properties cannot be contained in the Necessary Existent, for if Its essence were realized with such properties, they would be together as parts. If its essence (*dhāt*) were realized and the properties were accidental (*ʿaraḍī*), then they would subsist in the Necessary Existent for their essence due to another cause. Consequently, the Necessary Existent would be a receptacle. But from what we have asserted it has become evident that the Necessary Existent is not the receptacle in essence. It cannot, moreover, be the case that these attributes are due to the Necessary Existent Itself, for It would then be a receptacle. From one idea no more than one thing can be realized, for we have proved that whatever comes from a cause is not realized until it becomes necessary. Consequently, when one entity becomes a necessity from a single idea (*yak maʿnā*) and another entity also becomes a necessity from the same idea, then something must become a necessity due to something else because of the nature of the former due to which something becomes a necessity. It becomes a necessity due to two reasons. One of these originates, for example, from this nature and this will, whereas the other comes from that nature and that will. Another duality is then placed into this context. Discourse would then be directed at this duality and the argument would start anew. Hence, there is no multiplicity in the Necessary Existent.

22. Finding That the Characteristic (Ṣifa) "Necessary Existent" Cannot Be Applied to More Than One Entity

We have found that if two entities were called "Necessary Existent," then without a doubt there would be a differentia (*faṣl*) or a distinguishing mark (*k͟hāṣṣa*) for each. We have also found that both the differentia and the distinguishing mark do not occur in the essence (reality) of that which is universal. Hence, the Necessary Existent is a Necessary Existent without that differentia and that distinguishing mark. If we imagine only the nonexistence of that differentia and that distinguishing mark, one of these two cases would follow. Either each would be like the Necessary Existent or each would not be like It. If they were like the Necessary Existent, they would be two different things without, however, the distinctions of differentia and distinguishing mark, which is impossible. If they were not like It, then having a differentia and a distinguishing mark would be an essential condition for the necessary existence of the Necessary Existent, and this condition would have to be the essence of the Necessary Existent. Thus, differentia and distinguishing mark would come under the common idea of essence (*maʿnā-i ʿāmm*), which is absurd. Indeed, if existence were other than essence, then this could be a legitimate alternative. But, for the Necessary Existent, existence is either due to essence or it is essence. Consequently, the Necessary Existent cannot be a duality (*du'ī*) in essence, in differentia, or in the distinguishing mark. For this reason, the "Necessary Existent" cannot be a characteristic that is applied to two things. Yet we have found that a cause is contained (*andar*) in the elements of any universal idea. For this reason, the Necessary Existent is not universal. If It were a universal, It would be an effect, and would not, therefore, be different from being a contingent being, which is impossible according to our demonstration.

23. Finding That the Necessary Existent Is Not Receptive to Change (Taghayyūr) and That It Necessarily Persists in Every Mode (Rūy)

Whatever is receptive to change (*gardish*) is also receptive to a cause. It is in a given condition (*ḥāl*) due to one cause, and in another condition due to another cause. Its being is not devoid of the property of "being in union with these causes." Thus, its being depends on "being in union with" the object with which it is united. We have established, however, that the Necessary Existent is not in union (*paiwand dār*) (with any other entity). Consequently, the Necessary Existent is not receptive to change.

24. Finding That the Essence (Māhiyya) of the Necessary Existent Can Be No Other Than Existence (Anniyya)

That whose essence (*māhiyya*) is other than existence is not the Necessary Existent. It has become evident that existence has an accidental meaning for that whose essence is other than existence *(anniyya)*. And it has also become evident that there is a cause for that which has an accidental idea (i.e., for that which has a contingent being). The cause of such a being is either the essence *(dhāt)* of that entity in which it subsists *(andar wai)* or something else.

The Necessary Existent cannot have an essence as the cause of Its existence for the following reasons. If such an essence should have being so that the existence of the Necessary Existent could be derived from it, or that this being were the cause of Its existence, then the being of the essence would have to be realized prior to itself. Since the second hypothesis could not be the reason (*kār*) for Its being, an inquiry (*su'āl*) into the first explanation would be legitimate. On the other hand, if the essence had no being, it could not be the cause of anything. For whatever does not exist is not the cause of the existence of anything. Thus, the essence of the Necessary Existent is not the cause of its existence. Its cause is, therefore, something else. Henceforth, there must be a cause for the existence of the Necessary Existent. The Necessary Existent must exist, therefore, due to something else. This, however, is impossible.

25. Finding That the Necessary Existent Is Neither a Substance (Jauhar) nor an Accident ('araḍ)

A substance is that whose essence (*ḥaqīqa*) does not exist in a subject when the substance exists. Furthermore, it is that which can be realized only in a subject matter (*mauḍu'*). From this point of view, there is no doubt that a body (*jism*) is a substance, though one can doubt the actual existence of that body which is a substance until one knows whether or not it is in a subject.

Hence, substance is that which has an essence, such as materiality *(jismī)*, spirituality *(nafsī)*, humanity *(insānī)* and horseness *(farasī)*. The condition of such an essence specifies that one does not know whether or not it has existence until its existence is realized in a subject. Whatever is of such a nature possesses an essence other than existence. Consequently, whatever has no essence other than existence is not a substance.

And with regard to accidentality *('araḍī)* it is obvious that the Necessary Existent does not subsist in anything. Since the existence of the Necessary Existent is not related by way of correspondence or generically to the existence of other things, this essence is neither in the subject (due to the subject), as it is for humanity and what is other than humanity, nor is the idea of genus *(jins)* applied to it, since existence is applied to what is posterior and prior, having neither opposite nor genus. And whatever is not in a subject *(mauḍu')* has neither posteriority nor priority. Accordingly, an existent which does not subsist in a subject cannot be a genus of things other than in the sense described previously, whereas substance is the genus of those things which are substances. The Necessary Existent is, therefore, not a substance. In brief, It is not in any category because existence is external to essence for each category (*maqūlāt*), and hence it would only be an accidental addition to the essence of the Necessary Existent if the Necessary Existent belonged to a category. Existence, however, is the essence of the Necessary Existent. From our discussion it becomes evident that there is no genus *(jins)* for the Necessary Existent. Consequently, It does not have a differentia (*faṣl)* and, thus, It does not have a definition. Since it has neither a place nor a subject, it has no opposite and no species (*nau')*. It has neither companion (*yār*) nor resemblance. Finally, it has become evident that It does not have a cause. Hence, It is not receptive to change *(gardish)* or to divisibility *(bahra padhīrish)*.

AL-GHAZĀLĪ

The outstanding figure among Islamic theologians of the Medieval time, often called the greatest Muslim after the Prophet Muḥammad, Abū Ḥāmid Muḥammad al-Ghazālī was born in 1058 in the village of Ghazal near Tus (Khorassan). He was educated first in his native town, then in Jurjan, and finally in Nishapur. After the death of his teacher al-Juwaynī, the great theologian of the age, in 1085, al-Ghazālī was invited to the court of the Seljuk vizier Niẓām al-Mulk, who appointed him to be the teacher of fiqh in 1091 in the Niẓāmiyya madrasah of Baghdad. In 1095, either because of a spiritual crisis, or of the change of the political situation caused by the murder of Niẓām al-Mulk, al-Ghazālī left Baghdad. He spent eleven years in wanderings visiting Damascus, Jerusalem, Mecca, and other places. He became a Ṣūfī. In 1106 on the invitation of the vizier Fakhr al-Mulk, al-Ghazālī began to teach in the

Niẓāmiyya madrasah of Nishapur. Not long before his death al-Ghazālī returned to Tus, where he died in 1111.

Al-Ghazālī is often compared with St. Augustine because of his dramatic story of spiritual and intellectual anxiety and doubt. Because of his skeptical bent of mind he turned away from the rigid dogmatism of the ulema and at the same time examined critically the main trends of thought existing in his age. Al-Ghazālī singled out four Islamic groups that claimed to be in possession of the truth: theologians, the Ismāʿīliyya, the philosophers, and the Ṣūfīs.

The study of Kalām brought Abū Ḥāmid to the conclusion that the teaching of the mutakallimūn, though it had some value, still failed to lead to the indubitable certainty he was seeking. Al-Ghazālī had found equally inaccessible the Ismā'īlī doctrine. The strongest attack he launched, however, was against the philosophers, particularly al-Fārābī and Ibn Sīnā.

It is quite significant and characteristic of al-Ghazālī that before starting criticism he considered it necessary to study thoroughly the object of his criticism. Hence he spent a number of years studying philosophy and summed up that period of his life by writing *Maqāṣid al-Falāsifa (Intentions of the Philosophers).* The exposition of Islamic Aristotelianism in that work was so skillful and objective that when it appeared in Latin in the thirteenth century it was taken as genuine philosophical writing influenced by Avicenna. Al-Ghazālī's actual refutation of the Aristotelians is contained in his *Tahāfut al-Falāsifa (The Incoherence of the Philosophers).*

He examined twenty propositions (sixteen metaphysical and four physical) of the Aristotelians, against which, as he thought, the Muslims should be warned. The three propositions al-Ghazālī found particularly dangerous were the eternity of the world, God's knowledge of universals only, and the denial of the resurrection of the body. Al-Ghazālī, in spite of his strong criticism of the philosophers, did not completely reject its validity. He had high regard for parts of natural philosophy and logic.

Al-Ghazālī found the answer to his own intellectual and spiritual quest in Sufism, in spite of some criticism against this trend, too. In mysticism he has discovered a knowledge "known in a manner which is not open to doubt at all." True knowledge is not a matter of discourse or argument, but of divine grace. It could be obtained only through mystical experience, through the outpouring of divine light. Al-Ghazālī dedicated his greatest work to that "discovery": the *Iḥyā' ʿUlūm al-Dīn (Revival of the Religious Sciences).*

Al-Ghazālī has become the most influential theologian by succeeding to bring "marriage" between mystical teaching of Islam and its law.

The following selection is al-Ghazālī's introduction to *Tahāfut al-Falāsifa* and his criticism of one of the twenty Aristotelian's propositions.

From Al-Ghazālī

Tahāfut al-falāsifa (Incoherence of the Philosophers). *Translated by Sābih Ahmad Kamali. Lahore: Pakistan Philosophical Congress Publication, 1963. Copyright, Pakistan Philosophical Congress*

Preface One

Let it be known that it would be tedious to dwell at length upon the differences among the philosophers themselves. For prolixity is their manner, and their disputes are too many, and their opinions are scattered, and their ways are divergent and devious. Therefore, we will confine our attention to the inconsistencies which are found in the theories of the premier philosopher who is called *the* Philosopher, or the First Teacher, for he systematized their sciences, and reformulated them, eliminating all that was redundant in the philosophers' opinions, and retaining only that which was close to the basic principles and tendencies of philosophical thought. This is Aristotle, who refuted all his predecessors—including his own teacher, whom the philosophers call the divine Plato. Having refuted Plato, Aristotle excused himself by saying: "Plato is dear to us. And truth is dear, too. Nay, truth is dearer than Plato."

We have related this story in order to show that in their own view there is nothing fixed and constant in the philosophers' position. They base their judgments on conjecture and speculation, unaided by positive inquiry and unconfirmed by faith. They try to infer the truth of their metaphysical theories from the clarity of the arithmetical and logical sciences. And this method sometimes carries conviction with the weak-minded people. But if their metaphysical theories had been as cogent and definite as their arithmetical knowledge is, they would not have differed among themselves on metaphysical questions as they do not differ on the arithmetical.

As far as the translators of Aristotle's works into Arabic are concerned, our problem is even more difficult. For the translations themselves have been subjected to interpolation and changes, which have necessitated further commentaries and interpretations. As a result, the translations are as much in dispute among the philosophers as the original works are. However, the most faithful—as Aristotle's translators—and the most original—as his commentators—among the philosophizing Muslims are al-Fārābī Abū Naṣr, and Ibn Sīnā. Therefore, we will confine our attention to what these two have taken to be the authentic expression of the views of their mis-leaders. For what they discarded and refused to follow must undoubtedly have been utterly useless, and should not call for an elaborate refutation.

Therefore, let it be known that we propose to concentrate on the refutation of philosophical thought as it emerges from the writings of these two persons.

For otherwise, the scattered character of the philosophical theories should have to be reflected in a proportionately loose arrangement of our subject-matter.

Preface Two

Let it be known that the difference between the philosophers and others is threefold.

In the first place, the dispute is centered upon a mere word. Take for instance their use of the word "substance" for God, meaning thereby a being which is not in a subject, or a self-subsisting being which does not need an external cause to continue it in existence.

We do not intend here to undertake the refutation of this terminology. For if the meaning of self-subsistence is agreed upon, the applicability of the word "substance" in this sense will have to be considered from the etymological point of view. If from that point of view, the application of the word is justified, it will still be debatable whether the Sacred Law approves of its use. For the permission to use words as names (of God) or the injunction against their use is based on what appears from the letter of the Sacred Law. Perhaps you will say: "This word was used by the Mutakallimūn in the discussion of the Divine attributes. In the Sacred Law, the Jurists never used it. It is, therefore, improper on your part to confuse the realities of things with matters of habit and custom (of which *Fiqh* treats)." But (this is inadmissible, because) I know that it amounts to a discussion on whether it is permissible to use a certain name which is truly applicable to the bearer of the name. And hence it is equivalent to a discussion on whether a certain (moral) action is permissible.

In the second place, there are those things in which the philosophers believe, and which do not come into conflict with any religious principle. And, therefore, disagreement with the philosophers with respect to those things is not a necessary condition for the faith in the prophets and the apostles (may God bless them all). An example is their theory that the lunar eclipse occurs when the light of the Moon disappears as a consequence of the interposition of the Earth between the Moon and the Sun. For the Moon derives its light from the Sun, and the Earth is a round body surrounded by Heaven on all the sides. Therefore, when the Moon falls under the shadow of the Earth, the light of the Sun is cut off from it. Another example is their theory that the solar eclipse means the interposition of the body of the Moon between the Sun and the observer, which occurs when the Sun and the Moon are stationed at the intersection of their nodes at the same degree.

We are not interested in refuting such theories either; for the refutation will serve no purpose. He who thinks that it is his religious duty to disbelieve such things is really unjust to religion, and weakens its cause. For these things have been established by astronomical and mathematical evidence which leaves no room for doubt. If you tell a man, who has studied these things—so that he has sifted all the data relating to them, and is, therefore, in a position to forecast when a lunar or a solar eclipse will take place: whether it will be total or partial; and how long it will last—that these things are contrary to religion, your assertion will shake his faith in religion, not in these things. Greater harm is done to religion by an inmethodical helper than by an enemy whose actions, however hostile, are yet regular. For, as the proverb goes, a wise enemy is better than an ignorant friend.

If someone says:

The Prophet (may God bless him) has said: "The Sun and the Moon are two signs among the signs of God. Their eclipse is not caused by the death or the life of a man. When you see an eclipse, you must seek refuge in the contemplation of God and in prayer." How can this tradition be reconciled with what the philosophers say?

we will answer:

There is nothing in this tradition to contradict the philosophers. It only denies that an eclipse has anything to do with the life or the death of a man. Further, it enjoins prayer at the time of an eclipse. The Sacred Law enjoins prayer at the time of sunrise or sunset or during the day; what is unusual if, with a view to finding greater favor (with God), it also enjoins prayer at the time of an eclipse?

If it is said:

At the end of the same tradition, the Prophet said: "When God reveals Himself to something, it prostrates itself before Him." Does it not follow from this tradition that an eclipse is an act of prostration caused by Revelation?

we will answer:

This addition is spurious. We must condemn its author as a liar. The Prophet's words are only those which have been reported above. However, if this addition were authentic, would it not be easier to interpret it than to reject the evidence (of astronomical and mathematical sciences) which is conclusive and definite? People have interpreted many a plain text by rational arguments which never attained to such clarity and cogency (as the astronomical and mathematical arguments in this case have done).

The atheists would have the greatest satisfaction if the supporter of religion made a positive assertion that things of this kind are contrary to religion. For then it would be easier for them to refute religion which stood or fell with its opposition to these things. (It is, therefore, necessary for the supporter of religion not to commit himself on these questions,) because the fundamental question at issue between him and the philosophers is only whether the world is eternal or began in time. If its beginning in time is proved, it is all the same whether it is a round body, or a simple thing, or an octagonal or hexagonal figure; and whether the heavens and all that is below them form—as the philosophers say—thirteen layers, or more, or less. Investigation into these facts is no more relevant to metaphysical inquiries than an investigation into the number of the layers of an onion, or the number of the seeds of a pomegranate, would be. What we are interested in is that the world is the product of God's creative action, whatever the manner of that action may be.

In the third place, there are philosophical theories which come into violent conflict with the fundamental principles of religion, e.g., the religious doctrines of the world's beginning in time: of the attributes of the Creator; and of the resurrection of bodies. All these things have been denied by the philosophers. Therefore, we propose to leave the rest of the sections (enumerated above) aside, in order to concentrate on this one, and on questions allied to it, in our criticism of philosophical theories.

Preface Three

Let it be known that it is our purpose to disillusion those who think too highly of the philosophers, and consider them to be infallible. Since I have undertaken to expose the incoherence and contradiction involved in philosophical thought, I will approach them in order to attack them, not to defend something of mine own. I will refute what they believe, by showing that it is a mixture of diverse elements which come from such schools as the Mu'tazilah, the Karramiyah, the Waqifiyah, etc. My attitude towards these sects themselves is that, while it is not necessary for me to defend any one of them, we are all equally opposed to the philosophers. For we differ among ourselves only in regard to the details; whereas the philosophers attack the very basis of our religion. Let us, therefore, unite against the common enemy; for at a critical juncture, we must forget our private quarrels.

Preface Four

One of the most artful methods employed by the philosophers is that, when in discussion they come up against a difficulty, they say: "The science of metaphysics is extremely subtle. Of all the sciences it is the most difficult even for a sharp intelligence to grasp." Those who follow the philosophers employ a similar trick in order to get rid of their difficulties. When they are unable to explain something in the work of their masters, they still glorify them and say: "Undoubtedly, a solution can be found somewhere in the sciences developed by the ancient masters. Perhaps our failure is the result of our inability to consult Logic and Mathematics on this question."

To these suggestions, we will reply as follows:

As far as Mathematics is concerned, one of its two branches, which is an inquiry into discrete quantity—viz., Arithmetic—has evidently nothing to do with Metaphysics. To say that it is not possible to understand Metaphysics without the help of Arithmetic is nonsense—like saying that Medicine, or Grammar, or Literature cannot be understood without the help of Arithmetic: or that Arithmetic cannot be understood without the help of Medicine.

As regards the other branch of Mathematics—viz., Geometry—which is an inquiry into continuous quantity, all that it tells us is that the heavens and all that is below them down to the Center, i.e., the Earth, are round in shape. Further, it tells us of the number of the strata of these things: of the planets revolving in the Sphere; and of the quantity of their movements. Now, we can grant them all these things—from conviction, or for the sake of the argument. They need not adduce scientific evidence to prove them. But there is nothing in these facts which proves or disproves metaphysical principles. To say that there is something which does so is like saying: "To know whether this house is the product of a knowing, willing, powerful, and living builder, it is necessary to discover whether it has six or eight sides, and what is the number of its beams and bricks." Obviously, such an assertion would be sheer nonsense. It would be like saying: "The temporal character of an onion cannot be known, unless the number of its layers be discovered"; or, "The temporal character of this pomegranate cannot be known, unless the number of its seeds be discovered." This sort of argument simply does not appeal to an intelligent mind.

As regards their contention that reference to Logic is unavoidable, it is right. But Logic is not their monopoly. Fundamentally, it is the same thing as in the Art of Scholastic Reasoning we call the Book of Theoretical Inquiry. The philosophers have changed its name to Logic to make it look formidable. We often call it the Book of Disputation, or the Data of the Intellects. When a gullible enthusiast hears the word "Logic," he thinks that it is a new subject, unknown to the Mutakallimūn and cultivated by the philosophers alone. In order to remove this misunderstanding, we propose to discuss the Data of the Intellects in a separate work, where we will avoid the phraseology used by the mutakallimūn and the Jurists, adopting for the time being the terms used by the Logicians, so that the whole thing might be cast into a different mold, and the methods of the Logicians might be followed in the minutest detail. In that book, we will speak to them in their language—I mean their logical terminology. We will show there that

> neither the conditions for the material validity of Syllogism—laid down by them in the section of Logic devoted to Demonstration—nor those for its formal validity—in the Book of Syllogism—nor the postulates which they have formulated in the Isagoge and Categories, and which form the parts and preliminaries of Logic

are of any help to them in metaphysical sciences. But it is necessary to reserve the discussion of the Data of the Intellects for a separate book. For, although an instrument for the understanding of the purport of this book, it is not indispensable to every reader. Therefore, we are going to postpone it; so that he who does not need it may not be bothered by it here. However, he who fails to understand some of the terms used here will be well advised to begin with mastering the contents of our book called *The Standard of Knowledge*—viz., the (branch of) knowledge they call Logic.

PROBLEM X
OF THEIR INABILITY TO PROVE BY RATIONAL ARGUMENTS THAT THERE IS A CAUSE OR CREATOR OF THE WORLD

We will say:

He who believes that all body is originated (for it is never free from changes) has an intelligible position, if he claims that body requires a cause or a creator. But what prevents the philosophers from saying—as the Materialists say—that:

> From eternity, the world has been as it is. It has no cause or creator. A cause is required by that which originates in time. No one of the bodies in the world originates in time; nor does it perish. It is only the Forms and Accidents which originate in time. The bodies—i.e., the heavens—are eternal. And the four elements, which are the stuff of the sphere of the Moon, and their bodies and Matter(s) are

> eternal. On these pass in succession the Forms resulting from combination and transformation. Further, the human soul and the vegetative soul originate in time. And the series of the causes of all those things which originate in time comes to an end at rotatory motion. And rotatory motion is eternal, its source being the eternal soul of the sphere. All this shows that the world has no cause, and that the bodies in the world have no creator. The world is as it has always been. Similarly, the bodies in the world are, and have been, eternally uncaused.

What do the philosophers mean by saying that the eternal bodies in the world have a cause?

If it is said:

That which is uncaused is a necessary being. In connection with the attributes of a necessary being, we have stated the reason why body cannot be a necessary being.

we will answer:

And we have exposed the invalidity of what you claim to be the attributes of a necessary being. It has been shown that rational demonstration does not prove anything but the impossibility of an infinite regress. And the Materialist cuts short—at the very outset—an infinite regress by saying that:

> The bodies have no cause. As regards the Forms and Accidents, some of them are causes of others, till at last the series comes to an end at rotatory motion.

And, as the philosophers themselves believe (the Materialist admits that) some of the rotatory movements are causes of others, but that the causal series reaches its end in rotatory motion.

So he who reflects over the points we have mentioned will see the inability of all those who believe in the eternity of bodies to claim that they have a cause. These people are in consistency bound to accept Materialism and Atheism—as some thinkers, who gave clear expression to the presuppositions of the philosophers' theory—have actually done.

If it is said:

Our argument is this: If these bodies are supposed to be necessary, it will be absurd. If they are supposed to be possible, all that is possible needs a cause.

we will answer:

The words "necessary" and "possible" are meaningless. All the confusion created by the philosophers has its source in these two words. We prefer substituting for them their sense—i.e., the denial of a cause, and its affirmation respectively. This would result in the philosophers' saying that these bodies may, or may not, have a cause. The Materialist will say that they do not have a cause. Why should the philosophers find fault with him? And possibility meaning what it does, we will say that body is necessary, not possible. If they say that it is not possible for body to be necessary, they make a groundless and arbitrary assumption.

If it is said:

No one can deny that body has parts: that parts constitute the whole; and that essentially they take precedence over the whole.

we will answer:

Let it be so. Let the whole subsist by the parts and their combination. Let, however, the parts as well as their combination be uncaused, eternal, and independent of an efficient cause. The philosophers cannot prove the impossibility of these assumptions, unless they use the argument which they advanced to prove the impossibility of plurality in the case of the Prime Being. We have refuted that argument. And the philosophers have nothing else whereby to defend themselves.

This makes it clear that he who does not believe in the origination of bodies has no basis on which his belief in the Creator may be founded.

SUFISM

Islamic mysticism—Sufism, or in Arabic, *Taṣawwuf*—has exercised considerable influence on the cultural and sociopolitical life of Muslims. It has been both product of elite consciousness and a popular religion, a form of social protest against the dominant political system as well as the legalized religious doctrine that warranted and sanctioned the system. Yet Sufism has also been used to quell, to pacify, and to repress social activity. Sufism counterposed irrationality to rational thinking while it also stood forth as a variety of religious free thought not infrequently contiguous with philosophic theorizing. It persuaded seekers of the Path to renounce mundane cares and bodily appetites, to practice ascetic self-discipline, and at the same time it gave inspiration to

Niẓāmī, Jāmī, 'Umar Khayyām, Rūmī, and many other poets with rapturously extolled love and life.

Most authors believe that the name *Sufism* goes back to the Arabic word *ṣūf*, meaning "wool," because ascetics' raiment was made of wool. Many Ṣūfīs themselves are prone to interpret their name as derived from *ṣafā*, that is, "to be purified," indicating the perfection of the human being, free from bodily desires and worldly affections. The name is also referred to the word *ṣaff* (a contraction from the phrase "The first row of the faithful at prayer"), the suggestion being that Ṣūfīs are among the most righteous. Another explication would connote Sufism with the noun meaning "bench" in the phrase *ahl al-ṣuffa*, "the people of the bench," that is, the homeless poor who used to gather about the bench at the Prophet's mosque in Madīnah in the early period of Sufism. There are other interpretations, including a conjecture that the term had no etymology at all, that it was not derived from any real root whatever but was merely a combination of sounds, denoted by the letters S, U, and F, inducing certain psychophysiological reactions (in analogy with the Sanskrit *OM*, a sacred term with Hindus, still unaccounted for by philologists).

To determine the sources of Islamic mysticism is even more difficult. Its ideas and images resemble those of other mystical teachings. For that reason certain scholars in the past (and a few recently) declared Sufism to be a derived, dependent system of ideals and looked for its roots in Neoplatonism, Zoroastrianism, Buddhism, and the like.

The role of external factors in the rise and development of Islamic mysticism was unduly magnified, partly due to the character of Ṣūfī sources (many of them in Persian or in languages other than Arabic). Also, the interaction of religious and philosophical theories and doctrines in the Near and Middle East, where the ideas of Christianity, Judaism, and Neoplatonism had been known long before the Prophet Muḥammad appeared, has been underscored.

Yet the mystical world outlook is actually uncircumscribed by any geographical, national, or chronological boundaries. Every religion has its own mystical tradition, and the religious dogmas and tenets determine its peculiar features. While Sufism was subjected to external influences as much as the whole of Islam, and was doubtless influenced by various non-Islamic schools, it would be more reasonable to consider Sufism as a product of Muslim spiritual evolution.

Sufism is a complicated phenomenon lacking a generally accepted ontology. Still, the most prominent idea is the "Unity of Being" (*waḥdat al-wujūd*), which presents the culmination of the development of Ṣūfī philosophy. It was first formulated by Ibn 'Arabī, though the very idea was shared, more or less, by Ṣūfīs preceding him (Abū Yazīd al-Bisṭāmī, Manṣur al-Ḥallāj, Ibn al-Fāriḍ, etc.). The term was first used in systematic fashion by Sa'īd al-Dīn al-Kunawī (d. 1300).

The selection below is from Ibn 'Arabī's treatise *Fuṣuṣ al-ḥikam* (1230), considered to be the Great Shaykh's most important work because it presents "the kernel" of his philosophy.

From Ibn 'Arabī

Fuṣuṣ al-ḥikam. *Translated by Angela Culme-Seymour. Reprinted from* Muhyiddin Ibn 'Arabī: The Wisdom of the Prophets (Fuṣuṣ al-ḥikam). *Aldsworth, Gloucestershire: Beshara Publications, 1975.*

Of the Divine Wisdom (al-hikmat al-ilāhiyah) in the Word of Adam

God (*al-haqq*) wanted to see the essences (*al-a'yan*) of His most perfect Names (*al-asmā al-husnā*) whose number is infinite—and if you like you can equally well say: God wanted to see His own Essence (*'ayn*) in one global object (*kawn*) which having been blessed with existence (*al-wujūd*) summarized the Divine Order (*al-amr*) so that there He could manifest His mystery (*sirr*) to Himself.

For the vision (*ru'yā*) that a being has of himself in himself is not the same as that which another reality procures for him, and which he uses for himself as a mirror: in this he manifests himself to his self in the form which results from the "place" of the vision; this would not exist without the "plane of reflection" and the ray which is reflected therein.

God first created the entire world as something amorphous and without grace comparable to a mirror not yet polished; but it is a rule in the Divine activity to prepare no "place" without it receiving a Divine spirit as is explained (in the Koran) by the blowing of the Divine spirit into Adam; and this is none other (from a complementary point of view to the former), than the actualization of the aptitude (*al-isti'dād*) which such a form possesses, having already the predisposition for it, to receive the inexhaustible effusion (*al-fayd*) of the essential revelation (*at-tajallī*).

There is not then (apart from the Divine Reality) other than one pure receptacle (*qābil*), but this receptacle itself comes from the Holy Effusion (*al-fayd al-aqdas*) (that is to say from the principal manifestation, meta-cosmic, where the "immutable Essences" are Divinely "conceived" before their apparent projection in the relative existence). For, the entire reality (*al-amr*) from its beginning to its end comes from God alone, and it is to Him that it returns. So, then, the Divine Order required the clarification of the mirror of the world; and Adam became the light itself of this mirror and the spirit of this form.

As for the Angels (of whom there is some mention in the Koran's account of Adam's creation), they represent certain faculties of this "form" of the world which the Sufis call the Great Man (*al-insān al-kabīr*) so that the angels are to it just as the spiritual and physical faculties are to the human organism. Each of these (cosmic) faculties finds itself as if veiled by its own nature; it conceives nothing which is superior to its own (relative) essence; for there is in it something which considers itself to be worthy of high rank and in the state nearest to God. It is thus because it participates (in a certain manner) in the Divine Synthesis (*al-jam-'iyat al-ilāhiyah*) which governs that which appertains, be it to the Divine side (*al-janāb al-ilāhī*), be it to the side of the Reality of Realities (*haqīqat al-haqāiq*), be it again—and by this organism, support of all the faculties,—to the Universal Nature (*tabī 'at al-kull*); this encompasses all the receptacles (*qawabil*) of the world, from its peak to its foundation. But this, logical reasoning will not understand, for this sort of knowledge is solely dependent on Divine intuition (*al-kashf al-ilāhī*), it is by that alone that one will know the roots of the forms of the world, in so far as they are receptive towards their ruling spirit.

Thus, this being (Adamic) was called Man (*insān*) and God's Representative (*khalīfah*). As for his quality as a man it designates his synthesized nature (containing virtually all other natures created) and his aptitude to embrace the essential Truths. Man is to God (*al-haqq*) that which the pupil is to the eye (the pupil in Arabic is called "man within the eye"), the pupil being that by which seeing is effected; for through him (that is to say the Universal Man) God contemplates His creation and dispenses His mercy. Thus is man at once ephemeral and eternal, a being created perpetual and immortal, a Verb discriminating (by his distinctive knowledge) and unifying (by his divine essence). By his existence the world was completed. He is to the world that which the setting is to the ring; the setting carries the seal which the King applies to his treasure chests; and it is for this that (Universal) Man is called the Representative of God, Whose creation he safeguards, as one safeguards the treasures by a seal; as long as the King's seal is to be found on the treasure chests, nobody dares open them without his permission; thus man finds himself entrusted with the Divine safe-keeping of the world, and the world will not cease to be safeguarded as long as this Universal Man (*al-insān al-kāmil*) lives in it. Dost thou not see, then, that when he disappears and is taken away from the treasure chests of this lower world, nothing of which God kept in them will remain and all that they contained will go, each part joining its own (corresponding) part; everything will be transported into the other world, and (Universal Man) will be the seal on the coffers in the other world perpetually.

All that the Divine Form implies, that is to say the total of the names (or Universal Qualities) is manifested in this human constitution, which, by this means, distinguishes itself (from all other creatures) by the (symbolic) integration of all existence. From there comes the Divine argument condemning the Angels (who did not see the "raison d'être" nor the intrinsic superiority of Adam); remember that, for God exhorts thee by the example of others and see from whence the judgment strikes that whom it strikes. The Angels did not realize what is implied by the constitution of this representative (of God on earth), and neither did they realize what is implied by the essential adoration (*dhātiyah*) of God; for each does not know of God except that which he infers from himself. But, the Angels do not have the integral nature of Adam; so they did not comprehend the Divine Names, the knowledge of which is the privilege of this nature and by which this "praises" Him (affirming His aspects of Beauty and Goodness) and "proclaims" Him "Holy" (attesting His essential Transcendence); they did not know that God possesses Names that were withdrawn from their knowledge and by which therefore they could not "praise" Him nor "proclaim" Him "Holy."

They were victims of their own limitations when they said, with regard to the creation (of Adam on earth): "Wouldst Thou, then, create therein a being that sows corruption?" Now, this corruption, what is it if not precisely the revolt that they themselves were manifesting? That which they were saying about Adam applies to their own attitude towards God. Moreover, if such a possibility (of revolt) was not in their nature, they would not have unconsciously affirmed it with regard to Adam; if they had had the knowledge of themselves they would have been exempt, by this very knowledge, from the limits to which they were submitted; they would not have insisted (in their accusation of Adam) so far as to draw vanity from their own "praise" of God and from that by which they "proclaimed" Him "Holy," whereas Adam realized Names of which the Angels were ignorant, so that neither their "praise" (*tasbīh*) nor their "proclamation of Divine Holiness" (*taqdīs*) were the same as those of Adam.

This, God describes to us so that we should be on our guard, and that we should learn the right attitude towards Him—may He be exalted!—free from pretentiousness on matters which we have realized or embraced by our individual knowledge; moreover, how could we think we possess something which surpasses us (in its universal reality) and which we do not really know (essentially)? So pay attention to this Divine instruction on the way God punishes the most obedient and faithful of His servants, His closest representatives (according to the general hierarchy of beings).

But let us return now to the (Divine) Wisdom (in Adam). We can say of it that the Universal Ideas (*al-umur al-kulliyah*), which evidently have no individual existence as such, are none the less present, intelligibly and distinctly, in the mental state; they always remain interior with respect to individual existence, yet determine everything that pertains to this. Much more, that which exists individually is no more or less than (the expression of) these Universal Ideas, without these latter ceasing, for all that, to be in themselves purely intelligible. They are, then, external in so far as determinations implied in the individual existence and, on the other hand, interior in so far as they are intelligible realities. Everything which exists individually emanates from these Ideas, which remain, however, inseparably united to the intellect and could not individually be manifested in such a way as to be removed from the purely intelligible existence, whether it is a question of individual manifestation in time or out of time; for the relation between the individual being and the Universal Idea is always the same, whether or not this being be subject to temporal condition. Only, the Universal Idea assumes in its turn certain conditions pertaining to individual existences following the realities (haqāīq) which define these same existences. Thus for example is the relationship which unites the knowledge and he who knows, or life and he who lives; knowledge and life are intelligible realities, distinct from one another; so, we affirm of God that He knows and lives and we affirm equally of the Angel that he knows and lives, and we say as much of man; in all these cases, the intelligible reality of knowledge or that of life remain the same, and its relationship to he who knows and to he who lives is identical each time; and yet one says of Divine Knowledge that it is eternal, and of man's knowledge that it is ephemeral; there is then, something in this intelligible reality which is ephemeral by its dependence with regard to a (limiting) condition. Now, consider the reciprocal dependence of ideal realities and individual realities: in the same way that knowledge determines he who participates in it—for one calls him knowledgeable—so he who is qualified by knowledge determines in his turn the knowledge, so that it is ephemeral in connection with the ephemeral, and eternal in connection with the eternal; and each of these two sides is, in relation to the other, at once determining and determined. It is certain that these Universal Ideas, in spite of their intelligibility, have not, as such, (their own) existence but only a principial existence; likewise, when they apply themselves to individuals they accept the condition (*hukm*) without however assuming thereby distinction or divisibility; they are integrally present in everything qualified by them, like humanity (the quality of man), for example, is present integrally in each particular being of this species without undergoing the distinction nor the number which affects individuals, and without ceasing to be in itself a purely intellectual reality.

Now, as there is a mutual dependence between that which has an individual (or substantial) existence, and that which has not and is, to tell the truth, but a non-existent relationship as such, it is easy to conceive that beings are bound between themselves; for in this case there is always a common denominator, meaning existence as such, while in the former case the mutual relationship exists in spite of the absence of a common denominator.

Without doubt, the ephemeral is not conceivable as such, that is in its ephemeral and relative nature, except in relation to a principle from which it derives its own possibility, so that it has no being in itself, but derives it from another to whom it is tied by its dependence. And it is certain that this principle is in itself necessary, that it is subsistent by itself and independent, in its being, of any other thing. It is this principle, which by its own essence, confers the being to the ephemeral which depends on it.

But since (the principle) demands on its own account the (existence) of the ephemeral (being), this proves itself in this respect as (not only "possible" but also) "necessary." And since the ephemeral depends essentially on its principle it must also appear in the (qualitative) "form" of the latter in everything that it derives from it, like the "names" and the qualities, with the exception however of the principial autonomy which is not applicable to the ephemeral being, even though it be "necessary"; that is, it is necessary by virtue of another, not of itself.

Since the ephemeral being manifests the "form" of the eternal, it is by the contemplation of the ephemeral that God communicates to us the knowledge of Himself: He says to us (in the Koran) that He shows us His "signs" in the ephemeral: ("We will show them Our signs to the horizons and in themselves . . ." XLI, 53). It is from ourselves that we conclude that He is; to Him we attribute no quality without ourselves having that quality with the exception of the principial autonomy. Since we know Him by ourselves and from ourselves, we attribute to Him all that we attribute to ourselves, and it is because of that, again, that the revelation was given by the mouth of the interpreters, (that is to say the prophets) and that God described Himself to us through ourselves. In contemplating Him we contemplate ourselves, and in contemplating ourselves He contemplates Himself, although we are obviously numerous as to the individuals and types; we are united, it is true, in a single and essential reality, but there exists none the less a distinction between individuals, without which, moreover, there would be no multiplicity in the unity.

In the same way, although we are qualified in every respect by the qualities which come from God Himself, there is (between Him and us) certainly a difference, that is to say our dependence towards Him, in so far as He is the Being, and our essential conformity to Him, because of our very possibility; but He is independent of all that which constitutes our indigence. It is in this sense that one should understand eternity without beginning (*al-azal*) and the antiquity (*al-qidam*) of God, which abolishes moreover, the Divine Primacy (*al-awwaliyah*) signifying the passage from non-existence to existence; even though God be the First (*al-awwal*) and the Last (*al-ākhir*) He cannot be called the First in the temporal sense, because then He would in that sense be the Last; but the possibilities of manifestation have no end: they are inexhaustible. If God is called the Last, it means that all reality returns finally to Him after having been brought to us: His quality of the Last is thus essentially His quality of First and inversely. We also know that God has described Himself as "Exterior" (*al-zāhir*) and as "Interior" (*al-bātin*) and that He manifested the world at the same time as interior and exterior, so that we should know the "interior" aspect (of God) by our own interior, and the "exterior" by our exterior. In the same way He has described Himself by the qualities of mercy and of anger, and He manifested the world as a place of fear and hope, so that we should fear His anger and hope for His clemency. He has described Himself by Beauty and Majesty and endowed us with a reverent awe (*al-haybah*) and intimacy (*al-uns*). It is thus for everything concerning Him, and by which He has designated Himself. He symbolized these couples of (complementary) qualities by the two hands which He held out towards the creation of Universal Man; this latter reunites in himself all the essential realities (*haqāīq*) of the world in his totality, just as in each of his individuals. The world is the apparent, and the representative (of God in it) is the hidden. It is for this that the Sultan remains invisible and it is in this sense that God says of Himself that He hides behind the veils of darkness—which are natural bodies—and the veils of light—which are subtle spirits; for the world is made of crude (*kathīf*) and of subtle matter (*latīf*).

(The world) is to itself its own veil and thus cannot see God, due to the very fact that it sees itself; it can never by itself get rid of its veil, in spite of knowing that it is attached, by its dependence, to its Creator. The fact is the world does not participate in the autonomy of the Essential Being, so much so that it can never conceive Him. In this respect God remains always unknown, to the intuition as well as to the contemplation, for the ephemeral has no hold on that (that is to say the eternal).

When God says to Iblis "What is it that prevents you from prostrating yourself before that which I have created with My two Hands?" the mention of two Hands indicates a distinction for Adam; God thus makes allusion to the union in Adam of the two forms, that is the form of the world (analogous to the passive Divine Qualities) and the Divine "form" (analogous to the active Divine Qualities) which are the two Hands of God. As for lblis, he is nothing but a fragment of the world; he did not receive the synthesized nature, by virtue of which Adam is a representative of God. If Adam had not been manifested in the "Form" of the One who entrusted to him His representation towards the others, he would not be His representative; and if he did not contain all that which is needed by the herd that he has to guard—it is on him that this herd depends, and he must suffice to all their needs—he would not be representing God for the other (creatures).

The representation of God belongs only to the Universal Man, whose exterior form is created of realities (*haqāīq*) and of the forms of the world, and whose interior form corresponds to the "Form" of God (that is to say to the "total" of the Divine Names and Qualities). Because of that God has said of him "I am his hearing and his sight"; He did not say "his eye and his ear," but distinguished the two "forms," one from the other.

It is the same for all beings of this world with regard to each their own (transcendent) reality; however, no being contains the synthesis similar to the one which distinguishes the Representative and it is only by this synthesis that this one surpasses the others. If God did not penetrate existence by His "form" the world would not be; in the same way as individuals would not be determined if they had not the Universal Ideas. According to this Truth, the existence of the world resides in its dependence with regard to God. In reality each depends (on the other: the "Divine Form" on that of the world and inversely); nothing is independent (of the other); this is the pure truth; we are not expressing ourselves in metaphors. On the other hand when I speak of that which is absolutely independent thou wilt know what I mean by it (that is to say the infinite unconditioned Essence). Each, (the "Divine Form" as the world), is then tied one to the other and one cannot be separated from the other; understand well what I tell thee!

Now, thou knowest the spiritual meaning of the creation of Adam's body, that is to say of his apparent form, and of the creation of his spirit, which is his interior "form." Adam is, then, at the same time, God and creature. And thou hast understood that which is his (cosmic) rank that is to say the synthesis (of all the cosmic qualities), synthesis by virtue of which he is the Representative of God.

Adam is the "unique Spirit" (*an-nafs al-wāhidah*) from which was created the human species according to the Divine Word, (in the Koran); "O you, mankind, fear your Lord, who hath created you out of one soul and out of him created his wife, and from them hath deployed many men and women" (IV, I). The words "fear your Lord" signify: make of your apparent form a safeguard for your Lord, and make of your interior—that is to say of your Lord—a safeguard for yourselves; every act (or every Divine Order) consists in blame or in praise (in negation or in affirmation); then be His safeguard in the blame (that is to say as limited creatures) and take Him for safeguard in the praise, so that you have, amongst all beings, the most just attitude (towards God).

After He had created him, God showed Adam all that He had put into him; and He held it all in His two Hands: one containing the world and the other Adam and his descendants, then He showed these the ranks that they occupied in the interior of Adam.

Since God made me see that which He put in the primordial generator I have transcribed in this book the portion which was assigned to me, and not everything that I have realized; for that, no book in the present world could contain. But, among the things that I have contemplated and which could be transcribed in this book, as far as was assigned to me by God's Messenger—May Benediction and Peace be on him!—was the Divine Wisdom in the Word of Adam: it is that which this chapter discusses.

IBN RUSHD (AVERROES)

The works of Abū al-Walīd Muḥammad Ibn Aḥmad Ibn Rushd (known in the West as Averroes) mark the climax of Muslim Aristotelianism and at the same time its virtual end. He was born in Cordoba in 1126 in a family of a Muslim judge (*qāḍī*). Ibn Rushd lived in Andalusia and Morocco. In 1169 he was appointed as the judge of Seville. Two years later Ibn Rushd returned to Cordoba where he probably also took the place of the judge. In 1182 he became the court physician replacing Ibn òufayl after his death. In 1195, for reasons that are not clear, Averroes fell in disgrace and most of his writings were burned. He stayed in exile for a short time. After being restored to grace, Ibn Rushd lived in retirement in Marrakech until his death in 1198.

Ibn Rushd got the title of "The Commentator" because of his creative commentaries on most of Aristotle's works. He also compiled commentaries on the works of Plato, Alexander of Aphrodisiac, Nicholas of Damascus, al-Fārābī, Ibn Sīnā, and Ibn Bājjah.

The great commentator sought to liberate the original Aristotelian teaching from the erroneous interpretations of Neoplatonics and Muslim commentators. His criticism was particularly strong against Avicenna and al-Ghazālī.

Ibn Rushd's position is characterized by his particular approach to the relation between existence and substance. It is here that he strongly disagrees with Avicenna. While the latter considered essence to be ontologically prior to existence and existence to be something added to essence, Ibn Rushd held that individual substances existed primarily and, though the mind distinguishes between essence and existence in them, ontologically the two are one.

Averroes is best known for his doctrine of the intellect. Like previous Muslim philosophers, he reflects on Aristotle's understanding of various intellects. Ibn Rushd follows Aristotle in many respects. However, he disagrees with the

"First Philosopher" by declaring that the passive human intellect also is eternal and incorruptible, and hence, it is universal to all mankind, like the Active Intellect.

Ibn Rushd created a scheme for the relation of philosophy, theology, and religion with five methods of argument, or "syllogistic arts," in the form they had been expounded by al-Fārābī and Ibn Sīnā. In his view, philosophy and religion are equally concerned with interpreting the utmost foundations of being. Their kinship resembles the relationship between foster sisters.

Altogether Averroes wrote thirty-eight commentaries on Aristotle's writings. Of these, twenty-eight are originally in Arabic, thirty-six in Hebrew translation, and thirty-four in Latin translation. One of his original works is *The Incoherence of Incoherence* (*Tahāfut al-tahāfut*)—a refutation of al-Ghazālī's *The Incoherence of the Philosophers* (*Tahāfut al-falāsifa*).

From Ibn Rushd (Averroes)

The Decisive Treatise Determining the Nature of the Connection between Religion and Philosophy. *Translated by G. F. Hourani in* Averroes on the Harmony of Religion and Philosophy. *London: Luzac & Co. Ltd., 1961.*

The Decisive Treatise, Determining the Nature of the Connection between Religion and Philosophy

[What is the attitude of the Law to philosophy?]

Thus spoke the lawyer, *imām,* judge, and unique scholar, Abū al-Walīd Muḥammad Ibn Aḥmad Ibn Rushd:

Praise be to God with all due praise, and a prayer for Muḥammad His chosen servant and apostle. The purpose of this treatise is to examine, from the standpoint of the study of the Law, whether the study of philosophy and logic is allowed by the Law, or prohibited, or commanded—either by way of recommendation or as obligatory.

Chapter One: The Law Makes Philosophic Studies Obligatory.

[If teleological study of the world is philosophy, and if the Law commands such a study, then the Law commands philosophy.]

We say: If the activity of "philosophy" is nothing more than study of existing beings and reflection on them as indications of the Artisan, i.e., inasmuch as they are products of art (for beings only indicate the Artisan through our knowledge of the art in them, and the more perfect this knowledge is, the more perfect the knowledge of the Artisan becomes), and if the Law has encouraged and urged reflection on beings, then it is clear that what this name signifies is either obligatory or recommended by the Law.

[The Law commands such a study.]

That the Law summons to reflection on beings, and the pursuit of knowledge about them, by the intellect is clear from several verses of the Book of God, Blessed and Exalted, such as the saying of the Exalted, "Reflect, you have vision:" this is textual authority for the obligation to use intellectual reasoning, or a combination of intellectual and legal reasoning. Another example is His saying, "Have they not studied the kingdom of the heavens and the earth, and whatever things God has created?": this is a text urging the study of the totality of beings. Again, God the Exalted has taught that one of those whom He singularly honored by this knowledge was Abraham, peace on him, for the Exalted said, "So we made Abraham see the kingdom of the heavens and the earth, that he might be" [and so on to the end of the verse]. The Exalted also said, "Do they not observe the camels, how they have been created, and the sky, how it is has been raised up?" and He said, "and they give thought to the creation of the heavens and the earth," and so on in countless other verses.

[This study must be conducted in the best manner, by demonstrative reasoning.]

Since it has now been established that the Law has rendered obligatory the study of beings by the intellect, and reflection on them, and since reflection is nothing more than inference and drawing out of the unknown from the known, and since this is reasoning or at any rate done by reasoning, therefore we are under an obligation to carry on our study of beings by intellectual reasoning. It is further evident that this manner of study, to which the Law summons and urges, is the most perfect kind of study using the most perfect kind of reasoning; and this is the kind called "demonstration."

[To master this instrument the religious thinker must make a preliminary study of logic, just as the lawyer must study legal reasoning. This is no more heretical in the one case than in the other. And logic must be learned from the ancient masters, regardless of the fact that they were not Muslims.]

The Law, then, has urged us to have demonstrative knowledge of God the Exalted and all the beings of His creation. But it is preferable and even necessary for anyone, who wants to understand God the Exalted and the other beings demonstratively, to have first understood the kinds of demonstration and their conditions [of validity], and in what respects demonstrative reasoning differs from dialectical, rhetorical, and fallacious reasoning. But this is not possible unless he has previously learned what reasoning as such is, and how many kinds it has, and which of them are valid and which invalid. This in turn is not possible unless he has previously learned the parts of reasoning, of which it is composed, i.e., the premises and their kinds. Therefore he who believes in the Law, and obeys its command to study beings, ought prior to his study to gain a knowledge of these things, which have the same place in theoretical studies as instruments have in practical activities.

For just as the lawyer infers from the Divine command to him to acquire knowledge of the legal categories that he is under obligation to know the various kinds of legal syllogisms, and which are valid and which invalid, in the same way he who would know [God] ought to infer from the command to study beings that he is under obligation to acquire a knowledge of intellectual reasoning and its kinds. Indeed it is more fitting for him to do so, for if the lawyer infers from the saying of the Exalted, "Reflect, you who have vision," the obligation to acquire a knowledge of legal reasoning, how much more fitting and proper that he who would know God should infer from it the obligation to acquire a knowledge of intellectual reasoning!

It cannot be objected: "This kind of study of intellectual reasoning is a heretical innovation since it did not exist among the first believers." For the study of legal reasoning and its kinds is also something which has been discovered since the first believers, yet it is not considered to be a heretical innovation. So the objector should believe the same about the study of intellectual reasoning. (For this there is a reason, which it is not the place to mention here.) But most masters of this religion support intellectual reasoning, except a small group of gross literalists, who can be refuted by [sacred] texts.

Since it has now been established that there is an obligation of the Law to study intellectual reasoning and its kinds, just as there is an obligation to study legal reasoning, it is clear that, if none of our predecessors had formerly examined intellectual reasoning and its kinds, we should be obliged to undertake such an examination from the beginning, and that each succeeding scholar would have to seek help in that task from his predecessor in order that knowledge of the subject might be completed. For it is difficult or impossible for one man to find out by himself and from the beginning all that he needs of that subject, as it is difficult for one man to discover all the knowledge that he needs of the kinds of legal reasoning; indeed this is even truer of knowledge of intellectual reasoning.

But if someone other than ourselves has already examined that subject, it is clear that we ought to seek help towards our goal from what has been said by such a predecessor on the subject, regardless of whether this other one shares our religion or not. For when a valid sacrifice is performed with a certain instrument, no account is taken, in judging the validity of the sacrifice, of whether the instrument belongs to one who shares our religion or to one who does not, so long as it fulfills the conditions for validity. By "those who do not share our religion" I refer to those ancients who studied these matters before Islam. So if such is the case, and everything that is required in the study of the subject of intellectual syllogisms has already been examined in the most perfect manner by the ancients, presumably we ought to lay hands on their books in order to study what they said about that subject; and if it is all correct we should accept it from them, while if there is anything incorrect in it, we should draw attention to that.

[After logic we must proceed to philosophy proper. Here too we have to learn from our predecessors, just as in mathematics and law. Thus it is wrong to forbid the study of ancient philosophy. Harm from it is accidental, like harm from taking medicine, drinking water, or studying law.]

When we have finished with this sort of study and acquired the instruments by whose aid we are able to reflect on beings and the indications of art in them (for he who does not understand the art does not understand the product of art, and he who does not understand the product of art does not understand the Artisan), then we ought to begin the examination of beings in the order and manner we have learned from the art of demonstrative syllogisms.

And again it is clear that in the study of beings this aim can be fulfilled by us perfectly only through successive examinations of them by one man after another, the later ones seeking the help of the earlier in that task, on the model of what has happened in the mathematical sciences. For if we suppose that the art of geometry did not exist in this age of ours, and likewise the art of astronomy, and a single person wanted to ascertain by himself the sizes of the heavenly bodies, their shapes, and their distances from each other, that would not be possible for him—e.g., to know the proportion of the sun to the earth or other facts about the sizes of the stars—even though he were the most intelligent of men by nature, unless by a revelation or something resembling revelation. Indeed if he were told that the sun is about 150 or 160 times as great as the earth, he would think this statement madness on the part of the speaker, although this is a fact which has been demonstrated in astronomy so surely that no one who has mastered that science doubts it.

But what calls even more strongly for comparison with the art of mathematics in this respect is the art of the principles of law; and the study of law itself was completed only over a long period of time. And if someone today wanted to find out by himself all the arguments which have been discovered by the theorists of the legal school on controversial questions, about which debate has taken place between them in most countries of Islam (except the West), he would deserve to be ridiculed, because such a task is impossible for him, apart from the fact that the work has been done already. Moreover, this is a situation that is self-evident not in the scientific arts alone but also in the practical arts; for there is not one of them which a single man can construct by himself. Then how can he do it with the art of arts, philosophy? If this is so, then whenever we find in the works of our predecessors of former nations a theory about beings and a reflection on them conforming to what the conditions of demonstration require, we ought to study what they said about the matter and what they affirmed in their books. And we should accept from them gladly and gratefully whatever in these books accords with the truth, and draw attention to and warn against what does not accord with the truth, at the same time excusing them.

From this it is evident that the study of the books of the ancients is obligatory by Law, since their aim and purpose in their books is just the purpose to which the Law has urged us, and that whoever forbids the study of them to anyone who is fit to study them, i.e., anyone who unites two qualities, (1) natural intelligence and (2) religious integrity and moral virtue, is blocking people from the door by which the Law summons them to knowledge of God, the door of theoretical study which leads to the truest knowledge of Him; and such an act is the extreme of ignorance and estrangement from God the Exalted.

And if someone errs or stumbles in the study of these books owing to a deficiency in his natural capacity, or bad organization of his study of them, or being dominated by his passions, or not finding a teacher to guide him to an understanding of their contents, or a combination of all or more than one of these causes, it does not follow that one should forbid them to anyone who is qualified to study them. For this manner of harm which arises owing to them is something that is attached to them by accident, not by essence; and when a thing is beneficial by its nature and essence, it ought not to be shunned because of something harmful contained in it by accident. This was the thought of the Prophet, peace on him, on the occasion when he ordered a man to give his brother honey to drink for his diarrhea, and the diarrhea increased after he had given him the honey: when the man complained to him about it, he said, "God spoke the truth; it was your brother's stomach that lied." We can even say that a man who prevents a qualified person from studying books of philosophy, because some of the most vicious people may be thought to have gone astray through their study of them, is like a man who prevents a thirsty person from drinking cool, fresh water until he dies of thirst, because some people have choked to death on it. For death from water by choking is an accidental matter, but death by thirst is essential and necessary.

Moreover, this accidental effect of this art is a thing which may also occur accidentally from the other arts. To how many lawyers has law been a cause of lack of piety and immersion in this world! Indeed we find most lawyers in this state, although their art by its essence calls for nothing but practical virtue. Thus it is not strange if the same thing that occurs accidentally in the art which calls for practical virtue should occur accidentally in the art which calls for intellectual virtue.

[For every Muslim the Law has provided a way to truth suitable to his nature, through demonstrative, dialectical, or rhetorical methods.]

Since all this is now established, and since we, the Muslim community, hold that this divine religion of ours is true, and that it is this religion which incites and summons us to the happiness that consists in the knowledge of God, Mighty and Majestic, and of His creation, that [end] is appointed for every Muslim by the method of assent which his temperament and nature require. For the natures of men are on different levels with respect to [their paths to] assent. One of them comes to assent through demonstration; another comes to assent through dialectical arguments, just as firmly as the demonstrative man through demonstration, since his nature does not contain any greater capacity; while another comes to assent through rhetorical arguments, again just as firmly as the demonstrative man through demonstrative arguments.

Thus since this divine religion of ours has summoned people by these three methods, assent to it has extended to everyone, except him who stubbornly denies it with his tongue or him for whom no method of summons to God the Exalted has been appointed in religion owing to his own neglect of such matters. It was for this purpose that the Prophet, peace on him, was sent with a special mission to "the white man and the black man" alike; I mean because his religion embraces all the methods of summons to God the Exalted. This is clearly expressed in the saying of God the Exalted, "Summon to the way of your Lord by wisdom and by good preaching, and debate with them in the most effective manner."

IBN KHALDŪN

A forerunner of Machiavelli and Vico, Montesquieu and Hegel, Darwin and Spencer, Marx and Toynbee, the one called 'Abd al-Raḥmān Ibn Khaldūn is one of the greatest thinkers of the Muslim world.

He was born in Tunis in 1332 into an Arab-Spanish family of scholars and statesmen. Ibn Khaldūn was brought up in both traditional religious and the rational philosophical sciences. He taught and occupied high positions in Tunis, Algeria, Morocco, Spain, and Egypt. He shared with many other outstanding minds the fate of having the privilege of those who served in medieval courts: the hardship of prosecution, imprisonment, and exile. Ibn Khaldūn spent his last years in Egypt until his death in 1406.

Ibn Khaldūn's greatest work is *Al-Muqaddimah (The Prolegomena)*. It is the first of seven volumes of his Kitāb al-'ibar, the historical narrative of the Arabs and Berbers. *Al-Muqaddimah* has brought to Ibn Khaldūn the fame and the recognition of the greatest philosopher of history. In Toynbee's words, Ibn Khaldūn's philosophy of history "is undoubtedly the greatest work of its kind that has ever been created by any mind in any time or place."

Ibn Khaldūn's study of history is not limited by the factual events because the latter represent nothing more than the surface of history. He looks into the inner meaning of historic developments, seeking their causes and the origins. Hence, for him history is the way to truth, and thus it could be accounted as a branch of philosophy.

Ibn Khaldūn originated the theory of history and of civilization. The starting point for his theory is the Aristotelian maxim that man is a political animal by nature, who is in need of assistance from fellowmen to meet material demands and protection.

The life of individuals as well as the existence of different human associations (societies, states, civilizations) go through cycles of emergence, growth, and decay. Ibn Khaldūn exposes the mechanism of this cyclic development. He recognizes dual determinism of the historic events. Following the traditional Muslim theology, Ibn Khaldūn conceives of God as the First cause of everything that exists. The death of the state, for example, according to him, is finally sealed by a timely decree of God. However, Ibn Khaldūn, being in accord with traditional Muslim ontology, introduced natural causality into history. He is of the belief that numerous factors determine the cause of history, including climate, geography, economics, religion, culture, education, and ecology. Though reason cannot see ontological causes, it can and it should see natural, historic causes.

From Ibn Khaldūn

The Muqaddimah: An Introduction to History. *In 3 volumes. Translated by Franz Rosenthal. New York: Routledge & Kegan Paul, 1958.*

First Prefatory Discussion

Human social organization is something necessary. The philosophers expressed this fact by saying: "Man is 'political' by nature." That is, he cannot do without the social organization for which the philosophers use the technical term "town" (*polis*).

This is what civilization means. (The necessary character of human social organization or civilization) is explained by the fact that God created and fashioned man in a form that can live and subsist only with the help of food. He guided man to a natural desire for food and instilled in him the power that enables him to obtain it.

However, the power of the individual human being is not sufficient for him to obtain (the food) he needs, and does not provide him with as much food as he requires to live. Even if we assume an absolute minimum of food—that is, food enough for one day, (a little) wheat, for instance—that amount of food could be obtained only after much preparation such as grinding, kneading, and baking. Each of these three operations requires utensils and tools that can be provided only with the help of several crafts, such as the crafts of the blacksmith, the carpenter, and the potter. Assuming that a man could eat unprepared grain, an even greater number of operations would be necessary in order to obtain the grain: sowing and reaping, and threshing to separate it from the husks of the ear. Each of these operations requires a number of tools and many more crafts than those just mentioned. It is beyond the power of one man alone to do all that, or (even) part of it, by himself. Thus, he cannot do without a combination of many powers from among his fellow beings, if he is to obtain food for himself and for them. Through cooperation, the needs of a number of persons, many times greater than their own (number), can be satisfied.

Likewise, each individual needs the help of his fellow beings for his defense, as well. When God fashioned the natures of all living beings and divided the various powers among them, many dumb animals were given more perfect powers than God gave to man. The power of a horse, for instance, is much greater than the power of man, and so is the power of a donkey or an ox. The power of a lion or an elephant is many times greater than the power of (man).

Aggressiveness is natural in living beings. Therefore, God gave each of them a special limb for defense against aggression. To man, instead, He gave the ability to think, and the hand. With the help of the ability to think, the hand is able to prepare the ground for the crafts. The crafts, in turn, procure for man the instruments that serve him instead of limbs, which other animals possess for their defense. Lances, for instance, take the place of horns for goring, swords the place of claws to inflict wounds, shields the place of thick skins, and so on. There are other such things. They were all mentioned by Galen in *De usu partium.*

The power of one individual human being cannot withstand the power of any one dumb animal, especially not the power of the predatory animals. Man is generally unable to defend himself against them by himself. Nor is his (unaided) power sufficient to make use of the existing instruments of defense, because there are so many of them and they require so many crafts and (additional) things. It is absolutely necessary for man to have the cooperation of his fellow men. As long as there is no such cooperation, he cannot obtain any food or nourishment, and life cannot materialize for him, because God fashioned him so that he must have food if he is to live. Nor, lacking weapons, can he defend himself. Thus, he falls prey to animals and dies much before his time. Under such circumstances, the human species would vanish. When, however, mutual cooperation exists, man obtains food for his nourishment and weapons for his defense. God's wise plan that man(kind) should subsist and the human species be preserved will be fulfilled.

Consequently, social organization is necessary to the human species. Without it, the existence of human beings would be incomplete. God's desire to settle the world with human beings and to leave them as His representatives on earth would not materialize. This is the meaning of civilization, the object of the science under discussion.

The afore-mentioned remarks have been in the nature of establishing the existence of the object in (this) particular field. A scholar in a particular discipline is not obliged to do this, since it is accepted in logic that a scholar in a particular science does not have to establish the existence of the object in that science. On the other hand, logicians do not consider it forbidden to do so. Thus, it is a voluntary contribution.

God, in His grace, gives success.

When mankind has achieved social organization, as we have stated, and when civilization in the world has thus become a fact, people need someone to exercise a restraining influence and keep them apart, for aggressiveness and injustice are in the animal nature of man. The weapons made for the defense of human beings against the aggressiveness of dumb animals do not suffice against the aggressiveness of man to man, because all of them possess those weapons. Thus, something else is needed for defense against the aggressiveness of human beings toward each other. It could not come from outside, because all the other animals fall short of human perceptions and inspiration. The person who exercises a restraining influence, therefore, must be one of themselves. He must dominate them and have power and authority over them, so that no one of them will be able to attack another. This is the meaning of royal authority.

It has thus become clear that royal authority is a natural quality of man which is absolutely necessary to mankind. The philosophers mention that it also exists among certain dumb animals, such as the bees and the locusts. One discerns among them the existence of authority and obedience to a leader. They follow the one of them who is distinguished as their leader by his natural characteristics and body. However, outside of human beings, these things exist as the result of natural disposition and divine guidance, and not as the result of an ability to think or to administrate. "He gave everything its natural characteristics, and then guided it."

The philosophers go further. They attempt to give logical proof of the existence of prophecy and to show that prophecy is a natural quality of man. In this connection, they carry the argument to its ultimate consequences and say that human beings absolutely require some authority to exercise a restraining influence. They go on to say that such restraining influence exists through the religious law (that has been) ordained by God and revealed to mankind by a human being. (This human being) is distinguished from the rest of mankind by special qualities of divine guidance that God gave him, in order that he might find the others submissive to him and ready to accept what he says. Eventually, the existence of a (restraining) authority among them and over them becomes a fact that is accepted without the slightest disapproval or dissent.

This proposition of the philosophers is not logical, as one can see. Existence and human life can materialize without (the existence of prophecy) through injunctions a person in authority may devise on his own or with the help of a group feeling that enables him to force the others to follow him wherever he wants to go. People who have a (divinely revealed) book and who follow the prophets are few in number in comparison with (all) the Magians who have no (divinely revealed) book. The latter constitute the majority of the world's inhabitants. Still, they (too) have possessed dynasties and monuments, not to mention life itself. They still possess these things at this time in the intemperate zones to the north and the south. This is in contrast with human life in the state of anarchy, with no one to exercise a restraining influence. That would be impossible.

This shows that (the philosophers) are wrong when they assume that prophecy exists by necessity. The existence of prophecy is not required by logic. Its (necessary character) is indicated by the religious law, as was the belief of the early Muslims.

God gives success and guidance.

MODERN ISLAMIC THOUGHT

The most significant, if not the only, attempt to interpret Islam in modern philosophical terms belongs to Muhammad Iqbal. It is often said that "in the entire gamut of Islamic modernism the only serious student of philosophy the Muslim philosophy can boast of is Muhammad Iqbal."

This great poet and philosopher was born at Sialkot, a border town of the Punjab, in 1877. He studied at one of the best institutions of higher learning in the subcontinent—the Government College of Lahore. Iqbal left for Europe to continue advanced graduate studies both in Britain and Germany. In 1907 he successfully defended the dissertation "The Development of Metaphysics in Persia" and was awarded the doctoris philosophiae grade.

Coming back from Europe, Iqbal started his career as an attorney, college professor, and poet—all at once. He was deeply involved in politics and contributed to the formulation and the spread of the two-nation theory, which ideologically justified the partition of India and the emergence of the state of Pakistan in 1947.

Iqbal's fame as a poet is so great that he is called the Jalāl al-Dīn Rūmī of modern times. The admirers of his poetic genius constructed a mausoleum on the grave outside the main entrance to the Badshahi mosque in the center of Lahore. The mausoleum has become a place of pilgrimage.

Iqbal's religious and philosophical views are widely expressed in his poetry, like his magnum opus *Asrar-i khudi* and poems *Bang-i dara, Darb-i kalim.* However, his major contribution in the field of philosophy is *The Reconstruction of Religious Thought in Islam,* the six lectures that he delivered in Madras in 1928–29.

The main aim of his "reconstruction" is to demonstrate the essential conformity of Islamic heritage with the Western outlook. Iqbal's attempt to bring about a synthesis of Western and Islamic ideas is sometimes compared in its magnitude to the synthesis attempted either by al-Ghazālī in his *Revival of Religious Sciences*, or by al-Kindī and Ibn Rushd, who sought to harmonize the Greek philosophical outlook with the religious world view of Islam.

In his attempt to reinterpret Islam and thus to bridge the gulf between philosophy and religion, Iqbal appealed to different sources, including Muslim mysticism, the atomism of Ash'arites, and the insights of Hegel, Whitehead, Bergson, and so on.

Though Iqbal's role is compared by some to that of Luther in the history of Christianity, his efforts to reform Islam were not so successful. Still Iqbal's call to Muslims to seek in their own cultural heritage the resources for the reconstruction of their life retains all its urgency.

The selection below is from the last lecture under the name "Is Religion Possible?"

From Muhammad Iqbal

The Reconstruction of Religious Thought in Islam. *Lahore: Sh. Muhammad Ashraf, 1962.*

Conservatism is as bad in religion as in any other department of human activity. It destroys the ego's creative freedom and closes up the paths of fresh spiritual enterprise. This is the main reason why our medieval mystic technique can no longer produce original discoveries of ancient Truth. The fact, however, that religious experience is incommunicable does not mean that the religious man's pursuit is futile. Indeed, the incommunicability of religious experience gives us a clue to the ultimate nature of the ego. In our daily social intercourse we live and move in seclusion, as it were. We do not care to reach the inmost individuality of men. We treat them as mere functions and approach them from those aspects of their identity which are capable of conceptual treatment. The climax of religious life, however, is the discovery of the ego as an individual deeper than his conceptually describable habitual self-hood. It is in contact with the Most Real that the ego discovers its uniqueness, its metaphysical status, and the possibility of improvement in that status. Strictly speaking, the experience which leads to this discovery is not a conceptually manageable intellectual fact; it is a vital fact, an attitude consequent on an inner biological transformation which cannot be captured in the net of logical categories. It can embody itself only in a world-making or world-shaking act; and in this form alone the content of this timeless experience can diffuse itself in the time-movement, and make itself effectively visible to the eye of history. It seems that the method of dealing with Reality by means of concepts is not at all a serious way of dealing with it. Science does not care whether its electron is a real entity or not. It may be a mere symbol, a mere convention. Religion, which is essentially a mode of actual living, is the only serious way of handling Reality. As a form of higher experience it is corrective of our concepts of philosophical theology or at least makes us suspicious of the purely rational process which forms these concepts. Science can afford to ignore metaphysics altogether, and may even believe it to be "a justified form of poetry," as Lange defined it, or "a legitimate play of grown-ups," as Nietzsche described it. But the religious expert who seeks to discover his personal status in the constitution of things cannot, in view of the final aim of his struggle, be satisfied with what science may regard as a vital lie, a mere "as if" to regulate thought and conduct. In so far as the ultimate nature of Reality is concerned nothing is at stake in the venture of science; in the religious venture the whole career of the ego, as an assimilative personal center of life and experience, is at stake. Conduct, which involves a decision of the ultimate fate of the agent cannot be based on illusions. A wrong concept misleads the understanding; a wrong deed degrades the whole man, and may eventually demolish the structure of the human ego. The mere concept affects life only partially; the deed is dynamically related to reality and issues from a generally constant attitude of the whole man towards reality. No doubt the deed, i.e., the control of psychological and physiological processes with a view to tune up the ego for an immediate contact with the ultimate Reality, is, and cannot but be, individual in form and content; yet the deed, too, is liable to be socialized when others begin to live through it with a view to discover for themselves its effectiveness as a method of approaching the Real. The evidence of religious experts in all ages and countries is that there are potential types of consciousness lying close to our normal consciousness. If these types of consciousness open up possibilities of life-giving and knowledge-yielding experience the question of the possibility of religion as a form of higher experience is a perfectly legitimate one and demands our serious attention.

The truth is that the religious and the scientific processes, though involving different methods, are identical in their final aim. Both aim at reaching the most real. In fact, religion, for reasons which I have mentioned before, is far more anxious to reach the ultimately real than science. And, to both, the way to pure objectivity lies through what may be called the purification of experience. In order to understand this we must make a distinction between experience as a natural fact, significant of the normally observable behavior of reality, and experience as significant of the inner nature of reality. As a natural fact it is explained in the light of its antecedents, psychological and physiological; as significant of the inner nature of reality we shall have to apply criteria of a different kind to clarify its meaning. In the domain of science we try to understand its meanings in reference to the external *behavior* of reality; in the domain of religion we take it as representative of some kind of reality and try to discover its meanings in reference mainly to the inner *nature* of that reality. The scientific and the religious processes are in a sense parallel to each other. Both are really descriptions of the same world with this difference only that in the scientific process the ego's standpoint is necessarily exclusive, whereas in the religious process the ego integrates its competing tendencies and develops a single inclusive attitude resulting in a kind of synthetic transfiguration of his experiences. A careful study of the nature and purpose of these really complementary processes shows that both of them are directed to the purification of experience in their respective spheres. An illustration will make my meaning clear. Hume's criticism of our notion of cause must be considered as a chapter in the history of science rather than that of philosophy. True to the spirit of scientific empiricism we are not entitled to work with any concepts of a subjective nature. The point of Hume's criticism is to emancipate empirical science from the concept of force which, as he urges, has no foundation in sense-experience. This was the first attempt of the modern mind to purify the scientific process.

Einstein's mathematical view of the universe completes the process of purification started by Hume, and, true to the spirit of Hume's criticism, dispenses with the concept of force altogether. The passage I have quoted from the great Indian saint shows that the practical student of religious psychology has a similar purification in view. His sense of objectivity is as keen as that of the scientist in his own sphere of objectivity. He passes from experience to experience, not as a mere spectator, but as a critical sifter of experience who, by the rules of a peculiar technique, suited to his sphere of inquiry, endeavors to eliminate all subjective elements, psychological or physiological, in the content of his experience with a view finally to reach what is absolutely objective. This final experience is the revelation of a new life-process—original, essential, spontaneous. The eternal secret of the ego is that the moment he reaches this final revelation he recognizes it as the ultimate root of his being without the slightest hesitation. Yet in the experience itself there is no mystery. Nor is there anything emotional in it. Indeed with a view to secure a wholly non-emotional experience the technique of Islamic Sufism at least takes good care to forbid the use of music in worship, and to emphasize the necessity of daily congregational prayers in order to counteract the possible anti-social effects of solitary contemplation. Thus the experience reached is a perfectly natural experience and possesses a biological significance of the highest importance to the ego. It is the human ego rising higher than mere reflection, and mending its transiency by appropriating the eternal. The only danger to which the ego is exposed in this Divine quest is the possible relaxation of his activity caused by his enjoyment of and absorption in the experiences that precede the final experience. The history of Eastern Sufism shows that this is a real danger. This was the whole point of the reform movement initiated by the great Indian saint from whose writings I have already quoted a passage. And the reason is obvious. The ultimate aim of the ego is not to *see* something, but to *be* something. It is in the ego's effort to *be* something that he discovers his final opportunity to sharpen his objectivity and acquire a more fundamental "I am," which finds evidence of its reality not in the Cartesian "I think" but in the Kantian "I can." The end of the ego's quest is not emancipation from the limitations of individuality; it is, on the other hand, a more precise definition of it. The final act is not an intellectual act, but a vital act which deepens the whole being of the ego, and sharpens his will with the creative assurance that the world is not something to be merely seen or known through concepts, but something to be made and re-made by continuous action. It is a moment of supreme bliss and also a moment of the greatest trial for the ego:

> Art thou in the stage of "life," or "death," "death-in-life"?
> Invoke the aid of three witnesses to verify the "Station."
> The first witness is thine own consciousness—
> See thyself, then, with thine own light,
> The second witness is the consciousness of another ego—

See thyself, then, with the light of an ego other than thee.
The third witness is God's consciousness—
See thyself, then, with God's light.
If thou standest unshaken in front of this light,
Consider thyself as living and eternal as He!
That man alone is real who dares—
Dares to see God face to face!
What is "Ascension"? Only a search for a witness
Who may finally confirm thy reality—
A witness whose confirmation alone makes thee eternal.
No one can stand unshaken in His Presence;
And he who can, verily, he is pure gold,
Art thou a mere particle of dust?
Tighten the knot of thy ego;
And hold fast to thy tiny being!
How glorious to burnish one's ego
And to test its lustre in the presence of the Sun!
Re-chisel, then, thine ancient frame;
And build up a new being.
Such being is real being;
Or else thy ego is a mere ring of smoke!

Jawid Nama

Index

About the Author

Marietta Stepaniants is the Director of the Center for Oriental Philosophies Studies at the Institute of Philosophy, Russian Academy of Sciences, where she has been working since 1959. For fifteen years she was a professor of the Diplomatic Academy; in recent years, she has been Chair of Oriental Philosophies at the Russian State University of Humanities (Moscow). She is the author of ten books including *Islamic Philosophy and Social Thought: 19th–20th Centuries; Sufi Wisdom;* and *Gandhi and the World Today*. Among more than twenty volumes edited by her are: *Rationalistic Tradition and Modernity* (in three volumes); *History of Indian Philosophy: A Russian Viewpoint*; *Feminism: East, West, Russia*; *Democracy and Justice: Cross-cultural Perspectives*. Her writings have been translated and published in eighteen countries.